THE FREEDOM HANDBOOK

THE FREEDOM HANDBOOK

LUKE DENIS AND CHRIS HAMPTON

Copyright © 2017 by Luke Denis and Chris Hampton.

Library of Congress Control Number: 2017901926
ISBN: Hardcover   978-1-5245-8254-8
          Softcover   978-1-5245-8253-1
          eBook   978-1-5245-8252-4

All rights reserved. No part of this book may be reproduced or transmitted in any form or by any means, electronic or mechanical, including photocopying, recording, or by any information storage and retrieval system, without permission in writing from the copyright owner.

Print information available on the last page.

Rev. date: 03/02/2017

To order additional copies of this book, contact:
Xlibris
1-888-795-4274
www.Xlibris.com
Orders@Xlibris.com

Contents

Preface xi
About The Authors xiii

- The Challenge - 1
- New Administrative Structures - 15
- Taxes and Social Programs - 34
- Education - 61
- Health Care - 88
- Food Systems - 109
- Legal Systems and Laws - 138
- The War On Drugs - 158
- War - 180
- Religious Institutions - 212
- Monetary Systems - 235
- The Problems: A Summary - 263
- A Whole World's Dark Night of the Soul - 290
- Moot Points and Potential Game Changers - 320
- Holes In the Plan - 344
- Freedom - 362

This book is dedicated to your ancestors, all of our ancestors. The brightest, bravest and strongest of humanity who for thousands of years fought, with every breath and every step, not only for survival, but for every scrap of freedom we know.

This book is also dedicated to your highest potential, all our highest potentials, and the awareness that this pursuit of self knowledge, and virtue, is the only work there is.

No Government No Problem

Preface

The Freedom Handbook. Second edition from Incite Insight.

This is an impassioned guide to breaking the chains that hold us back. Every day we see what could be. The quest to live a good life. To be free to embrace a warmer culture, happier people, better systems of managing our resources. This is what this book is all about, we have some very powerful ideas about what we can do and how to get there.

Help plant the seeds of a better tomorrow. Join us online at Incite-Insight.com and in the streets. All power to the people.

About The Authors

Luke Michel.

Luke married his highschool sweetheart and they have two terrific children together. Although he's a self-made, highly successful entrepreneur and visionary, Luke firmly believes that it's much more important to understand where someone wants to go in life, rather than where they've been. In this way Luke wants to help build a world where human potential is freed and we live free from tyranny, oppression and authority; where personal accountability is paramount and people have stopped forcing their will on one another.

He has an especial interest in technology and human potential - feeling that the rightful inheritance of human accomplishment is unjustly held hostage by the ruling class. He leads a private life and respects everyone's right to choose all elements of our own lives, provided these choices cause no harm to others.

Luke's surprisingly calm, except when it comes to arbitrary authority or harm being done to his fellow human family. He's a strong, vibrant human being full of curiosity, optimism and care for the world around him. Although, he's careful to draw the distinction between a helping hand and a hand-out.

Luke's the kind of person who stands for what he believes in, walks the walk he talks and isn't afraid to stand up to the ruling class and autocratic authority in all forms. Luke is tough, honest, a big dreamer and a capable visionary, he's also a big supporter of other people's dreams and capacity. Luke cares deeply about his fellow human family.

Chris Hampton.

Chris builds bridges - between ideas, and people - relishing the intersection between creativity and knowledge. Driven by the relentless curiosity of a consummate generalist, he's fascinated with the connections between, and inner working, of all things. A gentle yet fierce and tenacious soul, Chris' a strong ally to virtue and a formidable enemy of arbitrary and oppressive rule. Working daily to realize our potential, Chris brings ideas and directness to all his interactions. Possessing a unique and unyielding vision of change, he's consistently focused on motivating others to both realize their dreams and unchain humanity. Bright and passionate, Chris is the biggest kind of dreamer and builder and has devoted his life to the idea of freedom – like Voltairine de Cleyre believing with every beat of his heart that ""This is the time to boldly say, "Yes, I believe in the displacement of this system of injustice by a just one; I believe in the end of starvation, exposure, and the crimes caused by them; I believe in the human soul regnant over all laws which man has made or will make; I believe there is no peace now, and there will never be peace, so long as one rules over another; I believe in the total disintegration and dissolution of the principle and practice of authority."

Together Luke and Chris wrote this book and then became the founders of Incite Insight. They want to help you stir up a deeper understanding of the world we live in. They want for you to discover your own problem solving potential and most of all, to help us change the world for the better. That's why they have published this book. That's why they are building a global forum, a changemaker's tool box, world-wide connections between changemakers, and a trailblazing new global media channel, Incite Insight Media. It's why you are here. Cheers to the Change Makers.

CHAPTER ONE

- The Challenge -

"Madness is something rare in individuals—but with groups, parties, peoples, and ages it is the rule."[1]
- **Friedrich Nietzsche** -

Do you feel a deep sadness seeing so much pain in your human family, down in your very core? Are you disgusted and angry? Are you left feeling hopeless and lost, like so many of us? Do you ask yourself in your private heart, "W*hat can really be done? What can I – what can any of us – do?"*

The ability to create, innovate, feel deep compassion, to love one another, to care, to imagine—these incredible human gifts should allow us to create the world of our dreams, and yet we live in a world of pain, starvation, and war. We are fed limitation, lies, hatred, violence, fear, and, ultimately, slavery from our earliest days. Our potential is wrapped in chains, leaving we common folk feeling impotent and powerless to solve the very real problems facing our world and us.

All our technology and ingenuity could provide food, shelter, and abundance for all. Instead, we have seen poverty grow to unbelievable heights, our people and planet getting sicker by the day, while our moral depravity grows to cancerous levels. Humanity's turmoil is summarized by grotesque gaps between rich and poor, between thriving and barely surviving, and the gap widens every day.

We all feel this gross contradiction. Human beings are astonishing. Enormous potential fills our hearts with hope, but too often see our dreams dashed against the cold, unfeeling shores of rampant systemic disease.

Even discussing our trials is no simple task.

---

[1] *Beyond Good and Evil,* eds. Rolf-Peter Horstman and Judith Norman, trans. Judith Norman (Cambridge: Cambridge University Press, 2002), 70.

They need to be discussed.

Our world is complex and there is no easy solution. However, if we focus our empathy, our potential, and our ability, to create viable solutions, then we will shine. This focus will allow us to create the positive changes we are all so desperately hungry for, though it is an arduous process.

What if within these pages, were blueprints for our complete rebirth? What if after reading this book, our blinding need for immediate and absolute change became clear? What if this book delivered a lucid plan, to affect an instantaneous worldwide, regional, and local revolution that is both nonviolent and healthy?

Viva la revolución! The time is now!

The Freedom Handbook is a deafening cry, a catalytic wake-up call designed to stir your blood and inspire sweeping change around the world. Using basic common sense, humanity needs to reform archaic systems and ideas that bind our potential. We can learn to live and thrive without oppression and arbitrary authority.

The truth is on the table. Look closely. Countless leaders, books, movies, articles, and whistle-blowers have diligently outlined the problems we face – the corruption, lies, and unmitigated disregard for basic human rights, all in the name of profit and power.

Over the last twenty years, changes in technology and information have sparked a revolution that is now a roaring fire. The Internet's power and digital media's thunderous voice are already totally redefining civilization.

In all of human history, there have been only two primary information revolutions. Once when we began writing information down, and again when the printing press unleashed information to the masses for the first time. Both shifts in how we access information brought about a complete metamorphosis in human existence, but these shifts did not happen overnight.

This time, due to the given opportunities inherent in a dual informational and technological revolution, the repercussions will be far more pervasive. This current evolution is also taking shape much faster. The groundswell is visceral and irreversible. The only real questions are, "*Where do we want to go?*" and, "*Who do we want to be?*"

> *This technical aspect of our current revolution launches already earth-shattering possibilities into a completely new universe of opportunities. The second chapter of this book, New Administrative Structures, will lay the "how" on the table.*

The shape of the earth is round. Nature is interconnected and symbiotic. The illusory world we humans have created for ourselves is pyramid shaped, compartmentalized, and divisive. Our decisions, information, and resources have come primarily from those at the top of the pyramid for centuries.

With the advent of cutting-edge technology, we can now say, *"No more."* No more will we suffer the yoke of those above us, of a ruling class, of any self-described elite. Humanity has finally figured out how to create circular, symbiotic solutions. It is time to replace all of our pyramids with circles.

Imagine a world where children teach themselves. Imagine a world where local, national, and global communities easily and joyfully co-create sustainable solutions for problems, which challenge us all. Imagine common sense ruling our relationships, and creating a deep, global calm.

In our hearts, we can see the truth. A few, if any among us, would ever cause violent, physical harm, kill our neighbors, or behave with sickness and fear if diseased systems and leaders were not brainwashing and coercing us.

Imagine the world's illnesses are healing and her resources have destroyed the false notion of scarcity. *There is abundance for all.* Imagine a world of people who have embraced their awareness of common good. *This is an understanding that making and writing rules is useless.* Imagine freedom, the imagination of the entirety of the human race truly liberated, once and for all. *There is no problem that we cannot overcome together.*

Freedom is the largest and most powerful kind of idea. We have titled this book *The Freedom Handbook* to help us focus on achieving this goal not just for us, but for everyone. Freedom – true, pure, and boundless – is within reach for every living human being. The time for us to claim our inheritance and free ourselves is now.

Around the world, governments, social programs, tax and monetary systems, legal structures, and violent conflict resolution tactics, such as war, are disgraceful and defunct. These structures are the depraved manipulations of ruling elite who enslaved humankind thousands of years ago and have become entrenched as a sort of axiom.

"They have to be there," we are told. "They've always been there. How would we function without them?"

The answer is simple: *easily*.

Therefore, it is time to draw a line. Opposing sides have been readying their forces and weaponry. We know defeat is inevitable for those who seek to limit humanity in any way. Victory is guaranteed for those of us seeking to unleash creative potential, and salve the wounds suffered by the societal chains we pretend exist.

You have been fighting all this time but do not worry, the rules have changed.

The weaponry of the enemy is extinct and powerless against the informed, cohesive, and inspired human race of today. For many who might not see this truth, the inspiring reality will become clear shortly.

It is often said that insanity is doing the same thing over and over but expecting a different result. This statement illustrates how mission critical it is for the global community to gather, and effect sweeping change immediately.

What will these changes look like?

"Those who cannot remember the past are condemned to repeat it."[2]
- George Santayana

This tiny book offers up readily available solutions and healthy changes for governance, social programs, education and health care, food systems, legal systems and laws. We will cover major changes in how we view the war on drugs, war in general, religious institutions, personal income, corporate and sales taxation, and the environment.

What this book does not do, is provide an already weary public with yet another perspective on our problems, served up with a depressing lack of tangible solutions. These frustrating efforts, although well-intentioned, play on our fears and outrage by using stories of enslavement and oppression, threats of civil collapse, and all out Armageddon. For those of you who have read books like William Cooper's *Behold a Pale Horse*[3] and watched movies like *Zeitgeist*,[4] reading the Freedom Handbook will be a vastly different experience.

It is important to regard this book as a means to begin a collective conversation. It is a fire starter. We do not claim to have all the answers in here. We will cover enormous ground, just by honing in on the core issues, while removing all the basic irrelevancies. Far too many of us are permanently sidetracked with questions about what is going on behind the scenes, within authority structures and elite circles. This handbook ignores the rabbit holes and evidences just how moot most of these issues truly are.

What is relevant to this discussion and to our collective future, is the intersection between humanity's pain and our potential to be so much more. This juxtaposition is driving us all toward solutions. We need to look at our roadblocks, in order to match them effectively

---

[2] *The Life of Reason* (New York: Dover Publications, 1980, repr. New York: Charles Scribner's Sons,1905), vol. 1, ch. XII, http://gutenberg.org/files/15000/15000-h/15000-h.htm

[3] (Light Technology Publishing), 1991.

[4] Directed by Peter Joseph (GMP, 2007), video and DVD.

with illustrations of our potential, and the best options available to make things better.

During this quick study of our problems and our best solutions, if you disagree with certain opinions or facts, refocus your attention on the solutions you do think will work. With so much to discuss, it is unrealistic to think you will agree with everything.

In the very beginning, as Luke and I began to share these ideas with friends, associates, and family, a few things became clear.

First, the ingenuity and imagination of humanity is truly untapped, unstoppable, and up to any challenge.

Second, it would be impossible to outline detailed solutions for all the world's various problems in a single book. However, this little manifesto does possess the pivotal beating heart of our freedom. It is up to all of us to continue the conversation this book aims to start and use that to create a plan of action. This is a roadmap of specific steps to affect total revolution, instantly and peacefully.

Third, people wondered, "What makes you think the entire world will listen to the two of you?" and, "Are you ready for the personal attacks and fight of a lifetime you will have to deal with if this hits the mainstream?"

To these questions, we answer that while a messenger can be a deviant, a pariah, or even insane, if the message itself has value then its *truth* cannot be diminished by the person who speaks it.

Therefore, Luke and I have decided to challenge our readers to ignore our failings. To throw away an important message in distaste of its deliverance is to wash away humanity's salvation with filthy rags of ego and judgment.

Luke and I have discovered in one another, a complete and resounding readiness. So, yes, mainstream – bring on your queries. We welcome them, because our message is stronger than we are, and necessary to fix the problems which are plaguing our entire species.

Luke and I feel humanity's monstrous need for change with incredible raw force, and we are committed to this course. Ever since we can remember, both of us have possessed abhorrence for the current discordant structure. Today, these feelings have grown so large that they live in a place where no words can convey them. This calling is a giant pressure, which has worked our flesh raw.

We are not great men with noteworthy contributions or admirable characters. We are just two normal guys approaching the middle of our lives who have had enough of the pain, injustice, and senselessness in our world.

Since we were young, we have both possessed an awareness that we cannot shake. It has driven us to fight the system we were born into with openness, to avoid and break more rules than some would care to. More importantly though, this awareness has focused both of us enough to understand our world, and has compelled us to face difficulties while hungrily seeking out solutions.

Today, our world is unbalanced, unhealthy, and, for many of us, a frightening, painful place. Some of you already fully understand the struggles that many people face, while others are less aware. Regardless, most of you feel and can acknowledge with open, honest, and difficult-to-swallow hopelessness the terrible strife of the human race.

You might be shocked when we confront you with horrors most cannot imagine yet none of us can refute, no matter how much we want to. We cannot afford to ignore the truth any longer, but that does not mean there is not hope. You are holding it in your hands, and we have done our best to weave hope, inspiration, and real solutions into this tale of humanity's troubles.

The coming truths will hit so hard that you will soon forget us, which is fine. We hope your excitement grows with each piece of the plan.

Imagine you are taking a trip in a NASA shuttle with a wonderfully comfortable sitting room and a huge transparent wall. Circling the earth, you soak up the beauty of our distant home below you. Around you, words drift out of a speaker system, describing the finer details of the portrait you are lucky enough to witness.

Who is speaking? Does it matter? The messenger is irrelevant when the message is about the whole world. Sometimes, you have to take a hundred steps backward, upward, or outside of yourself when faced with ideas that challenge your current beliefs.

This perspective is often referred to as a satellite view.

Our ability to be objective and detached from personal prejudice is essential.

This book may prompt what some refer to as a dark night of the soul, a terrifying experience in which we realize we do not know anything about the world we inhabit. Tightly held beliefs about our society, ourselves, and everything we know may be completely shattered.

Examine carefully the things that make you most uncomfortable. Why are you uncomfortable? Follow those feelings to their deceptive roots and discover where they really come from. Be gentle with yourself and give these big ideas and hard questions time to percolate.

No one has ever experienced pure freedom - no one. Here is a very basic and current world example. You decide to buy a truck from a person who is advertising online. You pay him or her and receive a bill of sale so you can prove it is now yours. The truck is your private property, right? Can you jump in the truck and bring it home? Nope. You have to get insurance, a transfer permit, registration, and a license plate, which mean stipulations, qualifications, and money. The list ends here only if you already have a driver's license.

Not even close to freedom. You are not free now, and you never have been. Church and state have always been around telling you what is what. The cost of rejecting those ideas or fighting back could mean robbery, imprisonment, torture, or death – tyranny in every imaginable form.

Humanity has come to understand that the stakes are of the highest kind. They are life and death, slavery and freedom. Yet, the information regarding this incredibly important topic is confusing and, because of this, frustration is peaking. Some of us are stuck in magnetizing cycles arguing about what is wrong or what to do about it.

This progression points to the vital need for massive increases in solidarity.

Togetherness around solutions is all the more difficult due to the way even our language has been debased. This bastardization misshapes and mutes our response to words such as solidarity, freedom, and revolution just to name a few.

Many of us are enraged but far too overwhelmed and frightened to take action or join the discussion. That fear becomes apathy, and then acceptance. Better the pain you know than the chance of freedom.

Make no mistake that apathy is our largest foe. Your greatest battle will be letting go of the things that you believe to be true, the tenants that strip away your will to fight. Apathy thrives even within the groups working for truth and healthy change. A pure, cultivated, and gargantuan fear has allowed the potential of an entire world to be captured and controlled by a greedy, shortsighted, and ultimately pathetic few.

> *"Science may have found a cure for most evils; but it has found no remedy for the worst of them all—the apathy of human beings."*[5] *- Helen Keller -*

Good people typically cannot comprehend the atrocity that our world has become when laid bare before them, or envision solutions that make real sense. As a result, they fall apart at the communicative seams. We know this. We have seen it happen, and so we want to make a deal with you, right here and now.

We need you to have the courage to read this book from cover to cover with an open mind and an open heart - really open up. Together, let us examine carefully and without prejudice the world we live in. Be ready to examine the plan with eyes that see only core, unbiased truth and ears that listen with meticulous discernment.

Sometimes a song's sad melody hurts, but we find acceptance and healing in knowing it is supposed to be uncomfortable.

When the going gets tough and you feel like throwing the book down in disgust, please, hang in until the end. If you finish this modern manifesto, we swear you will be properly informed and inspired, like never before. You will be ready to hash out solutions within your community and solve problems that seemed insurmountable before.

Remember that when taken to task, and hammered to the wall with the most basic truths, ideas, and principles that you hold dear, the work you now hold in your hands has stood up to all criticisms and challenges thus far.

If you want applicable, easy examples of healthy solutions to the problems and troubles that assail you, we have provided answers throughout this book, along with snippets from the debates that sparked those answers when we first started sharing these ideas. We are hoping you will insist on hearing the final deliberations that put these ideas to the test.

---

[5] *My Religion* (San Diego: The Book Tree, 2007; orig. pub. New York: Swedenborg Foundation Inc., 1927), 162.

The time has arrived for the human race to investigate and create a global movement, a worldwide campaign for freedom.

Robust discussion alone among average people, committed to honest and open conversation about any perceived holes in this plan, quite often ends in a consensus based upon viable solutions.

Luke and I hereby call out the global media, our leaders from every field of thought on earth, as well as our human family at large and ask that you chew on these ideas, try them on for size. Live them, internalize them, and by all means, call us. We would love to hash out all the grimy little details with you and help build solutions around what the world needs.

Be assured that the world as a whole is far better equipped than we two alone, to try and design the intricate nuances of our future mechanisms and structures. This is only a part of the start to something so much larger than any of us.

What humanity needs, right now and more than anything, is a viable plan of action with absolute merit. We need a common understanding, a common goal, and an agreed-upon stratagem that we can all follow. Leaders need solid direction as information rules the day, but consensus is nowhere to be found. Leaders are everywhere, but humanity desperately needs a place to gather, and ideas to gather around.

We are helping to create that space, and you, with this book in your hands, are a part of that process.

Cut to the core, this manuscript was crafted to accomplish two things.

The first is to offer many of the world's brightest solutions, in one spot, in the strictest common-sense form. Second, to create awareness of the vast problems we face. For those of you desperate for the perfect tool to pass to someone you know, regardless of their current beliefs, this book is something you can count on. It addresses more advanced questions, while also offering a highly effective wake-up call for people, at any stage of awareness.

The wounds that the current power systems inflict every single day are designed to keep you asleep. This book is designed to help you wake up.

Luke and I did our utmost to bring together the very best ideas we have come across. These are real, palpable, workable solutions and ideas that pave a luminous and revolutionary path.

> *Did you know that every single day, the speed with which humanity collectively solves crossword puzzles increases as the day wears on? We get faster by the hour because our collective awareness, which is caused by the ethereal conversations around the answers, increases as time passes.*[6]

> *We feel that Luke's original decision, followed by our collective one, to pen these thoughts is indicative of the bubbling need for their expression. Humanity's collective consciousness is speaking, telling us, "It's impossible not to continue this discussion and follow it through to new and inevitable comprehensive solutions."*

The global palaver has begun, and it is becoming a tidal wave. Creating a birthing action that transforms and transcends. We are all growing into an accountability that lies to our local, regional, national, and global communities rather than the abstract power structures of the past that we have all been trained to take for granted. Thus will we come to rule ourselves in the name of that accountability to our communities and ourselves.

We will all be free.

---

[6] Rupert Sheldrake, *The Presence of the Past: The Habits of Nature* (Rochester, VT: Park Street Press, 1988), 182-196.

Truly free.

In so many dreams around the world, humanity has come together. It is time for tribes of visionaries and idea-folk to dream and stretch for an entire race. We can dream together, all we free thinkers and revolutionaries, tech-friends and young visionaries, armies of mothers and daughters, professionals, laborers, academics, artists...even children.

We all must come together like never before. We must build a new, online, in-your-face community. We must create an integral, perpetual, transparent, and unstoppable tool in our new organization and understanding of freedom. Let us craft together a new administration, a battle plan, and find salvation together.

Brothers and sisters, we hope you find this book a collection of truths, and if you find a flaw in our work, so much the better. Doubt inspires thought, and thought is the tool of freedom. We hope this book builds high the fire of your inspiration, and that you find it embodies the soul of humanity's new freedom.

This book is meant to be challenging. The Freedom Handbook is meant to get your blood boiling and raise the hackles on the back of your neck. We need to get you thinking, cursing, doubting. Ultimately, we need to get you to engage and shed the chains of apathy that have been placed upon you.

Be warned again: you may feel like giving up the discussion at some point. When that happens, please remember our deal. If you continue past these next few sentences, then you are committing to reading the entire book before solidifying your opinions.

It is just a mere few hundred pages, you can do this.

For our part, we promise to keep things concise, based in fact, and informative enough to shape conversation but rough enough to keep you involved as needed. This is going to be an exhilarating trip focused primarily on designing our world's future. You will properly understand our present situation as well as the execution plan for freeing ourselves from the systematic oppression that enslaves us. A plan that moves towards a global liberation, abundance, and freedom for all.

We wrote this book to stir the pot, to get people upset and talking. Many views are strong and may offend some people, but everyone is entitled to his or her own opinions and these are ours. We make absolutely no apologies. In fact, we relish the idea of getting some people fired right up – the tough statements herein are intended to shatter the foundation of corrupt ideas and systems, to poke you and make you think, to draw you to try these solutions within your community.

The challenge is everyone's. If you think our ideas are unfeasible, then let us come up with better ones together. Humanity cannot help but improve on the tired ideas still in use today. As change makers, Luke and I are always willing to listen. We are very aware that the common sense of our fellow humans will eventually rule the day.

Radical and unhealthy ideas must be weeded out and distilled. We are ready for honest debate on all fronts, ready to shed old and expired ideas in favor of something better. Get yourself ready to abandon *your* old ideas. It is time to stop complaining. It is time to start the official discussion, to instigate real working solutions and create healthy change.

Hang on for one of the wildest rides of your life.

CHAPTER TWO

- New Administrative Structures -

Through careful collusion we have been made to feel impotent. We have been tricked into feeling powerless when the simple truth is that any single one of us can reshape the world. A small number of us, collected and working together are more powerful than all the chains that keep us from the freedom that is our birthright.

> *"If humanity does not opt for integrity we are through completely. It is absolutely touch and go. Each one of us could make the difference."*[1]
> *- R. Buckminster Fuller -*

Each and every one of us has the opportunity to turn the tide of humanity's most dire moment – the time we are living in right now. Rejoice, friends! We have a strategy, a workable way to save the world, and here is the beginning of our plan for rebirth.

> *"What I'm thinking about more and more these days is simply the importance of transparency, and Jefferson's saying that he'd rather have a free press without a government than a government without a free press."*[2]
> *- Esther Dyson -*

---

[1] L. Steven Seider, "Bucky Fuller: Every person makes a difference and integrity is critical," *Examiner* Web site (November 25, 2012), http://www.examiner.com/article/bucky-fuller-every-person-makes-a-difference-and-integrity-is-critical.

[2] "Esther Dyson." BrainyQuote.com. Xplore Inc, 2014. 2 March 2014. http://www.brainyquote.com/quotes/quotes/e/estherdyso352080.html.

> *"In reality the workings of your governing systems are opaque and covert, while hiding in the chattering spotlight of an ostensible transparency, even though the ultimate objective is clear."*[3]
> - Breyten Breytenbach -

Governments are not necessary anymore.

Take a moment to consider that. We have evolved past the old methods of organization. Now, we are not saying that we do not need an administrative structure. Structure remains, but the world we are looking to build is governed by the people and for the people, not by a few elites for the rest of us.

The new establishment we are looking to build organizes information and decision-making processes. Decisions can no longer be top down, arbitrary, or individual, they must be based on relevant, completely transparent data. What exactly does this mean and how will it all work?

To serve its community dependably and lovingly, a country, state, provincial, regional, or city-level administration needs to operate based on three simple pillars:

1. All data must be handled with complete transparency, at all times, within the administration, and must be made available to any member of the community that desires it.
2. The administration cannot make high-level decisions. Its purpose is to facilitate the community decision-making process by sourcing and sorting available data. This data is then presented to the community as a whole, and the community votes on the options to ensure the healthiest choices are made.

---

[3] *The Nation* Web site (September 23, 2002), http://thenation.com/article/letter-to-america-4.

3. Wages in the new administration are performance based, and volunteers are encouraged to fill as many positions and perform as many functions as possible.

Let us examine and qualify the merit of these essential pillars.

> *"I just think we need more accountability and more transparency."*[4]
> *- John Thune, US Senator -*

In political arenas, terms such as "transparency," "accountability," "freedom," and "democracy" are used to make us feel good, to inspire us to vote, or to make us believe that our elected powers actually embody these terms. In reality, these words have been poisoned, twisted, and ultimately interlaced with blatant lies to incite support and confidence for a system in which transparency, efficiency, ethics, true liberty, and common sense are mathematical and logistical impossibilities. We will prove that this is so in the next chapter.

> *"At the dawn of his administration, President Obama opined: 'A democracy requires accountability, and accountability requires transparency.' Magical rays of white-hot sunlight emanated from his media-manufactured halo. And then bureaucratically engineered darkness settled over the land."*[5]
> *- Michelle Malkin –*

---

[4] Neil Cavuto, "Sen. John Thune on Legislation to Block Bailout of State Pension Plans," *Fox News* Web site (February 9, 2011), http://www.foxnews.com/on-air/your-world-cavuto/transcript/sen-john-thune-legislation-block-bailout-state-pension-plans.

[5] "Obama's Cloud-Based Transparency," Michelle Malkin Web site, http://www.michellemalkin.com/2011/11/30/obamas-cloud-based-transparency/ (Nov. 30, 2011).

Complete transparency is, without question, the number one requirement for the highest levels of organization. The world's governments and private organizations could all use a definitive transparent twist.

> *"If human beings are fundamentally good, no government is necessary; if they are fundamentally bad, any government, being composed of human beings, would be bad also."[6]*
> *- Fred Woodworth -*

We need to plan our future with critical questioning and sense. This chapter is based on clean and unyielding common sense. It is one of the shortest in the book and was the easiest to put together because the ideas are naturally simple and starkly obvious. Humanity's natural and abundant common sense is often the keystone in this book's discussions, and in any life worth living.

> *"Common sense is the genius of humanity."[7]*
> *- François Guizot -*

Right now, we are going to begin exploring human potential, common sense, administrative solutions, and a few key transformative realities. These transformations have already begun and affect every stitch of life, though they are often unnoticed. They are proof of a changing world and even though they are only beginning to take shape, these potent new tools and strategies form the basis of what we call "cooperative infrastructure."

We have two questions for you to think about as we move forward, and they are not easy. We are going to have to come back to them

---

[6] *The Match* (n.d.).
[7] Quoted by William Maxwell Wood, *A Shoulder to the Wheel of Progress* (Applewood Books, 2009, orig. pub. 1853), 65.

throughout our discussions. *Why do some people still believe we need a government to solve our problems and assuage our fears? If there were no ruling authority in our world, other than common sense and community, would we really have some sort of meltdown and start rioting in the streets?*

We have a third question that is more implied than directly addressed, but it is food for thought. *Why the heck have we lived with this unsuccessful government structure for so long?*

To make the second pillar a reality, we simply need to use the Internet.

Casting votes online allows the public to easily make decisions for the community. For example, if the community needs a new bridge, the administrative volunteers and staff responsible for local bridges post online a list of quotes from qualified vendors. Then the public votes to decide who should win the bid.

The administrative people also manage suppliers and ensure that they are doing a great job. The administration cannot be bought off, as the staff and volunteers making up the establishment are not making the decisions – it is up to the community to decide. Vendors are then forced to influence the people in order to win the contract of the day, not to mention our continued loyalty. This process demands nothing short of honest, quality work.

The third pillar of humanity's new, bare bones yet highly effective administration for self-governance, asks some of us to volunteer a little time to aid administrative and social processes.

The world is full of all kinds of different people who enjoy lending their skills to help out in all types of ways. Some will love to be top officials and public speakers, others will contribute to, or take on, the duties of major positions or even aid with average administrative needs. Undoubtedly there are huge numbers of people who would be happy to contribute to their communities through volunteering. It is clear we will have no problem filling many high-profile positions and accomplishing substantial amounts of the basic tasking with volunteers.

Look at how Wikipedia is able to accomplish mountains of work and achieve most of its objectives by using the public at large. Wikipedia is one of the largest websites in the world and is run by a non-profit organization, the Wikimedia Foundation.[8] It relies on millions of volunteers' steady contributions.

To pay staff, the new administration uses a common-sense tiered remuneration system. Periodically throughout the year (perhaps quarterly), compensation is paid out at varying levels depending on the reviews and decisions the community as a whole has made. This final safety check affords the community an opportunity to openly, routinely, and fairly regulate the administrative staff's performance and compensation.

Luke and I fleshed out this performance based pay principle together, and it was hardly a challenging conversation compared to some others. Each community needs to decide on fine details that will work for them, and it will. The point is that committed, open-minded discussion is all that is needed to arrive at solutions that make healthy sense.

Do you have a suggestion to improve any of the ideas presented by your community? The world is listening, waiting for you to get out of that chair. On the other hand, go ahead and stay put and simply join the conversation via your favorite electronic device.

Now that we have laid a very loose foundation, let us go back and add a touch more depth to the first pillar. Our new administration must fund all activities with completely transparent fiscal systems. For example, let us say a localized and agreed-upon fuel tax was used to fill coffers that pay for road maintenance. All revenue received from fuel tax would be visible for the first time. If everyone could view the actual bank accounts, imagine how this one act of transparency would change things.

How much is your government collecting currently? Try to find out and you will discover that you would have had better luck trying

---

[8] Wikimedia Foundation, http://en.wikipedia.org/wiki/Wikipedia: Wikimedia_Foundation.

to nail water to a wall. This complete lack of transparency feeds the gross mismanagement and corruption currently running rampant in all government systems around the world.

At some point you might think, "I do not want to be involved. I do not want to be responsible for taking care of complicated things. The world is way too complex. We need smart people and governments and rulers to take care of things."

Here is a quick word of warning to you. Humans have never thought this way before, in centuries or even millennia, past. Only the pleasures of modern society have dulled our wits so effectively. A few short generations before ours and all the way back through time, humankind watched rulers with a steely eye. We had to fight for our lives for every ounce of liberty and freedom in the land. After securing some measure of freedom, we knew that holding on to the scraps we had bled for meant maintaining a vigilant, watchful readiness. We opposed, with every ounce of our beings, the ruling authority's tyranny and oppression.

Here is another truth, not everyone needs to concern themselves with everything. As the existence of current charities and volunteers indicate, there are more than enough people concerned about various social issues. Typically, all that will be asked in the future is that you help a little bit more than before, in the areas you care most about, gathering with your community to build collective strength or vote on the odd social issue.

Self-governance asks that we all work together instead of looking to authorities for answers. This means that you will have to discuss local issues with your neighbors, friends, family, and communities. That is not asking so much, is it? A heightened sense of our collective responsibility and a small set of individual responsibilities is the basic price of freedom.

Our modern apathy is the reason current governments can manipulate us to any end, revoke our most basic human rights, steal from us at every turn, and tax us to death. Governments can arbitrarily throw us in jail with little or no evidence and can even take our homes, cars, or businesses away, for not following their rules or, heaven forbid, not paying those taxes. They have routinely, in the interest of "national security" or some other rubbish, stolen our property, sent us off to fight and die in endless wars, or thrown us in prison. These are just a few of the horrific and daily occurrences that happen because we allow them to.

In our system, all you would have to do to play your part in a new and better world would be to look up some local issues online and cast a vote by clicking. That is a very small price to pay for freedom.

Furthermore, who says everyone has to vote? Do you agree that a certain very low percentage (10 percent or less perhaps) of an entire population will represent the views of the majority? In essence, for a population of ten million people, even a half- or quarter-million people can speak for the remainder. If the remainder spoke, the result would surely be the same.

The self-governance solutions for administration truly are this simple and efficient.

Many of the innovative ideas we will discuss under the term "cooperative infrastructure" are already active and slowly being accepted as the new standard operating procedures (SOPs) for the healthiest parts of the private sector.

Responsibly and with love, this system shall serve us, our children, and our humanity well into the future. Where is the love in any of our current systems? History reveals that even the strongest among us can rarely, if ever, withstand the pressures of politics without succumbing to corruption. A system cannot love unless it is a collection of us all, and if it cannot love than it is doomed to failure.

> *"Power tends to corrupt, and absolute power corrupts absolutely. Great men are almost always bad men."*[9]
> *- Lord Acton -*

---

[9] Lord John Emerich Edward Dalberg-Acton, "Letter to Bishop Mandell Creighton, April 5, 1887," in *Historical Essays and Studies*, eds. John Neville Figgis and Reginald Vere Laurence (London: MacMillan and Co.,1907), 504.

In the last chapter, we promised to lay out the implications of the current technological revolution in our administrative conversation. When this monster concept is woven into the three pillars of self-governance that we just presented in an effort to support the infinite potential of humanity as a whole, only then will freedom stand revealed.

Freedom in administration means fiscal sustainability, security, and common sense. It means communal social responsibility through equal access and never-before-seen levels of collaboration and sharing. This technical revolution turns old information-revolution models on their heads and paves the way for widespread, sustainable, healthy, and relatively easy changes to our fiscal systems.

> *"Non-disclosure in the Internet Age is quickly perceived as a breach of trust. Government, corporations and each of us as individuals must recalibrate how we live and share our lives appropriate to the information now available and the expectations of others."*[10]
> *- Simon Mainwaring -*

How does our world currently accomplish anything? By organizing itself through what we call "institution." People gather together to fulfill a desired goal, setting in place various costly methods and physical locations to forward the pursuit of stated agendas. Human agendas of all kinds, for profit or not, always require enormous amounts of money and the gathering of qualified professionals and necessary materials. Institutionalizing our goals has been the only paradigm for a long time and, again, involves huge infrastructure

---

[10] "The Coming Decade of Radical Transparency," *The We First Blog* Web site, http://simonmainwaring.com/social-networking/the-coming-decade-of-radical-transparency (December 16, 2010).

and coordination costs. Our city's downtown landscapes are a terrific example.

Whether you are starting a business, spreading a message, or chasing your dreams, institutionalizing goals has always been far too expensive for the common person or even the common good. Many of us can personally attest to this painful reality.

These worn-out models are insanely expensive due to the cost of moving people and resources together around our problems.

The logistical, financial, and even moral disgraces of old institutional models are already beginning to be eradicated and transformed by emerging technologies and social practices.

Let us use the term *cooperative infrastructure* to describe the fruits of our technical revolution, which affords game-changing differences that we are only beginning to discover and understand. Consider the following five points:

Cooperative infrastructure shifts problems to individuals and teams.

When people can work from wherever they are, horrendous costs are eliminated and productivity is bolstered to impressive new heights. This evolution also removes large archaic expenses and cumbersome processes tied to managing employees and resources in the traditional manner.

Through the Internet, every single individual can be actively engaged in access, input, and sharing. These things allow suitable solutions and self-governance to develop.

> *"The internet is becoming the town square for the global village of tomorrow."*[11]
> *- Bill Gates -*

---

[11] A. Jeff Ifrah and Steven Eichorn, "Commentary: Banned from the Internet," *National Law Journal* (October 11, 2010).

2. Cooperative infrastructure replaces institution's costly habits regarding projections and planning with new, robust efficiencies in testing and agility.

The fashion industry provides a stunning example of this point. The industry has a long history of unpredictable customer behavior tied to costly seasonal design and manufacturing guesswork. I heard a story years ago, about one perceptive company that decided to put a selection of clothes online and ask customers to vote on their favorites. They eliminated all risk, guaranteed record sales, and ensured never-before-seen levels of customer satisfaction. They were pioneers, using a strategy for interaction with customers and communities that is now heavily established and highly effective.

These days, the public helps develop various products, services, and even the operations of many institutions. Numerous companies have begun to recognize the value of surveying and involving the public more. Imagine how humanity could leverage the full power behind this still-emerging technique for the public good.

The cell phone exemplifies another way technology eliminates and/or radically simplifies planning methods. Look at how mobile phones have affected the way we meet with friends for drinks or stay in touch as they move locations. This is just one small example in a sea of technological changes. Technology at each new turn saves people both time and resources.

In today's world, change makers understand that no matter how they envision their creations being used, the world may reinvent them and take them to a completely new level. Look at how we have used the Internet in a million unforeseen ways and totally recreated it with common people's collective actions, voices, and imaginations.

Our instant access to information and the ever-growing ways we can manipulate and learn from data, share what we have learned, and thus improve on past performance is astounding. The tools and strategies we use to project and plan for our future are shifting considerably.

Tim Berners-Lee is accredited by some for inventing the World Wide Web, as we know it today. Though many individuals, such as J.C.R. Licklider, Paul Baran, Donald Davies, Vint Cerf, Robert Kahn, and hypertext pioneers Vannevar Bush, Ted Nelson, and Douglas Engelbart, just to name a few, helped with pieces of the ideas and technology we know of as the Internet.[12]

In a TED Talk called The Next Web, Tim Berners-Lee talks about a new technology he calls Linked Data, an Internet-sized example of innovation and new opportunities[13] that is still in infant stages.

Linked Data is the difference between the Internet's current content and the raw data that is constantly being collected, manipulated, and scrutinized by small parties of unconnected people in all areas of life. Some of the advantages of Linked Data are better understood in the context of our experiences with our private data and its potential value to corporations like Facebook.[14]

Massive stores of valuable information are unused. Enormous potential is just waiting to be discovered from all our scientific research data alone, loads of which is still locked away in private databases and computers all over the world and not yet being shared.

In his talk, Tim describes a complicated research question which delivers no viable search results on the Internet, but when faculties

---

[12] "Internet History Timeline," *Internet Hall of Fame* Web site, http://www.internethalloffame.org/internet-history/timeline; "Inductees," *Internet Hall of Fame* Web site, http://www.internethalloffame.org/inductees/all.

[13] "The Next Web," *TED Talks* Web site (March, 2009), http://www.ted.com/talks/tim_berners_lee_on_the_next_web.html; "Inductees: Innovator Tim Berners-Lee, *Internet Hall of Fame* Web site, http://internethalloffame.org/inductees/tim-berners-lee.

[14] Christian Bizer, Tom Heath, and Tim Berners-Lee, "Linked Data—The Story So Far," http://tomheath.com/papers/bizer-heath-berners-lee-ijswis-linked-data.pdf; http://www.ted.com/talks/tim_berners_lee_on_the_next_web.html; "Inductees: Innovator Tim Berners-Lee, *Internet Hall of Fame* Web site, http://internethalloffame.org/inductees/tim-berners-lee; "Linked Data—Connect Distributed Data Across the Web," http://linkeddata.org/; Linked-open-data-Europeana-video.ogv; "Linked Data," *Wikipedia* Web site, http://en.wikipedia.org/wiki/Linked_data.

with varying elements of Alzheimer research combined their raw data and posed the same question, thirty-two proteins that matched the complicated search query were instantly located.

Linked Data's huge implications point out the infinite potential to make better collective decisions as we upload and learn to share and sort all our pure data.

If you have access, you can help get raw data online. The rest of us can help best by adding our voices to the public pressure, which is already encouraging the world's organizations to start doing so. Shortly, we will lay out ways to get involved in this issue and any others you might like to help with.

Municipal, educational, and health-systems data, for example, could and should be shared by all. Imagine what we will learn and how we will improve on past performance when humanity has all the facts about all areas of life on the table. The sky is hardly the limit here.

For many of us, the full scope of Linked Data's potential can be a stretch to understand. If possible, talk to anyone who works with raw data in a research capacity to better grasp the infinite possibilities that come from manipulating that data.

3. Cooperative infrastructure allows the common person to create and share books, art, news, science, etc. Sharing this media is nearly free in comparison to older and more conventional forms of print, radio, and TV media. With this ability to create and share, the common collective can change and even govern the world.

Before the Internet, you had to be extremely wealthy or secure the support of large media corporations to get any message out to the world. Now, the raging debate over blogger and citizen journalism in the mainstream media already signals our victory.

This modern time we so lovingly refer to as "the information age" is characterized by an explosion of online media, movements, and common participation. We have joined the ranks of content creators and global co-creators. We have helped shape political movements by discovering the power of our voice. We have already begun creating the world we want through better news gathering and sharing, no longer relying on pre-approved snippets of information that someone, somewhere, thinks that we should know.

These are small but widely visible examples of the new technical efficiencies we learn more about every day.

The true power of cooperative infrastructure is only just being discovered. Visible, viable applications throughout private organizations and governments are already apparent and producing astounding results, even if our governing bodies are doing so with the usual ineffectual slowness.

If you need more proof for such outrageous statements, have patience. The evidence is coming. Be ready to mine for truth amidst personal prejudices and fear.

4. By using volunteers, cooperative infrastructure outperforms the old model in leaps and bounds. It replaces an overly heavy reliance on paid professionals and captures enormous lost creative and collaborative potential without fiscal cost.

There's a mathematical principle that applies to much of the world, a principle that we call "the power law." Interestingly, it also appears in many unrestrained social systems where people are allowed to contribute as much or as little as they want. The law is more commonly referred to as the 80/20 rule. This mathematical certainty dictates that roughly 20 percent of contributors account for about 80 percent of the results in any effort.[15]

The following images show this math by comparing Flickr and Wikipedia to normal institutionalized efforts. Most of the people who contribute to both new systems are not part of standard institution's "paid potential."

---

[15] Clay Shirky, "Institutions vs. Collaboration," *TED Talks* Web site (TEDGlobal 2005), 7:40, http://www.ted.com/talks/clay_shirky_on_institutions_versus_collaboration.html; Clay Shirky, "Power Laws, Weblogs, and Inequality," *Clay Shirky's Writings About the Internet: Economics & Culture, Media & Community, Open Source* Web site (February 8, 2003), http://www.shirky.com/writings/powerlaw_weblog.html.

People in new models will volunteer their time to sort data and contribute in small, individually manageable ways to the larger communal goal. Do not worry needlessly about whether we will be able to find enough volunteer staff to organize the data for our administrative needs. We already know the systems we will put in place and the people needed to run them will find one another.

In the newer systems we are speaking of, 20 percent of us are still responsible for about 80 percent of the results. However, by inviting anyone and everyone to volunteer their time and abilities, the world captures invaluable free contributions.

Cooperative infrastructure unleashes humanity's full problem-solving potential by securing the missing 80 percent of individual contributions and corresponding 20 percent of value. It accomplishes this mighty feat with no cost when compared to the institutional model of hiring and managing staff.

This new, near-free, connected, and creative workforce outperforms institutions that are more traditional by engaging the community at large. Essentially, more heads and hands on deck mean more efficient and successful activities.

For anyone who would like to learn more about how collaboration shatters institutional paradigms, Clay Shirky presents some of these ideas in video format. Clay is an adjunct professor in New York University's graduate Interactive Telecommunications Program, and the author of several books. His TED Talk on SOPA/PIPA,[16] a legislative attack on freedom, had over one million views in its first forty-eight hours online.

Clay Shirky's ideas about collaboration and institution have significantly affected millions of people, not to mention the impact his ideas are having on groups and organizations. Clay uses the term "cognitive surplus" to describe some of the benefits of cooperative infrastructure we have been discussing.

---

[16] "Why SOPA is a bad idea," *TED Talks* Web site (TED Salon NY 2012), http://www.ted.com/talks/defend_our_freedom_to_share_or_why_sopa_is_a_bad_idea.html.

If you like inspiring and engaging speakers, Clay is fantastic at delivering fact-based motivation. You can have a look at the following three talks Clay gave for an even more in-depth look at some of these amazing, transparent, and healthy changes by clicking the following links:

> Institutions versus Collaboration[17]
> How Cognitive Surplus Will Change the World[18]
> How the Internet Will Transform Government[19]

In the last of those three links, he crushes all debate about open-sourced solutions across social structure by discussing new technologies from Linus Torvalds.

5. Cooperative infrastructure allows us to focus on and eliminate the corruption of our motivations, goals, and heartfelt intentions.

Self-preservation trumps all concerns that our global organizations were built to serve. Many problems humans face today can be attributed, in part, to this structural flaw. As it stands, while any classic orgnaization's inception papers are still wet with ink, the community's focus immediately moves from the original goal to new primary directives supporting the institution's preservation.

Take some time to absorb the implications of this. The root of all institutional failure to meet humanity's needs lies here, and is one of the quietest and most subtle ways our goals are corrupted.

When an institution's motivations shift this way, our world's integrity crumbles and humanity's dreams and liberties disappear amidst profit and power's insatiable call. Therefore, our future will be constructed of unshakable, omnipresent transparency.

---

[17] *TED Talks* Web site (TEDGlobal 2005), 7:40, http://www.ted.com/talks/clay_shirky_on_institutions_versus_collaboration.html;

[18] *TED Talks* Web site (TED@Cannes, 2010), http://www.ted.com/talks/clay_shirky_how_cognitive_surplus_will_change_the_world.html.

[19] *TED Talks* Web site (TEDGlobal, 2012), http://www.ted.com/talks/clay_shirky_how_the_internet_will_one_day_transform_government.html.

> *"The internet treats censorship as a malfunction and routes around it."*[20]
> *- John Gilmore -*

By now, a glimpse of our potential may have emerged in your mind. Understand that we will never again attempt a projection before setting sail on a venture. Projection is a concept of the past and was always an illusory, human-made construct, much like government itself. Every outcome has always been out of our hands. Co-creation and the mysteries of life always bring the unexpected.

We can successfully face the problems of today and our future only with open acceptance, communal responsibility, and imaginative, ever-agile decision-making. Transparency must run through our blood. It will be the life force of our emerging communicative culture.

> *"A lack of transparency results in distrust and a deep sense of insecurity."*[21]
> *- The Dalai Lama -*

> *"Transparency is not the same as looking straight through a building: it's not just a physical idea, it's also an intellectual one."*[22]
> *- Helmut Jahn -*

---

[20] Barlow, John Perry. "Passing the Buck on Pornography," http://w2.eff.org/Misc/Publications/John_Perry_Barlow/HTML/porn_and_responsibility.html; Judith Lewis, "Why Johnny Can't Surf," *LA Weekly*, 43 (Feb. 21, 1997).

[21] "Dalai Lama: I shout and say harsh words," *The Telegraph* (May 13, 2012), http://www.telegraph.co.uk/news/worldnews/asia/tibet/9261176/Dalai-Lama-I-shout-and-say-harsh-words.html.

[22] Quoted by Norman Weinstein in "Book Review: 'Immaterial World: Transparency in Architecture': Marc Kristal crystallizes increasingly complex notions of transparency with a light touch," *ArchNewsNow* Web site (March 25, 2011), www.archnewsnow.com/features/Features355.htm. (Wilhelm 2011)

Does the plan look radical to you so far?

Do the administrative suggestions seem a tad socialist? At this infant stage of our adventure, perhaps you think the plan seems solid, simple even. On the other hand, maybe you are not so sure, but underneath the skepticism and fear, your hope runs high. Despite a plethora of unanswered questions, general feedback at this stage has been positive and inspired. This says a lot about our need for massive change.

> *"Compassion is not weakness, and concern for the unfortunate is not socialism."*[23]
> *- Hubert H. Humphrey -*

> *"Everything proceeds as if of its own accord, and this can all too easily tempt us to relax and let things take their course without troubling over details. Such indifference is the root of all evil."*[24]
> *- I Ching -*

Indifference is apathy's closest cousin. Do not worry if you are not quite on board yet, because there is a lot of encouraging and provocative material left to cover. Many will take longer to adjust, and that is okay too. You will get there. We believe in you. Just be prepared, for considering the more difficult truths within this book will involve tearing your perceived reality to pieces.

You have heard a few small yet absolutely key pieces of humanity's best plans for a new world. There are new ways to organize our local and global administration. You were promised a thrilling and frightening snapshot of our world alongside a fresh and compelling road map for global coup and rebirth.

---

[23] Antony Jay, *Lend Me Your Ears: Oxford Dictionary of Political Quotations* (Oxford: Oxford University Press, 2010), 140.

[24] Helmut Wilhelm, *The I Ching or Book of Changes* (Princeton University Press, 2011).

The snapshot begins in earnest on the next page. Trust us.

To gather the world's common folk, or enough to change the world, we all must travel in trust together across this tale and bear honest witness to everything, as it is laid out, with patience.

Use the quiet spaces in between chapters to engage your imagination, to awaken your involvement, to broaden your acceptance and sense of responsibility. With each section, as tidbits and pieces come together, know that the excitement and impatience you feel is good.

In fact, it means you are listening, you are alive and human. This process can be nasty, gritty, and terribly tough, as much as it is wonderful, empowering, and life changing. We will do our best to feed your appetite.

It is time to get serious and really shake things up. Let us discuss zero percent tax, the extinction of all social programs as they exist today, and methods for meeting humanity's needs in healthier ways. Let us evidence how every single government program the world over is the very definition of insanity and inefficiency.

Again and again, we keep bumping into the insanity cliché about using old, flawed ideas. Luke and I define insanity as follows: attempting to silence the voices in your head and heart with popular behavior and thought.

CHAPTER THREE

- Taxes and Social Programs -

A word of warning: this chapter's going to rock your boat. Once you are done with the initial shock, roll up your sleeves, because there is inner and collective work to be done.

> "My humanity is bound up in yours, for we can only be human together."[1]
> - Desmond Tutu -

> "Wisdom ceases to be wisdom when it becomes too proud to weep, too grave to laugh, and too self-ful to seek other than itself."[2]

> "Where is the justice of political power if it executes the murderer and jails the plunderer, and then itself marches upon neighboring lands, killing thousands and pillaging the very hills?"[3]
> - Kahlil Gibran -

Let us start with a difficult truth and move forward from there. Income and corporate taxes are no longer needed. Our new administrations will not arbitrarily collect any, and this means that all the money you earn is yours and yours alone.

---

[1] *The Words of Desmond Tutu,* 2nd ed. (New York: Newmarket Press, 2006), 71.
[2] *Sand and Foam* in *Kahlil Gibran: The Collected Works*, Everyman's Library ed. (New York: Alfred A. Knopf, 2007), 208.
[3] *The Treasured Writings of Kahlil Gibran* (Edison, NJ: Castle Books, 1975), 849.

That would mark the end of social programs as they exist today – no more government health care, welfare, pensions, subsidies, bailouts, or black budgets. No more mismanaged and wasted community resources. From now on, a community's resources stay within the community. Our own wealth, back in our own pockets, will equip us to solve our own problems.

If the community needs something done, people will naturally respond by creating common sense solutions. Some people will likely disagree with the last statement, and that is okay because if you feel as though humanity's innate goodness and problem-solving abilities are not a sure bet, wait, watch, and listen. We will come back to the idea a few times over the course of this book.

The law of supply and demand is as applicable to unrestrained social behavior as it is to today's economic societies. This math ensures that my amazing grandmother and all seniors who currently receive a government pension check will be taken care of. The check she receives and her financial security were hot topics for Luke and me during my introduction to these ideas, but honest debate between open-minded people eventually led to a healthy consensus.

Here are the five items we are going to discuss in this chapter:

1. Governments are not built by the people or for the people. They are built by the few to control the many.
2. All state social programs the world over are fiscally unsustainable.
3. Government social programs create more problems than they solve.
4. No government or organization should take money from you to look after you later in life.
5. Cash handouts offer no lasting help and facilitate the further decay of a people or situation.

Before jumping into things, let us quickly revisit the concepts of taxes and freedom. Income tax should not have been allowed in the first place. It is actually illegal, but this has not deterred the desirous few. Somehow, this glaring fact has provided little fuel for dissent among us apathetic many.

Many would argue that income tax is legal today and that it was made legal through various forms of legislation. For example, the Sixteenth Amendment to the United Stated Constitution made the collection of federal income tax legal, as thirty-eight of the forty-eight states in the union in 1913 ratified it. As of 1992, forty-two states had ratified the amendment. The Library of Congress provides up-to-date information on the Constitution, such as recent court cases, <u>through an app</u> or <u>other web-based resource</u>.[4]

All sorts of atrocities have been legalized throughout human history. Laws are always changing, and the concept of taxation is actually a moral issue. Regardless of the way you choose to perceive the law, or history, consider your true nature. Think about the common sense facts of life with respect to property and human rights. Questions about tax are ones we all need to answer for ourselves.

Even if taxes are legal, any law can change if the public chooses to change it. In a few moments, if you still feel strongly that income tax is legal then try instead to focus on this chapter's surrounding discussion.

Here is a link to a 1942 Disney featurette film, "<u>A New Spirit</u>,"[5] funded and approved by the US Department of Treasury that was used to *persuade* Americans to pay the voluntary income tax. The following year, after a large increase in filings as a result of the film,

---

[4] U.S. Congress, *Constitution Annotated*, Congress.gov Web site, http://beta.congress.gov/constitution-annotated/; Library of Congress, "U.S. Constitution: Analysis and Interpretation," Application, https://itunes.apple.com/us/app/u.s.-constitution-analysis/id692260032?mt=8.

[5] *The New Spirit*, directed by Wilfred Jackson and Ben Sharpsteen, written by Joe Grant and Dick Huemer (Walt Disney Productions and U.S. Department of the Treasury, 1942).

Disney was asked to make another film to increase the percentage of filing Americans yet again. The detailed backstory and more on the illegality of income tax can be found in an <u>article written by Jim Korkis</u>, an award-winning teacher and a recognized animation historian and Disney authority.[6]

Why would authorities need to use propaganda like this at all when they could easily reference any *supposed* legal requirement? There is only one possible reason and that is because there was no legal requirement. There still is not.

It is not about the laws that humankind wrote or not. It is about humanity's intrinsic and inalienable rights. When we take a moment to investigate our rights, we learn that any products of our labor and our property are, in fact, the only physical assets that our inalienable rights protect.

The following facts illustrate the beginnings of a staged process for shifting popular opinion about income tax. <u>According to a 2001 study</u> by economist Emmanuel Saez of the University of Berkeley, California, and Professor Thomas Piketty of the Paris School for Advanced Studies in the Social Sciences, only 13.6 percent of American people filed federal income tax returns in 1939, and subsequently paid any federal income taxes at all.[7]

Amazingly, the same study shows that in 1946, 89.1 percent of Americans were filing and paying federal income tax. That's a 75-percent increase only seven years later and a complete flip of the ratio of filers versus non-filers.

Naturally, you might wonder whether there was an increase in legal action or government or IRS threats during this period as a result of any legal changes to the income tax laws. The answer is no.

---

[6] Jim Korkis, "Donald Duck Pays His Taxes," *Korkis' Kartoon Korner* on *Larry's Toon Institute* Web site (undated), http://www.awn.com/tooninstitute/toonnews/korkus.htm.

[7] Thomas Piketty and Emmanuel Saez, "Income Inequality in the U.S. 1913-1998," *NBER Working Paper 8467* (Cambridge, MA: National Bureau of Economic Research: 2001), 4, Table A0 Reference Totals for Tax Units and Income, 9, http://www.nber.org/papers/w8467.

No major alterations were made to Title 26, the Internal Revenue Code as it was first published in 1939.[8] The Revenue Code is still largely the same to this day, as a matter of fact.

So why did this huge increase in voluntary compliance happen? The patriotic spirit of the American people was challenged, fed, grown monstrous, and leveraged to convince Americans that as a result of the *purported* global threats of Hitler, Mussolini, and Hirohito's Axis of Evil, they were obligated to contribute to the price of potential war.

President Franklin Delano Roosevelt, along with the help of <u>Disney's Donald Duck</u>, convinced the public that paying their income tax to fund the war against Hitler was the "privilege" of every true-blooded American. Not many could argue with that kind of a statement at an hour of "national crisis." Very few, if anyone, did or could resist at the time. They would have been ostracized and persecuted as un-American, even anti-American, and as traitors. Here's the famous FDR quote from the fireside chat radio broadcast:[9]

> *"It is not a sacrifice for the industrialist or the wage earner, the farmer or the shopkeeper, the train man or for the doctor to pay more taxes, to buy more bonds, to forgo extra profits, to work longer or harder at the task for which he is best fitted. Rather, it is a privilege."*[10]
>
> *- Franklin Delano Roosevelt -*

---

[8] Peter Hendrickson, *Cracking the Code* (2003, 10th printing 2008).

[9] http://www.toolsforjustice.com/stop-irs/70-year-irs-tax-scam-started-with-fdr-donald-duck/

[10] Thomas Piketty and Emmanuel Saez, "Income Inequality in the U.S. 1913-1998," *NBER Working Paper 8467* (Cambridge, MA: National Bureau of Economic Research: 2001), 4, Table A0 Reference Totals for Tax Units and Income, 9, http://www.nber.org/papers/w8467.

That quote comes from a speech delivered into the homes of every American on December 9, 1941, two days after Pearl Harbor and about 24 hours after Congress declared war on the Axis Powers of Germany, Italy, and Japan. Sixty years later, another tragedy would spark a similar speech, though with more disastrous consequences.

Throughout history, the propagation of war for the political gain of the few at the expense of the many has always been one of the most devastating forms of public distraction and division.

For now, while we are discussing taxes, here is a hard, fast, and viable solution to the income tax issue. Everyone can apply this immediately and watch our world begin to shift accordingly. This solution is also one that people who already believe in small government, no-government, or who simply hold anti-war beliefs will be especially fond of.

Ed Hedemann of the National War Tax Resistance Coordinating Committee has redirected the federal portion of his tax bill to non-profits and humanitarian efforts for over forty years without any prosecution or retribution.[11]

A year after being drafted for the Vietnam War and refusing to go, he decided to take his resistance to violence a step further and stop paying for others to go to war via his own federal income tax portion. For over forty years, he has not paid a cent to the federal government in income tax. Instead, he notifies them of the total figure he is choosing to donate to various humanitarian efforts each year.[12] That is it.

If you live in the US and are interested in what forms to fill out and how, watch this terrific television interview with Amy Goodman on Democracy Now.[13]

---

[11] "Billions of Reasons to Resist," *National War Tax Resistance Coordinating Committee* Web site, http://www.nwtrcc.org/.

[12] "Ed Hedemann," *National War Tax Resistance Coordinating Committee* Web site, http://www.nwtrcc.org.

[13] "Tax Day: While Millions Rush to Meet Deadline, Resisters Continue Longstanding Refusal to Fund War" (April 15, 2013), http://www.democracynow.org/2013/4/15/tax_day_while_millions_rush_to

Ed Hedemann's courage, actions, and model are within our rights as planetary citizens, so let us follow his inspiring example and begin redirecting our resources into programs we are building together. From now on, instead of supporting war, corruption, and government, you can decide what is most important to you and to whom you write your checks.

Arguments over the legality of income tax based on various human-made laws are beside the point anyway. If any human being, institution, or authority demands – never mind enforces entitlement to - a portion of the fruits of your labor, then this is slavery. It is also wrong, and no human-made written rules, bills, or amendments will ever make it right.

The founding fathers of the United States of America strictly forbade the collecting of people's wages by the federal government.[14] If this sage advice had been followed, few, if any government programs would even exist. Instead, the public would have created healthier private solutions.

The United States is used here as the example, but the reality is that all countries around the world are identical in principle; only the details of oppression vary. Even if you agree to it, if the government removes any portion of your earnings, you're still in the same boat and the rules are the same. It is slavery.

You might say, "Well we need all the government programs, so I am happy to pay," or "It is my patriotic duty to do so." Remember, this is really about your basic human rights. It is about your right to the fruits of your labor. By forgoing this right in exchange for the protection and provisions of institution, we are unwittingly and willingly submitting to rule and surrendering our freedoms.

Luke and I understand the need and desire to help support the communities we all share through fiscal contributions. We are not suggesting ignoring very real, human issues. We are saying let us stop

---

[14] Article I, section 9, clause 4, *Constitution of the United States of America.*

allowing arbitrary authority to dictate how we contribute, or how we deal with our social issues. We, the people, are much more capable of creating solutions and change than the government has ever been.

> *"The thing people need to understand is that the government is something that, while doing small things badly, does large things badly, too."*
> *- Unknown -*

Here is an interesting way to look at things. If government is truly working for the common person's benefit, then the suggestions we have put forth for transparency and systems that are more efficient should be acknowledged and quickly implemented. Instead of building replacements, we could simply remodel our existing infrastructure. However, very few, if any, governments would be willing to entertain the suggestions for transparency, never mind adopt any other solutions to the problems of corruption which run rampant in the halls of power.

Face the facts. Governments are institutions we pay to provide services for us. The problem is, government activities are kept secret from us when they happen at all, and their solutions are too inadequate to solve the problems that we are facing. The situation gets worse, the government does nothing, and we are still allowing them to make our lives worse for us, and we do it by paying them.

Instead of handing over decisions to others, let us manage our own lives. We can do a better job. We have surrendered our rights repeatedly under violent pressure, though none of us has ever wanted the government making decisions about our lives, bodies, families, homes, or businesses. For most of recorded history, we have lacked the wherewithal to fight back, but, finally, the Age of Authority is coming to an end. Shared knowledge alone has changed the game.

Let us move on the first quick issue in our list of five. Governments are not built by the people, or for the people. They are built by the few to control the many. According to popular theory, government is an institution comprised of us common folk, both employees and elected officials. In theory, the institution collects our wealth and then redistributes it to those who require it and uses it to pay for the services everyone uses and needs.

However, government in practice is a very different beast. The world's elite and royal families built government institutions to continue control the common people under a much more evolved, presentable, and modern guise. This might be exactly the kind of statement you do not want to hear or discuss.

Even if you think it does not apply to our country at this time, you can still see some of the worst forms of tyranny all over the world. Many of us can openly acknowledge that most of our elected officials are awfully bourgeois and elitist. No matter how you look at it, our politicians, their messages, and their agendas seem far removed, disconnected, and more than a touch opposed to the needs of the average individual.

Then there are the heavily supported left-versus-right-debate distractions, which have proven to be irrelevant. The two opposing parties are only appendages of the same animal and are controled by those who support both sides of the illusory political debate.

Furthermore, our governments' laws, regulations, policies, and actions consistently serve the lobbying efforts of big business and the rich and powerful. When these efforts are supported, rarely if ever do the common people truly receive the care they need.

The old idea that a few people can somehow get together and make healthy decisions for the rest of us is crazy and unnecessary. We have the ability to govern ourselves.

With freedom comes responsibility. Responsibility means personal and collective accountability. We will keep coming back to this idea, as it is the crux of our new world. We need to become both mutually and individually engaged in our new collective awareness and acting authority.

If you want to live without asking questions or challenging authority, sheltered by an ignorant hope, believing that the *powers that be* are doing all that can be done on our behalf, then the choice you are ultimately making is slavery.

We need to think for ourselves.

> *"Rarely do we find men who willingly engage in hard, solid thinking. There is an almost universal quest for easy answers and half-baked solutions. Nothing pains some people more than having to think."*[15]
> *- Martin Luther King, Jr. -*

On to numbers two and three of our five points. State social programs around the world are fiscally unsustainable and exacerbate the problems they were created to solve.

When it comes to government projects, quality and efficiency go right out the window. Everyone milks the system for all it is worth. The government's inherent corruption, expired operational systems, and inability to compete effectively in today's markets is visible everywhere.

We can see it in the political and corporate fat cats trading questionable contracts back and forth, and we can see it in the overpaid city worker who leans on a shovel for half of his or her career until retirement. These same city workers then collect a pension from empty coffers, essentially picking the pockets of the current working class.

We are not saying all government workers are bad or lazy people. Simply, if efficiency's the goal, government produces the opposite. The nature of the system cripples the natural good sense and innovative human capacity of the people working for the state. Few government workers can honestly disagree with either of the last two statements.

---

[15] Martin Luther King, Jr. Day Web site, http://mlkday.gov/plan/library/communications/quotes.php

Let us look at it another way. What if you wanted to renovate your bathroom but the government was in charge of bathroom renovations across the country, the same way it is currently in charge of the road systems. Before you can even begin renovations, you must follow a hundred bureaucratic steps. The government will require all kinds of paper, time, money, and effort from you up front, only to make some autocratic decision regarding the type of renovation you are going to receive, if any.

> *"The difference between stupidity and genius is that genius has its limits."*
> - Unknown -

Once work begins, after you somehow came to an agreement with the government, how easy will it be to make sure the quality of work is up to your standards with the government-appointed workers relaxing on the job?

Governments produce subpar work when compared to private-contract work, and that is before you start to factor in the costs. Government employees the world over make two-to-three times as much as their private-sector counterparts. It is tough to imagine keeping your bathroom renovation costs in check as comfortably as you would with, say, one of the most reputable private contractors around.

After weeks, months, or even years, no one could even predict the total debauchery and disaster. There is a very realistic chance your project will run in the red or even leave you bankrupt. Not many of us would ever consider doing business this way, for anything.

> *"If stupidity got us into this mess, then why can't it get us out?"* [16]
> - Will Rogers -

---

[16] Will Rogers. BrainyQuote.com, Xplore Inc, 2014. http://www.brainyquote.com/quotes/quotes/w/willrogers161549.html, accessed March 26, 2014.

Nothing can be accomplished properly or efficiently this way. Effective answers to any social challenge we face arise only after complete control over the mechanism is turned transparent and given back to the people to run. Solutions need to be managed by the community in question and executed with the good sense of any successful private organization.

Overpaid? Really?

Just in case you stumbled at the "overpaid" statement regarding government employees, here is an example from Luke's experience.

Luke had a friend whose wife worked for Parks and Recreation within the Alberta Government for years. She had been recently laid off. His friend expressed how frustrated his wife was that she could not find anyone in the industry willing to pay her anything close to her government rate of thirty to thirty-five dollars an hour.

The going rate for raking leaves and landscaping work in Alberta at the time was ten to fifteen dollars per hour. The private sector tells the honest story about the value of the type of work being provided. In this case, landscaping was obviously not worth thirty to thirty-five dollars an hour in that market period.

The government is consistently overcharged not only for labor, but also for many of the supplies they purchase. Also, consider the numerous corporations added to many development projects that are simply a long list of inactive contributors, happily padding the project cost.

In his book *Myths, Lies, and Downright Stupidity,* published in 2007, John Stossel bets his readers one thousand dollars that they could not name a single thing government does better than the private sector.[17]

As far as we know, no one has collected to date.

In an article entitled "Private Enterprise Does It Better,"[18] Stossel continues to lay things bare for the uninitiated with brilliant examples – two from the US and one from Paris – of private enterprises "putting on a clinic" and turning government systems and infrastructure on its head. These businesses turned large profits where deficits were the rule before.

The bottom line is that if private enterprise is not efficient, it loses money and perishes. Government, on the other hand, has the power to tax us to cover losses. The institution has somehow even perpetuated the insane idea that government programs do not have to be fiscally viable. This type of thinking is precisely the kind of garbage that transfers our debts to our children and the generations to come after them.

Our epidemic-like habit of postponing inevitable financial, ecological, and social burdens is the most irresponsible and diseased practice that government is responsible for.

The only way such counter-intuitive and unhealthy realities can exist is through the subversion of the systems we perceive as being built for our betterment. Ugly agendas made strictly to control us are behind almost every government-backed program.

Now, nothing is purely black and white. Yes, there is tremendous good and truth in our government systems. Most people who work

---

[17] (New York: Hyperion Books).
[18] Reason.com Web site (August 5, 2010).

within our planet's institutions certainly mean well and do their best to make the world a better place, at least at first.

However, in our pyramid-shaped world, where decisions, information, and authority move in a very narrow hierarchy down to the common masses, it is also painfully clear how so many can be deceived so easily.

Compartmentalized information, conditioned secrecy, abuse, fear, and blackmail tactics pave the way for hidden agendas. Informants against injustice and innovators with cheap, healthy solutions across every industry on earth are constantly intimidated or bought into silence.

If industry continues to dictate the rules of human life, profit-and-power mongers become the sole beneficiaries. Each of us knows this truth far too well. We struggle to stay ahead and struggle to see a way out in a system that is rigged to see us fail.

When faced with undeniable evidence of injustice, human beings have been carefully conditioned to respond with "I am just following orders," "I am sorry, I need this job," or even "I did not write the law, I just enforce it."

Moreover, all of us come crashing up against the feeling that it just does not seem possible for a small few to deceive and frighten the entire world, unless the perceived normal healthy debate itself *is* the distraction.

Selling the Lie

There's a close in the sales world called the "choice close."

In this scenario, the sales person offers the potential customer a choice, like a blue or green option. This emotionally distracts her from the choice of whether or not the product is even worth purchasing by moving

> *on to the next question, implying that the customer's decision to buy the product has already been made.*
>
> *The easy, exciting question about color makes her feel that she already owns the product and secures her commitment. In similar fashion, much current public debate is a distraction from the real issues.*

The completely irrelevant debate about whether to vote right or left wing is one of the most visible manipulations of our thoughts. For the best lesson on the value in voting, watch the animated film "<u>The Story of Mouseland</u>," most famously told by Tommy Douglas in 1944 and introduced by his grandson, actor Kiefer Sutherland.

Let us look specifically at the second point in our list of five.

Here is the stark reality of the situation. There is not one government social program on the planet that has ever been fiscally viable or successful - not a one. We have already spoken about government inefficiency in general. When it comes to pensions, it is equally obvious that government cannot produce sustainable operations.

"People are getting pension checks now, so how is this possible," you ask? Pension checks are paid for by stealing from those of us working. In some American cities, up to 80 percent of the municipal budget goes to retired city workers' pensions. Detroit even admitted that their city's pension commitments were the central reason for their recent bankruptcy. It is a big fat Ponzi scheme, as is the entire set of current government systems.

A government cannot guarantee you any benefit or service without first taking it from someone else. This is why the promise of government social programming is merely the promise of slavery – you are being asked to thank the people that are robbing you for the crumbs they leave you, and whether or not you see any actual benefit depends on where you stand.

Let us look at it another way. The government is just a middleman between humanity and our social issues. Imagine what will happen when we eliminate the extra costs alone, not to mention the perversion of reason and our compassionate goals. We need to stop placing autocratic mechanisms between our issues and ourselves.

When we delve a touch deeper into this third point, we discover how in each and every case, anything akin to a pension plan and even private insurance, regardless of which country you live in, is a financial farce that strips us of our rights via our property yet again.

> *"There is no worse tyranny than to force a man to pay for what he does not want merely because you think it would be good for him."*[19]
> *- Robert A. Heinlein -*

With respect to pensions specifically, you might ask "Did they not realize it would not work when they came up with the idea in the first place?"

Of course they knew.

The day the pension system was dreamed up, it was designed to fail. Why would our own governments lie? This lie is central, as are many, to facilitating your obedience.

Governments, by their very nature, create subservience. They force our reliance on them to solve our problems. They boil down to an institution that is focused on its own self-preservation at all cost. These institutions lie because they need our votes and our loyalty. They want to ensure some of us will continue working for or supporting them for all our lives.

The insurance industry, on the other hand, presents an intriguing mathematical tale of cold hard profits driven by complex actuarial

---

[19] *The Moon Is a Harsh Mistress* (New York: G.P. Putnam Sons, 1968), 242.

calculations. Money is one of the largest instruments of control. Therefore, robbery on a massive scale is always about control.

We will come back to these concepts of long-term financial robbery and deep layers of control in the chapter on monetary systems. For now, let us focus on accepting an obvious truth.

We can do things better.

Everyone has the right to accumulate property via the *sole* entitlement to the fruits of his or her labor.

Let us finally abandon this crazy notion that any authority on earth, much less a small group of specialists, can provide healthier solutions than we can. The research is everywhere. We cannot take the time to lay every piece of data in front of you. It is up to you. If you do not agree with certain statements or facts by the end of the book, then go investigate them for yourself.

You and you alone are and always have been the final authority of your life.

By that token, we all need to become better investigators and be more engaged in our communities.

> *"In times of change learners inherit the earth, while the learned find themselves beautifully equipped to deal with a world that no longer exists."*[20]
>
> *- Eric Hoffer -*

Even if people's opinions about how to go about things are vastly different, our potential for improving every aspect of human life is still the most undeniable truth of all.

As we start learning to discuss and solve our own issues *en masse,* we will quickly discover our individual needs are not as different as we might have thought. Think about all the conversations that you have had where everyone involved was committed to understanding

---

[20] *Reflections on the Human Condition* (New York: Harper & Row, 1973), section 32.

each other. Consensus, compromise, and creative solutions all come out of the woodwork.

We hope you are feeling a bit better about all this, but we suspect that there is still the lingering sense of being owed something because you were promised by your government that you would get a pension for life, so that is what you want.

Okay, that is fine, we understand those promises were made, but you were lied to and that is just all there is to it. There is no need to panic or worry, though, as money and solutions will be provided. Just do not look to the government that got you into this mess to get you out of it.

Let us come back to my grandmother as an example.

If her government checks stopped, in part because everyone in my family stopped paying federal income taxes, we could easily direct a portion of our former contributions to my grandmother to equal her current pension. The remainder could be redirected wherever we feel, as individuals, is best, as is our right.

Using humanity's remaining collective portion of reclaimed personal property, the community at large will easily address our social issues.

One can argue that some seniors do not have enough family to support them. I personally might choose to support education and senior care, because those are issues that I care about.

When we care, we respond with money and active contributions.

As discussed, the laws of supply and demand will always play a part.

We will cover much more of the specific details about how to structure and implement these changes as best we can throughout the book. A full review of the plan and a few key pieces must wait until the final chapters – we need to make sure all the pieces of the puzzle are on the table before we can explain how they all come together.

Perhaps you, dear reader, rely on some form of government support or programming. If mismanagement of public money is rectified and our money is put back in the hands of the people, real changes will be effected. Our resources will actually be put to work in our communities the way we see fit and so there will be more to go around.

Simply put, if the government is performing an action, then the problems of performing that action are perpetuated until they explode, causing countries to go bankrupt and implode.

We must stop the madness now!

On to point number five: handouts destroy our creative spirit and desire to work.

History teaches us that even in socialist regimes, when few control the resources of many, absolute power always corrupts absolutely. A nation cannot create wealth by plundering its own citizens in the name of social programs.

The Canadian Aboriginal people were victims of genocide and the very worst of human atrocities as European settlers stole their land, resources, culture, and dignity. The history behind the devastation is not up for debate.

What is up for debate is what to do about it. Consensus is hard, no doubt, when considering how to recompense these people for such heinous behavior. We respectfully draw your attention to the core of the matter which is that handouts have not helped. They have only further denigrated and destroyed a people's hope for health and prosperity.

Luke sat in family court for a few hours on several occasions and witnessed approximately forty cases. Most were related to Aboriginal families living on reservations. The sheer horror of the stories turned his stomach.

Social Programs Cause Social Problems

When I was in my youth, my mother was deeply committed to working with children who had all kinds of disabilities. Today, she continues to help and work with children with her new husband. One little Aboriginal girl's situation heavily impacted our entire family. For years, she was repeatedly sent to visit her parents, and until very recently was under constant threat of eventually being sent back to live with her family permanently. After each visit, she showed signs of physical and emotional abuse. Our family was also in contact with one of the little girl's older sisters, who suffers from a severe case of fetal alcohol syndrome. Other older siblings have made accusations of incest and rape, and have dealt with malnutrition, physical abuse, and worse.

My mother's husband is one of the most dedicated and caring educators I have ever known. Between the two of them, and with the help of many others including one dedicated government employee that vowed to quit if this case was not handled properly, they have done everything they could to work with the government to protect this little girl from abuse.

Common sense was evident with all the facts on the table – however, standardized protocol for reintegrating Aboriginal children into their "rehabilitated" families contributed to years of sporadic painful visits.

Thankfully, reason eventually ruled out in this case, but many other children fall through the cracks.

We can do better.

The Canadian government segregated the Aboriginal population in small chunks of territory and sent money as the major solution, thus stripping these people of the need to work in order to make a living for themselves and their families. This is a recipe for trouble.

Imagine what would happen if controlled tests were run with groups of people that needed various forms of support. If money was offered as the primary solution for these people in the test groups, likely less than 5 percent would benefit. This educated guesswork becomes based in fact momentarily.

It has been said that of you can teach a man to fish and feed him for a lifetime, or give him a fish and feed him for a day. The lesson misses a critical point though, which is that if we feed a man for a day, that man will show up with family and feasibly some friends on the following day, all hands out.

Consider that the North American Aboriginal population has received more government money and attention than any other group on earth. They have not prospered or significantly bettered themselves collectively or in most individual cases, despite all the government handouts.[21]

I was raised in Winnipeg, Manitoba, which has one of the largest Aboriginal populations in Canada, and I feel most connected to life and spirituality through native and shamanic traditions, along with Buddhism.

I love the Aboriginal people of the world, these brothers and sisters of mine, in the most familial way you could imagine. The

---

[21] Jesse Klein, "Killing Aboriginals with Our Kindness," *National Post* (May 14, 2013), http://fullcomment.nationalpost.com/2013/05/14/jesse-kline-3/. (Klein 2013)

preceding horribly distressing facts, as well as the ones to follow, literally tear at me as I touch their scathing truth.

This tale becomes a thousand times more horrific when you consider that these reservations are smack in the middle of Canada and the US, the most advanced, wealthiest Western countries in the world. Moreover, many Aboriginal people do not live on reservations but in the cities.

Aboriginal people in Canada have the highest substance-abuse and suicide rates, lowest life expectancy, and an incomprehensibly lower standard of living compared to those of us not living on reservations or even right next door in the cities.

Look at government-run housing projects. They are all a complete disgrace. The houses are built, and then, sometimes only a few years later, they are torn down after the communities turn them into absolute squalor.

This bears repeating: the government is often forced to tear down Canadian reserves, as they become the epitome of humankind's natural digression given said conditions.

Go to any kind of government- or city-run low-income housing district in your area and ask yourself, "Is this a shiny success?" Simply giving money to people, for any reason whatsoever, usually ruins their lives.

We do not want the Aboriginal people to think we are singling them out, so let us look at another example that covers a comprehensive cross section of the population: lottery winners.

Did you know that 70 percent of million-dollar lottery winners are penniless in seven years or less?[22] You read that right.

Money does not change your habits. If you save more than you make, then given a million, you would continue this behavior. If you

---

[22] Christina Commisso, "Why Most Lottery Winners End Up Losing Their New Fortune," *CTV News* (March 26, 2013), http://www.ctvnews.ca/business/why-most-lottery-winners-end-up-losing-their-new-fortune-1.1211569.

are broke all the time and spend more than you make, you would be among the 70 percent.

Money only magnifies who you already are. You are the creator of your life. Struggling people do not need financial help – they need education, support, compassion, and understanding. They need a brain tune-up and likely an attitude and perspective adjustment. There are many connected issues at play here, as well as options to help people in need, but the bottom line is that blindly throwing money at problems only perpetuates and often amplifies the problems.

Despite the endless dollars governments spend on social programs, we are not much better off. More to the point, we are miles away from our readily visible potential, never mind humanity's true innovative reach just over the horizon.

We can and must stop this insanity and try something different.

> *"As we approach each of the great social challenges of our time, we must acknowledge that old thinking will not provide the new solutions we need. These solutions will be uncomfortable, hard to sell and risky to execute. But the cost of not doing so is even greater."*[23]
> - Simon Mainwaring -

For those of you ready to get to work and wondering where to start, here are the beginnings of a few big pieces of solution that you can easily plug right into.

We can build replacements for our current government institutions and social programs, both large and small, while the current systems continue to falter along.

---

[23] "Why Even the Way We Innovate Must Change," *The We First Blog* (2011), http://simonmainwaring.com/future/why-even-the-way-we-innovate-must-change/

We can involve our communities as a whole as our new systems reach various stages of readiness as this will help us prevent any temporary lack of access to services and provide a more comfortable changeover.

Everything humanity needs to rebuild the world falls into one of two categories: first, sharing information and making decisions, and second, developing the creative and constructive activities that are required to build the things that we decide on together. Both begin online and then almost immediately develop physical roots in our local communities as a result.

We have built an online hub for discussions, connections to global resources, and examples of working solutions here. This is a home for ideas, tools, and sharing, built for both individuals and organizations.

It is an online gathering place with living examples of healthier options as well as a platform to facilitate the discussion and creation of more new solutions. We are not claiming to or planning on housing all the world's solutions ourselves, we just want to help by offering another way to connect and plug in.

We need to build many different web homes for all manners of our human existence, from local, regional, and national social services, to cities', towns', and countries' road and infrastructure requirements. We need people to begin building online platforms for discussion and data sharing and the framework for providing the services themselves.

We can do this through discussions at first, and, after agreeing on various starting points, we can start building the assorted components of all shapes and sizes.

People can also work on building these platforms from within the government or the private sector, where all the social issues now reside. With a less and less capable government, more people will be working in the private sector anyway.

To replace the largest systems, we will need to implement longer-term projects, as many current large-scale systems are overly centralized. They would benefit from a smaller, more localized approach. For example, we need localized solutions for the issues in our food systems.

Smaller systems can be replaced more quickly. It is tremendously exciting to think about how these smaller systems will offer us many early testing opportunities. They will be huge momentum-building examples for the whole world to share in.

Looking at food systems, we can see the increasingly popular phenomenon of singular large institutions being replaced by many smaller ones. Therefore, many of the large global changes we are talking about in this book might happen faster than you think, as we break our big issues into smaller, bite-sized, local pieces.

Longer-term projects involve collecting data and implementing decision making at a global level. We should certainly start immediately framing and building these bigger solutions, as they will take a little bit longer to reach full service capacity.

For now, let us focus on the original invitation to make safe local, regional, and national online hubs for data collection, discussion, and decision-making processes regarding all aspects of human life.

Not the technical sort? Get involved in the strategy and discussion or action and implementation side of the equation. Either you help build the structures, or build on the ideas.

For those of you with a special love for computers, we need a means to *secure* these online activities. The safety of voting processes and the fiscal side of our operations are obvious early nodes that need to be crafted and protected.

Most of our future's solutions will likely be localized and small, rather than overly centralized and large. Further into our discussions, more details on the makeup and funding of these solutions will become clear.

The Freedom Handbook

One of the things covered later, for instance, is how to employ the tens of millions of unemployed people in the United States and offer them aid that does not come in the unhealthy form of handouts.

We have some pretty exciting answers coming, but for now know that our new systems are already under construction and recruiting volunteers. Qualified and passionate folks like *you* are needed to build, drive, and maintain these vehicles.

Let us get to work.

Volunteers from all lifestyles, along with the professionals required for the tasks, will easily build online and then on-the-ground systems to replace our existing ones.

All we have to do is work together. We already do this now – at work, during leisure time, and even out in public, we need to get along with completely different people. Self-governance is just a bigger, more technological job.

It is also called freedom, and the pay is out of this world.

To start on the right foot, let us mesh the inspirational spirit of two famous calls for public support in our hearts: John F. Kennedy's passionate call to a country – which a whole world responded to – to race to the moon, and Wikipedia's global call to average citizens to build a better encyclopedia.

Let us acknowledge our greatness, our genius, and our togetherness and build a worldwide web of self-governance.

At this point in the book, our test readers wanted more concrete solutions. They wanted to be assured that the holes they perceived would be attended to.

We understand.

When Luke laid some of this stuff on me for the first time, it took me a few weeks to finally get it, and I had already been exploring these issues for my entire adult life. I asked him most of the questions you are probably thinking right now. We are going to get there. Be patient and remember to focus on accepting some difficult truths about our world's corruption, inefficiency, and slavery.

These criminal realities can act as catalytic motivators for change but only become potent through terrifying, vulnerable awareness.

CHAPTER FOUR

- Education -

"I have never let my schooling interfere with my education."[1]
- Mark Twain -

Education is one of my favorite topics of discussion for many reasons. It is one of the most important things that any of us can talk about, both as an investment in the future through our children and in ourselves, later in life. Yet I hated school, for reasons which will become uncomfortably apparent throughout this chapter.

To start, we need to acknowledge the simple fact that our educational system is defunct.

It destroys human creativity and intelligence while driving a compartmentalized, divisive, and stifling sense of obedience over all else. Expertise has been the sole model for education. We cannot allow this to continue.

Instead, we need to draw natural, symbiotic connections between all life's subjects. We must reclaim the role of the educated generalist who can think for him or herself. We also need to successfully encourage and engage the natural curiosity and creativity of youth through teachers and programs that are involved and invested in their communities.

Once Upon a Time

One day in first grade, I walked out during the middle of class and straight down the hall to

---

[1] Andrew Robinson, Chapter 3, *Genius: A Very Short Introduction* (Oxford: Oxford University Press, 2011).

> *the principal's office, where I stated, right to his eye-bulging face, "This school is for babies and I'm not doing it." To say that my criticism of the curriculum was not appreciated would be an understatement.*

We are inevitably going to need a new paradigm in education, as we are with every other part of life. We need to evolve a new way to learn, share, create, and collaborate with children and adults alike, rather than stifling the finest minds among us at an early age.

Thankfully, we have already made a strong start towards this change with large swaths of the planet's information stores now accessible to anyone with internet. Humanity is now able to look into an undiscovered sea of history and potential.

This is vital, because education is the most direct and has the most far-reaching effect on the public good. We must realize that our intellectual integrity is the very backbone of freedom, and that without the ability to think, we lose everything.

Given this understanding, the discordant nature of our current systems can be seen as a truly harrowing quagmire that is devouring the best and brightest among us.

To guide this part of our discussion, we will lean heavily on the work of three accepted thought leaders in modern education. The dialog from Sir Ken Robinson, Liz Coleman, and Sugata Mitra is invaluable. These three have, as a matter of course, laid out the most obvious common sense problems and solutions facing education in the modern era. However, while considering their arguments, it is important to remember the crossword puzzle story. More and more of us every day are coming up with and coming back to, in some cases, these very same ideas.

In December 2010, Sir Ken Robinson's brilliant eleven-minute animated video, entitled "Changing Education Paradigms," was posted on TED's Best of the Web.² In fact, he champions a radical rethink of educational systems in four separate TED Talks, going back to 2006. We cannot recommend more fervently his TED Talks "How Schools Kill Creativity"³ and "Bring on the Learning Revolution!"⁴ as well as his most recent, "How to Escape Education's Death Valley."⁵

"Bring on the Learning Revolution" just might be the most-viewed TED Talk of all time. What does that tell us? It tells us that education is one of the single most important aspects of human life.

> "A real decision is measured by the fact that you've taken a new action. If there's no action, you haven't truly decided."⁶
> - Anthony Robbins -

> "Do you want to know who you are? Don't ask. Act! Action will delineate and define you."⁷
> - Witold Gombrowicz -

> "Action may not always bring happiness; but there is no happiness without action."⁸
> - Benjamin Disraeli -

---

2. RSAnimate (2010) http://www.ted.com/talks/ken_robinson_changing_education_paradigms.html.
3. (2006) http://www.ted.com/talks/ken_robinson_says_schools_kill_creativity.html
4. (2010) http://www.ted.com/talks/sir_ken_robinson_bring_on_the_revolution.html.
5. (2013) http://www.ted.com/talks/ken_robinson_how_to_escape_education_s_death_valley.html.
6. *Awaken the Giant Within* (New York: Free Press, 1991), 49.
7. *Diary*, Vol. II (Chicago: Northwestern University Press, 1988), 130.
8. *Lothair* (1870).

> *"Action is a great restorer and builder of confidence. Inaction is not only the result, but the cause, of fear. Perhaps the action you take will be successful; perhaps different action or adjustments will have to follow. But any action is better than no action at all."*[9]
> — *Norman Vincent Peale* —

Let us consider how action directly connects to education. We cannot help but improve on the world we have, but we must begin re-imagining and re-creating it quickly as we are able. We learn best when we act and experiment, and we face rotting digression and loss of potential when we let the mire of inaction claim us.

Education is not about memorizing an intellectual idea—it is about understanding how to apply intellectual concepts to life. This understanding is gained only through action.

What role does failure play? Failure is just another name for the action required to achieve success. Courageous and repeated agile action, combined with measurement and study, pave the road to success' door.

Ultimately, we need to experiment and refine.

Let us further consider Sir Ken Robinson's celebrated musings on education. The animated film we linked to above begins by examining why every country on earth is reforming its public education system. This trend is telling indeed as it shows that most people already believe that education needs reform. It also speaks again to the importance humans instinctively place on education.

> *"The problem is, they're trying to meet the future by doing what they did in the past."*
> — *Sir Ken Robinson* —

---

[9] As quoted by John C. Maxwell, *Talent Is Never Enough Workbook* (Thomas Nelson Inc., 2007), 27.

Sir Ken Robinson describes the heart of the problems as being "deep in the gene pool of public education." He identifies that archaic ideas about academia lead our society to mass produce "smart" and "non-smart" people.

This central problem is clear when we consider how education is compartmentalized into infinite disciplines. The model of "expertise" produces staggering limitations.

In plainer language, we're using tired educational ideas that devastate human potential. Current systems, in essence, shovel our kids into a maze of pre-dug ditches that cuts life and our creative spirit into sterile, stifling, and unconnected pieces.

> *"Over the past century the expert has dethroned the educated generalist to become the sole model of intellectual accomplishment."*[10]
> - Liz Coleman -

At the end of his educational animation, Ken describes a study conducted to determine genius levels regarding divergent thinking, a primary skill for everyday problem solving. The study determined that 1,500 children in kindergarten who started off at over 98 percent genius were dulled in their abilities to only 32 percent five years later.

Think about that for a second.

After another five years, the number dropped to below 10 percent. This single study sums up the reality of our current education systems perfectly.

We could end the argument on our education systems' quality and productivity with that study on its own. There is no question that we can do better than reducing our creative genius and our natural capacity to solve problems, to almost nothing.

---

[10] "Education: Agent and Architect of Democracy," *Teacher-Scholar*, Vol. 2, No. 1 (Fall 2010) 43, http://www.fhsu.edu/teacher-scholar/volume2/Education/page1.html.

We cannot stop here, though.

There is still too much incredible raw material with which we can rebuild our education systems still to discuss.

We hope you love the fact that this book is not just packed with problems but also stacked with solutions. It sure gets our blood racing as we imagine what you will do – what the world will do – when you come to the end of our summary of problems and hold a viable and terribly exciting action plan in your hands.

On that note, let us examine Sir Ken Robinson's newest talk: "How to Escape Education's Death Valley." You have got to hand it to our friendly knight because he is superbly funny, and humor can be a valuable tool in education.

Ken begins by telling us that in some parts of the United States, 60 percent of kids drop out of high school, with 80 percent of kids leaving school before graduation in the Native American community.

If the US halved the drop-out rate, it's estimated that the economy's net gain over ten years would be nearly a trillion dollars.[11]

Let us all take a moment and agree on what we already know to be true. Investing in education means huge dividends.

He points out that the drop-out crisis is only the tip of the iceberg when it comes to our educational woes. What those staggering figures do not include are all the disengaged kids, the ones who go to school but do not enjoy it and feel as though they do not get any real benefit from it.

The US spends more on education than most countries, has smaller class sizes, and creates hundreds of initiatives every year to improve on education. Sir Ken tells us that the trouble is that all of these efforts are going in the wrong direction before introducing the three principles under which human life flourishes, three simple thing that our education system contradicts.

---

[11] Sir Ken Robinson, "How to escape education's death valley," (TED Talks Education, April 2013); "TED star Sir Ken Robinson offers solutions for Chicago's schools," *The Grid, Chicago Sun Times* (April 9, 2013), voices.suntimes.com/business-2/grid/ted-star-sir-ken-robinson-offers-solutions-chicagos-schools.

Diversity

Humans are naturally diverse; however, the United States' No Child Left Behind[12] program perfectly illustrates how our education systems are most often based on *conformity,* diversity's natural opposite.

Curiosity

Our natural curiosity opposes a heavy focus on *compliance* in our education systems, which rely far too much on standardized testing. This testing does play a role, but it should not be the sole rule. Our children and teachers are forced to follow routine algorithms instead of the exciting power of imagination and curiosity.

Creativity

Human life is inherently creative - lives are unique, vibrant, and diverse. Education should awaken and develop the power of creativity, which helps us successfully navigate life. Instead, education centers on *standardization* by way of command-and-control-style programming, mandated by the state.

Ken offers Finland as an example the whole world could follow. In terms of standardized testing, Finland often comes out on top in math, science, and reading.

Bear in mind this testing is painting quite an incomplete picture, as it leaves out all other subjects. Finland doesn't obsess about these three disciplines though. The country takes a very broad approach to education that includes humanities, physical education, and the arts, and Finnish students rarely take standardized tests.

---

[12] The No Child Left Behind Act of 2001, Public L. 107-110, January 8, 2002; 115 Stat. 1425.

"What do you do about the drop-out rate?" an American once asked.

"Well, we don't have one," A bemused Finn responded. "Why would you drop out? If people are in trouble, we get to them quickly and help them and we support them."

For those thinking that Finland, with a population of only five million people or so, cannot be compared to the US, Ken points out that Finland equals some smaller states and regions in terms of population.[13] He explains that the same methods can be applied anywhere, though perhaps in smaller sections as required.

Ken also says that higher-performing educational systems – like those in Australia, Canada, South Korea, and Singapore – understand the following concepts and apply them much better than the United States does. As Canadians, Luke and I can say without question that every country needs *much* more focus on these three key ideas:

Individualized teaching and learning

These systems recognize that they must engage each student and their individuality, creativity, and curiosity. This is how we learn.

Status and support for teachers

These systems recognize the importance of selecting great teachers and then continually investing in their professional development.

Giving back responsibility to the local schools

These systems recognize that education does not go on in the committee rooms of our legislative buildings—it happens in classrooms and schools, and therefore the power of discretion should be in the hands of the teachers, the students, and their families.

---

[13] Finland's population is about the same as Maryland, Wisconsin, Minnesota, Colorado, Alabama, or South Carolina.

We will conclude our exploration of Sir Ken Robinson's inspiring work with the following list of attributes of some successful alternative education programs Ken has encountered:

- Highly personalized
- Strong support for teachers
- Close links with the community
- Broad and diverse curriculum
- Programming outside and inside of school
- They work [better]

Not far from Ken's house is a place called Death Valley, where it never rains and nothing grows because it is the hottest, driest place in America. In the winter of 2004 seven inches of rain fell in Death Valley, and in the spring of 2005 the whole valley floor was carpeted in flowers, which showed us that Death Valley was dormant not dead.

Right beneath the surface are the seeds of possibility waiting for the right conditions. In organic systems, if the conditions are right, life thrives.

If we take a dormant area, school, or district and change the conditions by giving people a different sense of possibility and a broader range of opportunities, life will flourish.

When considering the limitations of our current educational models, people often ask, "What's the purpose behind dumbing the entire human population down?" It is the only way to contain the amazing capacity and compassion of the human race.

For some terrific information on some of the history behind the corruption of our education systems, read the book *The Deliberate Dumbing Down of America* by Charlotte Thomson Iserbyt, who served as senior policy advisor in the US Department of Education in the Reagan administration.[14]

Holding the country's top job in education, she had access to all kinds of documented evidence of our education systems' complete

---

[14] 2nd ed., Conscience Press (2011).

subversion. Iserbyt discusses this in an interesting video interview, "Deliberate Dumbing Down of the World."[15] Her views are extreme as far as some of the deeper roots of these problems, so she needs to be taken with a grain of salt.

It is pretty typical for many whistleblowers and authors who expose and continue to investigate injustice's roots to get caught in the magnetizing web of who, why, and how.

We cannot take the time to go through the historical documents and evidence, which so many other authors have done before us. Iserbyt's book is one of many on the subject of education, which has recently been made available free online and contains some great information.[16]

Perhaps the single best book that provides a comprehensive look at some of the control systems in these discussions is *Tragedy & Hope* by Carroll Quigley.[17]

For education specifically, read *Dumbing Us Down: The Hidden Curriculum of Compulsory Schooling, 10th Anniversary Edition* by John Taylor Gatto.[18] John was named New York City Teacher of the Year in 1989, 1990, and 1991 and New York State Teacher of the Year in 1991.[19] If you would prefer video format, *The Ultimate History Lesson: A Weekend with John Taylor Gatto* by tragedyandhope.com is available on YouTube in parts, starting here.[20]

---

[15] http://www.youtube.com/watch?v=DDyDtYy2I0M (2006).
[16] http://www.deliberatedumbingdown.com/MomsPDFs/DDDoA.sml.pdf.
[17] (GSG and Associates, 1975), http://www.amazon.com/Tragedy-Hope-History-World-Time/dp/094500110X/ref=sr_1_1?s=books&ie=UTF8&qid=1390823481&sr=1-1&keywords=tragedy+and+hope
[18] (Gabriola Island, BC: New Society Publishers, 2002); see also *Weapons of Mass Instruction* (Gabriola Island, BC: New Society Publishers, repr. 2010).
[19] "I Quit, I Think," *The Odysseus Group: John Taylor Gatto* Web site (n.d.), http://www.johntaylorgatto.com/underground/prologue2.htm; "John Gatto," *Thrive* Web site (n.d.), http://www.thrivemovement.com/pioneer/john-gatto; "John Taylor Gatto Bio," *The Odysseus Group: John Taylor Gatto* Web site (n.d.), http://www.johntaylorgatto.com/aboutus/john.htm.
[20] Interviewer Richard Grove, tragedyandhope.com (January 1, 2012), http://www.youtube.com/watch?v=YQiW_l848t8.

The Freedom Handbook

After nearly 30 years in the classroom, after winning his last award in 1991, Gatto wrote an article announcing his retirement entitled, "I Quit, I Think" for the *Wall Street Journal*.[21] It reads, "If you hear of a job where I don't have to hurt kids to make a living, let me know. Come fall I'll be looking for work."

On his website, he says, "In [the letter] I explained my reasons for deciding to wrap it up, even though I had no savings and not the slightest idea what else I might do in my midfifties to pay the rent."

Gatto supports home schooling and also promotes unschooling[22] and open source education. These models deserve way more attention and offer a wealth of functioning examples of improved educational systems and strategies.

Naturally, we often run out of time and space not just for discussing our problems but also for exploring all the amazing solutions out there,[23] so look to our bibliography, which includes many of the best resources we've encountered to date.

If you are interested in learning about alternative education, start by researching *unschooling* and *open source education*.[24] In an effort

---

[21] John Taylor Gatto, "I Quit, I Think," *The Odysseus Group: John Taylor Gatto* (n.d.), http://www.johntaylorgatto.com/underground/prologue2.htm.
[22] "Unschooling," *Wikipedia* Web site, http://en.wikipedia.org/wiki/Unschooling.
[23] "John Taylor Gatto," *Wikipedia* Web site, quoting education professor Wade A. Carpenter, Berry College, http://en.wikipedia.org/wiki/John_Taylor_Gatto.
[24] "Open Source Learning," Wikipedia Web site, http://en.wikipedia.org/wiki/Unschoolingwww.en.wikipedia.org/wiki/open_source_learning (updated December 5, 2012); Canadian Open Source Education and Research, *Canopener* Web site, http://canopener.ca; Richard Baraniuk, "The Birth of Open Source Learning Revolution," TED Talks Web site (August, 2006) http://www.ted.com/talks/richard_baraniuk_on_open_source_learning;; Open Source Curriculum," Wikipedia Web site, http://en.wikipedia.org/wiki/Open-source_curriculum; Open Source, Education, Open Source Initiative Web site, http://opensource.org/osi-open-source-education; MIT Open Courseware, http://ocw.mit.edu/index.htm; *Open Source Education Foundation* Web site, http://www.osef.org/.

to incite insight, we have included a few links to especially interesting material in the bibliography.[25]

Later, we'll introduce a few key documentary films that also explain and evidence the ruling elite's controlling mechanisms exceptionally well. So well in fact, that when the time comes, we will insist above all that you watch these few short films.

There are many easy-to-understand ways to improve education. In our discussion, it really does not matter who or what exactly is undermining human potential. This type of distracting discussion becomes completely irrelevant when we agree on a few easy improvements and start driving the bus ourselves.

There are many paths to the mountaintops of our dreams. We are proposing certain shortcuts that will allow us to surpass monumental difficulties with ease and grace. If you are struggling to come to terms with the dark and tyrannical realities of our world, then follow the more scrumptious path of our potential unleashed, for once we understand that the world is not flat, the old arguments supporting that fallacy become moot.

This book is attempting to educate an entire world – the whole human race – about a necessary paradigm shift that will affect every facet of human existence. Imagine attempting to introduce and effectively guide someone or, better yet, a group of a hundred random people, through radical shifts in their beliefs.

With such incredible heights as our goal, we are forced to employ every imaginable literary, human, and intuitive tool to reach out and

---

[25] Kate Hammer, "More Families Are Discovering School's Out—Forever," *Globe and Mail* (September 10, 2010), http://www.theglobeandmail.com/news/national/education/more-families-are-deciding-that-schools-out---forever/article570684/?page=all; "Creating Our Own Structure," Unschooling Canada Web site (n.d.), http://www.unschooling.ca/; "Unschooling," Ontario Federation of Teaching Parents (n.d.), http://ontariohomeschool.org/unschooling.shtml; Tim Johnson, "Unschooling: Forget Homeschooling, They'll Figure It Out for Themselves," *Canadian Family*, http://www.canadianfamily.ca/kids/baby/unschooling-forget-homeschooling-theyll-figure-it/.

touch you. Even though our main focus is on solutions, at times it helps to steady our gaze on the horror of all current structures and institutions to uncover why those solutions are necessary.

Only when more have accepted the stifling limitations that have been placed upon humanity will we all be ready to reach out in action to create a new and better world. It can be tricky to balance this juxtaposition between humanity's potential and our personal pain, and so we've carefully staged this process.

It is vital that we see this though and not falter under the storms of the world that was.

Abundance, joy, and the best parts of everything that lives inside you, are our goals. We need to grow these things, so we can reach our unrestrained creative spirit. The rewards that wait for us are worth the difficult parts of this book, we promise. The work ahead and the turbulent change will be worth it in the end.

> *"There is no coming to consciousness without pain....[26] People will do anything, no matter how absurd, to avoid facing their own souls....[27] One does not become enlightened by imagining figures of light, but by making the darkness conscious."[28]*
> *- Carl Gustav Jung -*

> *"It is precisely because we resist the darkness in ourselves that we miss the depths of the loveliness, beauty, brilliance, creativity, and joy that lie at our core."[29]*
> *- Thomas Moore -*

---

[26] *Contributions to Analytical Psychology* (1928), 193.
[27] *Psychology and Alchemy* in *Collected Works*, vol. 12, par. 126.
[28] *Alchemical Studies* in *Collected Works*, vol. 13, par. 335.
[29] *Dark Nights of the Soul* (Gotham, 2005).

After all that talk of darkness and coming to terms, let us speak of the coming light.

Liz Coleman is a glorious orator and thinker who gave a poignant TED Talk on education reform in June 2009 entitled "A Call to Reinvent Liberal Arts Education."[30] She argues with stirring and logical grace for the rebirth.

"What kind of a world *are* we making?" she asks. "What kind of a world *should* we be making? What kind of a world *can* we be making?" She reminds us how readily these questions are treated with skepticism and moved off the table.

"In so doing, the guardians of secular democracy in effect yield the connection between education and values to fundamentalists," she warns. "You can be sure, (they) have no compunctions about using education to further their values: the absolutes of a theocracy."

We can readily admit that we, too, would rather not talk about the horror of our slavery, about the motivations or machinations of the ruling elite, any more than are necessary for the purposes of this book. Some light must be shed, however, if we are to focus on our preference – activating plans to re-imagine and re-create our world. Remember, shortcuts up the mountain can be found amidst a positive, open-minded, and agile focus on change.

Further, Luke and I agreed not to delve into the identities or the darkest motivations of the world's dominating powers, which certain circles love to debate. These issues are inconsequential. The future is our oyster, and these dying powers do not matter in the world we must create. We should not be bothered with such sick, twisted irrelevancy; and we are confident enough in the power that we – Luke, I, and all of you – possess.

We, the people, shall free and rule ourselves.

In the pursuit of all that is good, education of our children is one of the most important keys. Abandon your tenured ideas and

---

[30] TED Talks, http://www.ted.com/talks/liz_coleman_s_call_to_reinvent_liberal_arts_education.html (2009).

structures, rotten with decay. Our future is emblazoned in the gossamer eyes and hearts of every child, everywhere.

> *"Someone should do a TedTalks on putting the ideas in TedTalks into actual action."*[31]
> - Henzo Bobo -

> *"(in modern academia, social values) remain emphatically extracurricular. In effect, civic-mindedness is treated as outside the realm of what purports to be serious thinking and adult purposes. Simply put, when the impulse is to change the world, the academy is more likely to engender a learned helplessness than to create a sense of empowerment. This brew—oversimplification of civic engagement, idealization of the expert, fragmentation of knowledge, emphasis on mastery, and neutrality as a condition of academic integrity—is toxic when it comes to pursuing the vital connections between education and the public good, between intellectual integrity and human freedom."*
> - Liz Coleman -

The idealization of the expert, the fragmentation of knowledge, and our emphasis on technical mastery are those pre-dug ditches we mentioned that are keeping us from reaching our fullest potential.

The idea of quantitative reasoning is also an important part and a vital aspect of our new world. We need quantitative reasoning, as

---

[31] Youtube comments section, Dan Pink, "The Puzzle of Motivation," TED Talks (August 2009), www.youtube.com/watch?v+rrkrvAUbU9Y; Comments, Henzo Bobo, http://www.youtube.com/user/HenzOOzo.

this is the heart of what it takes to manage change when measurement is crucial. Through quantitative reasoning, we can systematically discriminate between what is core and what is periphery.

> *"The problem is there is no such thing as a viable democracy [society] made up of experts, zealots, politicians and spectators."*
> *- Liz Coleman -*

If you look to the sidebar, you'll see that we added the word *society* to a quotation made by Liz Coleman. We did this because democracy is not a viable modern-day social solution to anything. Collaboration and transparency will birth a new form of governance, and as such, a new term needed to be coined. Therefore we introduce symbiotic transparency, which we define as follows:

1. Symbiotic Transparency - *a form of administration founded on the unbridled transparent, symbiotic, and organic nature of humanity's organizing self.*
Antonyms: Democracy, Communism, Government
Similar to: Liberty, Equality, and Freedom

> *"No one has the answers and everyone has responsibility."*

> *"The hard choices are not between good and evil, but between competing goods. This discovery is transforming. It undercuts self-righteousness, radically alters the tone and character of controversy, and enriches dramatically the possibilities for finding common ground. Ideology,*

zealotry, unsubstantiated opinions simply won't do. This is a political education, to be sure. But it is a politics of principle, not of partisanship."
- Liz Coleman -

One of the single most transformative ideas we have recently rediscovered as a species was presented in the context of education. In the following TED Talk, "Build a School in the Cloud,"[32] Sugata Mitra provides irrefutable proof that children, when organized around a given problem, can effectively teach themselves better than we as adults can. Let us dream with Sugata of new practices in education that allow children to teach themselves.

The implications of child self-education are widespread and not limited to educational paradigms. By unwrapping this big idea, another core concept of freedom is revealed, a concept that will repeatedly arise as we move forward.

In his early experiments, Sugata would place computers with complex questions in languages completely alien to the children in small holes in the wall and then leave the room. When he came back, he would be met with educated answers that met or exceeded the quality of the answers provided through modern education systems.

Think about that; these findings are game changing. We have also seen the same learning principles breaking comparable new ground in business and organizational models.

Throughout the rest of the book we will use the term "setting the stage" to refer to this concept of enhanced learning through empowerment over firm directives. Setting the stage dramatically reduces planning costs and efforts. We have already learned that the keys are diversity, curiosity, and creativity. The right tools and a can-do attitude are all that we need.

---

[32] (2013), http://www.ted.com/talks/sugata_mitra_build_a_school_in_the_cloud.html.

The untapped potential of the human race is enormous, but people have to take action to achieve it. We need to cultivate that potential with creativity and curiosity, rather than smother it under rote memorization, and we all have to do, is agree to do something together. For the sake of our children, and our children's children, we need to take action now.

History shows us the failures of what has come before us, so why do we keep repeating the same mistakes and suffering the same consequences?

Let us do something different, right now, together.

Slowly, slowly, we are learning through the evidence provided by Google's "20 percent time" and the even more telling ROWE (Results Only Work Environment) that people work better when they are encouraged to pursue their own agendas and interests.

ROWE, a concept created by Jody Thompson and Cali Ressler, creates an environment in which employees are paid for results rather than hours worked.[33] In these environments of fewer rules, productivity, engagement, and satisfaction all go up, and turnover takes a dive.

The bottom line is that we merely have to set the stage for human greatness and then watch it unfold in grand style.

By allowing people to unchain their imaginations in a fresh space loaded with tools, information, openness, and curiosity, we will produce larger, superior results. This immediately applicable idea has incalculable, widespread relevance and needs to be instituted as quickly as possible.

Let us finish our chapter in education with a look at how it ties to social programs, in this new world that we must create. After that, we can lay out some detailed solutions that everyone can start working on right now.

First, eliminating a government-funded public education system means that private citizens are free to organize ideas that are funded

---

[33] Results Only Work Environment, http://www.gorowe.com.

privately. We, the people, are solely responsible for all social issues and educating our children, and so we will feel compelled to contribute and act accordingly with the best interests of our children at heart.

Not everyone cares about every issue out there, and not everyone has to. However, since people and all forms of organizations will pay no taxes in this new world, we are afforded the right to choose for ourselves what is important.

Luke has decided not to contribute to education once his children are finished their schooling, which he has every right to do. Parents should be the primary contributors to their child's education anyway. There will always be additional philanthropic contributions from those who feel a connection to education and a desire to bolster our education as a species. Luke did add that if one of his children decides to pursue more education, he will begin contributing again to whichever organization he and his child feel is best suited to meet their unique needs, interests, and goals.

This should be the way it works for everyone.

If anyone in any region on the planet is concerned about funding any social need, he only needs to communicate fundraising messages to his community to receive the aid he asks for. Local parents and legions of other dedicated individuals and corporate supporters will step up and provide what is needed in the interest of preserving the species as a whole.

As it stands, our educational system excels only at destroying human creativity and curiosity. Remember, roughly 90 percent of our creative problem-solving skills are sterilized by schools, which are modelled after Prussian education systems created hundreds of years ago to create a subservient warrior class.

We can do better.

The question is where to start, and what can we do for our kids today, for their education and humanity's future? Here are our answers:

Let us home school our kids whenever possible while we make adjustments to improve education and make it a fully collaborative institution.

Our children, as proven by Sugata Mitra's studies alone, all have the capacity to learn necessary life skills and surprise us with solutions if we would simply get out of the way while engaging their curiosity.

Given that understanding, let us give kids access to adult information and teaching processes online and watch them improve and redesign our best efforts.

Studies show that the number of children being home schooled is rising 7 times faster than the number of kids enrolling in schools every year in the United States. You can read an article here that states "As homeschooling has become increasingly popular, common myths that have long been associated with the practice of homeschooling have been debunked."[34]

Homeschooled kids have better standardized test results[35] and the achievement gaps between sexes, income levels, and ethnicity that plague public schools do not exist in homeschooling environments.[36]

It is easy to see we have everything we need to create a global network of tools that communities and parents can use to re-invent education. We simply expand on all the great stuff going on and create increasingly collaborative online and on-the-ground resources for public education. If homeschooling and other forms of solution are proven to outperform current systems, then let us better support and utilize them.

---

[34] Dr. Susan Berry, "Report: Homeschooling Growing Seven Times Faster than Public School Enrollment," *Breitbart* Web site (June 8, 2013), http://www.breitbart.com/Big-Government/2013/06/07/Report-Growth-in-Homeschooling-Outpacing-Public-Schools.

[35] "Home-schooling: Outstanding results in national tests," *Washington Times* (August 30, 2009), http://www.washingtontimes.com/news/2009/aug/30/home-schooling-outstanding-results-national-tests/.

[36] "A brief look at comparisons of standardized test results for home educated students and public school students," *Ontario Federation of Teaching Parents* (1998), http://ontariohomeschool.org/comparison/.

Jack Andraka Invents Early Detection Test for Pancreatic, Ovarian and Lung Cancer

At 15 years old, Jack created a new early diagnostics test for the detection for pancreatic, ovarian and lung cancer that is 28 times faster, 26,000 times cheaper and over 100 times more sensitive than previous testing methods.

It took Jack over 200 submissions of his written proposal for research before Dr. Anirban Maitra, Professor of Pathology, Oncology and Chemical and Biomolecular Engineering at John Hopkins School of Medicine, finally offered him a chance. Motivated by recent loss, he worked after school every day, weekends and holidays at Maitra's lab, until he developed his test.[37]

As we really embrace and refine the practice of setting the stage, picture the possibilities. Imagine the things Jack and the rest of our kids could do if we gave them that kind of opportunity.

---

[37] Jack Andraka, "A Promising Test for Pancreatic Cancer—from a Teenager," TED Talks (July 2013), http://www.ted.com/talks/jack_andraka_a_promising_test_for_pancreatic_cancer_from_a_teenager; Brad Aronson, "Jack Andraka—15-year-old Jack Andraka invents cancer test 10x more sensitive and 26,000x chaper than current tests," *Brad Aronson's Blog* (n.d.), http://www.bradaronson.com/jack-andraka/; Lihn Bui, "Local Teen Scientist Invents Test for Pancreatic Cancer," *CBS Baltimore* (October 13, 2013) http://baltimore.cbslocal.com/2013/10/13/local-teen-scientist-invents-early-detector-for-pancreatic-cancer/

Teen Inventor Devises Plan To Clean Billions of Tons of Plastic from the World's Ocean's

Boyan had a big idea and a can-do attitude. He developed a plan to rid our oceans of over 7 billion tons of plastic.[38] *The Ocean Cleanup Array project comes with a few issues to iron out, and it has its fair share of critics as noted in the following article http://www.ryot.org/19-year-olds-invention-save-ocean-met-skepticism/373377.*

At the end of the article, Michael Palumbo of RYOT News says, "…the real issue is our continued use of plastics and the need for an alternative method of packaging. Perhaps he should try to invent that instead."[39]

This kind of sideline skepticism does not help. We need to support each other and build on successes

---

[38] Sarah Griffiths, "Could a teenager save the world's oceans? Student, 19, claims his invention could clean up the oceans in just five years," *Daily Mail* Web site (September 9, 2013),. http://www.dailymail.co.uk/sciencetech/article-2415889/Boyan-Slat-19-claims-invention-clean-worlds-oceans-just-years.html; David Knowles, "19-year-old Dutch engineering student Boyan Slat devises plan to rid the world's ocean's of 7.25 million tons of plastic," *New York Daily News* Web site (March 25, 2013), 19-year-old Dutch engineering student Boyan Slat devises plan to rid the world's oceans of 7.25 million tons of plastic (March 26, 2013), http://www.nydailynews.com/news/world/plan-aims-rid-oceans-7-25m-tons-plastic-article-1.1299892

[39] Michael Polumbo, "Is a teen's invention to clean up the ocean legit?" RYOT News (September 17, 2013), http://www.ryot.org/19-year-olds-invention-save-ocean-met-skepticism/373377.

The Freedom Handbook

instead of picking apart attempts at healthy change and tearing each other down.

Reality forces humans to be realistic while solving problems, but encouragement is necessary as well. Apathy is at the root of this constant negative chattering, so prevalent today. Free from unhealthy levels of skepticism and worthless cynicism, imagine what kids like Boyan could do with our full support. Let's empower our kids and each other.

Aaron Swartz: A life-size hero and Julian Assange for the academic legacy of mankind

Aaron Swartz is an icon for today's generation. He stood for freedom. He fought for everyone's right to access humanity's knowledge and academic research; he fought for education.[40]

A shockingly prolific teen innovator, as a young man he helped develop the Web feed format RSS, the idea of Creative Commons, and the social media news site Reddit, among other impressive contributions. Aaron killed himself at the age of

---

[40] David Amsden, "The Brilliant Life and Tragic Death of Aaron Swartz," *Rolling Stone* (February 28, 2013), www.rollingstone.com/culture/news/the-brilliant-life-and-tragic-death-of-aaron-swartz-20130215; Valerie J. Nelson, "Aaron Swartz dies at 26; Internet folk hero founded Reddit," *Los Angeles Times* (January 12, 2013), articles.latimes.com/2013/jan/12/local/la-me/0113-aaron-swartz-20130113.

26 facing thirty-five years in jail and a one million dollar fine. If you are not familiar with Aaron's life or his criminal prosecution by the US justice system for "borrowing too many books from the library," we encourage you to do some research. His story is one of the most important of our time.[41]

He represents, for many of us, the inalienable right we each have to our collective information and technology, as well as our education, liberty, and freedom.

Aaron was dubbed Commons Man by the Economist for his advocacy of the Creative Commons model of authorship, in which creators choose to give away their work for free. One of the most natural places to apply this ethic is academia.[42] *Tim Berners-Lee*

---

[41] "Exclusive: Aaron Swartz's Partner, Expert Witness Say Prosecutors Unfairly Targeted Dead Activist," *Democracy Now* Web site (January 17, 2013), www.democracynow.org/2013/1/17/exclusive_aaron_swartzs_partner_expert_witness; Bernard Keane, "Online activists and exemplary punishments," *Crikey* Web sit (Januaruary 21, 2013), http://www.crikey.com.au/2013/01/21/online-activists-and-exemplary-punishment/; Simona Chose, "Aaron Swartz: A Julian Assange for the Academic Crowd," *The Globe and Mail* Web site (January 20, 2013), http://www.theglobeandmail.com/news/national/education/aaron-swartz-a-julian-assange-for-the-academic-crowd/article7544023/; Samantha Murphy Kelly, "The 'Internet's Own Boy' Is a Powerful Homage to Aaron Swartz," *Mashable* Web site (January 21, 2014), http://mashable.com/2014/01/21/the-internets-own-boy-review/; Aaron Swartz, http://www.aaronsw.com/; "Taren Stinebricknever Kauffman," *Wikipedia* Website, http://en.wikipedia.org/wiki/Taren_Stinebrickner-Kauffman.

[42] G.F. and M.G., "Remembering Aaron Swartz: Commons man," *Babbage: Science and Technology* Blog, *The Economist* Web site (January 13, 2013), www.economist.com/blogs/babbage/2013/01/remembering_aaron_swartz_#sthash.sbiTFPI5.dpbs.

showed us earlier that to realize human potential, we must share Linked Data and knowledge. Not only that, but public funds have paid for most of the research and data in question.

Let us connect with the best proven education solutions available right now online. We can build global, national, and local platforms to share our experiences and use the best lessons we have learned to co-create new, vibrant education systems for our kids.

This global web of classrooms shared by kids and adults alike is guaranteed to facilitate improved results during a child's early years. Both adults and kids learn skills and absorb new information online so readily these days. We can easily learn from each other all that's needed to better educate our kids.

With the aid of our online systems, let us first target smaller test areas with all the potency of the best we have got globally to support them. We use smaller sample regions to build on what we know and inevitably produce smashing success stories on a larger scale than ever seen before, which will enliven and encourage the whole world to follow suit. This strategy is so strong that it can and should be applied to many aspects of our changing world.

After we build the space for our conversation, and creative action sees some success on the ground, we then scale the solutions online and on the ground fast, far, and wide.

Picture building momentum together through agreed-upon new channels at the local and global level, and it becomes clear that we do not need to ask any authorities of old for permission. Much like coming of age as an adolescent, our freedom requires only our readiness and capacity to claim it. As we begin to learn and care for ourselves, all current power structure's capacity to control us disappears and drops away naturally.

Any institutions truly invested in humanity's happiness and health will surely support positive change. If not, we can identify them as objectors. We might even compare the objectors or any human control systems to the bully who loses all power and will to fight in the face of fearless opposition. For this strategy to work best, we need large numbers at the end of the day. To start, there are more than enough of us committed to change—if we agree upon some starting points, we can begin to set the smaller examples, which will give rise to the groundswell needed for total rebirth.

Be warned: history is littered with cases of smaller groups and even individuals being harassed and abused by the systems that they push back against or work to replace. This issue was addressed earlier and will be again. Just be mindful that there is sometimes a price attached to doing the right thing. It is always worth paying.

As far as post-secondary education goes, Luke and I are not really qualified to comment on reform, other than as educated generalists that is. Joking aside, let us begin the conversation and construct new ideas. Then we will all figure out together how best to tweak or reinvent our world of higher education.

We are really excited to invite Liz Coleman into the post-secondary education reform discussion and to ask Sir Ken Robinson and Sugata Mitra to help with the homeschooling programs online and on the ground. Humanity has more than enough teachers and leaders. We have more than enough ideas and lessons we can apply immediately to see our kids really flourish.

All the dots connect in the end. You are almost a quarter of the way through. Have patience and the holes will fill. Here are three small quotations to help prepare you for the next bloodcurdling story of global limitation and intensely perplexing corruption; this time, through the lens of our health care systems.

sidebar

> "The world is indebted for all triumphs which have been gained by reason and humanity over error and oppression."[43]
> - James Madison -

> "Don't believe everything you hear. Real eyes, realize, real lies."
> - Tupac Shakur -

Liberating humankind's healthy potential is not easy by any stretch. However, the fun part is that it is way easier than making sense of the current senselessness.

> "Tis strange—but true; for truth is always strange; Stranger than fiction."[44]
> - Lord Byron -

---

[43] Report on the Response of Virginia to the Alien and Sedition Act, Virginia House of Delegates (1798), http://awww.fjc.gov/history/home.nsf/page/tu_sedition_hd_madison.html.

[44] Lord George Gordon Byron, *Don Juan*, canto 14, st. 101 (1823).

CHAPTER FIVE

- Health Care -

"It takes a great man to be a good listener."[1]
- *Calvin Coolidge* -

We need to be quiet and instruct our minds to listen.

We need to ask where our anger and frustrations come from when something makes us twitch.

Most of us have been deeply affected in some way, by our current health systems. Many have turned their frustration into appropriate, inquisitive, and solution-oriented action, but some continue to hold on to a diseased and distorted reality. This death grip is built with the difficulty of vulnerability and the fear of change.

Humanity is far from as healthy as it could be, and not just because of that extra piece of cheesecake. Our bodies are so much more vibrant than we are allowed to realize.

Our health systems are designed to kill, maim, mentally incapacitate, and physically weaken the population. They offer few real choices and persecute, with gross prejudice, any healers with alternate solutions, especially cheap and effective ones.

Nothing is black and white. Obviously, there is enormous good and truth in our allopathic health systems too, because most of you working within the health industry have the best of intentions.

Let us examine some facts about the cancer *industry* – one of the clearest indicators of Western medicine's dismal success and rampant corruption. Disagree with the previous statements all you want, but these stats speak for themselves:

---

[1] As quoted by Timothy Rasinski and Lorraine Griffith, *American History* (Shell Education, 2007), 20.

In the early 1900s, one in twenty people developed cancer
In the 1940s, one in sixteen people developed cancer
In the 1970s, it was one in ten
Today, it is one in three.[2]

Dr. Joseph Mercola, New York Times best-selling author and anti-corruption health practitioner, runs one of the top-ten health sites on the net, yet for his efforts, the corporate medical establishment has deemed him a "quack."[3] The stats listed above and some other facts we will discuss come from a terrific article he wrote, posted August 3, 2013 and entitled "Why Medicine Won't Allow Cancer to Be Cured."[4]

Cancer is big business. In fact, according to the National Cancer Institute, in 2010, the cost of cancer was 124.57 billion dollars[5] – yet the cancer industry spends virtually nothing on proven prevention methods, such as education regarding proper diet and exercise. Funding for prevention and cures is almost off the table altogether. Instead, industry allocates almost all its money to treatment.[6]

If you are honest with yourself, it is easy to realize that there is no motivation for curing cancer and altering these profitable patterns. The simple fact is that corporations and businesses do not do altruism

---

[2] Dr. Joseph Mercola, "Why Medicine Won't Allow Cancer to Be Cured," mercola.com (August 3, 2013), www.articles.mercola.com/sites/articles/archive/2013/08/03/natural-cancer-treatment.aspx

[3] Bryan Smith, "Dr. Mercola: Visionary or Quack?" *Chicago Magazine* (January 31, 2012), www.chicagomag.com/Chicago-Magazine/February-2012/Dr-Joseph-Mercola-Visionary-or-Quack.

[4] *Dr. Mercola* Web site (August 3, 2013), http://articles.mercola.com/sites/articles/archive/2013/08/03/natural-cancer-treatment.aspx.

[5] The National Cancer Institute projects cost of cancer care rising from $158 billion in 2010 to as much as $207 billion in 2020. "The Cost of Cancer," National Cancer Institute (2010), http://www.cancer.gov/aboutnci/servingpeople/cancer-statistics/costofcancer.

[6] Dr. Joseph Mercola, "Why Medicine Won't Allow Cancer to Be Cured," mercola.com (August 3, 2013), www.articles.mercola.com/sites/articles/archive/2013/08/03/natural-cancer-treatment.aspx

unless it's part of their charitable tax deductions for the year, which, really, is proof of concept.

Most importantly, *all* agendas die in corporations when profits are on the line.

This raises a big question. How do we ensure the integrity of our private institutions if government is not the answer? The chapter on the legal system outlines exactly how judicial systems will function, and further on, we will come back to ethics in commerce with a vengeance. For now, rest assured that an easily accomplished plan would shift corporate motivations from *bigger* and *more* to *better* and *healthier*.

Better is a pretty simple idea. For a glimpse of just how diseased current human goals are, and how a simple adjustment could make things better, watch this nine-minute video called The Story of Solutions[7] from http://storyofstuff.org/.

Dr. Mercola tells us that the typical American cancer patient spends fifty thousand dollars fighting the disease. Chemotherapy drugs are among the most expensive of all treatments with a one-month supply ranging from three thousand to seven thousand dollars.[8]

Again, no motivation exists for medi-business to cure paying customers, but how did business usurp medicine in the first place? We will use the United States as our par-for-the-course example, but make no mistake - the rules are basically the same in almost every country on earth.

Here are three quick points Dr. Mercola lays out to summarize the history behind the private interests' takeover of the United States medical industry.[9]

---

[7] Story of Stuff Project and Free Range Studio, storyofstuff.org.
[8] Dr. Joseph Mercola, "Why Medicine Won't Allow Cancer to Be Cured," mercola.com (August 3, 2013), www.articles.mercola.com/sites/articles/archive/2013/08/03/natural-cancer-treatment.aspx
[9] See, for example, Dr. Joseph Mercola, "How Corrupted Drug Companies Deceive and Manipulate Your Doctor," mercola.com (May 18, 2010),

"International bankers who own the drug and chemical companies gained control over the medical education system over 100 years ago.

"They gave grants to the AMA and leading medical schools in exchange for seats on their boards and the ability to control policy.

"Finally, they cleverly engineered control of virtually every federal regulatory agency pertaining to the practice of medicine."[10]

Dr. Mercola mentions a fascinating documentary called <u>Cancer— The Forbidden Cures</u>.[11] The film provides detailed evidence of our health systems' systemic corruption. It also covers the extreme lengths the establishment will go to, in order to discredit, imprison, and professionally derail any physician who treats cancer patients naturally.

The story of Dr. Nicholas Gonzalez and his predecessor Dr. William Kelley is one of countless examples of how healers who actually heal are persecuted. Dr. Gonzalez's entire career, which included decades of research and numerous patients with "impossible" recoveries, was completely derailed.

Dr. Mercola explains, "Dr. Gonzalez's mentor and supporter, Dr. Good, was one of the most published authors within scientific literature at that point, with over 2,000 scientific articles to his name. He had been nominated for the Nobel Prize three times, and yet he was refused because the findings were 'too controversial,' and flew in the face of conventional medical doctrine."

---

articles.mercola.com/sites/articles/archive/2010/05/18/how-corrupted-drug-companies-deceive-and-manipulate-your-doctor.aspx; Jeffrey Kluger, "Is Drug-Company Money Tainting Medical Education?" *Time* Web site (March 6, 2009), www.content.time./time/health/article/0,8599,1883449,00.html.

[10] Mercola, "Why Medicine Won't Allow Cancer to Be Cured," *Mercola.com* Web site (August 3, 2013), http://articles.mercola.com/sites/articles/archive/2013/08/03/natural-cancer-treatment.aspx.

[11] Written and directed by Massimo Mazzucco (2010).

Robert Good was at the top of his profession: President of Sloan-Kettering, father of modern immunology, and did the first bone marrow transplant in history. Yet, he couldn't get it published...He couldn't even get a single case report published.

In fact, I have a letter from one of the editors, dated 1987, who wrote a blistering letter to Good saying, "You've been boondoggled by a crazy quack guy. Don't you see this is all a fraud?"

It was just the most extraordinary, irrational letter... [Because] the patients' names were there, the copies of their pertinent medical records were there...Any of them could have called these patients, like Arlene Van Straten who, 29 years later, will talk to anyone...But no one cared. They wouldn't do it; they didn't believe it.

They couldn't believe it.

It was very disturbing to me because I say, "It is what it is." I come out of a very conventional research orientation, and it was astonishing to me—I had assistance; I had the president of Sloane-Kettering who couldn't get this thing published because it disagreed with the philosophy that was being promoted in medicine; that only chemotherapy, radiation, or immunotherapy can successfully treat cancer, even though the success rate was abysmal.

> *The idea that medical journals are these objective and unbiased repositories of the truths about science is total nonsense. Most of them are owned by the drug companies. They won't publish anything that disagrees with their philosophy.*[12]
>
> *- Dr. Nicholas Gonzalez -*

Dr. Gonzalez still actively helps people heal with natural alternatives to toxic drugs and radiation. If you are interested in the cancer treatment he promotes, his patient success stories, and his backstory, here is a great article.[13]

A few common-sense reality checks and eye-opening cancer resources can also be found in an article by S.D. Wells entitled "Top Seven Natural Cures for Cancer That Got Buried by the FDA, AMA, CDC."[14]

Any and all regulated health systems are a complete disgrace. Everyone in the world deals with the Center for Disease Control (CDC) in the U.S. Department of Health and Human Services.[15]

In Canada, Luke and I deal with entities like Health Canada,[16] while in the United States it is the American Medical Association (AMA)[17] and the United States Food and Drug Administration

---

[12] Dr. Joseph Mercola, "Kelley Treatment: The Cancer Treatment So Successful—Traditional Doctors SHUT It Down," mercola.com (April 23, 2011), articles.mercola.com/sites/articles/archive/2011/04/23/dr-nicholas-gonzalez-on-alternative-cancer-treatments.aspx.

[13] "Kelley Treatment: The Cancer Treatment So Successful—Traditional Doctors SHUT It Down," mercola.com (April 23, 2011), http://articles.mercola.com/sites/articles/archive/2011/04/23/dr-nicholas-gonzalez-on-alternative-cancer-treatments.aspx.

[14] S.D. Wells, "Top seven natural cres for cancer that got buried by the FDA, AMA, CDC," *Natural News* Web site (October 24, 2013), www.naturalnews.com/042688_natural_medicine_cancer_cures_government_agencies.html.

[15] www.cdc.gov.

[16] www.hc-sc.gc.ca.

[17] www.ama-assn.org.

(FDA).[18] Regardless of what these organizations call themselves, they provide complete and utter disaster for you and your health.

Medical institutions stifle and suffocate balanced views and solutions from numerous invaluable schools of thought.

Governments and "health" organizations around the world have been working furiously to criminalize the purchase and sale of nature's natural herbs and plants, which happen to be the source of all synthetic healing compounds as well. This is appalling because the dark (hopefully just profit-driven) purpose is enough to make you shiver to your core.

> *"Nearly 100 years ago, the AMA began removing nutritional education from medical schools in America. Medical doctors would no longer understand anything about using food as medicine (or be allowed to suggest it), and all mid-wives, Native American herbalists and natural healers would be referred to in medical journals as 'quacks.' The Western Medicine philosophy would soon come to be that no food in the world could ever heal a human being or cure any disease or disorder; in fact, only pharmaceuticals and vaccines would ever be able to make that claim (legally) and get away with it, whether in peer reviews, medical and science journals (JAMA), scientific 'studies' or labeled as such on products."*[19]
>
> *- S.D. Wells -*

---

[18] www.fda.gov.

[19] S.D. Wells, "Top seven natural cures for cancer that got buried by the FDA, AMA, and CDC" *Natural News* Web site (October 24, 2013), http://www.naturalnews.com/042688_natural_medicine_cancer_cures_government_agencies.html.

Bill C-51 and similar pieces of legislation around the world aim to criminalize nature. This article by The Independent reports on some of these laws and their costs in Europe. Canada's C-51 is explored in this incredibly revealing article from the Centre for Research on Globalization.[20]

In the United States, Obama signed Executive Order 13544 of June 10, 2010,[21] for the continued prosecution of nature's healing sources and remedies, as detailed in an article by the Examiner.[22]

Consider all the existing (and pending) legislation that outlaws the sale and use of nature's plants and herbs.

The government, institution, and structure are not set up to care for us. The very idea is a lie designed to further profits and power, and the truth of this is so immense that the inevitable and necessary realization of it can be one of the most uncomfortable experiences for a modern person – but it is necessary and vitally so, if we are going to fix the problem.

Consider how the Pharmaceutical Industry has been caught selling tainted drugs, even pills infused with AIDS. In 2003, the *New York Times* reported details of the Bayer Scandal, in which the pharmaceutical giant sold millions worth of AIDS infected medicine in Asia and Latin America in the mid-1980s. The law firm Lopez

---

[20] Global Research, "Canada's C-51 Law to Outlaw 60% of Natural Health Products," *GlobalResearch* Web site (April 30, 2008), http://www.globalresearch.ca/canada-s-c-51-law-to-outlaw-60-of-natural-health-products/8850; but see "About Natural Health Product Regulation in Canada," *Drugs and Health Products* page, *Health Canada* Web site, http://www.hc-sc.gc.ca/dhp-mps/prodnatur/about-apropos/index-eng.php.

[21] The White House, *Executive Order 13544—Establishing the National Prevention, Health Promotion, and Public Health Council* (June 10, 2010), http://www.whitehouse.gov/the-press-office/executive-order-establishing-national-prevention-health-promotion-and-public-health.

[22] James Williams, "Obama signs legislation to make supplements and alternative health remedies illegal," *Examiner.com* Web site (September 14, 2010), http://www.examiner.com/article/obama-signs-legislation-to-make-supplements-and-alternative-health-remedies-illegal.

McHugh posted an article on its website entitled "Report says Bayer sold AIDS-tainted medicine."[23]

Bayer is just one example of a corporation driven by profit and controlling interests at all costs. This article details some of this organization's history.[24] This is not a single rogue company – it is an example of a systemic and pervasive infection of greed.[25]

It is established fact – not an assertion – that business by its very nature is sociopathic. This fact has been used to defend the human beings running the largest companies in the world, which are beholden to their shareholders and profits at all costs. Regardless of where the psychopathy originates or how it is currently perpetuated, ethics need to be infused into human activity. This is not debatable. What we need to agree on, is how we get there.

The current medical establishment is the number one killer of healthy people on the planet. In addition, doctors from around the world have been tortured, killed, and ruined to suppress viable solutions for all manner of human medical ailments.

According to the 2003 report "Death by Medicine,"[26] written by doctors Gary Null, Carolyn Dean, Martin Feldman, Debora Rasio, and Dorothy Smith, doctors in the United States cause the deaths of

---

[23] "Report says Bayer sold AIDS-tainted medicine," *Lopez McHugh LLP* Web site (October 10, 2012), http://lopezmchugh.com/2012/10/10/report-says-bayer-sold-aids-tainted-medicine/index.html; Walter Bogdanich and Eric Koli, "2 Paths of Bayer Drug in '80s: Riskier One Steered Overseas," *New York Times* Web site (May 22, 2003), http://www.nytimes.com/2003/05/22/business/2-paths-of-bayer-drug-in-80-s-riskier-one-steered-overseas.html?pagewanted=all&src=pm.

[24] "Featured Articles on GMO Issues: Bayer resources," *GMWatch* Web site (n.d.), http://www.gmwatch.org/gm-firms/11154-bayer-resources

[25] *See also* Ben Goldacre, *Bad Pharma* (Faber and Faber, 2013).

[26] *Death by Medicine* (Axios Press, 2011); http://www.second-opinions.co.uk/deathbymedicine.pdf; also available at http://www.whale.to/a/null9.html.

The Freedom Handbook

over 783,000 patients every year. The original detailed report can be found here,[27] and there is a more user-friendly version here.[28]

Finally, an overview with significant statistical breakdowns and additional resources can be found here.[29]

The report's authors estimate that over 106,000 deaths per year are caused by prescription drugs, taken as prescribed, with over 37,000 deaths caused by "unnecessary procedures" and another 100,000 by "medical errors."

> *"It is evident that the American medical system is itself the leading cause of death and injury in the United States. By comparison, approximately 699,697 Americans died of heart disease in 2001, while 553,251 died of cancer."*[30]
> *- Life Extension Magazine -*

These statistics represent just the tip of the iceberg when it comes to the damage that orthodox medicines cause all over the world.

This ridiculous situation has arisen because people allow groups or institutions to dictate how to manage their health. In a regulated system, if you are diagnosed with a disease the treatment options will be the same no matter which doctor you visit. This is because

---

[27] Gary Null Ph.D.; Carolyn Dean MD, ND; Martin Feldman MD, Debora Rasio MD, and Dorothy Smith Ph.D., *Death by Medicine* (December 2003), http://www.webdc.com/pdfs/deathbymedicine.pdf.

[28] Null, Dean, Feldman, Rasio and Smith, *Death by Medicine* (n.d.), http://www.webdc.com/pdfs/deathbymedicine.pdf

[29] Null, Dean, Feldman, Rasio, and Smith, "Death by Medicine," *Life Extension Magazine* (March 2004), http://www.lef.org/magazine/mag2004/mar2004_awsi_death_01.htm.

[30] Null, Dean, Feldman, Rasio, and Smith, "Death by Medicine," Life Extension Magazine (March 2004), http://www.lef.org/magazine/mag2006/aug2006_report_death_01.htm

these doctors can only treat you with methods the regulators have approved.

If the doctor offers you an alternative treatment, he or she loses their license to practice medicine. Consequently, you do not get the best advice or the best treatment. You only get the type of care your doctor is allowed to provide.

This disgraceful and unethical reality is only one piece of our medical nightmare.

Existing regulations and continuing attacks on natural supplements and therapies are creating a global monopoly in our health systems. In addition, these efforts are seemingly motivated by more than pure monetary gain. Reducing health care options guarantees a corresponding increase in adverse health reactions and a sicker population.

There is no one size/cure fits all when it comes to human health.

Luke spoke with segments of the traditional Chinese medical community here in Calgary while writing the book, and in this community the opinion was strong that people need to remove themselves and their communities from the institution's oppressive rule. The topic of plant medicine piqued the interest of these doctors and healers, as current constraints have disallowed the use of many forms of traditional healing plants.

For anyone who takes issue with Dr. Nick Gonzalez's story, there are loads of evidence supporting the fact that many doctors who have helped their patients heal have had their licenses revoked, been sent to jail, or worse.

However, if Luke and I were to spend too much time with this issue, you might start calling us a couple of conspiracy nuts.

The *Conspiracy*

This is the one and only time we will tackle the term "conspiracy." Despite its infinite application throughout the book, the hot-button phrase has been purposefully avoided for fear of alienating common folk left and right. We cannot let our message be diluted because of the presence of a single word.

The dictionary definition of conspiracy, "a secret plan by a group to do something unlawful or harmful," means nothing to people anymore.[31] The entire world, it seems, has been slowly pitted against the term. It has become dirty and disgraced. Its use generates revulsion and disgrace among our peers.

How happy we make authorities when we ostracize and oppress our fellow humans. We fight each other in an extension of their distraction and division strategy. Enslaving one another like automatons, we attack our own salvation wherever it courageously first shoots up from the earth.

Here is a terrific article that explores the findings of a recent study on conspiracy, "<u>New studies: 'Conspiracy theorists' sane; government dupes crazy, hostile</u>."[32]

---

[31] "Conspiracy," dictionary.com Web site, http://dictionary.reference.com/browse/conspiracy?s=t; "conspiracy," (the act of conspiring; an evil, unlawful, treacherous or surreptitious plan formulated in secrecy by two or more persons; plot; a combination of persons for a secret, unlawful, or evil purpose); Oxford Dictionaries Web site, http://www.oxforddictionaries.com/definition/english/conspiracy?q=conspiracy.

[32] Dr. Kevin Barrett, "New studies: 'conspiracy theorists' sane, government dupes crazy, hostile," *Press TV* Web site (July 12, 2013), http://www.presstv.com/detail/2013/07/12/313399/conspiracy-theorists-vs-govt-dupes/.

Logic dictates that some of these so-called conspiracies are true and many are likely rooted in reality. Understandably, for many people, the thought of this can trigger intense emotions. Considering these things can become an overwhelming labyrinth too complex to comprehend.

The good news is that you do not have to. This book is meant to ease the pain and help you come to terms with some hideous things and move past them – tearing a Band-Aid off quickly is the only surefire way to minimize the pain, and so our manifesto pulls very few punches. It is time for us to wake up, think for ourselves, and really listen to each other.

People are screaming for solutions, starved for direction, and desperate for leaders who can guide us to a better place. The plan to save the world is not complicated, and it does not seek to place blame for what came before. We do not care who is to blame for what has gone wrong, we only care about what has gone wrong and how to make it better.

The core of our plan is contained here. It is time for you to govern your own life and for humanity as a whole to self-govern the world.

The Freedom Handbook

Do some research into Dr. Harvey Bigelsen or Dr. Stanislaw Burzynski. Here is Dr. Bigelsen's site,[33] with two links to Dr. Burzynski's work here and here.[34]

Ask yourself about these healers' stories and then ask what make sense and what does not. Both of these doctors have survived heavy legal attacks which supports the truth in, and adds strength to, their work. Much worse has been the case for an untold number of health practitioners ever since medical institutions were implemented worldwide.

It is horrendous, and it has to stop.

Dr. Bigelsen's work has been an inspiration for me. In 2007[35] and again in 2008,[36] I heard his interview with Regina Meredith of the Conscious Media Network, which has since been amalgamated with GaiamTV.

In his original interview with her, he talks about the damage done to the body's immune system from surgery and introduces his groundbreaking discovery of the holographic nature of blood.

---

[33] drbigelson.com Web site (n.d.), http://www.drbigelsen.com/DrBigelsen/Home.html; "Preview of Interview with Harvey Bigelsen," http://www.youtube.com/watch?v=yD2AZ-eLnyQ&list=PL7ADA98F8C79BDFB7&index=1; "Preview of Interview with Harvey Bigelsen II," http://www.youtube.com/watch?v=CiVJBeqNvfw&list=PL7ADA98F8C79BDFB7; "Preview of Interview with Harvey Bigelsen III," http://www.youtube.com/watch?v=IyqVBOshQ6M&list=PL7ADA98F8C79BDFB7.

[34] "Tomorrow's Cancer Treatment Today," *Burzynski Clinic* Web page (n.d.), http://www.burzynskiclinic.com/; *Burzynski Research Institute* Web page (n.d.), http://www.burzynskiresearch.com.

[35] "Harvey Bigelsen on Holographic Blood," host Regina Meredith, GAIAM TV (2007), http://www.gaiamtv.com/video/harvey-bigelsen-holographic-blood.

[36] Harvey Bigelsen on Hepatis C and Inflammation," http://www.gaiamtv.com/video/harvey-bigelsen-hepatitis-c-and-inflammation.

> *"The day may yet arrive when one may take a drop of blood and diagnose the condition of the entire physical body."*[37]
> - Edgar Cayce -

GaiamTV and Regina introduce Dr. Harvey Bigelsen in a 2011 interview about his book, *Medical Conspiracy in America*, by saying "Dr. Bigelsen is the first medical doctor to practice isopathy (biological medicine) in North America. As the first president of the Arizona Homeopathic Medical Board, Dr. Bigelsen drafted guidelines and standards for the practice of Holistic Medicine in Arizona that set the precedent in the United States."

In the interview, he discusses "how the medical establishment uses its power to keep new and alternative treatments away from their client base through coercion, legal witch-hunts and law making." He also talks about stem cell therapy.[38]

For those interested in this exciting topic, he also wrote a book called *Holographic Blood*, which was published in 2007.[39] His other books, *Your Cure for Cancer*[40] and *Doctors Are More Harmful Than Germs*,[41] are also highly recommended reading for anyone walking around in a human body.

You might want to watch the Dr. Burzynski Movie[42] and a second documentary, *Burzynski: Cancer Is a Serious Business, Part II*,[43] and

---

[37] *Dr. Bigelsen* Web site, http://www.drbigelsen.com/DrBigelsen/Home.html.
[38] "Harvey Bigelsen on the Medical Conspiracy," host Regina Meredith, CMN (Season 8, Episode 5: February 2011), http://www.gaiamtv.com/video/harvey-bigelsen-medical-conspiracy.
[39] (HERFF Publishing, 2007), http://www.drbigelsen.com/DrBigelsen/Store.html.
[40] http://www.drbigelsen.com/DrBigelsen/Store.html
[41] http://www.drbigelsen.com/DrBigelsen/Store.html
[42] http://www.burzynskimovie.com/
[43] Directed, written and produced by Eric Merola (2013).

then take a look at both Dr. Burzynski's patient group[44] and a skeptical blog[45] written by Bob Blaskiewicz.

There are some important things to note about Bob's blog and the campaign by SPCP (Skeptics for the Protection of Cancer Patients) and SBM (Science-Based Medicine) to criminalize Dr. Burzynski's practices. This post from the SBC website[46] and Bob's blog are full of complaints about primarily two things. First, it covers grievances about the costs of the treatments, and, second, the cases where his terminal cancer patients died.

Think about how people's complaints with the current medical establishment are identical. The number of people who lose their homes and businesses and are financially ruined by the institution of medicine in general is a substantial problem. These are obviously much bigger issues not caused by one single doctor.

It is standard practice for doctors working on new or alternative therapies to ensure that their cancer patients have already been deemed a lost cause by allopathic medicine. Patients rarely choose new or alternate treatments unless they have exhausted all the more popular options.

Either way, no matter the treatment, patients sometimes die.

Eliminating competition in any market *does not* help pricing or the customer's experience in any way. Monopolized markets are unquestionably bad for the consumer. Everyone who does not already know this desperately needs to understand. This continuing trend in all industries is one of the most talked about and dangerous in our society today.

---

[44] *Burzynski Patient Group* Web site (2011), http://www.burzynskipatientgroup.org/.
[45] "Burzynski Patient Kyla F.'s Story," *The Other Burzynski Patient Group* Web site (January 12, 2014), http://theotherburzynskipatientgroup.wordpress.com/.
[46] *Science-based Medicine* Web site, http://www.sciencebasedmedicine.org/the-skeptics-for-the-protection-of-cancer-patients-need-your-help/.

Bob and other likeminded skeptics need to tweak their approach, though they almost have the right idea. Think about how many people currently look up products and services online and read reviews before making a purchase. Aggressive, transparent reviews help inform everyone about the various products and services in the world.

Legislation and restriction around choices are not the answer. With lots of honest reviews, the problem solves itself.

Consider how many doctors only prescribe drugs and tout mainstream messages. Perhaps you have even met some yourself. Many are practicing with more concern for their own pocketbooks and a safe ride in a corrupt system than for their patients.

Imagine a global directory that catalogues customer experiences with all the doctors and healers. Measuring online integrity is already quickly gaining traction as an additional and improved way to rate personal and corporate credibility. As we integrate all fiscal systems with new forms of what is being called "social credit," we will have a creditability reporting system that is much better than anything we have now.[47]

When it comes to your health – or any part of your life – you deserve the right to make your own choices. It is amazing how we allow others to govern our bodies and our decisions about them. It is time we demand the freedom to decide on our health care.

Our doctors also need to possess the freedom to heal as they see fit.

At this, people still worry, "What if some quack starts treating people with wacky ideas and people die?"

Safety, just like morality and good behavior, cannot be legislated into existence. Besides, people are dying every day from a lack of access to health care, not to mention that as studies have shown, many still die from modern treatment, not just the illnesses.

---

[47] "Social credit," *Wikipedia* Web site (February 9, 2014), http://en.wikipedia.org/wiki/Social_Credit.

A global "Medi-Yelp" or online "IntegrityPages" is all we need to ensure integrity in human systems and practitioners of all kinds, from the handyman to the healer.

As a race, when we more fully engage our curiosity, imagination, and potential, we will inevitably create a healthier future that is better, especially for our physical bodies.

Do you know someone who died of cancer or heart disease?

Luke and I share the opinion, along with millions of others that most similarly categorized deaths, were actually caused by the treatments.

Consider what would occur if a voodoo doctor wants to treat people with goat's blood and people choose this form of treatment and ultimately die. The fact remains that it was their choice to make. Common sense says that with free choice on the table, people will gravitate and support methods with the best results, *period*.

Freedom means people decide for themselves how they should be treated and by whom.

Additionally, Luke feels that people should be able to end their own lives if they so choose. He would put up suicide booths.

Do you disagree with that idea? Let us discuss it and come to a common-sense consensus then. In the coming chapter on laws, we will examine together the best ways to govern human behavior.

These days, many people have concerns about overpopulation, which is addressed later in the book. For now, consider all the speculation about hidden depopulation policies, and even the potential manufacturing of many of today's modern illnesses for deliberate use against minorities and the public.

It can be difficult to ascertain what is true and what is not. What is blatantly apparent is that humanity has never been sicker. Our health systems certainly play a leading role, no matter how you slice it.

We can do better and we can live healthier.

The Bill & Melinda Gates Foundation is a large stock holder in Monsanto.[48] It's also heavily invested in the vaccine industry.[49] Though we don't want to single these two individuals out, their portfolio seems to dovetail awfully well with the apparent depopulation agenda among elite circles. Similar to Bayer, these folks seem to be an example of systemic moral crime within the ruling class and financial elite.

Vaccines, like genetically modified foods, are not properly tested for safety. Injecting the population with substances that have not undergone long-term testing is medical experimentation on *you* and *me*. No one knows for sure yet what the costs are. That in itself is a big enough point on which to end the discussion.

Mercury is one of the most toxic substances to human beings that we know of, no matter how you look at, and it is still used in some of today's vaccines. Mercury toxicity is explained in this interview with Dr. Chris Shade.[50]

Vaccinations seem to be causing untold long and short term health problems, but the debate is so messy that it would take too much time to cover here, as is the case with lots of big rabbit holes addressed in this book. If you're interested, use your common sense and do a bit of research.

Dr. R.E. Tent is a fairly quirky speaker and character, but even if his style bothers you, it is a small price to pay for his knowledge of health and the human body. In the following video, The Exploding Autoimmune Epidemic - Dr. Tent - It's Not Autoimmune, you have Viruses, he talks a fair bit about vaccines.[51] You will also find a few extra resources on vaccines in the bibliography to help.

---

[48] John Vidal, "Why is the Gates Foundation in GM Giant Monsanto?" *The Guardian* Web site (September 29, 2010), http://www.theguardian.com/global-development/poverty-matters/2010/sep/29/gates-foundation-gm-monsanto.

[49] http://www.gatesfoundation.org/Media-Center/Press-Releases/2011/03/Liquida-Technlogies-Receives-Investment-to-Bolster-Development-of-Vaccines

[50] http://www.quicksilverscientific.com/; http://www.naturalnews.com/044011_mercury_toxicity_Chris_Shade_quicksilver_scientific.html#ixzz2uKQbq9QA;

[51] Dr. R.E. Tent (December 27, 2012), http://www.youtube.com/watch?v=r8FCJ_Vpyns; http://www.pinterest.com/4thehealthofit/drrandy-tents-lectures/;

This past summer, I met a doctor who had also done additional doctoral work in clinical psychology. "What's the book about?" she asked, after we had time to get to know each other over some food and a couple of drinks.

To make a long story short, I could not surprise, shock, or get her to disagree with nearly anything I said, on any topic. She also told me that she wholeheartedly agreed that most, if not all, modern super illnesses were born in labs and purposefully injected into the human population by government and medical institutions around the world.

Reality is scary and ugly sometimes. You might be reeling at this stage because it gets worse, but do not worry because viable answers are coming *en masse*. This is not Zeitgeist, a great movie but one that left most of us asking, "Now what?"

That said, Peter Joseph's trilogy of Zeitgeist films are well worth watching.[52] His first takes a good hard look at humanity's problems in many areas. Unfortunately, the film offers only vague solutions via links to Jacque Fresco's beautiful but incomplete answer of the Venus Project and a resource-based economy. This trend continues throughout all three films.

The *Zeitgeist* series spawned the Zeitgeist Movement, which also promotes a resource-based economy as the solution to humanity's problems.[53] However, the steps to create one out of the economy we have are fuzzy, or, as Peter admits, missing completely.[54]

Humanity needs a plan.

Here is a list of a few things you can do today to help improve your own health, as well as cure the world's health systems:

---

https://archive.org/details/CancerPreventionAndNutrition-Dr.Tent
[52] *Zeitgeist (2007); Zeitgeist Addendum (2008), Zeitgeist Moving Forward (2011).*
[53] www.thezeitgeistmovement.com.
[54] Peter Joseph and Stefan Molyneux "Debate," *TZM Official Channel* (September 23, 2013), http://www.youtube.com/watch?v=jaP2GjvZlWY.

Feed your body healthier foods.
Exercise your body.
Exercise your mind.
Love and laugh.
Stop paying taxes in protest and invest in healthier alternatives.
Join online and on the ground and make change with our global voice.
Build new collaborative institutions to handle our decisions and activities (e.g., a transparent IntegrityPages/platform for people to vet healers).
Build self-governed health systems in smaller regions (with all our global solidarity and strength)—success stories will motivate the rest of the world to follow suit.

At the end of this book, we will talk about health systems again and paint a clearer picture of the problem and the plans. The world may currently restrict our potential for healthier lives and bodies, but not for long.
Imagine the real potential of human health.
Shake off the toughness of this journey so far. If you are caught up in our voice, remember your relaxed interstellar view. Listen to something calming, get a quick snack and fix yourself something to drink.
Next, we talk food.

> *"Let food be thy medicine and medicine be thy food."*
> *- Hippocrates -*

CHAPTER SIX

- Food Systems -

The human body is nothing short of miraculous in its resiliency. We are all capable of healing from almost every ailment you can think of, and we are far from fully understanding the mysteries of human life.

Food and water are the body's fuel. Your cells break down what you eat to remake your body entirely every seven years, so when we say that you are what you eat, we mean that literally.

> *"Chronic disease is a foodborne illness. We ate our way into this mess, and we must eat our way out."* [1]
>
> *- Mark Hyman -*

Yet, despite this importance, our food supply and agricultural systems are in big trouble. Currently, we are poisoning the foods that keep us alive and, in turn, keep our bodies functional. We are not suffering from rampant disease just because unhealthy things taste good, we are also suffering because we are letting the ruling elite and corporations decide what is best for us.

We desperately need to self-govern our own food production, which is not nearly as difficult as we have been led to believe. Most can agree that we do not need rulers to help us figure out how to grow food. The only concern that arises in modern civilization is the ability to feed larger numbers of people, sometimes in some very dense settings.

Therefore, the real question is how we will feed the world.

---

[1] "Pharmageddon: Can a New Weight Loss Drug Really Save Us?" *Huffington Post* (February 27, 2013), www.huffingtonpost.com/dr-mark-hyman/qnexa_b_1303050.html.

To arrive at an answer, we must first acknowledge two facts:

Food production is historically the fastest and easiest problem to remedy.

Food production is the first problem human beings instinctively remedy first when under duress.

Life can be complicated. Monetary systems, legal systems, and social programs are big and complex issues. Food, on the other hand, is as simple as can be. Despite humankind's best efforts, it is pretty tough to complicate eating and growing food.

The laboratories and factory farms that produce the majority of the world's food supply today may look like they came out of the worst parts of a science fiction novel, yet this is no fantasy.

Life may sometimes feel like a grand movie we are all starring in together, but it is very real. Look around. We cannot let this continue any longer. The solutions are going to come fast and furious in this chapter, but, first, we need to identify the diseased aspects of the world's food systems.

> *"High-tech tomatoes. Mysterious milk. Super-squash. Are we supposed to eat this stuff? Or is it going to eat us?"* [2]
>
> *- Annita Manning -*

On November 10, 2007, then Senator Barack Obama was working his way toward the 2008 presidential election and spoke in front of an audience in Iowa of more than four hundred farmers and rural activists. He pledged to promote local foods, sustainable agriculture, and the labelling of GMO (genetically modified organism) foods if elected.[3]

---

[2] As quoted in *Awakened Mind: One-Minute Wake Up Calls to a Bold and Mindful Life* (Conan Books: 2009), 175, by David Kundt.

[3] Tom Philpott, "Will Barack Obama break his GM food labelling promise?" *The Guardian* (October 6, 2011), http://www.theguardian.com/environment/2011/

"Here's what I'll do as President. I'll immediately implement Country of Origin Labeling because Americans should know where their food comes from. And we'll let folks know whether their food has been genetically modified because Americans should know what they're buying."[4]
- President Barak Obama -

In 2010, President Barack Obama appointed former Monsanto VP Michael Taylor to the top position in Foods at the FDA.[5] This happened despite multiple large public petitions, such as the one started through MoveOn.org, which opposed the widely criticized appointment.[6]

---

oct/06/barack-obama-gm-food-labelling; Tom Philpott, "Obama's Broken Promise on GMO Food Labeling," *Mother Jones* (October 6, 2011), http://www.motherjones.com/tom-philpott/2011/10/fda-labeling-gmo-genetically-modified-foods; Dave, "Breaking Video: 2007 Campaign Promise, Obama Says He'll Label GMOs if Elected," *Food Democracy Now* Web site (October 3, 2011), http://www.fooddemocracynow.org/blog/2011/oct/3/obama_promises_to_label_gmos/.

[4] Quoted in "Breaking Video: 2007 Campaign Promise, Obama says he'll label GMOs if elected," *Food Democracy Now* blog (October 3, 2011), by Dave, http://www.fooddemocracynow.org/blog/2011/oct/3/obama_promises_to_label_gmos/.

[5] Melanie Warner, "Obama Gives Former Food Lobbyist Michael Taylor a Second Chance at the FDA," Moneywatch, CBS News Web site (January 15, 2010), http://www.cbsnews.com/news/obama-gives-former-food-lobbyist-michael-taylor-a-second-chance-at-the-fda/; Jeffrey Smith, "You're Appointing Who? Please, Obama, Say It's Not So!" Huffington Post (February 23, 2009), http://www.huffingtonpost.com/jeffrey-smith/youre-appointing-who-plea_b_243810.html.

[6] See, for example, "Tell Obama to Cease FDA Ties to Monsanto," by Frederick Ravid, *MoveOn.Org Petitions*, http://petitions.moveon.org/sign/tell-obama-to-cease-fda; Connor Adams Sheets, "The 'Monsanto Protection Act': Five Terrifying Things to Know about The HR 933 Provision," *International Business Times* Web site (March 27, 2013), http://www.ibtimes.com/monsanto-protection-act-5-terrifying-things-know-about-hr-933-provision-1156079; Natasha Lennard, "How the Monsanto Protection Act Snuck Into the Law," *Salon* Web site (March 27, 2013) http://www.salon.com/2013/03/27/how_the_monsanto_protection_act_snuck_into_law/; Ashley Pinkerton, "The

In 1992, the FDA decided that GMO foods were not "materially" different from non-GMO foods, so it would require the same testing from both. As a result, the producer or manufacturer is currently the only party required to do testing, not independent scientists.[7]

Even earlier, in the 1980s, the FDA granted "GRAS" (generally regarded as safe) status to GMO foods, which meant that producers were spared from doing long-term testing for safety.[8]

Companies today with patents of GMO seeds are often able to prevent scientists from doing independent research.[9] This is even more devastating to our ability to ascertain the truth of GMO safety. GMO companies try to portray the other side as "anti-science," which makes anti-GMO scientists scoff.[10]

Since the 1990s, the FDA has not required companies to label their products as GMO or non-GMO, again because of the view that they are not different, though they did recently introduce voluntary guidelines for labelling.[11]

Unfortunately, the FDA has long had two conflicting roles: regulating GMO foods and promoting the biotechnology industry.[12]

'Monsanto Protection Act' of Betrayal," *Food First* Web site (April 10, 2013), http://www.foodfirst.org/en/node/4226.

[7] Ramona Bashshur, "FDA and Regulation of GMOs," ABA Health eSource, http://www.americanbar.org/content/newsletter/publications/aba_health_esource_home/aba_health_law_esource_1302_bashshur.html.

[8] Tom Philpott, "Does GMO Corn Really Cause Tumors in Rats?" *Mother Jones*, http://www.motherjones.com/tom-philpott/2012/09/gmo-corn-rat-tumor.

[9] Tom Philpott, "Does GMO Corn Really Cause Tumors in Rats?" *Mother Jones*, http://www.motherjones.com/tom-philpott/2012/09/gmo-corn-rat-tumor.

[10] Peter Melchett, "The Pro-GM Lobby's Seven Sins Against Science," *Soil Association* Web site (December 7, 2012). http://www.soilassociation.org/motherearth/viewarticle/articleid/4752/the-pr%2012/2012;.

[11] Ramona Bashshur, "FDA and Regulation of GMOs," ABA Health eSource, http://www.americanbar.org/content/newsletter/publications/aba_health_esource_home/aba_health_law_esource_1302_bashshur.html.,

[12] Bashshur.

What is changing the labelling landscape is what is going on at the state level.

The Non-GMO Project reports that thirty-seven state initiatives are underway to require labelling. At least seven state legislatures are considering the mandatory labelling and two states have already passed them.[13] We believe that consumer pressure and the supply and demand of the people as opposed to politics, will force this change to happen.

The illusion of democracy is fading as people all over the world are waking up to the lie they were told. We are increasingly realizing the fruitlessness of voting for any other human being in hopes that he or she will make anything but self-serving decisions about our lives and our shared world.

Absolute power corrupts absolutely. To infuse all human activity with ethics we need transparency and society as a whole to watch over each individual's proceedings. What we propose is a change in leadership, from an individual pyramidal model to a circular group model.

We must acknowledge that the government, banks, and corporations are extensions of one another. In truth, they are all one and the same. This corporatocracy is vying for global domination.

This is not a theory. This is the world we live in.

As we teeter on the edge of something far, far worse, the human race needs you, and we all need each other. We need to start working together. The ruling class is so well organized at the game of control and divide, while all of us working to make the world better spend most of our time fighting with each other about semantics.

Think about how much we can achieve as we learn to work together and use our working hands for the betterment of ourselves. We need to focus our collective efforts with a laser's intensity. Only then will our authority demand the respect it requires to make decisions and the big changes that must happen.

---

[13] *Non-GMO Project* Web site, http://www.nongmoproject.org/take-action/mandatory-labeling/.

It is important to realize how many generations have passed with a ruling class and, consequently, how practiced and well organized these authorities have to be.

Look at this <u>famous series</u> of web memes created by Stephanie Herman.[14] Her work is a stunning visual display of the crossovers between the government and Comcast, Disney, General Electric, Goldman Sachs, green energy, defense contractors, Enron, Keystone Pipeline, the media, Monsanto, Big Oil, the pharmaceuticals, Planned Parenthood, and social networking sites.

For our discussion on food, have a look at Stephanie's Venn diagram for Monsanto:

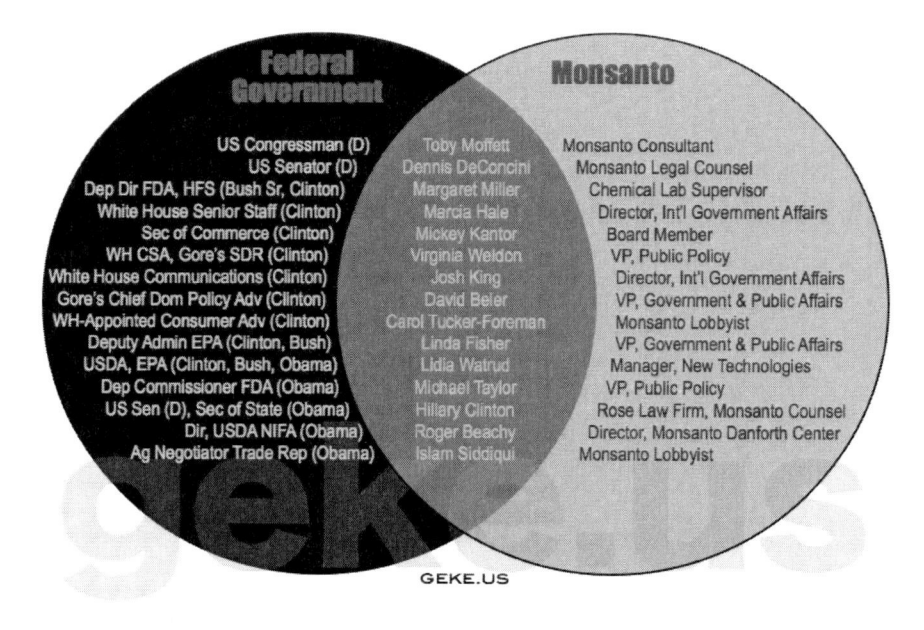

Twenty-eight countries, Poland and Russia most recently, have banned Monsanto's GMO foods outright.[15]

---

[14] "The Venn Diagram Meme," *Geke Econmeme,* Geke.us, http://www.geke.us/VennDiagrams.html; http://geke.us/MonsantoVenn.html; http://creativecommons.org/licenses/by-nc-nd/3.0/; http://geke.us/.

[15] Walden Bello and Foreign Policy in Focus, "Twenty-six countries ban GMOs: Why won't US?" *The Nation* Web site (October 29, 2013), http://www.thenation.

Anything created in a laboratory, and all chemically treated food, is making us sick. GMOs are killing us. What is worse is that from certain angles, it can look as though these products are killing us on purpose. Population control does make sense if control is the name of the game, which it most definitely is.

If you have seen the movie *The Matrix*, you will especially enjoy the critically acclaimed three-minute animated cartoon "The MEATRIX."[16] The film spawned "The MEATRIX II"[17] and "The MEATRIX II ½"[18] which are both pretty entertaining and well worth the few minutes. All three family friendly shorts explore factory farming, and the third addresses fast food.

Jeffrey Smith is the executive director of the Institute for Responsible Technology[19] and a best-selling author who is recognized as one of the world's foremost experts on GMOs. He has lectured in thirty-seven countries, counselled leaders from every continent, and has been quoted by hundreds of media outlets, including the *New*

---

com/blog/176863/twenty-six-countries-ban-gmos-why-wont-us; "List of Countries that Ban GMO Crops and Require GE Food Labels," *Natural Revolution* Web site, (June 19, 2013), http://naturalrevolution.org/list-of-countries-that-ban-gmo-crops-and-require-ge-food-labels/; Arjun Walla, 'Russia Considering a Complete Ban on All GM Food Products," *Collective Evolution* Web site (February 6, 2014), http://www.collective-evolution.com/2014/02/06/russia-considering-a-complete-ban-on-gm-food-products/; Case Adams, "Many Countries Ban GMO Crops, Require GE Food Labels," *R.E.A.L.* Web site, http://www.realnatural.org/many-countries-ban-gmo-crops-require-ge-food-labels/; *Non-GMO Project* Web site, http://www.nongmoproject.org/; "Poland Announces Complete Ban on Monsanto's Genetically Modified Corn," http://www.whydontyoutrythis.com/2014/02/poland-announces-complete-ban-on-monsantos-genetically-modified-corn.html.

[16] Louis Fox (director), Louis Fox and Jonah Sachs (writers), Free Range Studios and Sustainable Table (prod. cos.), Sustainable Table (distribution), (2003), http://www.themeatrix.com/.

[17] *The Meatrix II (Revolting)* (GRACE and Free Range Studios, 2003, 2006), themeatrix.com.

[18] *The Meatrix II ½* (GRACE and Free Range Studios), themeatrix.com.

[19] http://www.responsibletechnology.org/.

York Times, the Washington Post, and the BBC World Service. He is also a familiar face to many people as a popular guest on TV and radio shows. His first book, *Seeds of Deception: Exposing Industry and Government Lies about the Safety of the Genetically Engineered Foods You're Eating*,[20] quickly became the world's best-selling and number-one ranked book on GMOs.[21] His second book, *Genetic Roulette: The Documented Health Risks of Genetically Engineered Foods*,[22] presents irrefutable evidence that GMOs are harmful.[23]

He has his detractors among the corporatocracy's paid scientists and their skeptic supporters, however, many people can see the common sense in his work despite the fact that he is not a medical doctor or a scientist. Instead, Jeffrey Smith relies on his critical thinking skills and thorough research. Similarly, the rest of us regular folks need to be able to use this method when confronted with complicated technical issues.

We now know, based on over four thousand FDA memos[24] that were made public in a lawsuit brought by the Alliance for Bio-Integrity,[25] that scientists at the FDA were deeply concerned about the

---

[20] (Yes! Books, 3rd ed. 2003).

[21] "Jeffrey M. Smith Biography," *Institute for Responsible Technology,* http://www.responsibletechnology.org/resources/media-kit/jeffrey-m-smith-bio; http://www.responsibletechnology.org/

[22] (Yes! Books, 4th ed. 2007).

[23] *Beyond Belief: Jeffrey Smith on Food Fight: Truth about GMOs,* George Noory (host), GAIAM TV http://www.gaiamtv.com/video/jeffrey-smith-food-fight-truth-about-gmos#play/29898; "Jeffrey M. Smith Biography," *Institute for Responsible Technology* Web site, http://www.responsibletechnology.org/resources/media-kit/jeffrey-m-smith-bio.

[24] See, for example, "Key FDA Documents Revealing (A) Hazards of Genetically Modified Foods and (B) Flaws with How the Agency Made Its Policy," *Alliance for Bio-Integrity* Web site (n.d.), http://biointegrity.org/FDAdocs/index.html.

[25] Steven M. Druker, "How a U.S. District Court Revealed the Unsoundness of the FDA's Policy on Genetically Engineered Foods: A Report on the Results of *Alliance for Bio-Integrity v. Shalala,* Alliance for Bio-Integrity (updated 2003), http://biointegrity.org/report-on-lawsuit.htm.

health dangers of GMOs. Jeffrey summed up what the scientists said in this way: "These crops need to be tested carefully for food safety, there are diseases that can occur, allergens, toxins and problems from eating milk or meat from animals fed GMOs, there should be long term studies, human studies etc."[26]

The changes made to the planet's gene pool can never be reversed. Doctors have been calling for this technology to be put back in the lab since its release into the ecosystem,[27] demanding that it be proven safe for long-term human consumption as well as the larger environment. In fact, the damage done and any changes to the gene pool will outlast the earth itself.

This irresponsible experimentation could not be any more reckless.

We are allowing the ruling elites to play God, giving them the ability to deem that this product is okay or safe without questioning them. We are permitting all this, while they do permanent genetic experimentation on a cosmic scale.

This is insane.

After Michael Taylor's appointment to the FDA's top position, a new policy was enacted into law that stated that there is no evidence of any difference between GMOs and non-GMOs to be concerned with, so no testing is necessary and no labelling is necessary.

Most worldwide testing on GMOs is done and paid for by the corporations that produce them. Jeffrey Smith has already informed millions of people that industry feeding studies last a maximum of ninety days.[28]

---

[26] *Genetic Roulette* Author Jeffrey Smith GMO Testimony," Occupy Hawaii (September 24, 2013), at 01:30, http://www.youtube.com/watch?v=gnVt5ktjsXc.

[27] See, for example, Paul Hatchwell, "Opening the Pandora's Box: The Risks of Releasing Genetically Engineered Organisms," *The Ecologist* vol. 19, no. 4 (July-August, 1989), 130-136.

[28] "Beyond Belief: Jeffrey Smith on Food Fight: Truth about GMOs," George Noory (host), Gaiam TV (December 2012), at 23:30, http://www.gaiamtv.com/video/jeffrey-smith-food-fight-truth-about-gmos#play/29898; Rady

More people need to know this.
Everyone deserves to know.

In these studies, rats are fed GMO corn, soy, etc. If the rats are fine after ninety days, the industry decides it is okay to feed the GM product to human beings for a lifetime.

Recently, independent scientists in France decided to conduct a feeding study over two years, which is the lifetime of a typical rat.[29]

In the first ninety days, everything was fine in these tests as well, but in the first month afterward, the rats started getting tumors. By the end of the study up to 80 percent of the female rats had mammary gland tumors, up to 50 percent of the male rats had died prematurely, and all of the rats suffered higher rates of liver, kidney, and pituitary gland damage than the ones on non-GMO diets.[30]

To date, this is still the longest-term, most comprehensive study on GMOs ever done.

It should have resulted in the immediate cessation of GMOs around the world. Instead, only Russia banned GMO corn, with Kurzikstan following suite a month later.[31]

Ananda, "The Effects of Genetically Modified Foods on Animal Health," *Global Research* (December 13, 2013), http://www.globalresearch.ca/the-effects-of-genetically-modified-foods-on-animal-health/16747?print=1.

[29] Tom Philpott, "Does GMO Corn Really Cause Tumors in Rats?", *Mother Jones* (September 21, 2012), http://www.motherjones.com/tom-philpott/2012/09/gmo-corn-rat-tumor.

[30] de Vendômois JS, Roullier F, Cellier D, Séralini GE. A Comparison of the Effects of Three GM Corn Varieties on Mammalian Health. *Int J Biol Sci* 2009; 5(7):706-726. doi:10.7150/ijbs.5.706. Available from http://www.ijbs.com/v05p0706.htm. For commentary on the issue of retraction of the article from the scientific journal *Food and Chemical Toxicology*, see, for example, Barbara Cassassus, "Study linking GM maize to rat tumours is retracted," *Nature* Web site (November 28, 2013), http://www.nature.com/news/study-linking-gm-maize-to-rat-tumours-is-retracted-1.14268; Jeffrey M. Smith, "Dangerous Toxins from Genetically Modified Plants Found in Women and Fetuses," http://action.responsibletechnology.org/o/6236/t/0/blastContent.jsp?email_blast_KEY=1165644.

[31] Joe Entine, "Anti-GM corn study reconsidered: Séralina finally responds to torrent of criticism," *Genetic Literacy Project* Web site (November 19, 2012), http://

The reason public outrage subsided and was largely avoided was because after the study was released, the biotechnology industry mounted a massive PR assault – estimated at costing over a million dollars a day – that said, "The study was bogus science because they used rats that were already prone to tumors."[32]

Yet, the biotechnology companies use the same kind of rats to establish their products' safety wrongfully in the first place. Their argument loses all weight when you consider that only the groups that were fed GMOs had dramatically higher percentages of tumors, early deaths, and organ damage.[33]

Independent scientists that looked at three separate studies, including French research and Monsanto research, said that either all satisfied, or failed to satisfy, evaluation criteria to a comparable extent. By this reasoning, the rejection of only one of them – the French study – for publication was not scientifically justified.[34]

You can hear Jeffrey Smith speak all over the Web. Here is an especially short and informative cartoon review of his film "Genetic Roulette," which is also the world's most popular and informative films on GMOs.[35] One of the better interviews with Jeffrey is with

---

www.geneticliteracyproject.org/2012/11/19/anti-gm-corn-study-reconsidered-seralini-finally-responds-to-torrent-of-criticism/#.UyNAgV6Xk5g.

[32] "Seralini and Science: An Open Letter," *Independent Science News* Web site (October 2, 2012), http://www.independentsciencenews.org/health/seralini-and-science-nk603-rat-study-roundup/

[33] See, for example, the response of the European Network of Scientists for Social and Environmental Responsibility (ENSSER), "ENSSER comments on Séralini et al. 2012," ENSSER Web site (October 5, 2012), http://www.ensser.org/democratising-science-decision-making/ensser-comments-on-seralini-study/, and their report, *Questionable Biosafety of GMOs, Double Standards and, Once Again, a "Shooting-the-Messenger" Style Debate*, ENSSER-Comments-Seralini-etal2012-en.pdf.

[34] Helmut Meyer and Angelika Hilbeck, "Rat feeding studies with genetically modified maize—a comparative evaluation of applied methods and risk assessment standards," Environmental Sciences Europe 2013, 25:33http://www.enveurope.com/content/25/1/33.

[35] Directed by Jeffrey M. Smith, produced by Institute for Responsible Technology (2012), http://geneticroulettemovie.com/.

Thom Hartmann on the television program <u>Conversations with Great Minds</u>.[36]

In the bibliography at the end of this book, there are additional resources on not only the problems with our food systems, but also on becoming part of the many solutions, some of which we will be discussing shortly.

Jeffrey is not alone when he says that people often heal in a very short period from all manners of ailments after switching to a non-GMO diet. In fact, there are doctors everywhere prescribing non-GMO diets to their patients.[37] Food, like all of nature, has always and can always sustain the human race, provided we do not play God and destroy the balance of nature itself.

Numerous movies, books, and websites discuss what is inside today's food. Two popular films for those interested in learning more are *Food, Inc.*[38] an award-winning documentary,[39] and *Farmageddon*.[40]

Food Inc. looks at corporate food and the chemical poisoning of the population. *Farmageddon* is the story of a boy whose allergies and asthma are healed after he starts consuming raw milk and real food from farms. It also features stories about people from all over the United States who formed food co-ops and private clubs to get these foods and were raided by state and local governments.

---

[36] *Conversations with Great Minds,*

[37] "*Genetic Roulette* Author Jeffrey Smith GMO Testimony," Occupy Hawaii (September 24, 2013), http://www.youtube.com/watch?v=gnVt5ktjsXc.

[38] *Food, Inc.*, Robert Kenner (dir., writer, prod.); Robert Kenner, Elise Pearlstein, and Kim Roberts (writers), Magnolia Pictures, Participant Media, and River Road Entertainment (prod. companies) (2008); "Welcome, Food Inc. Fans!", *Food, Inc.*, takepart.com/foodinc/.

[39] "Food Inc.," *Top Documentary Films,* http://topdocumentaryfilms.com/food-inc/.

[40] *Farmageddon*, Kristin Canty (dir.), Kristin Canty and Paul Dewey (prods.) (2011); "The Film," *Farmageddon: The Unseen War on American Family Farms,* http://farmageddonmovie.com/film/.

> *"Apparently I am farmed and dangerous...But I am not a criminal. I'm a shepherd, farmer and writer..."*[41]
>
> - Montana Jones -

It is a terrifying and criminal reality. Your right to grow your own food and eat what you choose is being attacked.

Montana Jones is a Canadian farmer who has been preserving Shropshire sheep, a rare breed, for the last twelve years, and farming various other heritage breeds and vegetables for the last thirty. This article includes a heart-wrenching two-minute video of her story.[42]

In her legal battle, which began in 2012 and is still underway in 2014,[43] she faces up to twelve years in jail and fines of up to 1.5 million dollars CAD. Her case involves the Canadian Food Inspection Agency (CFIA) and raw milk activist Michael Schmidt.

The evidence of an agenda for clamping down on organic farming is rarely, if ever, mentioned but hard to deny when you take a few steps back and look at these trends nationally and even internationally.

Another example of corporate interests targeting small and natural farmers is evidenced in this video interview with Michigan pig farmer Mark Baker.[44] There is more on his family's struggle found in articles here and here.

Mark is a down-to-earth, hard-working guy just trying to support his family. People like Mark and Montana losing everything at the hands of state regulators certainly spells disaster for our food supply.

---

[41] *Farmed and Dangerous?* http://shropshiresheep.org/farmedanddangerous/

[42] Montana Jones, "Canadian Food Inspection Agency destroys shepherd's life and sheep," (November 19, 2013), http://www.realfarmacy.com/cfia-destroys-shepards-life-and-sheep/?fb_ref=recommendations-box-widget; Montana Jones, *Farmed and Dangerous,* http://www.gofundme.com/farmedanddangerous.

[43] "Disappearing Sheep Case Still Stuck in Procedural Wrangling," *Better Farming* (February 3, 2014), http://www.betterfarming.com/online-news/disappearing-sheep-case-still-stuck-procedural-wrangling-54294.

[44] "Hogwash! Authorities kill feral pigs in Michigan," *RT* (April 19, 2012), http://www.youtube.com/watch?v=H-w-ULR_bqA.

The scope of this problem on a global scale is both sad and alarming. With this undeniable trend of squeezing out (especially organic) small family farms in mind, consider the corporatocracy's established history of impoverishing third-world farmers by stealing their lands= and imposing large-scale agriculture projects that destroy the local ecosystems.

Corporations do all this without feeling, and certainly without sharing in the profits. In fact, they often end up raising both starvation and poverty levels.

We need to reclaim the earth's arable land for the common people of the world. Corporations have no right to that land whatsoever.

Speaking of land rights, this article[45] covers a widespread and tactical attack on people living off the grid altogether, not just growing their own food.[46]

Some might consider global land rights a debatable topic. The common human being's rights to grow food on his or her own land and to live sustainably off the grid are not up for discussion. Rather, they should not be.

Our right to do as we like with food and energy, provided we cause no harm to another, is inalienable. Humanity needs to defend against the persecution of people living free in any way. The 'how' comes later in this book, along with answers to many more of the larger questions.

Another deeply disturbing case of authorities criminalizing freed behavior is the story of Robin Speronis, a retired woman living off the

---

[45] Mac Slavo (January 3, 2014), http://www.shtfplan.com/headline-news/gov-swat-teams-target-rugged-individuals-who-grow-their-own-food-produce-their-own-electricity_01032014.

[46] *Battle for the California Desert: Why Is the Government Driving Folks off Their Land?"* Reason TV, Nick Gillespie (editor-in-chief), Zach Weismueller and Tim Cavanaugh (prods.) (August 23, 2011), http://www.youtube.com/watch?v=yw3RiMdS7sE; see also Tara Dodrill, "Are You A Target If You Live Off-the-Grid?", *OfftheGridNews* (May 8, 2013), http://www.offthegridnews.com/2013/05/08/are-you-a-target-if-you-live-off-the-grid/.

The Freedom Handbook

grid.⁴⁷ In this February 13, 2014, article, you will also find a terrific radio interview with the spunky Mrs. Speronis.⁴⁸

This is her story:

After her husband died, Robin decided to live off the grid. She uses a hanging water bag for bathing and a camping stove for cooking, but the state says she is not allowed to do this. After months of harassment, she now faces a thirty-day compliance order – connect to the municipal water supply or appeal the court's decision.

Ultimately, if she does not comply she faces eviction from the home she owns free and clear.⁴⁹ You can read all about this travesty of justice here.

The reasons for the order are quite simple. Robin represents a threat to municipal monopolies on water and power. Authorities cannot allow Robin Speronis to easily live off the grid, because then other people might get the idea that they can do the same thing.

This is the same strategy used around the world, no matter the nature of the liberated behavior. Authorities rely on legislation first, even if new regulations need to be written to enable said persecution. Next, public opinion needs to be swayed to support these unethical but costumed attacks on the targeted group or behavior.

Authority's monopoly on force is then deployed to enforce the law.

---

⁴⁷ Liza Fernandez, "Cape Coral Serves woman living off the grid with amended notice," WFTX-TV (Fox) (January 27, 2014), http://www.fox4now.com/features/4inyourcorner/C-242287801.html; Felicia Dionisio, "Widow faces eviction for 'living off the grid,'" WND-TV (December 16, 2013), http://www.wnd.com/2013/12/widow-faces-eviction-for-living-off-the-grid/.

⁴⁸ "City threatens widow with eviction for living off the grid," *OffTheGridNews* (February 13, 2014), http://www.offthegridnews.com/2014/02/13/city-threatens-widow-with-eviction-for-living-off-the-grid/; Darren Pope, "City cites 'international code' in eviction of woman 'living off the grid,'" *Myrtle Beach Independent Examiner* (December 16, 2013), http://www.examiner.com/article/city-cites-international-code-eviction-of-woman-living-off-the-grid;

⁴⁹ "Cape Coral Gives Woman Living 'Off-the-Grid' 30 Days to Join Water System," *News Press* (February 20, 2014), http://www.news-press.com/article/20140220/NEWS0101/140220003/Cape-Coral-gives-woman-living-off-grid-30-days-join-water-system?nclick_check=1.

We need to stand up for our innate right to live off the land, free and clear of interaction with the state. We need to stand together and protect our farmers. We need to protect our rights to grow our own gardens and keep animals.

All humanity has the right to do as we wish provided we cause no harm to other human beings, and we need to reclaim that right.

We will discuss how to handle personal disagreements and the law, shortly. For now though, think about how you have the right to grow and eat whatever you want.

It is criminal for anyone, or any authority, to challenge that.

Denise Morrison is a woman living in Tulsa, Oklahoma, whose herb and food garden was illegally destroyed by the city despite the fact that she had worked diligently to ensure she was well within her rights and had adhered to the city's local laws.[50] Think hard about the statements from <u>this</u> article.[51]

An Excerpt from the article, "Tulsa Officials Destroy Woman's Survival Garden"

Every word out of their mouth was, 'we don't care.'

Morrison, who was unemployed at the time of her property's unauthorized destruction, used her yard as a sort of survival garden, growing over 100 varieties of edible and medicinal plants. From fruit trees to herbs that helped ease pain from her

---

[50] Rob Richard, "Gov Criminalizes Self Reliance: Woman's Survival Garden Seized and Destroyed by Authorities," *SHTF Plan* Web site (June 19, 2012), https://www.shtfplan.com/headline-news/gov-criminalizes-self-reliance-womans-survival-garden-seized-and-destroyed-by-authorities_06192012.

[51] Marlene Kruvells, "Tulsa officials destroy woman's survival garden," *Hit & Run Blog,* Reason.com (June 21, 2012), http://reason.com/blog/2012/06/21/tulsa-destroy-survival-garden.

arthritis, Morrison had a purpose for every single one of her plants—that, under local law, meant that she was well within her legal right to maintain her garden. According to Tulsa city ordinances, plants may only grow over 12 inches tall if they're fit for human consumption. Since Morrison had dealt with local code enforcement in the past, she made sure that she could chow down on all her plants.

So last August, when city inspectors sent the Tulsa resident a letter telling her they wanted the garden to go, she took it up to the local courts, knowing that she was within her legal growing rights. She knew she'd win. Or, at least, that she should've won.

The day after she went to the courthouse, Morrison came home to men chopping down everything in her garden down—walnut trees, garlic chives—you name it, it was gone.

Not only are the plants my livelihood, they're my food and I was unemployed at the time and had no food left, no medicine left, and I didn't have insurance,' Morrison told reporters. 'They took away my life and livelihood.
- Marlene Kruvells -

Jason Helvenston was also ordered to destroy his home garden. A local news program talks about the concerns other residents in Orlando have about how his story affects their own rights to grow food on their own properties here.⁵² The article you can find here is another good article on Jason's story.⁵³

In Toronto, authorities deliberately destroyed a community garden without warning or giving people a chance to harvest the food just because the people did not have permission to grow free food on public land,⁵⁴ a story that you can read about here.

On a much more positive note, check out Beacon Food Forest's amazing website⁵⁵ and this article,⁵⁶ and then imagine what kind of possibilities really exist for cities and gardens. Beacon Food Forest is a seven-acre forest in Seattle where anyone can eat for free.⁵⁷

Stay-at-home dad Karl Trimaco is a gardener with fifty-five heirlooms who dislikes GMOs and pesticides. "I just thought [gardening] would be an excellent way to help provide for my family," he said. "People have been gardening since the beginning of human civilization, and the First Lady has even been setting an example by gardening at the White House! I never expected it to be so controversial." Read his story here.⁵⁸

Alternatively, you can watch police raid a grocery store with guns at the ready and listen to investigative journalist John Stossel's

---

[52] "Neighbors react to vegetable garden," WKMG TV (November 8, 2012), http://www.clickorlando.com/news/Neighbors-react-to-vegetable-garden/-/1637132/17336024/-/13gdtwsz/-/index.html.

[53] "FL Man Refuses City Order to Destroy His Garden," *Activist Post* (November 8, 2012), http://www.activistpost.com/2012/11/fl-man-refuses-city-order-to-destroy.html.

[54] "City of Toronto Workers Destroy Free Community Food Garden Amid Growing Food Crisis," *Activist Post* (September 30, 2012), http://www.activistpost.com/2012/09/city-of-toronto-workers-destroy-free.html.

[55] http://www.beaconfoodforest.org/.

[56] Dan Stone, "Seattle's Free Food Experiment," *Change Reaction, National Geographic* (April 29, 2013), http://newswatch.nationalgeographic.com/2013/04/29/seattles-free-food-experiment/.

[57] *Beacon Food Forest Permaculture Project,* http://www.beaconfoodforest.org/index.html.

[58] Heather Callaghan, "Landlord Charged for Front Yard Garden—Tenant and Neighbors Fight Back," *Activist Post* (August 5, 2012), http://www.activistpost.com/2012/08/landlord-charged-for-front-yard-garden.html.

common sense commentary on what he calls "the food police" in America here.

Andrew Wordes' story is included last because his story is so powerful and tragic that it tends to arouse the compassion and humanity in people.

The city of Roswell, Georgia has harassed and prosecuted Andrew for raising chickens and producing organic eggs, for over three years. They threatened to steal his land, threw him in jail, bankrupted him, and eventually foreclosed on his home, causing him to lose everything – including his life.

"On Monday, 3/26/2012, faced with foreclosure eviction, Mr. Wordes called an AJC reporter, telling him to watch what was about to happen. He poured gasoline in the house and lit it, resulting in an explosion and fire. His body was found in the house."[59]

Glenn Horowitz wrote a passionate story about Andrew for the *American Daily Herald,* which you can read here.[60] You can hear Andrew Wordes interviewed on the radio by clicking here.[61]

He also wrote a detailed account of all the senseless persecution, a first-hand account of his trial and tribulations that you can read right here.

Dr. Matthias Rath, a medical doctor, scientist, and advocate of natural, affordable, and effective health care, spoke about how the corporatocracy is running the world at the Cancer Free World conference in Berlin, Germany, on March 13, 2012. He called on the people of Europe to stand up and take responsibility for creating a

---

[59] Dave Kell, "Rusty Humphries Interview with Andrew Wordes in late Feb, 2012," (May 27, 2012), http://airbornecombatengineer.typepad.com/dave_kell/2012/03/rusty-humphries-interview-with-andrew-wordes-in-late-feb-2012.html.

[60] "In Memoriam: Andrew Wordes, Enemy of the States, *American Daily Herald* (March 30, 2012), http://www.americandailyherald.com/pundits/glenn-horowitz/item/in-memoriam-andrew-wordes-enemy-of-the-state.

[61] offgridsurvivalist, "The Roswell Chicken Man, Andrew Wordes Interview" (March 27, 2012), http://www.youtube.com/watch?feature=player_embedded&v=D0Md7aIudZE.

new democratic government for the people.⁶² The speech from that event, now called "Dr. Rath's Call to the people of Germany and Europe, Berlin 13-3-2012" can be seen here.⁶³

Dr. Rath also wrote a book called *Why Animals Don't Get Heart Attacks — But People Do,* and it is available free here.⁶⁴ In it, he speaks out openly against GMOs and the direct connection between a healthy natural diet and health.⁶⁵

Bear in mind that our point is not how amazing these doctors are or are not. What matters is that all doctors have the right to use alternative methods and promote anything they like. Dr. Rath has some great books, talks, and resources, which you can find out more about here and here.⁶⁶

The human body is sicker than it has ever been. Modern allopathic medicine is largely based on isolated and selective thinking.

> *"Bernard is right; the pathogen is nothing; the terrain is everything."* ⁶⁷
>
> - Louis Pasteur -

---

62 "Auschwitz Survivors Propose Constitution for New Europe," *Dr. Rath Health Foundation* Web site (November 13, 2007), http://www4.dr-rath-foundation.org/THE_FOUNDATION/relay_of_life/; European Referendum Initiative, http://www.eu-referendum.org/english/petitions/europe_for_the_people_info.html.

63 Rath Foundation (April 4, 2012), http://www.youtube.com/watch?v=6GZlKxrmdyA.

64 http://www.why-animals-dont-get-heart-attacks.org

65 "GMO News: U.S. Farmers Report Widespread GM Crop Contamination," *Dr. Rath Health Foundation* Web site (March 3, 2014), http://www4.dr-rath-foundation.org/THE_FOUNDATION/News/2014/gmo_news/index.htm; "Brussels EU approves GM corn and demonstrates yet again that it represents corporate interests," *Dr. Rath Health Foundation* Web site (n.d.), http://www4.dr-rath-foundation.org/index.html.

66 Dr. Rath Health Foundation, http://www4.dr-rath-foundation.org/ and WikiRath, http://www.wiki-rath.org/.

67 As quoted in *Oxford Handbook of Clinical Medicine* (Oxford: Oxford University Press, 2010), 417, by Murray Longmore *et al.*

When it comes to the question of healing the human body so that disease and illness cannot thrive, the first answer we must consider is food.

Even without GMO labelling, and despite higher prices, many of us can make healthier choices as to what we eat. In so doing we support the local farmers and organic channels. These channels, when developed properly, can change how we feed the world.

Humanity already has all the tools needed to grow food locally, eat healthily, and thrive.

Look at how the demand for more natural and health-giving food has changed the world we live in already. Imagine if everyone demanded fast, convenient, and healthful food instead of the typical fast food joints.

> *"You can find your way across this country using burger joints the way a navigator uses stars."*[68]
> *- Charles Kuralt -*

Pressure from those of us who demand better is the only reason almost all food has not become GMO. This pressure, grown bigger, can just as easily change the rest of the world's food-production habits.

> *"Oh yes, there's lots of great food in America. But the fast food is about as destructive and evil as it gets. It celebrates a mentality of sloth, convenience, and a cheerful embrace of food we know is hurting us."*[69]
> *- Anthony Bourdain -*

---

[68] As quoted in *Hamburger America* (Philadelphia: Running Press, 2011), Foreword, by George Motz.

[69] *Medium Raw: A Bloody Valentine to the World of Food and the People Who Cook* (HarperCollins, 2010).

Let us get responsible and change food. It is easy. First, we need to consider two questions:

Why is food production the fastest and easiest problem to remedy?

Why is the lack of food the first problem human beings instinctively remedy under duress?

Whenever a human population struggles against the state, local food production goes up. Look back in history and use your common sense. We human beings, like all living creatures, possess a survival instinct that lets us know we will starve to death without a plan to feed ourselves. There have always been efforts by the state and the ruling class to centralize food systems, but even in the best of times and, especially under duress, these centralized systems cannot provide for everyone. Therefore, we humans do what we do best. We solve the problem in a practical sense.

Simply put, the need to consume food is always going to be the most important issue we face. However, people are not as sure that the world's food systems as they exist today are as fast or easy a problem to fix.

They are, however. Here are five things we can immediately support within existing food systems that will make a huge difference to those systems, and start changing them for the better, quickly and easily.

Family Farms

We need to support local farms and ensure they are not shut down or prosecuted anymore. This can be done using our global voice and our pocketbooks. Learning to focus our global voice like a laser is discussed later. For now, think about buying local. Demand more healthful foods, and the market will respond.

Montana Jones and Mark Baker are two tiny examples of a problem that "The MEATRIX" visualized perfectly: industrial factory farms are aggressively trying to squeeze out the last of the world's family farms. Most of them are already gone. We need to get more people back into farming, which is already happening. This positive trend is indicative of the primary need and response we spoke of.

The market's been responding to humanity's sloth, to our love of convenience and our addiction to apathy. We need to grab ahold of the parts of us that love to care in order to create beauty, function, and innovation and to be responsible for ourselves and our communities. The state loves and depends on apathetic citizens. It needs your subservience to exist. Your independence and health destroy authority's power.

Urban Farming and Permaculture

Let us fill the world's cities with gardens that can easily and completely supply all the produce (and more) for the local population. During WWII, twenty million Americans planted "Victory Gardens." These gardens grew 40 percent of the US produce supply.[70]

Over the past two decades or more, common people all over the world have begun planting more gardens again. We have started reclaiming the right to grow our own food—since we have seen the corporate food supply visibly poisoning the people around us.

Millions of people around the world have been leading the charge, re-educating the population on gardening and developing new methods for the task while preserving the old ones. Urban gardening needs to grow in size and scope to meet the needs of so many people living together in a dense space. Living in cities is fun, and urban living can be sustainable.

Many of us already have people in our lives from whom we can learn—people who can help grow our self-sustainability and self-governance. In addition, there is always an abundance of terrific information online. A good organization with a fantastic video right on its home page is Urban Farming:[71] http://www.urbanfarming.org/. By employing more of the urban farming techniques all the people in

---

[70] Urban Farming video, http://www.urbanfarming.org.
[71] http://www.urbanfarming.org

this chapter are using, and learning from examples such as Seattle's Food Forest, we can feed our neighbors and ourselves food that is much better for us.

> *"Preserve and treat food as you would your body, remembering that in time food will be your body."*[72]
> - B.W. Richardson -

Permaculture is a branch of ecological design, ecological engineering, and environmental design that develops sustainable architecture and self-maintained agricultural systems, modeled from natural ecosystems.[73] Australian's Bill Mollison and David Holmgren first coined the term "permaculture" in 1978.[74]

One of the best sites on the twelve principles of permaculture can be found here.[75] At the bottom of that page is a great five-minute video that gives an overview of how ethics and design principles relate to each other and how they can be used together. Here is a strong article on the topic by David Holmgren.[76]

---

[72] As quoted in *Plain Words About Food* (Rockwell and Churchill Press: 1899), 16.

[73] "Permaculture," *Wikipedia* Web site (March 4, 2014), "permaculture," http://en.wikipedia.org/wiki/Permaculture; "permaculture," http://www.oxforddictionaries.com/definition/english/permaculture?q=permaculture'; "permaculture," http://dictionary.reference.com/browse/Permaculture?s=t;

[74] Bill Mollison and David Holgren, *Permaculture One: A Perennial Agricultural System for Human Settlement* (Australia: Corgi Publishing, 1978); see also Toby Hemenway, *Gaia's Garden: A Guide to Home Scale* Permaculture (White River Junction, VT: Chelsea Green Publishers, 2009); Ross Mars, *The Basics of Permaculture Design* (White River Junction, VT: Chelsea Green Publishers, 2005); Peter Bane, *The Permaculture Handbook,* eBook ed. (Gabriola Island, BC: New Society Publishers, 2012); Nicole Faires, *The Ultimate Guide to Permaculture* (New York: Skyhorse Publishing, 2012).

[75] http://permacultureprinciples.com/principles/.

[76] "12 Principles of Permaculture by David Holmgren," *Reach and Teach's Just Lists* blog (January 14, 2010), http://justlists.wordpress.com/2010/01/14/principles-of-permaculture/.

Using the principles of permaculture, people have been hard at work creating the most innovative, beautiful, and sustainable solutions that the world has to offer. As this technique becomes more fully embraced, the integration of nature, design, humanity, and sustainable function will free the human race from the limitations of our past. This technique is not a leap, permaculture solutions exist today. People just need to get more involved in either feeding themselves or supporting healthy choices.

Even more important is the opportunity for everyone who is already working on a better world to start agreeing on simple strategies like permaculture instead of focusing attention on disempowerment, divisive behavior, and distracting versus decisive discussion.

Family Gardens

If you do not want to get involved in larger community projects, plant a small garden at home. Each harvest, which can happen as often as every few weeks when gardening indoors, you will get better. We will learn together by supporting each other.

Not everyone needs to garden, but if you do not then you should support those that do. Their food can better nourish your body, your soul, and our shared world.

Aquaponics

Aquaponics is a combination of aquaculture or aquafarming and hydroponics. Fish and plants are grown together in an integrated system that creates a symbiotic relationship between the two.[77]

---

[77] Graham Slaughter, "Aquaponics brings fish-fuelled veggies to Toronto," *The Star* (January 3, 2014), http://www.thestar.com/news/gta/2014/01/03/aquaponics_brings_fishfuelled_vegetables_to_toronto.html.; Venus Rizing, "Aquaponics and Sustainable Living Go Hand in Hand," *Ground Report* Web site (February 16, 2014), http://groundreport.com/aquaponics-and-sustainable-living-go-hand-in-hand/; "Aquaponics," http://www.growingpower.org/aquaponics.htm;

Incidentally, aquaponics completely mitigates the undesirable effects of both hydroponics and aquafarming (fish farms).

Aquaponics is one of the most exciting revolutions to ever happen in agriculture. It is tough to pin down the exact origin of the idea, but only in recent years has it really taken off. What makes aquaponics so amazing is that you can grow food and fish together without any soil, chemicals, or pollution. You do not even need to clean the fish tank. The entire system is self-sustaining, it is often faster than traditional farming, it uses less water, and it is much healthier than any institutionalized farming methods.

Learn more in the exciting article "Aquaponics is Changing the Face of Food Production,"[78] which tracks the success of some aquaponics efforts in India. Australia has been a global leader in aquaponics since its recent explosion. Learn about the country's established practices and expertise here.

Two industry leaders in the United States that have a wealth of experience and information, as well as the materials themselves, are Nelson + Pade[79] and Backyard Aquaponics.[80]

Crowdfunding is another new and powerful trend. It allows common people to both introduce and fund one another's innovative ideas. If you're unfamiliar with the process and want to learn about a hugely successful crowdfunding campaign in aquaponics that not only changed the lives of two Berkeley students but also the lives of millions of people all around the world, check out the story of Nikhil Arora and Alejandro Velez.

"Aquaponics," *Homestretch,* CBC Radio Web site (June 5, 2013), http://www.cbc.ca/homestretch/episode/2013/06/05/aquaponics/; "Aquaponics," *Wikipedia* Web site (March 12, 2014), http://en.wikipedia.org/wiki/Aquaponics; *The Aquaponics Association* Web site, http://www.aquaponicsassociation.org/; "Aquaculture," *Wikipedia* Web site (March 11, 2014), http://en.wikipedia.org/wiki/Aquaculture.

[78] Venus Rizing (February 18 2014), http://groundreport.com/aquaponics-is-changing-the-face-of-food-production/.

[79] http://aquaponics.com/.

[80] http://www.backyardaquaponics.com/.

The Freedom Handbook

A fun video account can also be found here, detailing the crowdfunding company these two chose to use.[81] More on their inspiring story and aquaponics is available on their site.[82]

GrowCube and Other New Innovations

GrowCube is a new technology developed by software developer turned inventor, Chris Beauvois. Using aeroponics, which uses mists instead of trays of water; GrowCubes effectively reduce the amount of water used by traditional farming methods by 95 percent.

In this article on the technology, Daniel Cooper explains: "On average, it promises to be faster than traditional methods of growing, with a cube full of strawberries taking between four and six weeks to grow. This is opposed to the shoving-seeds-into-dirt-and-waiting method, of course, as you can grow the same produce throughout the year. The technology can also be used to grow both grapes (with a few tweaks) and hops, so perhaps it'll garner the interest of the brewing industry looking for ever greater control of its crops."[83]

Innovations are being developed all the time and will continue to be developed, provided we do not limit our options and continue to narrow our approach to food production by using primarily unhealthy chemical and industrialized farming techniques.

Corporate food's mandate – to synthesize the entire edible seed species on the planet, needs to be prevented. On the bright side, the

---

[81] Nikhil and Alejandro, "Home Aquaponics Kit: Self-Cleaning Fish Tank that Grows Food," *Kickstarter* (December 15, 2012), https://www.kickstarter.com/projects/2142509221/home-aquaponics-kit-self-cleaning-fish-tank-that-g.

[82] https://www.backtotheroots.com/.

[83] "GrowCube promises to grow food with ease indoors (hands-on)," *engadget* (November 8, 2013), http://www.engadget.com/2013/11/08/insert-coin-growcubes-hands-on/.; Growcubes, https://www.facebook.com/GrowCube; "The Grow Cube," *Garden Culture* Web site, http://www.gardenculture.net/indoor-garden-design-build/the-growcube-2017; "Agri-Cube grows mass quantities of vegetables in a one-car parking spot," *Gizmag* Web site (August 14, 2012), http://www.gizmag.com/prefab-garden-greenhouse-housing-complex-daiwa/23607/

potential does exist for GMO foods to become a healthy alternative one day.

In the meantime, let us support our innovative capacity for change instead of methods that, no matter where you stand, have serious room for improvement as evidenced by the continued issue of global poverty despite the claims that GMOs would eradicate hunger.

We have already developed numerous techniques for growing food indoors, and these techniques help us grow it faster and with much less water and waste. We can reduce harmful farming practices and the toxic pollution of our food supply, global water table, and arable land.[84]

Scarcity, as we have come to understand it, is a lie. We are getting better and better at growing food, but we are not using these techniques *en masse*. If we did, food could be grown almost anywhere and we could feed the world.

Have you ever fed someone a meal that really needed it? It is an amazing feeling. We can feed ourselves better. Think about how good it feels to reclaim your strength, balance, and vitality from unhealthy habits. Imagine how the whole world will feel when we are stronger and healthier. Imagine how incredible it will feel to feed all your poor and starving brothers and sisters.

In the following chapter, Luke's largest gift to me during this process is revealed. This gift took roughly three weeks to unwrap, and I wrestled with it the whole time.

We will attempt to unwrap it for you in just a few pages, but because this central concept is such an anchor, we will consistently tie back to it throughout this book. Quotations from some of the most respected leaders and minds in human history are used to help explain it.

---

[84] "Arable land" *Wikipedia* Web site (February 22, 2014), http://en.wikipedia.org/wiki/Arable_land.

Be patient with it. Worst case, you can just plow ahead while focusing on different problems and your favorite of their matching solutions.

Expect to disagree with a measure of the ideas and solutions offered. The key is developing a can-do attitude and the willingness to work on the things you agree with and work toward consensus on the more difficult issues.

CHAPTER SEVEN

- Legal Systems and Laws -

> *"Rightful liberty is unobstructed action according to our will within limits drawn around us by the equal rights of others. I do not add 'within the limits of the law' because law is often but the tyrant's will, and always so when it violates the rights of the individual"*[1]
> *- Thomas Jefferson -*

The above quote reminds us of life's golden rule, which no one has ever had to write down to remember. Do no harm, and we can do as we please.

Then he warns us that laws themselves are all too often tools of control.

We do not need written rules to help us understand the difference between right and wrong. We all feel a similar tug in our hearts and bellies if we do wrong or hurt another living being.

The purpose behind most of today's unending legislation, rules, and law is strictly control. A readily visible, though superficial, example is the monopolization of industry and profits.

> *"Any fool can make a rule, and every fool will mind it."*[2]
> *- Henry David Thoreau -*

If we want freedom, the assumption that we require written rules needs to unravel. We cannot look to government, for anything, ever

---

[1] Letter to Isaac H. Tiffany (April 3, 1819).
[2] Entry for February 3, Journals (1860), http://www.walden.org/Library/The_Writings_of_Henry_David_Thoreau:_The_Digital_Collection/Journal.

again. Most importantly, we need to accept the fact that it is irrational and absurd to allow any ruling body to make imperious decisions on our behalf, in exchange for promises of maternal care.

This makes us the very definition of a subject class or, more plainly, slaves.

Fortunately, all we need to do to free ourselves is learn to trust one another and ourselves. With a quick glance around the world, or across the street, we see that humans are not creatures of harm but rather, are built of caring.

When harm takes place, as exceptions always will, we can easily create consensus and justice that makes sense. In fact, we regular everyday humans are responsible for every scrap of good in our present systems.

Self-governance means realizing, even more than trusting, that common people already do understand and act on human issues. When we remove the middleman, which we will define here as any ruling body, then humans are left without any restrictions to create the healthiest outcome in each unique case through collected and transparent common sense.

Our challenge will be helping segments of our human family realize that adults do not require parenting. The centuries-old habit of outsourcing individual thinking and responsibilities will die hard. Believing that a few of us humans in charge can capably guide the rest altruistically, without massive corruption, is a pipe dream.

One of our toughest evolutionary tasks will be relinquishing the pattern of looking for guidance and authority from up on high. Instead, we can look to each other and look within our own hearts. We can work together as communities to form justice that makes sense.

Good behavior cannot be legislated into existence. Furthermore, let us completely abandon the notion that anyone has the right to tell another human being how to live. We need to stop telling each other what to do.

The United States is a newer country that started out with the best of intentions and wrote a great constitution based around the idea of "we, the people."3 Unfortunately, not one president has ever adhered to it.

Every single one of them has violated the basic tenant upon which their country is founded. They could not help themselves. They had the power to do so and pressure no one person should bear. Big business and lobbyists have too much influence on our various nation's laws and policies. If we allow laws to be passed, my dear friends, they will be used as chains to rule us.

How do we fix things and govern ourselves without any laws written down and only the golden rule in our hands and hearts? It is easy. We already do it every day during private mediation that spans industries and our private lives.

If you work in justice, or just care about it and want to be a part of the positive changes being made, there is a complete road map for a new justice system further on in this book.

Before we celebrate the success of some amazing people from around the world evidencing the fact that we can do better and invite you to join in, it will be helpful to gain a better understanding of the purpose of law.

Law's primary purpose is control and deception. The legal system is another deeply ingrained, ancient masquerade in our society. The ruling classes are not devilish beings, and yet we have allowed power to corrupt our brothers and sisters with devilish absoluteness.

> *"You say you got a real solution, well you know we'd all love to see the plan."*4
> *- John Lennon -*

---

[3] U.S. Constitution, Preamble(U.S. Constitution, Preamble 1789).

[4] *Revolution,* performed by the Beatles, written by John Lennon and Paul McCartney, produced by George Martin (Apple, 1968).

Remember, this plan is not Luke's or mine. No, it is simply bits from yours and bites from theirs making up a patchwork of common sense that is a natural part of us all. This is an essential collection of the best ideas we have come across, and all woven together into one cohesive plan. Our role is to gather everyone around, harness attention, and connect all the incredible dots humankind has left as a trail to reach our highest potential.

Remember, our focus needs to remain on our agility. There is no such thing as a perfect plan, but success will require our best efforts and the agility to adjust as we progress. The best equipped out there, please step forward and tweak the sense into our collective efforts where required.

Relax.

Let everything you have read so far percolate in your mind. Remember orbiting the earth in space. Sit and think. By the time you've circled our miraculous planet for a little while longer, contemplating life, asking bigger questions in a matter of minutes or hours than some of us do in a whole year, the road map to uncensored freedom for the common human will be plain as day.

This process is rich, complicated, and challenging, regardless of your current views or beliefs. Take things slow. If you disagree or see holes, this is good, it means you are thinking and you care.

The holes we will fill together, and by the end of this discussion most people will end up on the same page. Some holes will not be filled until we have covered more ground together in the physical world. By growing bigger many of the best things already going, we will all learn together how to tweak the largest initiatives.

Let us jump back to the task at hand and wrap our hearts and minds around improved formulas for social justice.

> *"It is not what a lawyer tells me I may do; but what humanity, reason, and justice tell me I ought to do."*[5]
> *- Edmund Burke -*

---

[5] Second Speech on Conciliation with America (1775).

We cannot allow any administration to write or pass any law, for any reason whatsoever. If we need to write something down, then no written law or rule shall bind any man or woman could be carved into stone at the entrance of every town or country.

This sanctioned and toxic obsession of governing others and enforcing our ideas on the next generation has become far too rampant. People need to seriously challenge this unhealthy impulse and act on it far less often. We will not and do not need to totally eradicate this all-too-human tendency, but we do need to recognize that it has gotten very out of hand and become a large cultural wound that needs treatment.

When I was growing up, a little old lady lived a few houses down the street. She ran a palliative care home, but despite doing good work she was a horrible person, filling the marble holes that my friend Isaak and I made in the boulevard. Even if we made them in our own yards, she would warn us of pending accidents and disasters.

She would rave to the whole street about this or that and would phone the police and waste their valuable time. I can still picture her waving her broom while yelling instructions to behave in one manner or another.

In short, she attempted to dictate the behavior of an entire block.

Yes, that includes the adults.

This angry old woman personifies the ancient human issue that has grown critically colossal in modern society. No one has the right to tell another human being how to act or what to feel.

Nobody wants to buy someone else's thinking.

Have you ever tried carrying someone, even a loved one, across a bridge that they were not ready to cross? Even if we manage to make it to the other side, the moment we plop that person down, they would run right back across.

At times, we all want to help someone understand or change. However, think about when the shoe is on the other foot. You will not even cross your own bridges before coming to terms in your own way.

The Freedom Handbook

Writing something down does not make it real, either. Fear of punishment for theft and crime does not disappear without written law, and neither do repercussions for causing harm. Strictly speaking, the mechanism and governing body are of real affair, and justice will thrive when we shift how we go about it and who is in charge.

When actual harm is caused, justice is unique.

The world is full of vastly different people with real problems getting along. All we are saying is, arbitrary authority, written rules, and categorized judgment is not working.

Our collective hearts and minds are the only wellspring of truth.

Debate will never end if we start discussing how to write a new set of rules that guarantee justice. Every year, we add streams of new laws and revisions to old laws without ever feeling like we have got it nailed. The same endless stacks of rules we use to try to create and protect freedom inevitably destroy any hope of it.

The laws of nature, consensus in our communities, and common sense are the laws that have always existed and will always remain.

For example, we all know in our hearts and minds without being told, not to steal, murder, or rape. Essentially, we know better than to cause harm to one another.

These ideas do not need to be written down. We all know the basic rules of life. The golden rule not only summarizes common sense, but also acts as a rally point, this central idea that all of our spiritual teachings share offers clarity in a world filled with complications.

We can use this single tool as a means to dispel all confusion and all conflict.

Ahimsa is Sanskrit for "do no harm," or, literally translated, "the avoidance of violence."[6] This concept can, when practiced by humans en masse, safeguard the world.

---

[6] "Ahimsa," *Wikipedia* Web site (March 9, 2014), http://en.wikipedia.org/wiki/Ahimsa.

If groups of people decide that they still wish to enforce rules, or adhere to some form of restrictive ideology, fine, no problem. These people just need a space to call their own and the freedom to express and share their beliefs. Provided no harmful lines are crossed, we have no right to enforce upon one another rules or laws about how to live. As a global community, we need only the golden rule to guide our watchfulness over one another.

Many people think that tolerance has a helpful role to play in assisting humans to follow the golden rule and live peacefully, however tolerance also has a dark side. We need to practice looking inside and asking ourselves where to draw the line between conflicting ideas in life.

For example, where exactly is the line between tolerance and apathy?

> *"Tolerance it a tremendous virtue, but the immediate neighbors of tolerance are apathy and weakness."*
> *- James Goldsmith -*

> *"Tolerance is the last virtue of a depraved society."*[7]
> *- D. James Kennedy -*

Think about what community really means.

All of history's unhealthy balance, as far as tolerance and apathy is concerned, whether with respect to slavery, women's rights, or anything else, was overcome through the common sense of the collective.

People wonder how we will all get along and none of those factions can ever agree. Simply, there will always be "radical" elements. Evidence that most of us in the global community know what is right and understand when and where to draw the line is gratifyingly

---

[7] "The New Tolerance," *The Christian Post* (May 17,2007), http://www.thechristianpost.com/news/the-new-tolerance-27459/.

abundant, and we will come back to this idea at the end of the chapter and again at the end of the book.

Warmth, direction, and purpose come from our hearts, though we are conditioned not to listen to ourselves. Self-governance demands that we take responsibility for ethics and justice ourselves, that we command the full faculties of our collective hearts and minds.

If you are struggling to figure out what new levels of personal responsibility and collective accountability really mean to your life and how to participate in your community's self-governance. Rest assured that everyone can find what he or she needs, including an ever-evolving place in the world, with help from an empowered community.

If you do not possess the wherewithal or desire to be a big part of new decisions or activity, so be it. Some people have other contributions to make to life, our planet, and our communities. Even today, not everybody works in government or on social issues.

Some of you must be asking, "What about the police?" Rest easy because there will still be police, courts, justice systems, and prisons. Police, court, and justice staff must be comprised of volunteers as well as paid employees, much like in the administrative arm.

In the years to come, the need for heavy policing may decrease. One might even imagine policing becoming largely irrelevant after a few generations have passed.

Under new commonly understood but unwritten law, no peace officer can bother you unless you're disturbing the peace. There will be no more tickets, no more victimless crime and punishment, and no more wasted resources.

Furthermore, only the people affected can claim someone is disturbing the peace or causing harm, not the police. If there is no injured party, there's no crime. This is known in our existing canon of human law as the central principle of common law.

Incidentally, common law, the purest form of law, is the very root of humanity's written law. If you are going to look anywhere other than to your common sense, look to common law for guidance.

Speaking of guidance, let us celebrate a few examples of the massive trends and powerful solutions that pertain to all of us.

Humanity is already shifting the world's police and security forces back to common sense and their rightful duty, which is to protect and serve the common citizen and freedom, instead of the status quo, the legislation of the day, or any authority.

If you know anyone who works with the military, police, or security forces of some kind, perhaps it is time you sat down together and talked about some of the things in this book and going on in the world. At rare times, security forces have heroically stood up for the public good, because they are part of that public.

Imagine what things will look like when the security forces of the world work for the common good all the time, in transparent fashion.

An article on the Thrive website covers two incidents from December 2013 where police in Thailand and in Italy honored their own sense of right and wrong by removing barricades, taking off their helmets, sitting down, and even marching with protestors.8 A terrific one-minute video clip of a CNN report covers the protestors' reactions as well as a sampling of the emotional and inspiring scene that day in Bangkok, Thailand.9

Thrive is an inspiring film seen by more than twenty-one million people around the world. It is now available in twenty-five different languages and, as of recently, can be seen free on the Thrive Movement site.10 Like other films of its kind, it leaves a little to be desired as far as solutions go, but it is still quite empowering.

An evolution is happening within the ranks of our global police forces, as indicated by organizations such as Law Enforcement Against Prohibition (LEAP), an international non-profit covered in Chapter Eight.11

---

[8] "When the Enforcers Become Allies," *Thrive* (December 13, 2013), http://www.thrivemovement.com/when-enforcers-become-allies.blog.

[9] "Thai Police and Protestors Remove Barriers, Call Truce," CNN, http://www.youtube.com/watch?v=t3y3WPL7Oko#t=14.

[10] *Thrive: What on Earth Will It Take?* Web site (n.d.), http://www.thrivemovement.com/.

[11] http://www.leap.cc/.

The Freedom Handbook

LEAP is important to our discussions for two reasons.

First, its experience on the front lines provides invaluable insight. Check out its vast wealth of terrific resources.

Second, LEAP represents an activity that is absolutely necessary in all industries, but especially within the security industry. It represents skilled professionals grouping together. This idea is covered in detail at the end of the book.

"Badges don't grant extra rights," says CopBlock, which self-identifies as a decentralized project united by the shared goal of police accountability.12 Common people have an established right to film the police, but many "peace" officers do not like being held accountable. Filing the actions of authorities while they perform their duties to protect and serve us is one of the most important things anyone can do. The Justice Department has said that people have the right under the First and Fourth Amendments to record the police.13

Veterans Against Police Abuse14 is another amazing organization that evidences an ongoing evolution in the ranks of uniformed men and women. On its homepage are two short videos, though if you only have time to watch one, make it the second rather than the first. Both videos document police brutality, but the second drives home the reason these organizations are necessary in a raw and brutal way.

Videos like these and stories like Kelly Thomas's or Robert Leone's can bring about feelings of devastation and anger.15

---

[12] Copblock.org, http://www.copblock.org/about/; Cop Block, "Spy Car Protects Against Unscrupulous Cop" (July 24, 2012), http://www.youtube.com/watch?v=VoWTd8TlaeU.

[13] Allen Etzier, "U.S. Justice Department Issues Letters Supporting Citizens Recording Police Officers," *Capital News Service* Web site (April 26, 2013), http://cnsmaryland.org/2013/04/26/u-s-justice-department-issues-letters-supporting-citizens-recording-police-officers/.

[14] Veterans Against Police Abuse, http://www.veteransagainstpoliceabuse.org/.

[15] Truth Be Known, "This Is What Happened to Kelly Thomas" (May 19, 2012), http://www.youtube.com/watch?v=1po6Sic5lOU#t=538; Larry Hohol, "Police Brutality Worse than Rodney King" (June 20, 2012); Larry Hohol, "Police

Kelly's torture, terror, and continued, senseless pain, and Robert's heartbreaking death are just two examples of an epidemic problem that has one simple solution: film the police. It is hard not to focus rage at the officers in these cases, though they are only symptoms of a systemic issue.

The state pits us common folk against one another by placing authority and murder in certain people's hands and encouraging them to beat the rest of us into submission. Policing is needed, yes, but all through history, the various authorities have absolved themselves of morality's constraints whenever it suits them.

Thus, transparency becomes all the more important where sanctioned violence is concerned.

To help us all understand the inner battle our women and men in uniforms of all kinds need to face, here is a phenomenal video that was just released in November 2013 by a woman named Josie the Outlaw. Her video is simply entitled "Message to Police."16

Josie begins with a terrific question that should be posed to the entire world's police and security forces: "Is there any law or order that you won't obey?"

If we will obey any order, there is no difference between the security forces of Stalin, Hitler, or any of the other tyrannical regimes the world has ever known, and us. All the way back through history, in the name of laws, democracy, religion, and countless other excuses, common people have been subverted into the tools of oppressive powers.

The most tyrannical moments in our history all have something in common – the security forces of the time falsely believed that they had the right to perform acts that were criminal and, more important, immoral because some authority told them so.

Brutality Worse than Rodney King—Official Robert Leone Updates," http://www.theluzernecountyrailroad.com/police-brutality.php.

[16] (December 1, 2013), https://www.youtube.com/watch?v=IOsN-P5abVg.

Josie reminds us that commonly held contemporary beliefs such as "it's not my job to decide what laws to enforce or not," and, most treacherous of all, "I can't be held responsible for just following orders," are gross, ugly lies.

This will become very clear when you take a moment to examine human history and even current written law.

For example, during the Nuremberg trials after WWII, Nazi law enforcers who used these common defenses were not exempted from personal prosecution. Josie finishes with simple common sense: "If something is not okay to do without a badge, you shouldn't do it with one either."

Talk to the people in your circle who use a gun at work. Talk about what orders just cannot be followed, no matter what. Get involved in the discussions online or the activity of our new justice system itself.

Let us use the scaling model we discussed in education as a prototype.

First, we will use small regions to test new systems and ideas with all the zeal and capacity of the global movement. New systems will be built while the old ones smash along. Once they are ready for testing, we transfer increasing amounts of public activity. When raging success stories start to occur (capacity is already evident in some areas), we scale the efforts around the world.

Think about what you would do if bound by no law. You could speed, or drink and drive. You could walk into a gun store and buy anything you want without getting a background check. Even a convicted criminal could buy any gun, strap it to her hip, and walk around in public. The world is one big oyster for all, so what would you do?

We are guessing you would finish work and go home to your family, like we would.

If you are worried that such lax gun practice would make the world more dangerous, think about the fact that if a criminal wants a gun these days, we can't stop him from obtaining one. Opportunity does not change. Safety cannot be forced. In fact, weapon control reduces public safety, not to mention it limits our freedoms and guarantees that the authorities of the day have a monopoly on force.

> *"The strongest reason for the people to retain the right to keep and bear arms is, as a last resort, to protect themselves against tyranny in Government."*17
> - Unknown -

When it comes to protecting ourselves from each other, we cannot legislate good behavior or write laws to guide people's choices – rules have not ever made us safer. The only things that make us safer are stronger communities and transparent, agile, and customized justice in the hands of the people versus any authority acting on our behalf.

We do not need rulers.

Absolute power causes even well intentioned humans to end up corrupted and disgraceful. Our current justice system leaves tens of millions if not hundreds of millions of people feeling, reasonably, as though justice itself has done them wrong or vanished altogether.

In our new world, you, Luke and I won't change the way we live, and unquestionably, the rest of our global neighbors are of the very same mind, despite mass media's fear mongering tales of violent crime around every corner. Studies have shown that in Canada and many countries around the world the crime rate has been in general decline for years and even decades.18

---

17 This is a quote often attributed to Thomas Jefferson, but the scholars who have studied all of his work say: "That sentence does not appear in the Virginia Constitution drafts or text as adopted, nor in any other Jefferson writings that we know of." Jefferson did write several drafts of a statement for the Virginia constitution—which were not adopted—such as: "No freeman shall be debarred the use of arms [within his own lands or tenements]." See "No freeman shall be debarred the use of arms" Quotation, *The Jefferson Monticello* Web site, http://www.monticello.org/site/jefferson/no-freeman-shall-be-debarred-use-arms-quotation.

18 Jill Mahoney, "Canadian crime rate hits four-decade low, Toronto leads the trend," *The Globe and Mail* (July 25, 2013), http://www.theglobeandmail.com/

The facts indicate that in many countries, such as the US and Canada, 95 percent or more of people (and that is being generous) are not involved in any sort of recorded crime at all in a given year, including even the smallest criminal offenses.

Speaking of which, we the people might soon deem many of these smaller crimes, such as marijuana prohibition, unnecessarily criminal. Here are the bare bones. Crime is rare, and most humans are trustworthy, caring, and will avoid harming others at almost all costs.

It is well documented that most crime stems from social inequality and poverty.19 This is known as structural violence.20 Much of today's crime would be eliminated at its root with alternate forms of social programming and social justice in place. Crime will also decrease as we address some of the financial woes of those in poverty.

The only people in the new world who might feel compelled to act criminally are the very same people who feel that way now. We can confidently assert that sweeping improvements in justice, as well as social programming, will eliminate large elements of crime.

Let us agree the world will not exactly burst into flames of rioting and chaos without written laws. Causing harm is and will always be criminal, both externally and internally. Policing and justice will still exist, and criminals will judged by us, their peers, in systems without a loophole in sight.

---

news/national/canadas-crime-rate-drops-with-homicides-at-46-year-low/article13416456/; Tobi Cohen,"Canadian crime rate hits lowest level in 40 years as Tories enact harsh new policies," *National Post* (July 25, 2013), http://news.nationalpost.com/2013/07/25/canadian-crime-rate-at-lowest-level-in-40-years-primarily-due-to-dip-in-non-violent-offences/.

[19] Sandro Contenta and Jim Rankin, "Solving Crime? Tackle the root causes first—pay now, or pay more later," *The Star* Web site (July 26, 2008), http://www.statcan.gc.ca/pub/85-002-x/2012001/article/11692-eng.htm#a1.

[20] "Structural violence," *Wikipedia* Web site (March 13, 2014), http://en.wikipedia.org/wiki/Structural_violence; Johan Galtung, "Violence, Peace, and Peace Research," Journal of Peace Research, Vol. 6, No. 3. (1969), pp. 167–191.

Imagine all people (from celebrities and organized criminals to bankers and corporate criminals) being truly accountable to their peers and community. Imagine the toughest criminals facing us instead of Crown prosecutors, who all too often have private agendas and price tags. Imagine all the world's potential criminals knowing they would have to face the entire world on a transparent global stage to plead their cases.

Imagine no loopholes and no laws, just common sense and the planetary, local, and victimized community to face for judgment.

As humanity embraces change on a mass scale – changes people have already begun to build – we liberate our well-being and healthiest potential. To cultivate self-governance, we remove the most obvious dysfunctional operating and decision-making habits from all human systems.

It really is that simple.

Here are a few things that will happen as we re-create our world. We will discover true peace of mind, rule our own bodies, and relish our inalienable right to travel the whole world. We will discover and grow empathy and compassion within ourselves for each other.

We will all realize that we are solely responsible for our own lives and futures, and are therefore accountable to our community as well as ourselves. Given these truths, we will invest our own money in communities and ourselves however we see fit.

Curiosity, inspiration, and innovation will take huge leaps forward as a result. Courage, compassion, and collaboration will rule the day.

These are healthy and liberating changes, millennia in the making.

This is the face of true freedom.

"Come on, we don't want drunk people driving around!" some people shout. No one does, but we want freedom. Individuals must and will adapt as they become accountable to their communities, and penalties will still exist for criminal behavior.

Unless a drunk driver hits someone, nothing can or should be done.

Police will not be running roadblocks anymore. Increasing penalties for harm done might be one way to deter this sort of activity, or MADD could increase campaigns and media exposure. We need a group of qualified people to better develop solutions than the one we have right now.

Naturally, some people will worry and say things like "we need a strong police presence to prevent crime." This sounds like a wonderful idea but we know now, that force makes that idea little more than a futile endeavor.

We cannot prevent bad things from happening and bad people from doing them. Rules and laws and the fear of punishment they incite have accomplished very little in the way of healthier, safer, or enlightened behavior.

Continuing to utilize current government systems when we know that they are honeycombed with corruption and inefficiency is sheer insanity. In doing so, we apathetically hand over control of our innate human rights.

> *"The world is in greater peril from those who tolerate or encourage evil than from those who actually commit it."*[21]
> *- Albert Einstein -*

Let us use this drunk driving example to suss out all the nitty-gritty details of how justice will work in the world that we will create together. The entire process is nothing but common sense, pure and simple.

Here is the scenario: someone drives drunk and injures or kills someone else. The victim or the victim's family charges him for the harm caused. He then pleads guilty or not guilty, and a hearing or trial takes place. If the jury finds him guilty then the victim and/or

---

[21] Quoted in Josep Maria Corredor, *Conversations with Casals* (1957), 11(Corredor 1957).

family proposes the sentence, which could be as severe as the death penalty. If the jury agrees with the sentence, justice has been served.

Do you disagree with the death penalty? It does not matter. You probably will not like many of the sentences that victims and their families will impose, but we cannot take anything off the table without imposing categorized opinions in the form of law. Furthermore, with ultimate transparency, preventing unfair sentencing is a breeze.

Common sense and aversion to violence should typically sway us away from violence in sentencing and all other collective decisions. There will be exceptions, but justice is only for victims, their families, and the courts via jury to agree on.

The community at large only gets involved in the rare instance that there is no living family to speak for the victim, otherwise our opinions are irrelevant and the matter should not concern us.

Again, justice is for victims, perpetrators, and the jury alone, on a case-by-case basis.

"If you have always believed that everyone should play by the same rules and be judged by the same standards, that would have gotten you labeled a radical 60 years ago, a liberal 30 years ago and a racist today." [22]
- Thomas Sowell -

If consensus dictates that victims or their families are being overly harsh, the jury fashions a sentence. This is an easy fail-safe.

Consider also that some victims or families may let the accused go free with little or no repercussions. That remains their choice, as victims, to make. Again, your opinion is irrelevant.

The people affected, and they alone, should decide what justice looks like.

Yes, there is potential for even a collection of people in a jury to form opinions that are unhealthy. In the distinctly rare case, that a

---

[22] Controversial Essays (Hoover Press, 2002).

The Freedom Handbook

jury manufactures justice in a manner that the global community finds unethical, the global community itself is a fail-safe of the grandest style.

This last line of defense is always prevalent in a system where transparency is the only rule. With the world watching all that goes on everywhere, injustice has nowhere to hide.

The relationship between justice and rehabilitation is an important consideration as we restructure our legal efforts. The current prison systems track record when it comes to creating healthy changes in individuals is dismal, to put it mildly. There are much healthier and more creative ways to encourage people to make better choices and heal from past trauma.

In fact, there is a lot of dialogue on this issue and some pretty obvious adjustments that can be made based on the healthiest rehabilitative systems in the world as indicated by the following article23 "<u>Sweden Is Closing Prisons Due to Lack of People to Put In Them</u>."

Use common sense and think about how some of the healthiest smaller communities of our past made decisions. They gathered the elders (jury) and those involved (victims and accused) when harm was caused. Often, they allowed the community as a whole to participate in the discussions (our community connected transparently through the internet).

After all information and parties had been gathered, decisions were made by consensus, in a manner of ways and with various ends. The common denominators have always been common sense and group consensus.

We can do anything we want as long as we do not harm others. If someone's actions offend another party, the people involved have to

---

[23] Adam Clark Estes, "Sweden Is Closing Prisons Due to Lack of People to Put in Them," GISMODO Web site (2013), http://gizmodo.com/sweden-is-closing-prisons-due-to-lack-of-people-to-put-1462950734.

work it out. If they cannot, then mediation and, worst case, the courts come into play, and with the help of a jury, an agreement can take shape.

This judicial activity must not be done for profit, and decisions need to be made with complete transparency. Legal and tribunal systems are a last resort, to be used only when men and women are at a complete loss.

Mediation and tribunal problem solving are relatively simple and commonplace solutions already in practice today. As basic, transparent, and common sense tweaks are made to these processes, human conflict is easily assuaged.

If these solutions for justice are not perfectly clear yet, they will become more so as we go further into the topics to come.

> *"I will accept the rules that you feel necessary to your freedom. I am free, no matter what rules surround me. If I find them tolerable, I tolerate them; if I find them too obnoxious, I break them. I am free because I know that I alone am morally responsible for everything I do."*[24]
> - Robert A. Heinlein -

Some people have asked, "Why are these methods better? The legal system has never failed me." This query comes from selfishness and/or ignorance of reality, a disconnection from our community.

We are communally responsible for all things. We need to honor our symbiotic connection to one another, to our communities. The question should not be "Does this work for you?" but "Is this working in general for all of us?"

Responsibility to your community and altruism aside, building a better world for everyone means that you, too, get to live in a safer, cleaner, more exciting world.

---

[24] The Moon Is a Harsh Mistress (1966)

The practice of writing law is a surefire slippery slope to corruption and servitude. Freedom goes right out the door, and freedom is the goal.

> *"The man with the gold makes the rules and one who makes the rules break the rules."*[25]
> *- Meek Mill -*

By this point, we hope some of you are feeling much more motivated and equipped to end the global regime of institution and law that is choking the life out of us.

> *"Hell, there are no rules here—we're trying to accomplish something."*[26]
> *- Thomas A. Edison –*

---

[25] "Use to Be," Dreamchasers 2 mixtape, Maybach Music Group (May 7, 2012).
[26] As quoted in How to Think Like Einstein : Simple Ways to Break the Rules and Discover Your Hidden Genius (2000) by Scott Thorpe, p. 124

CHAPTER EIGHT

- The War On Drugs -

"I don't do drugs. I am drugs."[1]
- Salvador Dali –

The war on drugs is an immoral assault on our freedom to rule our own minds and bodies.

We have never been able to force certain behavior on people, and we never will be able to, no matter how long we beat the visibly broken drum.

This war's inability to create healthy change has been staring us in the face for over sixty years now. Throughout history, the demonized substance of the day has constantly changed. What is important about this concept is the idea of it. There is an ongoing war against something that infects some of us. We are fighting to save people that want to hurt themselves, and that conflict will inevitably pit us against one another.

The only reason for these grossly ineffective types of legislation is division and control.

"There has never been a 'war on drugs'! In our history we can only see an ongoing conflict amongst various drug users — and producers. In ancient Mexico the use of alcohol was punishable by death, while the ritualistic use of mescaline was highly

---

[1] Quoted by Howard Pousner, "The High Art of Selling 'Dali: the Late Work'," Atlanta Journal-Constitution (July 27, 2010), http://www.accessatlanta.com/news/entertainment/calendar/the-high-art-of-selling-dali-the-late-work/nQ4MJ/.

> *worshipped. In 17ᵗʰ century Russia, tobacco smokers were threatened with mutilation or decapitation, alcohol was legal. In Prussia, coffee drinking was prohibited to the lower classes, the use of tobacco and alcohol was legal."2*
> *- Sebastian Marincolo -*

In 1920, the United States banned alcohol and named that ban Prohibition.3 There was evidence supporting claims that alcohol destroyed lives and was responsible for thousands of deaths each year even back then, however the measures taken at that point were proven to be completely ineffective.

In fact, the government's only achievements during Prohibition were turning good people into criminals, dividing the population against itself, killing God-only-knows how many innocent people, and funneling vast sums of money into organized crime.

People like you and me, honest people, were thrown in jail at the swipe of a pen. They were imprisoned for selling the same substance that was legal the day before. The entirety of Prohibition was a complete debacle that strengthened organized crime and destroyed what integrity the government pretended to have, as people were tossed in jail and killed.

All because an arbitrary group of politicians were given authority to pass laws which everyone felt obligated to follow because, well, they were laws.

Here we see again how government and institution rely primarily on the concept of law to control. Our new world, built of unchained human potential, relinquishes the expired ideas of categorized and written law with the recognition that, in reality, manmade rules are fruitless.

---

2   https://www.goodreads.com/author/show/4125666.Sebastian_Marincolo
3   Eighteenth Amendment to the Constitution of the United States of America (January 17, 1920).

> *"If you support the war on drugs in its present form, then you're only paying lip-service to the defense of freedom, and you don't really grasp the concept of the sovereign individual human being."*
>
> *- Neal Boortz -*

Prohibition led to steady increases in violence and failed miserably to accomplish the task for which it had been created.4 When the government ended this program, massive levels of violence immediately subsided, we got our lives back, and people did what people do – they went back to living and working peaceably.

Of note, over 500,000 jobs were re-created when Prohibition was repealed.5 When Prohibition was ended, the domestic wine and beer industries were revitalized, all of which put people back to work.6

The opinion that drugs are somehow different from alcohol is still popular. Remember, there was a time when all drugs were legal and people were free to use them at their own discretion. Then, one day, just like they did with alcohol, the ever-despotic governments made drug use and sale illegal.7

---

4 The homicide rate rose steadily during Prohibition, from 1920-1933, and started to decline sharply when Prohibition ended. See, for example, charts on "The End of Prohibition: What Happened and What Have We Learned?" http://www.albany.edu/~wm731882/future1_final.html.

5 Deborah Brookshire, "The Secret Eeconomy of the Appalachian Mountain Folks," http://academic.evergreen.edu/curricular/ageofirony/aoizine/deborah.html; https://www.google.ca/search?q=prohibition+repealed+500,000+jobs+re-created+&ie=utf-8&oe=utf-8&rls=org.mozilla:en-US:official&client=firefox-a&channel=sb&gfe_rd=ctrl&ei=wlwmU_PiKcPP8gfp0oHQCw&gws_rd=cr.

6 Michael Lerner, "Unintended Consequences," *Prohibition*, PBS Web site, http://www.pbs.org/kenburns/prohibition/unintended-consequences/; "The New Deal," *AP U.S. History Notes,* http://www.apstudynotes.org/us-history/topics/the-new-deal/.

7 For example, see Comprehensive Drug Abuse Prevention and Control Act (Controlled Substances Act of 1970), Pub. L. 91-513, Oct. 27, 1970, 84 Stat. 1236

Bam!

A worldwide fiasco emerges. Institutions around the world clamped down happily on the use of various substances in authoritarian fashion in service to the ultimate aim, which is and always has been the same - to weaken, divide, and control.

"Empire," "Propaganda," and "Apocalypse" are the three ninety-minute parts of the documentary The Power Principle.8 This film explains many things discussed in this book in far greater detail. It is grounded in history and includes top academic opinions, such as that of Noam Chomsky. The film is widely renowned as one of the most intellectually sound examinations of plutocracy and empire in the modern world.

John Perkins, the Daniel Ellsberg of today, is a man whose life and career is covered in some detail next chapter. He is also one of the people interviewed in this film. In the chapter on education, we promised to list a few key documentaries that everyone needs to see. The Power Principle is number one of three and by far the most important and insightful.

Accepted or legal behavior is always shifting in the eyes of human culture. Actions that got us killed yesterday are likely to be in fashion and all the legal rage tomorrow, and vice versa.

> *"The war on drugs is wrong, both tactically and morally. It assumes that people are too stupid, too reckless, and too irresponsible to decide whether and under what conditions to consume drugs. The war on drugs is morally bankrupt."9*
> *- Larry Elder -*

(21 U.S.C. 801 et seq.); http://facultypages.morris.umn.edu/~ratliffj/psy1081/drug_laws.htm.

[8] The Power Principle: Corporate Empire and the National Security State (Metanoia Films), http://metanoia-films.org/the-power-principle/; http://topdocumentaryfilms.com/power-principle/.

[9] The Ten Things You Can't Say in America (New York: MacMillan, 2001), 253.

We are talking about our bodies, folks, and giving some outside authority the right to govern them. The bottom line in our perfect world is simple; if no harm has been caused, no crime exists.

The debate about whether to legalize drugs has been going on for decades. Valid points exist on both sides, but the core truth is that corralling human behavior through institutionalized rules has had its day. We can do better.

Our new approach to drugs not only recognizes humanity's expired need for written law, but also the need for drug use to be treated as a health issue instead of a legal one.

Interestingly, Luke and I are on opposite ends of the spectrum when it comes to drug use. Luke has never tried any illicit drugs. He has never taken an Aspirin or smoked a cigarette, and he very rarely drinks alcohol. This is his choice; he does not believe these substances add any value to his life, but he's not about to stop anyone else from doing drugs. He would only intervene if a loved one were using hard, harmful substances.

In this case, like many of us, he would offer support, therapy, or tougher tactics of love.

On the other hand, Luke has tried both San Pedro and ayahuasca. Both are hallucinogenic plant substances that certain aboriginal communities have been using for hundreds or thousands of years in healing and sacred ceremonies as a means to explore human consciousness.[10]

The topic of human consciousness experimentation is taboo in today's society, and this should tell us all we need to know about this legislation's true purpose.

If our own minds and bodies are not safe from enforced rule and tyrannical response, then nothing is. Our inalienable right as adults to explore our own consciousness provided we cause no harm

---

[10] Kira Salak, "Peru: Hell and Back," National Geographic Adventure Web site (2006), http://www.nationalgeographic.com/adventure/0603/features/peru.html.

to another, is the most sacred of all human rights. If our bodies and minds are our truest temples, we cannot allow institution to rule over them.

> *"Is it possible that we have demonized hallucinogens because we fear the contents of our own minds?"*[11]
> *- Daniel Pinchback -*

It is critical to understand the monstrous ethical issues arising today regarding your body and authority's attempts to control it. When you hear about privacy and the ethical use of technology, you might assume the discussion is about your private Facebook data and the way corporations use it without your permission to drive profits.

Certainly, these practices fly in the face of our freedoms and ethics, but there is a much more serious, even lethal, issue at hand.

To start with, think about how mandatory medication and identification chipping fit into this discussion of our bodies and our rights. Subjecting the body of another to anything "mandatory," such as immunization or identification, is a blatant attack on her human rights.

Cory Doctorow is one of the most respected people on the planet when it comes to digital rights. He tells us that digital rights management is a very bad way to solve social programs.

Without tripping down a very large rabbit hole, think about how many small computers are making their way into our bodies. Think about how even our homes and cars are, in essence, computers of various sizes and shapes that we put our bodies into. Hearing aids and pacemakers represent the beginning of our modern ability to computerize and replace many parts of the human body.[12]

---

[11] Breaking Open the Head: A Psychedelic Journey into the Heart of Contemporary Shamanism (New York: Random House, 2002)

[12] See, for example, Victoria Wollaston, "We'll be uploading our entire minds to computers by 2045 and our bodies will be replaced by machines within

Imagine being late on payments to large medical corporations for your cochlear implant or your replacement legs. The 2010 movie Repo Men13 outlines the distinct possibility of a human race dependent on corporate authorities to manage the computers and body parts that keep them alive.

We are living in such an Orwellian world now.

Many of the predictions in George Orwell's novel 1984 are staring modern man in the face.14 Cory Doctorow tells us in the interview "Hacking Politics" with Steve Paikin from The Agenda"15 that we're also living in "Homeland," the name of one of his fictional attempts at social education, activism, and empowerment.16

Cory Doctorow talked to an audience at Google about "The Coming Civil War over General-purpose Computing,"17 about how there are no easy answers to difficult ethical questions about what defines a user as opposed to an owner of a system, as well as the rights of each party.

Transhumanism is another huge part of our modern world, one that we would need to write another book to fully examine. If you are interested in transhumanism for the advent of cybernetic additions and improvements to the human body, including being able to upload human consciousness onto a computer, or just want to learn more about the potential pitfalls and dangers, Cory Doctorow's work is a

---

90 years, Google expert claims," Mail Online Web site (June 19, 2013), http://www.dailymail.co.uk/sciencetech/article-2344398/Google-futurist-claims-uploading-entire-MINDS-computers-2045-bodies-replaced-machines-90-years.html; http://en.wikipedia.org/wiki/Digital_rights_management.

[13] Directed by Miguel Sapochnik, written by Eric Garcia and Garrett Lerner, produced by Scott Shuler (Universal Studios, 2010), http://www.universalstudiosentertainment.com/repo-men/.

[14] Nineteen Eighty-four (1949).

[15] "Cory Doctorow: Hacking Politics," The Agenda with Steve Paikin (July 10, 2013), http://www.youtube.com/watch?v=E4y3btcBD-o.

[16] Cory Doctorow, Homeland (Tor Teen, 2013).

[17] Talks at Google (August 22, 2012), http://www.youtube.com/watch?v=gbYXBJOFgeI.

The Freedom Handbook

strong and ethical place to begin. His talk at Google addresses some of the most important issues in our modern world.

Every single one of us needs to hear that talk.

Cory Doctorow met and became friends with Aaron Swartz, whom we discussed in Chapter Four, and he talks about Aaron with Steve Palkin again in another insightful interview "Aaron Swartz and Hacktivism."[18]

Let us circle back though to drug use. Unlike Luke, I have tried a few different drugs. I went through a one-year period when I was about twenty years old where I consumed cocaine, ecstasy, hallucinogenic mushrooms, and marijuana. I do not condone heavy drug use, but I do not regret the experience. The consciousness expansion and exploration possibilities inherent in drug use can hold enormous value for the human spirit.

Currently, the United States locks up nonviolent drug offenders, some for twenty years or more. These people make up a huge percentage of the United States' incarcerated population and have a horrendous cost.[19] Consider for a moment the enormous resources the ATF and all the other federal, state, and local law enforcement bodies waste in chasing this so-called offense.[20]

Now add the court time, lawyers' fees, and the rest of the costs attached to lengthy incarceration. Without access to all the real data, the true costs are unknown, but it is estimated that most of the budget spent by law enforcement goes toward locking up nonviolent drug offenders.

Last chapter we introduced LEAP, an organization fighting the war on drugs. LEAP provides invaluable insight from inside the war

---

[18] "Aaron Swartz and Hactivism," The Agenda with Steve Paikin (July 11, 2013), http://www.youtube.com/watch?v=ZEEgb1cAwvk.

[19] "Drug Offenders in the Correctional System," Drug War Facts Web site, http://drugwarfacts.org/cms/Prisons_and_Drugs#sthash.4obhyiRS.dpbs.

[20] Kathleen Miles, "Just How Much the War on Drugs Impacts Our Prisons, in One Chart," Huffington Post (March 10, 2014), http://www.huffingtonpost.com/2014/03/10/war-on-drugs-prisons-infographic_n_4914884.html

on drugs. The organization's efforts are commendable and can be leaned on as inspiration to group together. We must focus on the common sense benefits of grouping together.

Imagine if our police and all our varied resources fought real crime and more effectively dealt with murder, rape, and robbery. We could easily eradicate more serious crimes just by switching our focus onto them.

Furthermore, our children come out of today's prisons worse off for the experience. It has become well understood that the criminal education our youth receive in jail, only better prepares them for a life of crime.

This is crazy.

Some people believe that drug dealers are scum and we should not care what happens to them, but consider this: the biggest drug dealers of all are our own countries and governments. Governments all over the world have been exposed repeatedly as main players in global drug manufacturing and distribution.21

Modern government has helped to fund wars off-the-books and black-budget projects through the sale of drugs. There are a number of references in the bibliography for those interested in proof. If these assertions are even only partially true, it is time to address the problem.

Even if our ruling bodies used the money to help their grandmothers, we need to emphasize this critical point again. The very same institutions that purport to be helping us fight this insanely destructive, criminal, immoral, and violent war on ourselves, actually help fund and facilitate the lion's share of global drug manufacturing and distribution.22 There is only one primary reason to play both sides like this - the desire to control and divide.

---

[21] Prof. Michel Chossudovsky, "The Spoils of War: Afghanistan's Multibillion Dollar Heroin Trade," GlobalResearch: Center for Research on Globalization Web site (June 14, 2005), http://www.globalresearch.ca/the-spoils-of-war-afghanistan-s-multibillion-dollar-heroin-trade/91.

[22] "Drug War? U.S. Troops Are Protecting Afghan Opium; U.S. Occupation Leads to All-Time High Heroin Production," GlobalResearch: Center

The secondary reason, which is the most visible and openly acknowledged in society, is profit — profit that also significantly strengthens control.

Far too much government activity currently falls into the categories of off-the-books, black-budget, and secret. A brief mention of shady activity happens sometimes in the mainstream media, but it is quickly shied away from and then we never hear about it again. We almost never act on our concerns, and we certainly gain almost no traction with when voicing them.

Thankfully, a good chunk of us are boiling mad about the ignored hypocrisy, inefficiency, immorality, and criminality of the war on drugs.

Back in 1998, over 400 billion dollars was spent on narcotics and cannabis alone.23

Even without any point of reference (a graph with more numbers comes next chapter) for those figures in regards to global spending, we should still be able to agree that the war on drugs has not been successful in any way, shape, or form.

All the persecution to date has not been able to stop or even substantially lower the rate of drug use. Inmates are even able to access drugs in prison. The violence, raids, drug seizures, and trillions of tax dollars have not kept drugs from anyone.

---

for Research on Globalization Web site (November 13, 2013), http://www.globalresearch.ca/drug-war-american-troops-are-protecting-afghan-opium-u-s-occupation-leads-to-all-time-high-heroin-production/5358053; Prof. Michel Chossudovsky, "The Spoils of War: Afghanistan's Multibillion Dollar Heroin Trade," GlobalResearch: Center for Research on Globalization Web site (June 14, 2005), http://www.globalresearch.ca/the-spoils-of-war-afghanistan-s-multibillion-dollar-heroin-trade/91

[23] "Spending on Illegal Drugs: Sources and Methods," Worldometers, http://www.worldometers.info/drugs/; see also Richard Branson, "War on Drugs a Trillion-Dollar Failure," CNN Web site (December 7, 2012), http://www.cnn.com/2012/12/06/opinion/branson-end-war-on-drugs/.

In fact, we see no positive return of any kind on our annual "drug-war" investment.24

Humanity can change this landscape for the better, right here and now, and you can help. It is easy. There are basic strategies already in action that, when adopted en masse, will almost instantly end the global war on drugs.

We need to employ our individual rights to decide what you will not support and how you will spend your income. Join those of us ready for change by removing your fiscal contribution to the war on drugs.

This can be easily done through the completely sound and safe methods outlined earlier by Ed Hedemann of the National War Tax Resistance Coordinating Committee.25 Write your government a letter explaining why it is not receiving your support and then explain the initiatives you are supporting instead.

Let us re-channel all our resources and act on our unrestricted freedom to cultivate social awareness, programming, and supportive new solutions.

Again, let us treat drug use as a health issue, not a criminal one.

Social justice, transparency, community, creativity, and compassion – these are solid and available investments that humanity can count on. Remember when Sir Ken Robinson told us that if the United States halved their drop-out rate, the country's net gain would be nearly a trillion dollars over ten years?26

Think about all the previously wasted human capital that we are beginning to support, invest in, and see titanic returns on.

---

[24] Claire Suddath, "Brief History: The War on Drugs," Time World (May 25, 2009), http://content.time.com/time/world/article/0,8599,1887488,00.html.
[25] http://www.nwtrcc.org.
[26] Sir Ken Robinson, "Ted Talks Education," Huffington Post (May 3, 2013), http://sirkenrobinson.com/?p=779.

The Freedom Handbook

If you are wondering how to invest in these guaranteed human stocks, we have already outlined ways to channel your tax dollars into the programs you decide to support. Crowdfunding is discussed a little later on, and is a terrific way for humanity to invest in the hottest new solutions, strongest trends, and targeted movements.

For now, let us continue our discussion on how to end the war on drugs. A new type of organization is looking for our support, involvement, and investment, and it has already proven that it has what it takes to deliver healthier options. Please get involved and join online and on the ground today.

What?

Where?

How?

Have you heard of Avaaz27 and SumofUS28?

These two organizations are just two of the largest in the field of online petition-based activism. Similar to MoveOn,29 mentioned in the chapter on food systems, they gather our global voice via petitions. Donations to these sites support a tidal wave of legal, advertising, and public relations campaigns that have proven highly effective against the world's most powerful governments and private interests.

This big tool kit of strategic activities is one of the very best for making massive changes across all aspects of human existence. As we wrote this book, there were already tens of millions of us making some big changes in the world through these organizations. When the rest of you join us, these numbers reach the hundreds of millions and complete and utter control of the entire world's policies will rest in the common people's transparent hands.

We can take back dominion of our own lives.

---

[27] http://avaaz.org/en/.

[28] http://sumofus.org/?

[29] http://front.moveon.org/.

Take a moment to be inspired. These models represent collaborative institution at its unstoppable finest, which, as we discussed in the chapter on education, significantly surpasses old models in every way.

Collaborative institution is unrelenting. It completely revolutionizes the world by collectivizing our voices and actions. It does all this at a fraction of the cost that traditional institutions incur and does so with remarkable agility. It is a method that can meet the needs of the public, no matter how quickly our needs change.

Let us be abundantly clear; the only collective model that is healthy, is a transparent one without a governing authority.

Critics have attacked these methods, suggesting they constitute slacktivism or clicktivism. They derisively claim that that these methods mute humanity's tenacious activists by encouraging passive online activity over physical action. An article from Wired Magazine UK30 describes how Avaaz counters accusations of so-called clicktivism and takes on the lion bone trade. Cory Doctorow even chimes in with his typical insight and good sense.

Important also are the accusations that Avaaz, SumofUs, MoveOn, and other similar organizations are just NGOs that have secretly merged with the media, the corporatocracy, and ruling class interests. For example, Cory Morningstar criticizes Avaaz and similar organizations in her extensive investigative report with two parts and five sections for The Wrong Kind of Green.31

---

[30] "Avaaz Counters Accusations of Clicktivism and Takes on the Lion Bone Trade," http://www.wired.co.uk/news/archive/2013-06/17/lion-bone-clicktivism.

[31] "Avaaz: Imperialist Pimps of Militarism, Protector of War," The Wrong Kind of Green, three parts, five sections: Part I, (September 10, 2012), http://wrongkindofgreen.org/2012/09/10/avaaz-imperialist-pimps-of-militarism-protectors-of-the-oligarchy-trusted-facilitators-of-war/; (September 11, 2012); http://wrongkindofgreen.org/2012/09/10/avaaz-imperialist-pimps-of-militarism-protectors-of-the-oligarchy-trusted-facilitators-of-war/; (September 18), http://wrongkindofgreen.org/2012/09/18/avaaz-imperialist-pimps-of-militarism-protectors-of-the-oligarchy-trusted-facilitators-of-war-part-i-section-iii/; (September 24, 2012), http://wrongkindofgreen.org/2012/09/24/imperialist-pimps-of-militarism-protectors-of-the-oligarchy-trusted-

"There are massive efforts on the part of the internet's corporate owners to try to direct it to become a technique of marginalization and control."32
- Noam Chomsky -

We learn from Avaaz's alleged subversion how easily humanity's best intentions and even some of our newly evolving solutions can be twisted into tools of distraction and control. Don't lose heart, though, as our collective voice is unstoppable in the face of corruption.

Why? Because the power is in our voice, not the microphone we use.

Let us be prepared to investigate all our activities and organizations for private interests. We need to be vigilant and transparent in all our collective online activity to ensure our systems' integrity. If Avaaz or any tool ever gets tarnished or subverted, we just polish or switch to an alternative.

With this in mind, let us assume that Avaaz's goals are truly altruistic for the sake of examining its basic model. Be aware that we can and should create our own open-source platforms for this type of activity.

As common folk, it is easy to participate. We choose the concerns and campaigns, and then the whole world helps by clicking its support and offering donations. The organization then focuses and leverages our collective voice's infinite power and contributed resources to wage campaigns that change the world.

This might sound trite and a tad like clicktivism on the surface, but look deeper and see what happens when a few million folks simply click a button. Check out Avaaz's Wikipedia page for a quick version of some of its successful actions and movements since its inception in 2007.33

---

facilitators-of-war-part-ii-section-i/;, http://wrongkindofgreen.org/category/non-profit-industrial-complex-organizations/organizations/sumofus/.

[32] Interviewed by Hamish Mackintosh, "Peace netter," The Guardian (October 17, 2002), http://www.theguardian.com/technology/2002/oct/17/internetnews.interviews.

[33] http://en.wikipedia.org/wiki/Avaaz.

Humanity can use the same set of tools to initiate positive change in the face of some of the strongest lobbying forces and corporate muscle out there. Avaaz's success barely scratches the surface of the platform's potential. To liberate ourselves from corruption and oppression, all we need to do is to work together. A few hundred million more of us adding our voices and lending a hand is all it takes.

Through Avaaz, we also learn a bit about mass activism in the new age. We do not always have to take to the streets to have our voices heard.

Most importantly, organizations like Avaaz teach us that we need to grow our solidarity and form habits for joining in collective action and voice. When it comes to ending the war on drugs and other old and toxic systems, turn to Iceland for inspiration and remember that our pots, pans, and walking shoes are sometimes needed to push the right buttons.

Imagine the potential to force outdated institutions and the ruling class to bend to our will in each and every case, via the use of our collected voice.

This force, when focused properly, will allow us to finally drive this bus called life.

Returning back to the war on drugs, prohibition was useless, as is this so-called war. If you are against drug use, here are a few basic ideas: do not use them, educate your kids and communities not to use them, and improve support systems for those who are using.

Let us turn drugs into a health problem, not a criminal one.

If you feel like you have heard us say that before and it is getting a little old, remember that this insane war on ourselves is getting old. Enough is enough. Let us end it.

Government should not be in charge of anyone's well-being, not even with something so simple as the legal drinking age. It is up to us, the people and parents, to decide what's best for ourselves and our children.

Yes, there are some awful parents out there who make horrible decisions. Many of us will not agree with how certain people govern themselves or raise their kids. Still, nothing changes the fact that it is none of our business.

There are many complicated ethical questions regarding the core principle of harm. Have faith—you are worried because you care; therefore, we will undoubtedly contrive methods to ascertain the identity of harm together.

> *"Once brave politicians and others explain the war on drugs' true cost, the American people will scream for a cease-fire. Bring the troops home, people will urge. Treat drugs as a health problem, not as a matter for the criminal justice system."*[34]
> *- Larry Elder -*

We must remember the following three things. First, it is important to relax. You do not always have to have all the answers or be right, and you definitely do not have to agree with everything anyone says.

Second and most important, you will not agree with everything in this book. That does not matter. If 5 to 10 percent of this book's problematic portrait is accurate in your opinion, then massive erupting volcanoes of hot, heaping manure surround you.

Anyone got an air freshener, a bloody match, anything?

Now think about the flip side. If 5 to 10 percent of the talk in this book regarding human potential is true, we are sitting pretty, ready to round the bend to a victory dance the likes of which humankind has never dreamed of.

We are already well on the way to creating a vibrant, peaceful, self-governed world, sure to last a millennia.

---

[34] Larry Elder. BrainyQuote.com, Xplore Inc, 2014. http://www.brainyquote.com/quotes/quotes/l/larryelder192359.html, accessed March 16, 2014.

Third, collective strength eradicates individual weaknesses. United we stand, divided we fall.

Let us end the discussion on our desperate need for a new set of solutions to replace the war on drugs with a look at Richard's work on the subject, along with a look at Portugal's stance. Richard Branson wrote an article astutely entitled "Time to end the war on drugs," which he posted on his personal blog in December 2013.35

> "Portugal's 10 year experiment shows clearly that enough is enough. It is time to end the war on drugs worldwide. We must stop criminalising drug users. Health and treatment should be offered to drug users—not prison. Bad drugs policies affect literally hundreds of thousands of individuals and communities across the world. We need to provide medical help to those that have problematic use— not criminal retribution."
> - Richard Branson -

Portugal's an interesting case. It addressed public outcry over drug problems by edging closer to the personal and collective responsibility we speak of.

The country's current drug policy was established in 2000 and has been legally effective since July 2001. In Portugal, it is still illegal to possess certain drugs, but someone with a small amount for personal use will get a summons and be dealt with administratively instead of in criminal court. People who manufacture or sell drugs, however, face criminal charges.36

---

[35] http://www.virgin.com/richard-branson/time-to-end-the-war-on-drugs.

[36] Richard Branson, "Time to End the War on Drugs," Richard Branson Blog Web site, http://www.virgin.com/richard-branson/time-to-end-the-war-on-drugs.

Using well over a decade's worth of evidence, the official case study shows that decriminalization and treating problematic users as patients rather than criminals is much more effective than war and imprisonment. Indeed, the authors of one study found that Portugal had less problematic drug use, less drug-related harm, and less crowding of criminal justice facilities.37

After only five years, fewer teens were using illegal drugs and there were fewer new cases of HIV caused by dirty-needle sharing. The number of people seeking treatment for drug use more than doubled.

Further studies in Portugal have shown that the number of deaths related to heroin and similar drugs has decreased by more than half, and the number of people seeking treatment continues to grow.

The United States is notably the largest consumer of cocaine and marijuana in the world. European Union countries, which take a much more relaxed stance on drugs, use less.

Richard Branson is a Global Commission on Drug Policy commissioner.38 He's written a number of articles on the topic that are short and well worth the read, including "The war on drugs is a broken business model,"39 "Time to overturn the 1971 drugs law,"40 "Banning cats (ok, khat) is a pointless backwards step."41 Also check out "Why the war on drugs must end," by Sam Branson.42

---

[37] Caitlin Elizabeth Hughes and Alex Stevens, "What Can We Learn from the Portuguese Decriminalization of Illicit Drugs?" British Journal of Criminology, vol. 50(6) (2010), 999-1022, http://bjc.oxfordjournals.org/content/50/6/999.

[38] http://www.globalcommissionondrugs.org/.

[39] http://www.virgin.com/unite/leadership-and-advocacy/the-war-on-drugs-is-a-broken-business-model (11 October 2013).

[40] http://www.virgin.com/richard-branson/time-to-overturn-the-1971-drugs-law (25 March 2013).

[41] http://www.virgin.com/richard-branson/banning-cats-ok-khat-is-a-pointless-backwards-step (5 July 2013).

[42] http://www.virgin.com/search?keywords=why+war+on+drugs+must+end&type=all (9 July 2013).

One of the best recent documentaries on the subject is Breaking the Taboo, which was narrated by Morgan Freeman.43 The trailer for the film is on YouTube.44

If you want a break from the tough stuff this book is chock-full of, watch True Facts About Morgan Freeman first, for full-on gut-busting comic relief.45

In another article, "The war on drugs has failed,"46 Richard Branson shares the results of a recent worldwide online survey: "In the global online poll, 91% agreed that the war on drugs has failed. Over 90% also thought that providing treatment for addiction would be a better approach than putting people in jail."

After more than sixty years of war there cannot be many of us left who think this approach is working.47 The survey indicates that over 90 percent might not have even needed to hear the problematic portion of this discussion. So, if we are all on the same page, get involved, recruit your friends and family, and let's change this nonsense once and for all.

In another article, "Decriminalizing Drug Possession"48 Sir Richard outlines a recent study, A Quiet Revolution: Drug Decriminalisation Policies in Practice across the Globe,49 which

---

[43] Fernando Grostein Andrade and Cosmo Feilding-Mellens (Dirs.); Cosmo Feilding-Mellens (Prod.); Sundog Pictures and Spray Filmes (5 December 2012.
[44] http://www.youtube.com/watch?v=i2vqpNT1kV4 (23 November 2012).
[45] http://www.youtube.com/watch?v=Ch5MEJk5ZCQ (January 10, 2013).
[46] http://www.virgin.com/richard-branson/the-war-on-drugs-has-failed
[47] Richard Branson, "War on Drugs a Trillion-Dollar Failure," CNN Web site (December 7, 2012), http://www.cnn.com/2012/12/06/opinion/branson-end-war-on-drugs/; see also Single Convention on Narcotic Drugs, 1961 (in effect August 8, 1975); Harrison Narcotics Act, Ch. 1, 38 Stat. 785 (1914); Controlled Substances Act (CSA) 21 U.S.C. 13, §801 et seq.; 84 Stat. 1236.
[48] http://www.virgin.com/richard-branson/decriminalising-drug-possession.
[49] Release, http://www.release.org.uk/publications/quiet-revolution-drug-decriminalisation-policies-practice-across-globe.

examines evidence from twenty-one countries, including the Netherlands, Estonia, Australia, Mexico, Uruguay, and Portugal, that have adopted some form of drug decriminalization.

The report states: "The harms of criminalization far outweigh those of decriminalization. Decriminalization does appear to direct more drug users into treatment, reduce criminal justice costs, and shield many drug users from the devastating impact of a criminal conviction."50

> "The illegality of cannabis is outrageous, an impediment to full utilization of a drug which helps produce the serenity and insight, sensitivity and fellowship so desperately needed in this increasingly mad and dangerous world."51
>
> - Carl Sagan -

The last word on pot we will give to a Canadian, and a famous politician at that. Justin Trudeau was ambushed by a concerned conservative mother who works with drug users; his response is a major step in the right direction,52 minus the regulations and legislation he proposes, of course.

It will be interesting to see how many brave and truly noble politicians join us common folk in dismantling authority and controlling structures and help create the self-governed world we are entitled to.

We are all responsible for creating a better world together. Load up your compassion and sense, leave your judgment and rules at home and prepare to leverage your imagination. These are the new

---

50 Quoted by Richard Branson, "Decriminalising drug possession."
51 Elliott Steve, The Little Black Book of Marijuana (Peter Pauper Press, 2011), 153.
52 "Justin Trudeau discusses Pot with a concerned Steinbach mother" (September 26, 2013), http://www.youtube.com/watch?v=gtHmO_wK7UI.

suggestions, though we will not persecute or enslave you for not following them.

> *"Bad people are less a problem than indifferent people."*
> *- Gerhard Kocher -*

You do not need to know where or how exactly to begin, you just need to use your heart and head to make a decision and then take those very first steps. This concept is absolutely central to setting the stage for communities to gather and form consensus and then solutions. We need to be prepared to take action before planning each and every step involved.

> *"Action is the foundational key to all success."*[53]
> *– Anthony Robbins –*

> *"Action speaks louder than words but not nearly as often."*[54]
> *- Mark Twain -*

Freedom requires hard work, at least at first.

In a world freed from oppression, many things will not feel like work anymore. Humanity is brimming with enlivening solutions driven by passion. The shift to self-governance is virtually assured after we take those first few steps, which can feel like the hardest of all.

The long-term day-to-day collaboration, agility, and compassion will be our real work, but these efforts will produce results we can all be more proud of than anything we have ever done.

---

[53] As quoted in Stack the Logs!: Building a Success Framework to Reach Your Dream (2003) by John Blaydes, 57.

[54] Mark Twain. BrainyQuote.com, Xplore Inc, 2014. http://www.brainyquote.com/quotes/quotes/m/marktwain162937.html, accessed March 16, 2014.

Are you happy with your job now? No? Want a super-cool new gig working to free and empower the planet? Come join us and do your part so that we can tear down the walls that have enslaved humankind for millennia together.

Together we are already building a healthier world, where there are engaging and rewarding jobs for everyone.

> *"It was character that got us out of bed, commitment that moved us into action, and discipline that enabled us to follow through."*[55]
> - Zig Ziglar -

Now, let us do things differently. We can do better.

As we come to the end of another large and imposing discussion, we hope you can agree we have a problem and you are open to trying new solutions. We need to be effectively detached from the need to agree on a problem's exact origin before deciding to make something new. When a ship is sinking, stopping the leak and bailing the water out of the boat precedes the investigation into what caused the leak.

Get ready to engage in the discussions and activities you are most passionate about and have faith that your brothers and sisters will create effective and agile solutions where you cannot.

Let us lay down our lawful weapons as prepare to fight for one another, and turn our attention to the current power structure. Let us end this tyrannical and dysfunctional war on ourselves and start a battle with something to gain - our freedom!

It is time for global coup. It is time to reclaim our right to self-govern.

---

[55] Over the Top: Moving from Survival to Stability, from Stability to Success, from Success to Significance (Thomas Nelson, 2007), 243.

CHAPTER NINE

- War -

"It is forbidden to kill; therefore all murderers are punished unless they kill in large numbers and to the sound of trumpets."[1]
- Voltaire -

"Mankind must put an end to war before war puts an end to mankind."[2]
- President John F. Kennedy -

Humanity has dreamed of the end of war, and those of us alive today can make this dream come true. Common people from all walks of life and all corners of the earth, we all must realize that it's time to make that dream a reality. Together, you and I together can abolish war, because each and every one of us can make all the difference in the world.

For all you women and men around the world in uniform, this is a special call to action. You know better than the rest of us, that the powers that corral your violence and demand silence, obedience, and "honorable" death, know nothing about honor themselves.

War brings no peace, only horror and pain. All wars are unjust. Your families, old friends, neighbors, and communities are begging you - please come home, alive and in one piece. Lay down your weapons and refuse to be violent. This is your own heart's noble and courageous cry.

---

[1] Alexander J. Nemeth, *Voltaire's Tormented Soul: A Psychobiographic Inquiry* (Associated University Presse, 2008), 110.
[2] Address before the General Assembly of the United Nations, September 25, 1961.

> *"If the machine of government is of such a nature that it requires you to be the agent of injustice to another, then, I say, break the law."* [3]
> *- Henry David Thoreau -*

Do it today. Do it proudly. Your help is needed at home. We have self-governance to guard and freedom to defend, a fight with real honor and real enemies. We have money and jobs. We have a community and a world to re-create.

Join us.

We need tough guys and gals like you.

On the home front, refuse to imprison your neighbors while government and the elite scramble to salvage control through martial law or collusion. Their lies have run out of merit. People know the truth.

Standing military, navy, air force - none of these are needed in their present capacity. This is hardly as radical an idea as it may seem at first.

Violence on the scale of war is only possible through a plague of propaganda. It is made conceivable with lies used to incite fear and hatred within groups of common people. The necessity of war is the largest and longest lie ever ingrained into the human psyche.

These are statements of fact, not argument. The evidence is sound and the truth lives in our hearts. If you are not quite there yet, do not be afraid. We have not yet begun our war story. By the end of this discussion, you will understand where we're coming from.

War's purpose is strictly to divide, control, and weaken the common masses. Fiscal benefits and squabbling amongst the ruling elite are the reasons given, and the real essence of this discussion is that humans will not war with each other without being lied to in the worst ways possible.

---

[3] *Civil Disobedience* (1849).

Paul Chappell teaches us this crucial lesson very plainly and with first-hand experience in hand and heart. Paul's father served in the army for thirty years, fighting in the Vietnam and Korean wars, and his mother lived in Japan during World War II and in Korea during the Korean War. Paul graduated from West Point and served in the army for seven years. He was deployed in Bagdad and left the army a captain.

In <u>this</u> talk, he explains that all the way back through human history, the single largest problem facing any army on earth is getting human beings to sacrifice themselves and die.4 A close second, as you might imagine, is getting human beings to kill.

The powers that be learned long ago that if our soldiers believe they're fighting to protect their friends, family, and loved ones, they'll sacrifice their lives. Our instinct to protect our loved ones is far more powerful than our self-preservation instinct.

If any of you were to see your loved ones in pain or injured, you'd rush to protect them. Consequently, authorities need only to play on these basic, loving, human instincts to convince us to war with the demonized enemy of the day to "protect" our loved ones and way of life from their purported evils.

On the surface, there often appears to be sound reasons for war – in World War II, for example, there was a belief that the conflict was necessary to face and defeat a global threat in the Axis of Evil. Later in this discussion, we will address the fallacy of that belief.

If Canada gave up its military, it would not affect our security as a nation at all. The only thing that would be different would be that a strong and violent weapon would be removed from the armory of our oppressors. Through our apathy, we peaceful Canadians allow ourselves and the world at large to be treated with vicious iniquity.

All Canadians reading this should be aware that the things that might make you most proud to be Canadian, specifically our nonviolent policies and reputation, are far from true. Have a look

The Freedom Handbook

at the Coalition to Oppose the Arms Trade, which you can find at http://coat.ncf.ca/.

This group, established in 1989, has a wealth of evidence documenting the Canadian military's secret engagement in the Iraq war.4

Though Canada participated in military action against Iraq in 1991, popular opinion is that Canada largely held to its refusal to join the second war against Iraq in 2003 or support it in any large military sense. There are three articles that provide more than enough evidence to shatter this misconception, and you can read them here,5 here,6 and here.7

In addition, this report shows that over an eight-year period, about 80 percent of Canadian war profiteering through military exports was hidden, to the tune of over $7.2 billion US dollars.8

Now, consider how through arms trade, Canada supports regimes guilty of blatant and repeated human rights violations. The top six pension plans in Canada had close to two billion of our dollars invested in the world's top twenty weapon producers. 9

Incidentally, each human being possesses the wholesome attributes that many Canadians believe our government aspires to and that we are famous for the world over. We can all be nonviolent,

---

[4] Coalition to Oppose the Arms Trade, http://coat.ncf.ca.
[5] Issue #65 *(Operation Silent Partner: Canada's Quiet Complicity in the Iraq War)* (December, 2010), http://coat.ncf.ca/P4C/65/65.htm.
[6] http://coat.ncf.ca/articles/Canada_Iraq.htm. Article was first published as "Canada's Secret Complicity in the Iraq War," *The CCPA Monitor* (September 2008), 7-8.
[7] http://coat.ncf.ca/articles/Natynczyk_Iraq.htm. Article was first published as "Canada's Real Role in Iraq: Our New Defence Chief Commanded U.S. Troops in Iraq," *The CCPA Monitor* *September 2008), 1, 6, http://coat.ncf.ca/articles/Natynczyk_Iraq.htm.
[8] Wikiweapons Canada database, http://coat.ncf.ca/research/US.htm.
[9] "The Six Largest Canadian Pension Funds and Their Investments in the World's Top 100 War Industries," (2012), http://coat.ncf.ca/research/Pensions-Top100.htm.

peaceful, pleasant, and powerful. Our fears about each other are illusions.

Like the cheap throwaway goods that mark modern society's toxic idea of creation, let us toss away all these bad ideas and never look back. Let us build things to last again, things we can be truly proud of.

Whether you live in Canada or not, we all need to set aside that fear which tells us that without a standing military, some rogue nation or the omnipresent and faceless threat of terror will surely attack our country. Consider instead the total amount of money spent worldwide on military endeavors.

In his book, The End of Poverty, renowned economist Jeffrey Sachs tells us that global military spending in 2012 alone totaled $1,735 billion.10 If we reinvested this gargantuan chunk of our resources, many of humanity's truly critical needs could be met.

Here's a quick breakdown of some key details from the Stockholm International Peace Research Institute (SIPRI) report on 2012 trends in military spending: global military expenditure in 2012 reached approximately $1.75 trillion. This corresponds to 2.5 percent of the gross world product,11 or approximately $236 for each person in the world.

The United States, with its massive budget derived from printing money out of thin air, is the principal determinant of current world trends. The United States military expenditure alone accounted for just under half of the world's total, with 39 percent.12 While military spending declined in some countries, such as Canada, Australia, and Italy, it increased in Russia, Saudi Arabia, and China.13

---

[10] (New York: Penguin Press, 2005).

[11] Sam Perlo-Freeman, Elisabeth Skons, Carina Solmirano, and Helen Wilandh, "Trends in World Military Expenditure, 2012: SIPRI Fact Sheet," (April, 2013), 1, http://books.sipri.org/product_info?c_product_id=458.

[12] Anup Shah, "World Military Spending," Global Issues (June 30, 2013), http://www.globalissues.org/article/75/world-military-spending.

[13] SIPRI Fact Sheet, 2012, 2.

The Freedom Handbook

An excerpt from a blog by Emptie Yaz entitled "War Costs," which looks at an earlier SIPRI report in greater detail, helps us put these figures into perspective:14

Consider the global priorities in spending in 1998

Global Priority	$U.S. Billions
Cosmetics in the United States	8
Ice cream in Europe	11
Perfumes in Europe and the United States	12
Pet foods in Europe and the United States	17
Business entertainment in Japan	35
Cigarettes in Europe	50
Alcoholic drinks in Europe	105
Narcotic drugs in the world	400
Military spending in the world	780

Now, compare that to what was estimated as additional costs to achieve universal access to the following basic social services in all developing countries:

Global Priority	$U.S. Billions
Basic education for all	6
Water and sanitation for all	9
Reproductive health for all women	12
Basic health and nutrition	13

These estimates of the cost of universal access to some pretty basic services are incredibly shocking. It is hard to believe how far we have come from our common sense.

All this spending has not made us common folks or the world as a whole any safer. As ever, autocratic establishment can be counted on to fail everyone but itself. The loathsome truth is that the ruling

---

[14] *Insight* (March 30, 2013), http://staticviews.blogspot.ca/.

class has never believed the propaganda it has used to promote its own military force.

If you ask the average person about the motivation behind war, many will point to fiscal benefits. However, above all else, war provides one monstrous distraction, the greatest opportunity and tool for those in power to control and enslave us. They promote the idea that we are dependent on governments for physical protection from enemies they have created.

Politicians, rulers, and war all tell us people are to be feared.

The majority of us are not actually scared of most people we meet unless we are taught to fear them. Despite radical differences in beliefs, people rarely if ever harm each other without highly organized propaganda.

People would never war if it were not for rulers of old and governments of modern day inciting us through stories about our neighbors' "evil" and "savage" activities that "must be dealt with violently before the terrors invade our lands and destroy our way of life." After thousands of years and hundreds of proven examples of deception, it is time stop listening to this garbage.

> *"It has too often been too easy for rulers and governments to incite man to war."*[15]
> *- Lester B. Pearson -*

Most people believe that a strong military is a necessary evil. We urge you to go find the truth inside yourself, after you examine the facts honestly and carefully. We are well aware of the dancing dichotomy of life, the bittersweet nectar of it all, but "necessary evil" is a ridiculous oxymoron in this case.

---

[15] Lester B. Pearson, "The Four Faces of Peace," in *Nobel Lectures in Peace,* ed. Frederick Habermen (World Scientific, 1999), 140.

The Freedom Handbook

When you look inside yourself and wait for the answer, you will find one simple truth. We don't need war.

If this idea of looking inside yourself for truth and seeking answers from some ambiguous place within seems too fluffy, sit tight; the external process will become clear as we delve deeper into this and provide solutions to so many of life's modern ills. For now, realize that there is no conversation more important than the consistent one you have with yourself.

> *"Of all the enemies to public liberty war is, perhaps, the most to be dreaded because it comprises and develops the germ of every other. War is the parent of armies; from these proceed debts and taxes... known instruments for bringing the many under the domination of the few...No nation could preserve its freedom in the midst of continual warfare."*[16]
> *- James Madison -*

Many presidents and global leaders are quoted in the margins of this book. When people in the very positions of authority and power we speak against have the courage to share the truth for no other reason than selfless service, and at risk of their careers, we should take note.

Consider the constant state of warfare the United States has been dealing out globally over the better part of the last century and into the early decades of this one. It is no wonder liberties and freedoms around the world have eroded so quickly in the wake of this. It is impossible to hide from the reality of our global war economy – it has been proven that more than anything else in the world, sustained war wears down and destroys public freedoms.

We need to fight for our sovereign rights and freedoms.

---

[16] "Political Observations," (April 20, 1795).

It is our responsibility.

> "God forbid we should ever be twenty years without such a rebellion. The people cannot be all, and always, well informed...If they remain quiet under such misconceptions, it is lethargy, the forerunner of death to the public liberty...And what country can preserve its liberties, if its rulers are not warned from time to time, that this people preserve the spirit of resistance? Let them take arms." [17]
> - Thomas Jefferson -

Many of us are disgusted by the global treatment of the so-called terrorists that were never tried and for whom all rights and protections have been stripped away, and, as has been revealed, should never have suffered this indignity.

Under the guise of national security, governments sanction secrecy, preemptive violence, torture, and human rights violations that are not legal, no matter what they might claim.

Thankfully, many are beginning to see these practices for the heinous, criminal lies they are.

Some think that terrorists must be dealt with harshly because they are crazy and do horrible things. First, we need proof that these so-called terrorists were actually behaving illegally. They deserve the same rights and trials as everyone else.

As a matter of fact, these people need their rights protected and deserve a trial the most.

"An eye for an eye" is a dark, perilous, and painful philosophy.

---

[17] Letter to William Stephens Smith (November 13, 1787).

Every day, people harm others on a small scale but few of us could torture another human being. None of us would want to be personally responsible for imprisoning someone indefinitely without any official due process.

So, the large-scale harm we've been talking about throughout this book – which is most clearly exemplified through war – requires one of two things, individual psychopaths or collective apathy. Since there are very few psychopaths on average, we are really in this mess because it is too easy to turn a blind eye.

"Ethical horror" is a tame way to describe how the United States creates serial killers out of the drone pilots who play video games with villagers' lives.

When drones blow up a single human, too few of us are outraged. These drone attacks are responsible for horrendous "collateral damage," aka innocent human deaths, in remote villages around the world. The attacks are carried out on suspected criminals who have never had a trial or been convicted. We kill the assumed-to-be guilty, as well as the absolutely innocent, without knowing anything for sure.

There is also tremendous evidence to support the fact that most of the "lone assassins" and "madmen" throughout history have been victims of government collusion and gross manipulation. Many of these people are documented employees of the world's various alphabet soup agencies and the various intelligence groups around the world that operate in secrecy to further their own interests.

Notice how these scapegoats are usually killed immediately.

We never get to hear their voices, their stories.

Realize that when you rationalize any reason to abolish someone's rights, regardless of what he or she may have done, you open the door to your own rights being stolen. If criminals have no rights, then none of us really has any rights if the authorities decide they do not want to honor them.

We must look at how terrorists and heinous criminals are treated so that we can understand how inseparable their rights are from our own.

It could happen to you. When governments can decide, unilaterally, what is right or wrong, you could easily end up on the wrong side. If the government decides that you are an enemy, for any reason whatsoever, you will be railroaded.

> *"It is dangerous to be right when the government is wrong."* [18]
> *- Voltaire -*

> *"Show me the man and I'll find you the crime."* [19]
> *- Lavrentiy Beria -*

Evidence is everywhere. Therefore, this dangerous reality demands our attention while we examine nearly every major subject. This horrible and universal practice stifles the voices of individuals and even whole social movements.

Let us better protect the courageous voices among us from now on.

Now, it is time to go back to the idea of no standing military and the fear surrounding it. A standing military inevitably engages in violent, non-training-related activities, not on its own accord, but at the behest of the powers that nominally direct it.

Switzerland shows us how countries can exist without standing armies. The country can rapidly respond to foreign aggression using

---

[18] «Catalogue pour la plupart des écrivains français qui ont paru dans Le Siècle de Louis XIV, pour servir à l'histoire littéraire de ce temps,» *Le Siècle de Louis XIV* (1752).

[19] «Catalogue pour la plupart des écrivains français qui ont paru dans Le Siècle de Louis XIV, pour servir à l'histoire littéraire de ce temps,» *Le Siècle de Louis XIV* (1752).

an armed militia. Swiss males are expected to undergo basic military training around the age of twenty and keep their military issued weapons at home for life. They remain part of the militia until the age of thirty (age thirty-four for officers).

This approach has been working for the Swiss for many decades and is a solution the whole world can easily and successfully embrace.

Military brothers and sisters, come home, but keep your guns just in case. We will have no standing military, but we will stand up against unjust rule and oppression. With a ready militia, national security concerns will be easily dealt with. Imagine standing together as one huge human family, and our uniformed men and women protecting us.

If you know someone who wears a gun at work, talk to them. Tell them you need them, their communities need them, and all of humanity needs them for protection. Talk about freedom, human rights, and all the positive changes taking place.

Let us ask our friends and family in uniform to decide what orders they will not follow.

For those who are a bit more passive minded and hope these changes can happen without bloodshed at all, Luke and I share the hope that you are right. We, too, have great faith in humanity's compassion and growing powers of organization and collaboration.

Still, with caution we must recall Thomas Jefferson's warning about the commitment necessary to avoid tyranny. Remember, too, how the printing press brought with it a few hundred years of strife alongside its own far-reaching revolution.

Humanity has one last great battle to fight against a tiny few. This global engagement will bring an end to hunger, war, and oppression. Victory will birth self-governance, transparency, and true freedom for us all.

This will be a very different kind of clash, fought at home, in our own lands, against the toughest kind of foes – our age-old ruling bodies and our fear of living without them. The fight might last only relative moments, depending on levels of cooperation and collective action, but it is a fight that needs to happen and that we need to win.

It's time to talk about guns and weapons for a moment.

With all due urgency, we call your attention to an article that Gary North published on his website in January 2013, "Bury Your Guns at Wounded Knee," written by an anonymous author:

"December 29, 2012, marked the 122nd Anniversary of the murder of 297 Sioux Indians at Wounded Knee Creek on the Pine Ridge Indian Reservation in South Dakota. These 297 people, in their winter camp, were murdered by federal agents and members of the 7th Cavalry who had come to confiscate their firearms "for their own safety and protection." The slaughter began after the majority of the Sioux had peacefully turned in their firearms. The Calvary began shooting, and managed to wipe out the entire camp. 200 of the 297 victims were women and children. About 40 members of the 7th Cavalry were killed, but over half of them were victims of fratricide from the Hotchkiss guns of their overzealous comrades-in-arms. Twenty members of the 7th Cavalry's death squad, were deemed "National Heroes" and were awarded the Medal of Honor for their acts of heroism[cowardice].

"We hear very little of Wounded Knee today. It is usually not mentioned in our history classes or books. What little that does exist about Wounded Knee is normally a sanitized "Official Government Explanation." And there are several historically inaccurate depictions of the events leading up to the massacre, which appear in movie scripts and are not the least bit representative of the actual events that took place that day.

"Wounded Knee was among the first federally backed gun confiscation attempts in United States history. It ended in the senseless murder of 297 people.

"Before you jump on the emotionally charged bandwagon for gun control, take a moment to reflect on the real purpose of the Second

Amendment, the right of the people to take up arms in defense of themselves, their families, and property in the face of invading armies or an oppressive government. The argument that the Second Amendment only applies to hunting and target shooting is asinine. When the United States Constitution was drafted, "hunting" was an everyday chore carried out by men and women to put meat on the table each night, and "target shooting" was an unheard of concept. Musket balls were a precious commodity and were certainly not wasted on "target shooting." The Second Amendment was written by people who fled oppressive and tyrannical regimes in Europe, and it refers to the right of American citizens to be armed for defensive purposes, should such tyranny arise in the United States.

As time goes forward, the average citizen in the United States continually loses little chunks of personal freedom or liberty. Far too many times, unjust gun control bills were passed and signed into law under the guise of "for your safety" or "for protection." The Patriot Act, signed into law by G.W. Bush, was expanded and continues under Barack Obama. It is just one of many examples of American citizens being stripped of their rights and privacy for "safety." Now, the Right to Keep and Bear Arms is on the table, and will, most likely be attacked to facilitate the path for the removal of our firearms, all in the name of "our safety."

Before any American citizen blindly accepts whatever new firearms legislation that is about to be doled out, they should stop and think about something for just one minute. Evil does exist in our world. It always has and always will. Throughout history evil people have committed evil acts. In the Bible one of the first stories is that of Cain killing Abel. We cannot legislate "evil" into extinction. Good people will abide by the law, and the criminal element will always find a way around it.

Evil exists all around us, but looking back at the historical record of the past 200 years, across the globe, where is "evil" and "malevolence" most often found? In the hands of those with the power, the governments. The greatest human tragedies on record and the largest loss of innocent human life can be attributed to governments. Who do the governments always target? "Scapegoats" and "enemies" within their own borders... but only after they have been disarmed to the point where they no longer pose a threat. Ask any Native American, and they will tell you it was inferior technology and lack of arms that contributed to their demise. Ask any Armenian why it was so easy for the Turks to exterminate millions of them, and they will answer "We were disarmed before it happened." Ask any Jew what Hitler's first step prior to the mass murders of the Holocaust was – confiscation of firearms from the people.

Wounded Knee is the prime example of why the Second Amendment exists, and why we should vehemently resist any attempts to infringe on our Rights to Bear Arms. Without the Second Amendment we will be totally stripped of any ability to defend ourselves and our families.

"The Tea Party Economist," as Gary likes to call himself, deserves thanks for publishing this moving account, written by an unknown author who first sent it to Common Sense Junction.20 Wounded Knee epitomizes how essential our right to individual arms is, especially concerning the security of our liberties and freedom.

Still, people express concern about school shootings and their potential ties to gun access. They wonder if better gun control could help protect our children. The answer is no. In the United States, the states with the toughest gun laws are also among those with the highest crime rates, including gun crime. Communities are safer with guns and weaponry in the citizenry's hands – this weaponry is the last defense any of us have against crime, not to mention tyranny.

Katie Worthman's a WWII survivor with a chilling account of the real history behind gun control in Austria and Hitler's political rise to power, which you can read here.21

---

[20] Frank, "A Little Bit of History to Think About," *Common Sense Junction* Web site (January 14, 2013), http://www.commonsensejunction.com/?p=21553.

[21] {Add details on this specific youtube; reference Kitty Werthmann, as some may know her]

The Freedom Handbook

She recounts a tale of a rising political star elected by a huge majority – one who sounds very much like the American politicians of today. This same politician slowly, through small measures, gained a firm and violent dictator's grasp on Austria's people, people who had no weapons left to defend themselves.

In summary, here is her final warning: "Keep your guns, buy more guns!"

If guns kill people, then pencils misspell words, cars make people drive drunk, and spoons make people fat.

Despite the fabricated controversy in the media, the truth about the direct relationship between gun and weapon control to tyranny is undeniable. Examples aplenty outline the weaponry control practices of Hitler, Stalin, and many other leaders throughout history. For those who enjoy the odd video to supplement all the reading, here is another.

> *"How a politician stands on the Second Amendment tells you how he or she views you as an individual; as a trustworthy and productive citizen, or as part of an unruly crowd that needs to be lorded over, controlled, supervised, and taken care of."* [22]
> *- Dr. Suzanna Gratia Hupp -*

State Senator R.C. Soles shot one of two intruders in his home recently, just outside Tabor City, NC. Senator Soles did not hesitate to defend himself with his own gun, when he believed he and his family were in immediate danger. Despite being accused of being an anti-gun advocate, this senator has an A rating from the NRA and, according to Grass Roots North Carolina, is an ally who has consistently supported gun rights.

---

[22] Testimony before committee, 2008, http://www.youtube.com/watch?v=M1u0Byq5Qis.

His true feelings and legislative voting history aside, we can see from his all-too-common story how universal our right to defend our families against crime and violence truly is. The actions he took to protect his family are actions all ordinary citizens like us should be free to take when faced with the identical situation.

This story might also prompt questions like "How can some of the elite think that their lives are more valuable than ours?" Unfortunately this type of attitude is to be expected from human beings who have been bred and trained to believe that they deserve to run common people's lives – our children, our bodies, our souls, and our rights.

> *"A ruling intelligentsia, whether in Europe, Asia or Africa, treats the masses as raw material to be experimented on, processed, and wasted at will."*23
> *- Eric Hoffer -*

However, there is no need to demonize these people. The process of rulership and arbitrary authority is to blame, and is truly a plague on even the oppressor's humanity.

School shootings are recognized as examples of a recent evolution in criminal behavior. The argument that guns encourage or increase the ease with which these types of crimes are carried out is absurd. It is the same as arguing that criminalizing drugs makes access more difficult for our youth, which the war on drugs has taught us is a devastating misconception.

School shootings are a result of the collective human spirit's perversion and fracturing. Our humanity has reached a breaking point through massive levels of cognitive dissonance24 and flat-

---

23 *The Passionate State of Mind* (New York: Harper, 1955).
24 "Cognitive dissonance" is having thoughts or beliefs that are inconsistent with attitudes or behaviors, such as someone deciding to smoke despite worry about the health issues. See *Oxford Dictionary*, http://www.oxforddictionaries.com/definition/english/cognitive-dissonance?q=cognitive+dissonance (": "the state

out pain. Our general apathy and moral degradation are further symptoms of humanity's repressed pain.

The only real protection parents have today, as in any age in human history, against any kind of violence, is stronger families and communities.

Gun control strips us of our ability to protect and defend ourselves and our families. Therefore, if we truly want to protect our children, we are responsible for removing individual authority and tyrannical rule. In so doing, we lead by example and teach our kids and ourselves to be free and to function in collectively accountable, healthy communities.

We need to be serious about slavery and prepared to be violent in our refusal to be ruled. Let us make our ancestors proud and help them breathe a sigh of relief by achieving the fullest expression of our freedoms and natural rights that the human race has ever seen.

Instead of shame, debt, and despair, let us leave a legacy of absolute freedom to the children of the world.

Hope and pray that we will establish our release through strictly peaceful means. However, we must be prepared to fight. All transition brings hardship along the way.

We cannot minimize the pain of those who will or have already suffered. Instead, let us make the deaths and work of people like Aaron Swartz and so many of our brave sisters and brothers mean something. Rejoice in knowing we will experience only a fraction of the pain of past change during this newer kind of transition.

Humanity's contemporary struggles are bound to be more evolved than the revolutions of our past. It is plain to see that we can do things better in every single facet of life.

Therefore, our modern revolution is innovative itself.

---

of having inconsistent thoughts, beliefs, or attitudes, especially as relating to behavioural decisions and attitude change"); *Simply Psychology* Web site, http://www.simplypsychology.org/cognitive-dissonance.html.

New kinds of tools bring new kinds of challenges. Normal ethical challenges will always arise as we develop new technologies, especially concerning the fields of nanotechnology and transhumanism, and we must be prepared to face these challenges with an open mind and open heart.

It is standard and logical for authority to use new forms of technology, often in secret and always first as weapons, to control the general population. This will hardly be news to most. It is a known and typically unchallenged policy of governments around the world, and this policy has been in place for all of human history.

We need to change that.

We need to use all of our innovation, our technology, and our brightest minds for the common good.

Our military kin were asked to keep their guns yet refuse to be violent. Let us take a moment to address this apparent conflict.

The ruling class will unquestionably oppose us reclaiming our sovereignty and global resources. They have also likely anticipated that these levels of resistance would arise eventually. It will not take long until their backs are against the wall, when their authority starts dying and their control slips away.

When the ruling intelligentsia begins watching us common folk everywhere reclaim our property and our rights through nonviolence, we need to be prepared and expect violent opposition. We need to be ready to defend our communities, our rights, and ourselves.

> *"A people can value nothing greater than their own freedom and dignity, and must defend these with their last drop of blood. There is no duty as sacred and no higher law. The pernicious belief that one can secure these without conflict and by avoiding danger is both false and poisonous. Danger can only be met with virile courage joined with a calm*

and firm resolve and a clear conscience. These virtues alone form the true leaders of a people and bring into being the martial forces that can win the deepest and cherished dreams of humanity."
- Karl von Clausewitz, 1831 -

Freedom like we have never known will be hard-won, like all good things.

Be warned though, if we lollygag and doddle around, thinking and talking about it without taking action, we'll quickly find more of us, if not the whole planet, in a real one-world-state of brutal slavery.

"If you want a picture of the future, imagine a boot stamping on a human face—forever."[25]
- George Orwell -

Our future is our choice. Orwellian squared or freedom.

The One World Government is something about which we have all heard a lot of speculation. Individual thoughts on the issue aside for a moment, we can all recognize that there are ongoing, definitive efforts to globalize much of our world. Structure is necessary for evolution, and large, centralized systems can and should always be a part of our future. That being said, all decisions on that level must be transparent and collective.

Many of humanity's systems can be localized. If a centralized element of supervision remains in most cases, it will become a rarely used fail-safe. We will continue to explore flourishing examples of and ways to meet human needs in smaller, localized ways. In military terms, Switzerland's militia is a terrific example.

The truth is, the current One World Government movement is an even greater threat to humanity than royalty, dictatorships,

---

[25] *Nineteen Eighty-four* (1949).

or national rulers of the world's past. Agenda 21, for example, like centralized order and collectivism, sound nice on the surface, but when you look more closely, you will discover that control is the principle intention.

At the start of her comprehensive investigative report on Avaaz,26 Cory Morningstar makes some strong statements about a great deal of today's green and social movements, as noted below:

"The Ivy League bourgeoisie who sit at the helm of the non-profit industrial complex will one day be known simply as charismatic architects of death. Funded by the ruling class oligarchy, the role they serve for their funders is not unlike that of corporate media. Yet, it appears that global society is paralyzed in a collective hypnosis — rejecting universal social interests, thus rejecting reason, to instead fall in line with the position of the powerful minority that has seized control, a minority that systematically favours corporate interests.

"This investigative report examines the key founders of Avaaz, as well as other key sister organizations affiliated with Avaaz who, hand in hand with the Rockefellers, George Soros, Bill Gates and other powerful elites, are meticulously shaping global society by utilizing and building upon strategic psychological marketing, soft power, technology and social media — shaping public consensus, thus acceptance, for the illusory "green economy" and a novel sonata of 21st century colonialism. As we are now living in a world that is beyond dangerous, society must be aware of, be able to critically analyze, and ultimately reject the new onslaught of carefully orchestrated depoliticization, domestication of populace, propaganda and misinformation that is being perpetrated and perpetuated by the corporate elite and the current power structures that support their agenda. The non-profit industrial complex must be understood as a mainspring and the instrument of power, the very support and foundation of imperial domination."

---

[26] "Avaaz: Imperialistic Pimps of Militarism, Protectors of the Oligarchy, Trusted Facilitators of War," *The Wrong Kind of Green* Web site (September 10, 11, 18, and 24, 2012), http://wrongkindofgreen.org/2012/09/10/avaaz-imperialist-pimps-of-militarism-protectors-of-the-oligarchy-trusted-facilitators-of-war/.

With the right perspective, however, we can discover encouragement in this one-world-government initiative's very existence. A perilous One World Government threat is simply the natural, unavoidable polar opposite of our growing global voice and our transparent, ever-healthy forms of self-governance.

Once again, the choice is ours.

Which model do you support? The voting is going on everywhere, right now.

There is also a new, very special kind of war going on right now all over the world. More and more of us are starting to take notice and join the fight. While discussing war itself, and on the heels of the war on drugs, let us examine the establishment's open declaration of war on whistleblowers.

Edward Snowden, Julian Assange, Chelsea Manning, Aaron Swartz, and Karen Hudes are just some of the most recent notable names, which many of us know well by now. For those unfamiliar, these contemporary heroes are some of the most important stories of our time.

Whistle-blowing is under attack by authorities and is currently the only method we have to expose unjust practices within authority-driven systems. Just as guns are humanity's last form of physical protection, freedom of speech and whistle-blowing practices are the sole defense humanity has in the world of information against tyranny and authority run amok. That is, until we completely transition to transparent collaborative institutions.

Jesselyn Radack is another contemporary whistleblower. Her case ties our discussion on the human rights violations of suspected terrorists to the critical nature of whistle-blower practices.

She worked for the US Department of Justice as an ethics advisor and exposed the torture of John Walker Lindh. Her story is outlined in her book Traitor: The Whistleblower and the American Taliban.[27] Jesselyn Radack now works as a lawyer for whistle-blowers and the common good. After serving on the DC Bar's Legal Ethics Committee,

---

[27] Whistleblower Press (January 30, 2012).

she represented government contractors blowing the whistle on fraud and has since served as the director of National Security and Human Rights for the Government Accountability Project.

The Obama Administration has openly declared war on whistle-blowers.

If you are not convinced that whistle-blowers need our protection, check out Mike Masnick's June 21, 2013, article.28 He details more key campaign promises President Obama made back in 2008 to protect whistle-blowers that proved to be blatant lies.

Whistle-blowing is such an important part of our world, our revolution, and our healthy future that everyone needs to understand the vital and fragile nature of the activity.

Have a look at the list of whistle-blowers on Wikipedia. Even if you just focus on the last decade or two, then you can be the final judge, for the need to protect this process as well as these global heroes.29

The story of the modern age's most famous whistle-blower, Daniel Ellsberg, should also shed light on just how important this process is to each and every one of us.30 His story also neatly connects the whistle-blower process to the lie of war.

In 1971, Daniel Ellsberg shook America to its foundation by exposing a secret Pentagon study detailing how five presidents systematically lied to the American people about the Vietnam War. President Nixon's administration took a predictably similar approach to Obama's; Nixon's national security advisor Henry Kissinger declared Ellsberg the most dangerous man in America.31

---

[28] https://www.techdirt.com/articles/20130620/18182823551/obama-administration-has-declared-war-leakers-claims-any-leak-is-aiding-enemy.shtml (June 21, 2013).

[29] "Whistleblowers," *Wikipedia* Web site, http://en.wikipedia.org/wiki/List_of_whistleblowers

[30] http://www.ellsberg.net/bio.

[31] Seymour M. Hersh, "Kissinger and Nixon in the White House," *The Atlantic Monthly* (May 1982), http://www.theatlantic.com/past/docs/issues/82may/hershwh.htm.

> "Politics, as a practise, whatever its professions, has always been the systematic organization of hatreds."32
> - Henry Brooks Adams -

In 2009, the documentary film The Most Dangerous Man in America was nominated for the Academy Award for best documentary feature.33 The film tells some of the real story behind the Vietnam War and Daniel Ellsberg's globally acknowledged heroism. The documentary's website features a four-minute introduction to the film by Woody Harrelson.

It is now common knowledge that false flags are used to instigate war. The LBJ Presidential Tapes,34 declassified and released in 2001, prove that LBJ knew that the Gulf of Tonkin incident never happened. Most important, they show he lied about the incident and used it as an excuse to go to war.35

In 1962, Secretary of State Robert McNamara presented Operation Northwoods to President John F. Kennedy, who thankfully refused to use it as a means to make the American people go to war with Cuba.

The weapons of mass destruction lie and the most recent sarin gas false flag in Syria are just two more examples of this perpetual collusion.

This endless plague of wars that humankind has been engaged in around the world for as long as we can remember is completely unnecessary. Yes, this might sound overly simplistic, but it is not. This is a tough pill to swallow, so let us just keep on truckin' and discuss our final topic in the soulfully corrosive canon of war: WWII.

---

32 *The Education of Henry Adams* (1907).
33 Judith Ehrlich and Rick Goldsmith (Dirs. and Prods.), Kovno Communications (Prod. Co.), (January 29, 2009).
34 http://www2.gwu.edu/~nsarchiv/NSAEBB/NSAEBB132/tapes.htm
35 http://www.opsecnews.com/gulf-of-tonkin-incident-false-flag-for-war-in-vietnam/

Many believe that WWII was a noble and just war, one that was fought to prevent a fascist empire from taking over the world. It is easy to forget that many of our "sanctioned" history books are chiefly propaganda. The real stories are often buried, burnt, and lost. It is human nature for people to recount events with a personal bias.

> "Chief among the spoils of victory is the privilege of writing the history."[36]
> - Mark Alexander -

One book that does a beautiful job of unearthing pieces of our real history is The Rise and Fall of the Third Reich.[37] This nonfiction work by William L. Shirer chronicles the history of Nazi Germany from 1932 to 1945. It was first published in 1960 by Simon & Schuster in the US, where it won a National Book Award.

The book was a best seller, both in the United States and Europe, and a critical success outside Germany, where harsh criticism stimulated sales. Academic historians were generally negative.

Rise and Fall is based on captured Third Reich documents. These were the diaries of propaganda minister Joseph Goebbels, General Franz Halder, and Italian Foreign Minister Galeazzo Ciano. They contained evidence and testimonies from the Nuremberg trials, the British Foreign Office reports, and the author's views based on six years of reporting for the Third Reich. He worked for newspapers including the United Press International (UPI) and CBS Radio, which was terminated by the Nazi Party in 1940.[38]

Shirer wrote the following in the afterword of the thirtieth-anniversary edition of the book: "And though the academic historians, on the whole, were cool to the book and to me (as if I were a usurper with no right to invade their field — to write good history, they said,

---

[36] [Add cite]
[37] (New York: Simon and Schuster, 1960).
[38] [add pages from the book with his background details]

you had to teach it), there were notable exceptions." His comments clearly point to the rigid control of human history.

Whether we are looking back in history, at present, or into the future, the primary purposes behind war can only be control, power, and monetary gain. These things are nearly synonymous in an authority-driven world. Authority is preserved through secret agendas.

It is not a possibility that authorities mislead the people – it is a mathematical certainty. Only the most elite of the ruling class can accurately say what is in their minds and hearts, or what is actually said in all those backroom discussions.

Telling you and me the truth only hinders the divisive and controlling goals that are innate in any authority structure.

Shortly, we will discover how individual madness, psychopathy, and illness cannot bring about war or large-scale problems for the world anymore.

From some angles, the facts seem to indicate that another large reason for WWII was preventing Germany from becoming too independently powerful and weakening its economic strength. Bear in mind that economics and power struggles might be the most visible reasons, but the control, division, and weakening of both populations for easier future manipulation is always the primary purpose of war.

At the time, Britain was in an economic downturn but acting as a world banking empire. Its fiscal model was unsustainable. Germany, on the other hand, was manufacturing goods and services the world needed. As well as transferring large amounts of real, sustainable wealth. It seems possible then, that Britain decided to destroy Germany instead of creating its own sustainable sources of wealth.

We are not trying to defend Germany. Rather, we want to demonstrate that the rest of the world has shared responsibility and that printed and disseminated history is little more than propaganda.

It is also well documented that Germany and the Third Reich were both heavily supported by hard-core capitalists from countries which would later fight against them in the war. This pattern of funding volatile leaders and regimes, instigating unrest, and profiting in record numbers off the entire conflict – from its developing stages to the aftermath and rebuilding phases – is literally textbook behavior for the ruling elite.

Not only was WWII orchestrated, but it was also carried out with systematic logic for nothing more than personal gain for a small number of people. Most of us can agree that war seems to be driven by money and resources on the surface. WWII is not difficult to expose as similar in this way.

Money's greatest purchasing power, though, is control.

The ruling elite's strategies at that time might always remain unknown. Ultimately, Howard Zinn says it best in the following speech, "The Problem Is Civil Obedience,"[39] which was read by Matt Damon in a tribute to Zinn in February 2013.[40] Zinn describes our world's leaders like this: "...they smile, they shake hands, they smoke cigars — they really like one another no matter what they say."[41] He continues:

"Civil disobedience is not our problem. Our problem is civil obedience. Our problem is the numbers of people all over the world who have obeyed the dictates of the leaders of their government and have gone to war, and millions have been killed because of this obedience. And our problem is that scene in All Quiet on the Western Front where the schoolboys march off dutifully in a line to war. Our problem is that people are obedient all over the world, in the face

---

[39] Transcript of debate remarks at Johns Hopkins, reprinted in Howard Zinn, *Violence: The Crisis of American Confidence* (Johns Hopkins Press, 1972), http://www.informationclearinghouse.info/article36950.htm; http://www.thirdworldtraveler.com/Zinn/CivilObedience_ZR.htmlhttp://www.democraticunderground.com/discuss/duboard.php?az=view_all&address=132x3598598; http://www.thirdworldtraveler.com/Zinn/CivilObedience_ZR.html

[40] http://daily.represent.us/matt-damon-blows-your-mind/

[41] http://www.goodreads.com/quotes/163932-civil-disobedience-is-not-our-problem-our-problem-is-civil#;

The Freedom Handbook

of poverty and starvation and stupidity, and war and cruelty. Our problem is that people are obedient while the jails are full of petty thieves, and all the while the grand thieves are running the country."[42]

All that being said, some are likely still left wondering about Hitler himself and the need to stop his criminal madness.

Hitler and atrocities like school shootings cannot survive in our new world for two huge reasons. First, with transparency as the central force of our new awareness and activities – this all-seeing eye in the hands of common people – lies and hatred will have no place to hide, no place to grow and spread. Second, arbitrary authority is over, so rulers themselves will not be used or needed.

Eradicating individual and autocratic authority completely eliminates the potential for a criminal to gain any real power in the world. Transparency's role is not quite as clear, so let us break it down again. We cannot prevent the rise of individual evil. However, we can easily stop this type of illness from gaining any real ground. It will be much easier to identify and nullify before it reaches the out-of-hand state that Hitler's reign became.

Serious criminals of all kinds, and even school shooters, have nowhere to hide in a transparent world. If the transparent collective cannot rehabilitate a person through healthier communities, families, and a much earlier diagnosis, then we would be able to incarcerate the individual or protect the public well before any large-scale violence transpires.

War in our world today is a picture of how it has always been: a construct of power mongers. We are now ready to remove all arbitrary controls enslaving us. The freedom spoken about in this book and that is already alive and growing in so many of our communities and homes everywhere, will stop this forever-old pain and lie of war, dead in its tracks.

---

[42] http://www.goodreads.com/quotes/163932-civil-disobedience-is-not-our-problem-our-problem-is-civil#;

It is time to end war.

> "No one wins. It's a war of man."43
> - Neil Young -

If dog is man's best friend, war has been the best friend of tyranny, ever ready to defend its master. Common people suffer manipulation, the autopsy of our potential, the fracturing of our souls.

> "The best weapon against an enemy is another enemy."44
> - Friedrich Nietzsche -

Let us consider the words of Nietzsche.

Like him or hate him, he did nail the centillion-dollar war and peace-on-earth problem in a nine-word sentence. Think about it – there is no better way to keep us busy. This war story is about fostering acceptance, but it could have begun and ended with Nietzsche's quotation.

Most of us, understandably, demand more evidence.

When we stop catapulting others into power, stop voting others into command and capitulating, when arbitrary authority has no money or power anymore because we outright refuse, watch nearly all humanity's collective pain, fear, and injustice disappear.

War is a distracting stick used to beat us, but only after convincing us to beat our cousins. Actually, it is as often used to maim and murder us, as it is to incite our families to fight on our behalf.

War is and always has been a buzzing lie used to confuse, divide, and conquer the common masses. Freedom needs us to be ready

---

[43] Quoted by Kenneth G. Bielen, *The Words and Music of Neil Young* (...add data), 75.

[44] Quoted by Roy D. Morey in *The United Nations at Work in Asia* (McFarland, 2013), 96.

to defend ourselves against individual power reaching arbitrary authority.

Here are three things we can do right now to end war forever:

Cut off our financial support. We are the ones actually paying for war, and we have the right to decide what we support and what we do not. Do not support war anymore. Instead, let us all send our money to organizations that heal and help. Together we can deem them truly interested in and capable of making a positive impact. With no money to spend, arbitrary authority and war will end quickly, and all the old tools and infrastructure will be left for us to re-purpose and re-create, transparently.

Refuse to go to war. Some of you might be already willing and able to walk away and take your weapons home. A militia is a common-sense, necessary force. Some will need to continue to work in the military until our communities can provide new forms of employment. The bottom line remains: no more fighting. Train, get paid, but refuse to kill.

Even those of you who have been trained to kill for the majority of your adult lives probably do not ever want to kill another human being, and it will not take long for those who have had illusions about the grandeur of murder and war to realize what the rest of us already know. Once again, we are left with only the psychopaths and sociopaths keen to continue this business of killing and war.

Stop voting altogether. If Mouseland did not convince you how fruitless and even counterproductive voting is, check out Russell Brand's interview with BBC Newsnight's Jeremy Paxman to stoke your conviction.[45] By refusing to vote, participate in, and fund the systems in power, we nonviolently remove all control these authorities have over us and can instead wield our collective voice in a healthier fashion.

---

[45] http://www.youtube.com/watch?v=BHDcOBgWZqc (posted October 24, 2013).

In closing, we turn to Aristotle – the philosopher who informed and created what would become western thought. As such, let us soak up his thoughts on tyranny:

"Such are the notes of the tyrant and the arts by which he preserves his power; there is no wickedness too great for him. All that we have said may be summed up under three heads, which answer to the three aims of the tyrant. These are, (1) the humiliation of his subjects; he knows that a mean-spirited man will not conspire against anybody; (2) the creation of mistrust among them; for a tyrant is not overthrown until men begin to have confidence in one another; and this is the reason why tyrants are at war with the good; they are under the idea that their power is endangered by them, not only because they would not be ruled despotically but also because they are loyal to one another, and to other men, and do not inform against one another or against other men; (3) the tyrant desires that his subjects shall be incapable of action, for no one attempts what is impossible, and they will not attempt to overthrow a tyranny, if they are powerless. Under these three heads the whole policy of a tyrant may be summed up, and to one or other of them all his ideas may be referred: (1) he sows distrust among his subjects; (2) he takes away their power; (3) he humbles them."[46]

"The penalty good men pay for indifference to public affairs is to be ruled by evil men."[47]
- Plato -

We all know in our hearts that we have no right to kill.

---

[46] *Politics,* Book V, Part XI.
[47] *Republic,* Book I, Section 347c.

> *"Man has no right to kill his brother. It is no excuse that he does so in uniform: he only adds the infamy of servitude to the crime of murder."*[48]
> — Percy Bysshe Shelley —

> *"If we don't end war, war will end us."*[49]
> — H.G. Wells —

> *"War is only a cowardly escape from the problems of peace."*[50]
> — Thomas Mann —

The infamy of servitude, war's lie, and humanity's fear compels us to act. Our shame can fuel the red-hot flame of liberty's righteous victory. We will burn down the walls of oppression quickly only if we share our acceptance and pain. When humans see pain in others, we feel. In the company of friends, the dark night of all souls becomes a warm sunny day.

Imagine…a world finally freed and at peace with its people the best of friends.

---

[48] "Declaration of Rights" (1812), article 19.
[49] *Things to Come* (1936).
[50] Quoted by Edward R. Murrow in *This I Believe* (1956), 16.

CHAPTER TEN

- Religious Institutions -

"The world is my country, all mankind are my brethren, and to do good is my religion."[1]
- Thomas Paine -

"This is my simple religion. There is no need for temples; no need for complicated philosophy. Our own brain, our own heart is our temple; the philosophy is kindness."[2]
- Dalai Lama -

Few subjects are more sensitive than religion, so we must preface this part of our conversation with the following statement. Luke and I have an abundant appreciation for all the world's spiritual traditions. We do not condemn any religion, belief system, or form of faith.

Religion is pure, and yet the institution of religion is an affront to freedom. The church, like all state installations, is nothing more than humanity's holiest intentions and capacities bent, borrowed, stolen, and twisted into weapons that divide and pit us against one another.

This chapter is a celebration of all that is good, true, and should remain in the practice of the world's great religions. Real religiousness, the compassion and good in us all, is the motor of our new strength. It is the heart of our new machine. Our last planetary war, our global coup, and all the new structures and solutions emerging in the world need our faith as well as our sense.

---

[1] *The Age of Reason* (1794).
[2] *Kindness and Compassion*, 52.

We respectfully ask the atheists among us to please substitute words such as "religion" and "faith" for "compassion," "love," "empathy," "courage," and "community," as you so often do anyway.

Humanity needs all the virtue our religions have ever offered in order to both decipher and compose the delicate nuances of our new rich communal song.

Seek in the fearful abyss within. It is time to surrender to the brutal, quiet honesty deep in our hearts, time to shred and burn to ash ideas filled with disease. It is time to distill the world's core spiritual messages and rewrite the truths therein openly, and without restraint.

Our sacred books were re-written once, twice, many times, and by many hands, so many years ago that their message has been diluted. Let us seize these old books and blaze a fresh trail, a translucent and transcendent interpretation of the truth that allows us to thrive. The only ideas that are left behind are the outdated and violent ones, the ones that breed division and hate.

Arguing that tradition is an essential glue holding religion together is the same as arguing that someone's culture is dependent on a country's borders. If the world had no borders, and all religious texts were lost forever, humanity's cultural and religious knowledge and practices would likely experience a glorious rebirth, a renaissance of appreciation, depth, and beauty.

Imagine there's no heaven
It's easy if you try
No hell below us
Above us only sky
Imagine all the people
Living for today

Imagine there's no countries
It isn't hard to do
Nothing to kill or die for
And no religion too
Imagine all the people
Living life in peace

You may say I'm a dreamer
But I'm not the only one
I hope someday you'll join us
And the world will be as one

- John Lennon -3

Religion is meant to be a powerful and healthy influence, but by allowing our spiritual melody to be warped into firm, clashing ideals, we serve darkness, hate and fear.

There are certainly pure sentiments at the heart of all religious institutions; however, this truth does not diminish the horrors and atrocities performed daily in the name of religious conviction.

Hate is spoken only by the most extreme religious fundamentalists, yet our media focuses on magnifying the problem. This focus spreads fear and more hate.

> *"I love you when you bow in your mosque, kneel in your temple, pray in your church. For you and I are sons of one religion, and it is the spirit."* 4
> *- Kahlil Gibran -*

---

[3] "Imagine,' John Lennon single, written by John Lennon, produced by Phil Spector, *Imagine* (Apple, 1971).

[4] Quoted in Foreword by Simon Parke, of Kahlil Gibran, *The Forerunner* (White Crow Productions: 2010).

Regardless of your specific views or beliefs, all you must do is look around to see that the religious experiments conducted over the past few thousand years have not led to any real advancement in our civilization.

Consider the word "experiment." Everything in life is only an experiment. Free will, the most sacred gift of all, joyfully sees to that.

Human beings are always free to choose something new, or to experiment with what they know. Even if you resist change, the choice to do the same things repeatedly is an experiment. With each passing day, more people realize that clinging to archaic ideas can be tragic and that humanity has a ton of old thinking and old practices invested in powerful institutions, entrenched authorities that must be purged for change to happen.

Religion is also dangerous when we think of it as the sole means for salvation. The renowned thirteenth-century Sufi poet and mystic Rumi provides us with the following story:

Trust God But Tie Your Camel

There was once a man who was on his way back home from market with his camel and, as he had had a good day, he decided to stop at a mosque along the road and offer his thanks to God.

He left his camel outside, went in with his prayer mat, and spent several hours offering thanks to Allah, praying and promising that he would be a good Muslim in the future, help the poor and be an upstanding pillar of his community.

When he emerged, it was already dark and lo and behold—his camel was gone! He immediately flew into a violent temper and shook his fist at the sky, yelling: "You traitor, Allah! How could you do this to me? I put all my trust in you and then you go and stab me in the back like this!"

A passing Sufi dervish heard the man yelling and chuckled to himself.

"Listen," he said, "Trust God but, you know, tie up your camel."

Common sense dictates that you lock your front door when you leave home.

Hoping that the divine will win our human rights battles is obviously much more dangerous than hoping it will protect against property theft.

Many of us also find ourselves wishing for the ever-hoped-for mass spiritual awakening, especially today, amidst such suffering.

> *"Hope in reality is the worst of all evils because it prolongs the torments of man."*5
> *- Friedrich Nietzsche -*

Hope is both a terrible danger and a beautiful seed waiting to blossom. Without loving, liquid action, hope becomes blind and impotent, and our ugliness is left unchallenged to reign.

Religion's guidance has certainly advanced our treatment of one another, but history also reveals old, oozing, open wounds, and foul, unnerving scars that cover our bodies. Religion has been used more than any other excuse to instigate suffering and war.

> *"When missionaries came to Africa they had the Bible and we had the land. They said 'Let us pray.' We closed our eyes. When we opened them we had the Bible and they had the land."*6
> *- Desmond Tutu -*

Now, think about how religion's steely fist has undeniably delayed our advancement as a race by tyrannically working to stifle the "ideas" humans now call science.

---

[5] *Human, All Too Human* (1878).
[6] Quoted in Steven Gish, *Desmond Tutu: A Biography* (Greenwood, 2004), 101.

We can learn from the efforts of our forefathers. Let us gently remove each other's apathetic blinders and follow the path to freedom carved for us in our ancestors' blood in the Magna Carta.[7] The charter, signed in 1215, required King John of England to proclaim that his will was not arbitrary.

Common folk stood up and fought to protect their freedoms. They had learned the hard way not to rely on an authority to speak for God or create the path to salvation.

Then, in two stunning displays of arrogance and elitist, tyrannical behavior – both King John and Pope Innocent III renounced the agreement immediately after signing it. The king renounced it publicly right after the barons who had forced him to sign it left.

The Pope then annulled the "shameful and demeaning agreement, forced upon the King by violence and fear."[8] He saw it as an affront to the Church's authority over the king and the "papal territories" of England and Ireland.

No individual rightfully holds religious authority over any idea or person. The moment we adopt beliefs or direction from any institution, religious or not, we are lost.

> *"The tyranny of a prince in an oligarchy is not so dangerous to the public welfare as the apathy of a citizen in a democracy."*[9]
> *- Charles de Montesquieu -*

It is time to look at the central thread of life again.

All of us are symbiotic at every level, as is our environment and every element in nature. All our spiritual texts point to an energetic

---

[7] "Magna Carta," *The History Learning Site* (n.d.), http://www.historylearningsite.co.uk/magna_carta.htm.

[8] "Featured Documents," *U.S. National Archives and Records Administration,* http://www.archives.gov/exhibits/featured_documents/magna_carta/legacy.html.

[9] *The Spirit of the Laws* (1748).

connection among all life. Thankfully, math and physics finally caught up to this great spiritual truth within the last seventy-five years.10

Eastern traditions call this life force, or energy permeating all living things, by a few names: "qi," "prana," "mana," and others. If you prefer a more scientific approach, Dr. Fred Alan Wolf's recent movie, What the Bleep Do We Know?!, brilliantly summarizes definitive scientific support for this spiritual fact.11

Everything and everyone is connected. All living things around the world are joined, animated, and sustained by the same fundamental energy. In fact, as we manipulate or affect energy in one place or moment in time, all other energy in the universe is affected as well across all planes of time and space, instantly.

Einstein referred to this phenomenon as the "spooky action at a distance" of quantum entanglement.12 Thus, if we are all one energetic milieu, we are all connected simultaneously to a source, no matter the name we attach to it.

No woman, man, religious institution, or leader can tell us anything about our souls, our places in the world, or God's will because we already know these ultimate truths. The answers have been inside of us, outside of us, and all around us for all of time.

This connection that we humans have with truth, with ourselves, with our hearts and minds, and with the divine could be far healthier and stronger than it is.

---

10 See, for example, Gary Zukav's summary of the discussions at a conference of eastern and western scientists at the Esalen Institute, CA, in 1976, in *The Dancing Wu Li Masters: An Overview of the New Physics* (Morrow: 1979).

11 William Antz, Betsy Chasse, and Mark Vicente (Directors, Producers) (2004.

12 "Einstein's 'Spooky Action at a Distance' Paradox Older than Thought," *MIT Technology Review* Web site (March 8, 2012), http://www.technologyreview.com/view/427174/einsteins-spooky-action-at-a-distance-paradox-older-than-thought/; "Quantum 'Spooky Action at a Distance' Travels at least 10,000 Faster than Light," *Physics News* Web site, http://www.physnews.com/physics-news/cluster510279516/.

In my darkest hour, life taught me to seek the truth within myself, to silence myself and listen for the answers I had forgotten. Early in life, I began watching the world and even myself from a secret place of objectivity.

When we watch ourselves, when we take even a half second and look for meaning within ourselves about the events that shape our lives, the answers become obvious.

For all of us, our deepest crises in life bring us to the Dark Night of the Soul, a powerful experience and an inescapable part of being human. The concept is so big and central to growing up, becoming a better person and revolutionary change, both inside and out, that it has its own chapter later in this very book.

Think about how often you hear of people abandoning previous beliefs and turning to the world's great traditions for answers when faced with the toughest moments in their lives. Some decide to study and investigate religious teachings while others take a more scientific or philosophical approach, which is in no way less valid. The path is different for everyone.

> *"God is a metaphor for a mystery that absolutely transcends all human categories of thought, even the categories of being and non-being. Those are categories of thought. I mean it's as simple as that."*[13]
> *- Joseph Campbell -*

Let us strengthen the inner faculties and communicative muscles that God, or the universe, or whatever term you prefer, gave us to wield our true power and potential.

---

[13] *Joseph Campbell: A Hero's Journey,* documentary (2000), at 00:04 point.

> "For to be free is not merely to cast off one's chains, but to live in a way that respects and enhances the freedom of others." 14
> - Nelson Mandela -

You need to let other people live their lives, express, and enjoy their beliefs in whatever ways their hearts tell them is right. You also do not need institutional authority to guide you in any way. Rules, laws, restrictions, and obligations of any kind are all potential keystones in the bridge to our slavery and oppression.

You cannot say you want freedom and then hand your soul over to a religious corporation. To be truly free, you must retain control of your whole being, your mind, spirit, and body. When we renounce decrepit doctrine, we reclaim our responsibility to self-govern and commune with the divine ourselves; anything less and we will never be free.

> "I share the belief of many of my contemporaries that the spiritual crisis pervading all spheres of Western industrial society can be remedied only by a change in our world view. We shall have to shift from the materialistic, dualistic belief that people and their environment are separate, toward a new consciousness of an all-encompassing reality, which embraces the experiencing ego, a reality in which people feel their oneness with animate nature and all of creation." 15
> - Dr. Albert Hoffman -

---

[14] *Long Walk to Freedom: The Autobiography of Nelson Mandela* (Hachette Book Group, 1995), 154.

[15] Foreword, *LSD: My Problem Child* (1980),

We must remind ourselves about the central thread of life, which is the symbiosis that is the most basic concept of biology. We use the term "symbiosis" throughout our discussions to focus attention on this central shift in mentality that we, as a species, must undertake.

Much has been said about this need to alter our collective thinking.

Luke and I have found through discussions with average people that many, if not most of us, are already developing a greater sense of symbiosis and are acknowledging the need to sustainably remodel all human activities. Essentially, most of us have already assumed a much more global and connected worldview.

This is encouraging.

By all means, joyfully worship, pray, and believe. Only the forced opinions and institutions of old are dead. Instead of relying on dead and meaningless words and rituals, gather together and organize however you desire, honor and distil the timeless virtue and depth in these ancient teachings, and drop the harmful dogma once and for all. Celebrate and share.

Humanity needs to prevent judgment and fear from being used as motivators. This is our shared responsibility.

With that said, it is time to talk about the idea of sin. Jesus Christ himself once said, "Let the one among you who is without sin, be the first to cast a stone."

> *"The most unpardonable sin in society is independence of thought."*[16]
> *- Emma Goldman -*

Religious institutions have made innumerable claims regarding judgment and sin. Again, we can clearly identify the desire to divide,

---

[16] Anarchism and Other Essays, 3rd rev. ed., ch. 2 (1917), http://quotes.dictionary.com/The_most_unpardonable_sin_in_society_is_independence#2wqbLYyZuO4YHGLT.99.

restrict, enslave, and oppress the populous with a set of arbitrary conditions.

Sin, even according to the Bible, is an idea for the divine to explore, not man. We are using the Bible as an example, as it is the easiest reference for many Western populations.

> *"Judge not, that you be not judged. For with the judgment you pronounce you will be judged, and with the measure you use it will be measured to you. Why do you see the speck that is in your brother's eye, but do not notice the log that is in your own eye? Or how can you say to your brother, 'Let me take the speck out of your eye,' when there is the log in your own eye? You hypocrite, first take the log out of your own eye, and then you will see clearly to take the speck out of your brother's eye."*
> *- Matthew 7:1 -*

According to the Christian faith, if a person does not accept Jesus Christ as their savior then they will go to hell. Yet, many Christians do not actually believe that their loved ones who hold different views are doomed to eternal damnation. This willingness to flex beliefs is indicative of the type of compromise and fresh, common sense thinking it takes to rewrite and reinterpret our spiritual texts.

Ideas about sin and judgment can be ascribed to human writers, translators, and church "editors." Moreover, these ideas enable religious institutions to place behemoth internal footholds within us to strengthen their authority.

> *"Eskimo: 'If I did not know about God and sin, would I go to hell?' Priest: 'No, not if you did not know.' Eskimo: 'Then why did you tell me?'"* [17]
> *- Annie Dillard -*

Not too long ago, church leaders had the audacity to charge people to wash away their sins. They claimed that they had divine abilities, that they alone could prevent us and our loved ones from going to Hell.

This practice sounds so insane, so corrupt and appalling to our modern ear, it is hard to believe humans lived that way. Hindsight always provides this kind of perspective for individuals and humanity as a whole. Think about how you feel when you look back on slavery in the United States. Think about the last hard lesson you learned about being a better human being.

Now, think about how all your previous errors in life make you feel today.

Imagine how we will all feel as we look back on the ways we have allowed religious institutions to subvert and pollute our minds, spirits, and most holy ideals. Imagine how we will all feel as we look back on the ways we have allowed small numbers to rule over us for so long.

Thankfully, humanity can prevent the further tarnishing of its religious goodness. We can eradicate individual tyranny and oppressive power. As our solidarity grows, all we need to do is stand together and not waver in our convictions.

We can completely destroy any power that arbitrary authority has over the greater population in short order if we only stand together. Somewhere along the road, we will reach the necessary level of solidarity to redefine ourselves and discover our true power and the path to self-governance.

---

[17] *Pilgrim at Tinker's Creek* (New York: Harpers Magazine Press, 1974).

The pace we set is up to us.

Examine the Gnostic Gospels[18] and compare them to the King James Bible if you do not believe that religion as we know it was manipulated for purely selfish ends. There is furious debate about the truth regarding the enormous and careful editing, cutting, and slicing of the bible.[19] It is established fact that before radio, television, public education, or any modern propaganda techniques, ruling powers manipulated our most hallowed teachings to better control the general population.

The victors in war can rewrite history as they see fit. Most conquering powers rewrote the spiritual traditions and histories of the natives. Often, the victors would blend two religious traditions, not to ease acclimation but to destroy the identity, history, unity, power, and will of an entire culture.

> *"The most effective way to destroy people is to deny and obliterate their own understanding of their history."*[20]
> - George Orwell -

Furthermore, the ruling elite have continually studied the best methods to control the common masses.[21] Influencing the minds of the people was understood thousands of years ago to produce far superior results than mere physical control.

> *"A tyrant must put on the appearance of uncommon devotion to religion. Subjects are less apprehensive*

---

[18] "The Nag Hammadi Library," *The Gnostic Society Library* Web site (n.d.), http://gnosis.org/naghamm/nhl.html.
[19] http://www.rense.com/general66/hide.htm
[20] *Nineteen Eighty-four.*
[21] Edward Bernays, *Propaganda* (New York: Ig Publishing, 2004).

> *of illegal treatment from a ruler whom they consider god-fearing and pious. On the other hand, they do less easily move against him, believing that he has the gods on his side."22*
> *-Aristotle -*

The idea of mass mind control is difficult to think about, but it is something that we must consider and study before dismissing outright. To this end, judge for yourself the extent of these control systems by exploring the works of Walter Lippmann and Edward Bernays.

The film <u>Psywar</u> 23 contains some of the most riveting and recommended material that we can offer in this study. In fact, this documentary is second in that list of top three must-sees mentioned back in Chapter Eight.

> *"The conscious and intelligent manipulation of the organized habits and opinions of the masses is an important element in democratic society. Those who manipulate this unseen mechanism of society constitute an invisible government which is the true ruling power of our country...we are governed, our minds are molded, our tastes formed, our ideas suggested, largely by men we have never heard of. This is a logical result of the way in which our democratic society is organized. Vast numbers of human beings must cooperate in this manner if they are to live together as a smoothly functioning society...in almost every act of our daily lives, whether in the sphere*

---

[22] *Politics,* Book V.
[23] Written, directed, and produced by Scott Noble (Metanoia, 2010), <u>http://www.openfilm.com/channels/Durrutix</u>.

> *of politics or business, in our social conduct or our ethical thinking, we are dominated by the relatively small number of persons... who understand the mental processes and social patterns of the masses. It is they who pull the wires which control the public mind."* [24]
> *- Edward L. Bernays -*

In ancient times, conquering rulers would have been remiss if they had not taken the opportunity to re-craft the spiritual traditions of the times. Doing so allowed them to significantly shape the minds of the masses for their own controlling ends.

With this in mind, it is absolutely necessary to reclaim the integrity of our holy books. We must distill the core truths from our many sacred texts.

Think back on how many children, women, and men have been persecuted and killed over the past ten, fifty, one hundred, or one thousand years over religious matters.

What is most upsetting is that we gave these few people the authority to kill, even if we were not in uniform at the time ourselves. Through our apathy and fear, we are ultimately responsible for every atrocity enacted upon us.

> *"I am not a victim. I am alive, wide awake and free from the numbness of apathy."* [25]
> *- Rokelle Lerner -*

After thousands of years of the same old thing, we continue to allow religion to pollute our minds and souls and those of our children, effectively spiritually crippling the generations to come.

---

[24] *Propaganda* (Ig Publishing, 2004), 37-38.
[25] *Daily Affirmations for Adult Children of Alcoholics* (HCI, 1991, 1996)

Will this go on forever? Logic tells us no, because all things die and change. When becomes the question we must ask, and the shift has already begun. With your help, we can and should speed things up.

> *"Those who choose not to empathize enable real monsters, for without ever committing an act of outright evil ourselves we collude with it through our apathy."*[26]
> - J. K. Rowling -

Religion and spirituality are not naturally comprised of fear. Guidance should take the form of reassurance rather than retribution.

Picture what would happen if you arrive in front of your God, waiting to receive your so-called judgment, and he or she asks you, "How could you go to war and kill your neighbor whilst professing to believe in me?"

Your only answer would be that of any good slave: "Our religious and political leaders said this war was just, good, and sanctified in the name of you, God, and our good country. They said the enemies were heathen terrorists and deserved their fate."

Good luck with that excuse.

Christians are likely familiar with the following statements: "Love your neighbor as yourself"[27] and "Do unto others as you would have them do unto you."[28] These perfectly simple ideas could create a world that is very different from the one we see.

The Golden Rule withers and eventually falls apart as we flap our lips, go to church to echo sentiments we never truly think about as we

---

[26] Harvard Commencement Address (June 5, 2008), http://vimeo.com/1711302.
[27] Leviticus 18:18; Matthew 19:19; Mark 12:31; Luke 10:27.
[28] Matthew 7:12.

turn around and support the military. We will even send our children off to die and vote for politicians who support the wars that kill them.

This hypocritical behavior exists everywhere, in every nation on earth and politicians and corporations twist the intent of religion, and then blame religion for being the root of all evil.

They are wrong to do so. Only we can perpetrate and condone evil.

We should all be ashamed of our inaction and lack of thought.

If we claim to be Christians, Spiritualists, Jews, or Muslims, to have faith of any kind, or claim to be upstanding citizens while supporting any of the decisions our states or churches make for us, then we are not spiritual, religious, or compassionate.

Doing any of those things makes us hypocrites.

There is no defense for this. The institution of religion has become just another lie that excuses us from our responsibility to govern ourselves.

People are loving, kind, and good as a whole. We need no rules or laws to remind us how to behave. There are always individual exceptions, but even if some of us are not as wholly "good" as others, common sense, transparency, the new conjoined community, and infallible justice is far too much for any individual evil to bear.

United for the first time, we will finally witness the full beauty of humanity.

This question of how to deal with those exceptions of that inherent goodness is always one of the last to remain in discussions on removing authority. People ask, "Not everyone's caring and good. What do we do about them?"

Let us clarify the previous paragraph and take one more run through the simple common sense truths and solutions.

Yes, some hear only hateful and murderous murmurs in their sickened hearts and minds, so communities will rise to their rightful, responsible, and transparent places as healers and keepers of sense, peace, justice and compassion. Community means thousands of local and global layers of union and coauthored guardianship of freedom.

The bottom line is that there is nowhere for individual criminal behavior to flourish anymore. Our transparent, all-seeing eye is incorruptible.

Religion is such a touchy subject because we have been divided a hundred times and then a hundred times again. We have been conquered and conditioned by manipulation in the form of religion for thousands upon thousands of years.

You might now clearly see the millennia-old relationships between war and fear and religion and fear. Not to mention the history, education, information and propaganda and all the underlying fear inherent in each of those institutionalized studies. Notice the heightened tensions between Islam and the rest of the religious and even secular world at present, yet again.

> *"The minority, the ruling class at present, has the schools and press, usually the Church as well, under its thumb. This enables it to organize and sway the emotions of the masses, and make its tool of them."*[29]
> *- Albert Einstein -*

All state and church institution are ineffective when it comes to offering true care, compassion, or solutions. Religion of old is designed only to constrain and contain a brilliant being - you.

You are nothing short of divine. We are all built of love and energy, and so before we talk of evil again, let us revel in dreams of us.

> *"When you are joyous, look deep into your heart and you shall find it is only that which has given*

---

[29] Quoted by Steven J. Bartlett in *The Pathology of Man: A Study of Human Evil* (Charles C. Thomas Publisher, 2005), 82.

> *you sorrow that is giving you joy. When you are sorrowful look again in your heart, and you shall see that in truth you are weeping for that which has been your delight."* 30
> - Kahlil Gibran -

Two messages sewn on pieces of cloth have hung in my home for the past fifteen years. They can be traced back to highly idealistic, youthful times, when I lived in Toronto and worked as a bicycle messenger.

The first was penned by His Holiness the 14th Dalai Lama, and it is kept in the bathroom so guests are forced to attend to business and think, "We are visitors on this planet for 90 or 100 years at most. During that period, we must try to do something good, something useful, with our lives. If you contribute to other people's happiness, you will find that goal. This is the true meaning of life."31

The second, also written by His Holiness the 14th Dalai Lama, outlines some universal religious responsibilities: "The very purpose of religion is to control yourself, not to criticize others. Rather, we must criticize ourselves. How much am I doing about my anger? About my attachment, about my hatred, about my pride, my jealousy? These are the things which we must check in daily life with the knowledge of Buddhist teachings.32

The Dalai Lama has also advised: "Taking your own body and mind as the laboratory, see if you can use these different techniques: that is to say, engage in some thorough-going research on your own

---

[30] *The Prophet in Kahlil Gibran: The Collected Works* (New York: Alfred A. Knopf/Random House, 2007), 116.

[31] "Tibetan Spiritual Leader Charms Calgary," *His Holiness the 14th Dalai Lama of Tibet* Web site (October 2, 2009), http://www.dalailama.com/news/post/407-tibetan-spiritual-leader-charms-calgary.

[32] "A Talk to Western Buddhists," *The Dalai Lama, A Policy of Kindness: An Anthology by and about the Dalai Lama*, ed. Sidney Piburn (Snow Lion Publications, 1990), 87.

mental functioning and examine the possibility of making some positive changes within yourself."33

> *"Your hearts know in silence the secrets of the days and nights. But your ears thirst for the sound of your hearts knowledge. You would know in words that which you have always known in thought. You would touch with your fingers the naked body of your dreams."34*

> *"Nor shall derision prove powerful against those who listen to humanity or those who follow in the footsteps of divinity, for they shall live forever. Forever."35*
> — Kahlil Gibran —

Let us relearn what kind of a transition we can expect.

> *"When God desires to destroy a thing, he entrusts its destruction to the thing itself. Every bad institution of this world ends by suicide."36*
> — Victor Hugo —

We have discussed rewriting our religious doctrines, but we may not need to. The suggestion is meant to focus our common sense on the core of the matter at hand, which is to consider the real value of our current religious ideas and systems, where this value comes from, and what to do with it.

---

[33] *The World of Tibetan Buddhism: An Overview of Its Philosophy and Practice* (Wisdom Publications, 1995), 4.
[34] *The Prophet*, 54.
[35] *The Treasured Writings of Kahlil Gibran* (Open Road Media, 2011).
[36] *The Works of Victor Hugo* (MobileReference, 2008).

The temptation to rewrite our holy books may be too great for our religious scholars and leaders to resist. We have encouraged this idea so far, to open minds and better prepare us all to re-create our beliefs about life, but thinking about re-writing our holy books should hopefully send shivers running down millions of spines.

If we just look in our hearts, we can see that humanity needs written instructions just as badly as it needs kings, queens, or rulers of any kind.

What exactly is being done and how can you plug into the positive changes being made to religion? Here are three ways to start:

Cut off your financial support. When you contribute to authority-driven systems, you agree to be ruled. Do not agree. Let us all pool our resources with like-spirited neighbors and re-form our spiritual organizations with transparency and our true peaceful natures.

Build new communities, organizations, and structures, first online and then offline, to house our spiritual practices. Do what you do now. Just join in a fresh setting, free from corruption.

Help dissolve our old institutions and redistribute the collected wealth of our spiritual establishments.

> *"Don't give your money to the church. They should be giving their money to you."*[37]
> *- George Carlin -*

We are the rightful owners of untold material wealth, art, and whole libraries of ideas and texts within intuitions like the Vatican.

Humanity owns all of this. We have contributed. It is time we open the vaults, see what's been hiding inside, and decide how best to re-purpose our treasures and resources. Imagine all the things we will have learned by the time we are through cataloguing the entire hidden human heritage.

---

[37] "Interview with Jesus," *A Place for My Stuff* (Atlantic, 1981).

Dissolving old institutions means voting for this change by joining the collected voice that grows in reach and power every day. This world belongs to the common people, to everyone.

By uniting our voices, we can deal out any changes decided on together. Become a part of humanity's global cry for self-governance, peace, and freedom by participating in online campaigns through new, open-sourced microphones and methods like those inspired by Avaaz[38] and SumofUs[39].

Let us create new agendas and incorruptible, transparent platforms if Avaaz and others have let us down. Let us be relentless.

Be prepared for when you are called to join us in the streets. We will be drumming our way to the dissolution of these expired institutions.

There is room for all types of choices in our new world, including the choice to stick with old patterns. If you are ready for healthy change, decide for yourself what feels comfortable.

Help rewrite our religious texts or join a group working with the existing ones happily. Get rid of your priests and religious leaders and elect new ones, or choose to work with the ones you have and help them purge themselves and your church from the larger institution of religion.

Remember, smaller localized test areas and initiatives allow us to experiment with ideas and systems that can later be scaled around the world to free us all.

Wait for the bandwagon to arrive at your doorstep and hop aboard, for your human family will be glad to have you. Alternatively, look us change-makers up and help us build more wagons.

The choice is yours.

More ways to plug in and find your change-making family are coming.

---

[38] *Avaaz* Web site, avaaz.org
[39] *SumofUs* Web site, sumofus.org.

Our danger meter must be golden-rulish. When we direct our fellow populace with too much force in our words or hearts, thereby clothing them in our ideas and cutting them off from their own, we are doomed.

If we guide each other through dynamic suggestions built of love, we will grow a healthy appreciation for the essence and purpose behind each and every opinion and religious message.

We need to become master artisans and join Michelangelo as we reach out and make God out of art supplies.

> *"Look. Art knows no prejudice, art knows no boundaries, art doesn't really have judgment in its purest form. So just go, just go."*[40]
> *- K.D. Lang -*

---

[40] "Happy Birthday, k.d. lang," *ReadReidRead* Web site (November 2, 2011), http://readreidread.wordpress.com/2011/11/02/happy-birthday-k-d-lang/.

CHAPTER ELEVEN

- Monetary Systems -

> *"Money plays the largest part in determining the course of history."*[1]
> *- Karl Marx -*

> *"Money is a new form of slavery, and distinguishable from the old simply by the fact that it is impersonal—that there is no human relation between master and slave."*[2]
> *- Leo Tolstoy -*

Monetary systems serve the system of slavery more quickly and with greater certainty than any other institutionalized form of control.

The real truth behind our money is authorities biggest secret.

> *"It is well enough that people of the nation do not understand our banking and monetary system, for if they did, I believe there would be a revolution before tomorrow morning."*
> *- Henry Ford -*

The truth is often incomprehensible at first. People become furious when they find out they have been robbed on a level that's difficult to even grasp as being possible. It is strange how money can sometimes

---

[1] Communist Manifesto.
[2] What Shall We Do Then? (1886)

stir emotion and even action more effectively than education and violations of our freedoms and body.

Each of us can agree that money is a huge driving force in our world. Let us use its motivating power for good for a change. As passionate as many people are about material wealth, most do not know the first thing about our financial systems.

> *"In our time, the curse is monetary illiteracy, just as inability to read plain print was the curse of earlier centuries."*3
> *- Ezra Pound -*

Money makes the world go round, we are told. It is the new root of ultimate evil, above any law, and its systems are so convoluted and confusing that they leave us common folk out in the cold and broke.

> *"Persecution readily knits friendship between its victims."*4
> *- Ralph Waldo Emerson -*

Worry not, friends. We know that this fiscal tale is grim as grim can be, but your human family will deliver simple solutions made of mirth, good sense, and transparent collaboration.

Most people are eager to share knowledge.

You likely enjoy telling other people about new things you have learned. Think about the last time you learned something new at

---

[3] Guide to Kulchur, pt. 4, sect. 8, ch. 31 (1938).
[4] Persecution_readily_knits_friendship_between_its_victims. Dictionary.com. *Columbia World of Quotations.* Columbia University Press, 1996. http://quotes.dictionary.com/Persecution_readily_knits_friendship_between_its_victims (accessed: February 03, 2014).

work that made your job easier. Everyone feels this same sense of enjoyment when sharing newfound knowledge and its benefits.

Even though humans do this naturally, we have gotten better at encouraging one another over the years of our civilization all the way until the present day. This book has outlined some of the many ways education itself is improving and shattering current systemic paradigms.

We are really learning how to learn. When it comes to social issues and human problems, education is always first on the list as a tool for making positive change. It is vitally important for everyone, people of all ages, to keep learning.

As people continue to increase focus on self-education and teaching others, the level of solidarity needed to secure our freedom will become a reality.

To understand the problems with the world's monetary systems, we need to understand and share only three key things:

1. Where money comes from
2. Who owns the International Monetary Fund (IMF), the World Bank, and institutions like the Federal Reserve
3. What the fractional reserve banking system is

If information is the great gift of our time, we need to be willing to examine what we learn with courage and then act based on what we know. Yet, the ramifications of these long-hidden truths are so terrifying, and the pressure from humanity's collective needs so consuming, that the forces behind our slavery beg you to stay on your knees.

They tell us that our lives hang in the balance, and they do – but not in the way those forces would like you to think.

The current monetary system is an almost inescapable prison.

Humans now live a tortured existence that shifts according to fiscal seasons, which the forces that would keep us enslaved command. To understand our situation we need to be able to recognize the tools both the proud-faced and camouflaged factions of our elitist leaders use to keep us in chains.

Worry not because you can fully escape those chains merely by helping build and support common sense and transparent replacement systems.

> *"Whoever controls the volume of money in any country is absolute master of all industry and commerce…And when you realize that the entire system is very easily controlled, one way or another, by a few powerful men at the top, you will not have to be told how periods of inflation and depression originate."*
> *- Unknown Author -*

The first two points in the list are positively inseparable.

Where does money come from? Privately owned institutions dictate when and how the world's supply of paper money is printed. Individual people actually own all global fiscal organizations and structures, such as the Federal Reserve, the IMF, the World Bank, and the Bank of International Settlements. As a result, our governments are irrefutably indebted into servitude to these few individual people.

> *"When a government is dependent upon bankers for money, they and not the leaders of the government control the situation, since the hand that gives is above the hand that takes.5Money has no*

---

[5] Quoted by Michael Seear in An Introduction to International Health (Canadian Scholars Press, 2012), 102.

> *motherland; financiers are without patriotism and without decency; their sole object is gain."6*
> *- Napoleon Bonaparte -*

> *"Some even believe we (the Rockefeller family) are part of a secret cabal working against the best interests of the United States, characterizing my family and me as 'internationalists' and of conspiring with others around the world to build a more integrated global political and economic structure – one world, if you will. If that's the charge, I stand guilty, and I am proud of it."7*
> *- David Rockefeller -*

All the world's currencies and our various nations' government monetary systems are owned and controlled by a handful of people. There is no benefit for common people and no morality built into this system. Almost all the smaller banks in the world are privately owned as well.

Finally, all our banks participate in the most complicated/simple swindle humankind has ever seen - the fractional reserve system of money creation. Simply put, private institutions literally print money out of thin air and then lend it to our governments - with interest. This same insanely criminal practice is employed on a different, more common level at almost every single bank in the world. With the click of a mouse, bankers create money out of thin air to lend to people, organizations, and us - with interest.

> *"The modern banking system manufactures 'money' out of nothing; and the process is, perhaps,*

---

6 Quoted by R. McNair Wilson in Monarchy or Money Power (1933).
7 Memoirs (2003), 406.

> *the most, astounding piece of 'sleight of hand' that was ever invented...They can, in fact, inflate and deflate, i.e., mint, and un-mint the modern 'ledger-entry currency."* 8
> - Major L.L.B. Angas -

If this sounds crazy and illegal, that might be because it is. This practice can often take a while for most people to fully process after hearing it for the first time. It took me some time. Nevertheless, these are the cold hard facts, and they leave no room for misinterpretation.

> *"History records that the money changers have used every form of abuse, intrigue, deceit, and violent means possible to maintain their control over governments by controlling money and its issuance."* 9
> - Olive Cushing Dwinell -

Global interest can never be paid back if there is not enough money to cover it.

This senseless math means blatant slavery forever, fiscal disaster in the short term, and unavoidable financial collapse in the long term. Up until recently, there have been few ways out and that was the plan set out by the ruling elite, to build a global money monopoly that enables vastly easier mind, spirit, and body control through a string of broken promises.

> *"If all the bank loans were paid, no one could have a bank deposit, and there would not be a dollar of coin or currency in circulation. This is a staggering thought.*

---

[8] Slump Ahead in Bonds (New York: Somerset Pub. Co., 1937), 20-21.
[9] Olive Cushing Dwinell, The Story of Our Money (Boston: Meador Publishing Co., 1946), 71.

> *We are completely dependent on the commercial Banks. Someone has to borrow every dollar we have in circulation, cash or credit. If the Banks create ample synthetic money we are prosperous; if not, we starve. We are absolutely without a permanent money system. When one gets a complete grasp of the picture, the tragic absurdity of our hopeless position is almost incredible, but there it is. It is the most important subject intelligent persons can investigate and reflect upon. It is so important that our present civilization may collapse unless it becomes widely understood and the defects remedied very soon."10*
> - Robert H. Hemphill -

If you are feeling nauseated, you need to move inside and then through this discomfort with open eyes. Do not fight it or run away. The deep sickness you feel as you process this information is needed and it comes with the territory.

Get excited, though, because all that frustration can be used as motivation to grow healthy solutions that will fix everything, and we are here to show you how. People are already busily planting the seeds of a healthier tomorrow together, and you can help.

First, however, we need to understand the problems a bit better before we are ready to roll up our sleeves and solve them.

While discussing war, we talked about whistle-blowers and mentioned Karen Hudes, one of the most talked about whistle-blowers in the world today. Karen studies law at Yale and economics at the University of Amsterdam. She worked at the Export Import Bank of the United States from 1980–85, and worked for over twenty years (1986–2007) at the World Bank in the legal department.

---

[10] Foreword to Irving Fisher, 100% Money (1935).

Her inside knowledge of the world's elite fiscal systems can help us both understand our problems and, perhaps, what to do about them. You can listen to one of her most recent interviews here.11

We have more backstory and links in the bibliography of this book, but that interview is the most important starting point we can offer you.12 In it, essentially, she confirms the private ownership of the world's fiscal systems, as well as many of the statements made about the nature of today's money.

One of the more exciting pieces to her most recent discourse is an apparent splintering of elite motivations and the widespread efforts that she says are apparently going on in elite circles to oppose the more negative factions and establish a moral system for managing the world's money. Karen claims to be in contact with a growing majority of world leaders, who are in full support of the reforms she advocates.

> *"The modern theory of the perpetuation of debt has drenched the earth with blood, and crushed its inhabitants under burdens ever accumulating."13*
> *- Thomas Jefferson -*

> *"In one year, the conditions [of the Colonels] were so reversed that the era of prosperity ended, and a depression set in, to such an extent that the streets of the Colonies were filled with the unemployed...The colonies would gladly have borne the little tax on tea and other matters had it not been that England took away from the colonies their money, which created unemployment and dissatisfaction (Currency Act of 1764). The inability of the colonists to get power to*

---

[11] https://www.youtube.com/watch?v=H5h1i-7qt88&feature
[12] http://kahudes.net/
[13] Letter to John Wayles Eppes, June 24, 1813.

> *issue their own money permanently out of the hands of George III and the international bankers was the PRIME reason for the Revolutionary War."*
> *- Unknown author -*

There are many surprises within this unknown author's account of those times. Despite not knowing when exactly the author lived, notice how different his report is from our history books. Through propaganda, popularized opinion about tea, national security, or even WMDs, are easily tuned to the desired frequency.

The buried truth is that, more often than not, bankers' interests are at the heart of war. Make no mistake, control is still the sole name of the game. Money, religion, and fear are simply the major tools used to cultivate control.

Money, it just so happens, is the most potent of all.

> *"I believe that banking institutions are more dangerous than standing armies."*[14]
> *- Thomas Jefferson -*

Today, our governments are in a form far removed from anything Thomas Jefferson would have recognized. How do we fix our monetary systems so they are sustainable in the long term?

In humanity's emerging symbiotically transparent world, four simple actions solve the world's financial problems:

1. Our new administration prints currency on behalf of the people, interest free.
2. Banks have reserves of 100 percent, up from the mere 2–10 percent or similarly unsustainable figures they are held to today.

---

[14] Letter to John Taylor, 1816

3. The global and national financial systems operate with complete transparency, collective and open decision-making processes, and large numbers of volunteer workers in addition to employees who are paid tiered, performance-based wages. We print our own money and watch the bankers with new, complete, transparency.

> *"The Government should create, issue, and circulate all the currency and credits needed to satisfy the spending power of the Government and the buying power of consumers. By the adoption of these principles, the taxpayers will be saved immense sums of interest. Money will cease to be master and become the servant of humanity."*[15]
> - Gerald Grattan McGeer -

We use and build alternate forms of currency and exchange.

It is that simple. Let us call this form of money "common currency."

For now, we will set aside the details of this last action. In a few pages, all kinds of readily available, positive solutions are provided.

Common currency has been introduced before as a way to free nations from banking oppression. The banking elite have done everything you can imagine to stop it. War was a favorite means of distraction from that conversation, but bankers and supporting governments have learned new fiscal means to more easily subvert opposing nations.

If you really want to understand global economic slavery on a modern scale, read Confessions of an Economic Hit Man by John

---

[15] Gary North, "Historical Error #!5: A Bogus Lincoln Quote on Men and Wages," Specific Answers Web site (n.d.), http://www.garynorth.com/public/6924.cfm).

Perkins.16 John is a real hero who made his government's criminal behavior public, much like Daniel Ellsberg did. The startling truth is that John Perkins's whistle-blowing revelations are somewhat similar in nature to Daniel Ellsberg's, but much larger than anything Ellsberg could have even imagined.

Nowadays, the media is owned outright, unlike during the Vietnam War. To get the real story, contemporary commoners often have to look to "alternative" media.

More and more people are turning to, and building, alternate platforms for investigation and discussion. Every day connectivity grows between citizen journalism and the mainstream media, which is also completely transforming to accommodate people's increasing demand for transparency.

It could be said that the mass media is slowly becoming open sourced.

Despite this, alternative media is still a bone of contention for the segment of humanity that have been duped into spreading lies of alienation, hate, and servitude as truth.

In the last five to fifteen years, as a result of access to so much information, huge swells of people are developing a deeper understanding of the world and the healthiest types of changes that can be made.

Naturally, there are also large numbers of people digging their heels in and resisting it. There is lots of discussion on this polarization, and many of us can see and feel it.

Take heart. Change can be hard, but we are coming along better than could have been expected. A little more modern-style conversation and action is all that has needed to help the rest see the truth.

---

[16] (San Francisco, CA: Berrett-Koehler Publishers, 2009).

Let us all think long and hard about the following list of mammoth media corporations and their subsidiaries, which own the production of approximately 90 percent of the media Americans consume.

Bear in mind that the following information and infographic17 are from 2011, and the monopoly of our global media has only gotten worse. More recently, Comcast and Time Warner Cable announced an agreement to merge in a forty-five billion dollar deal you can read about in the Democracy Now article ""Former FCC Commissioner Warns About Comcast-Time Warner Merger, "Mindless" Media Consolidation."18

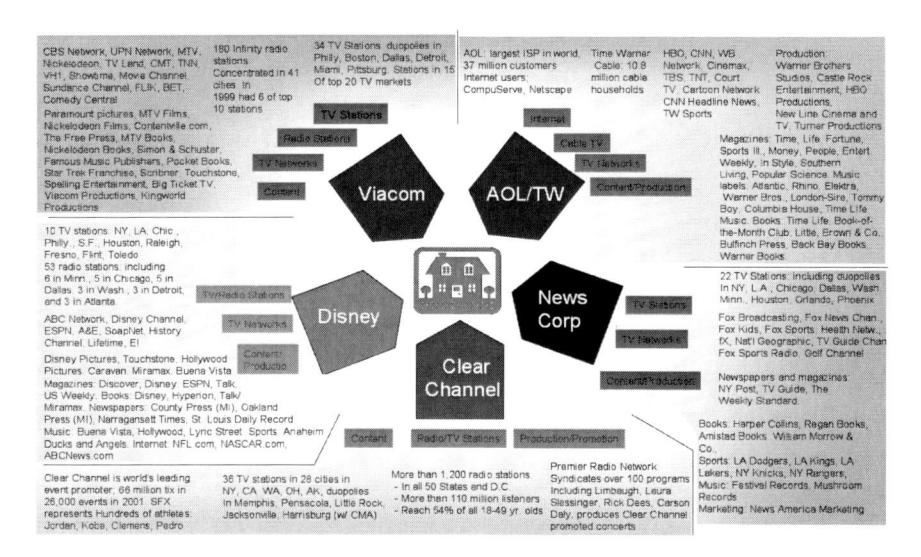

---

[17] http://rawwscoop.com/2012/12/24/who-owns-the-media/

[18] See also http://www.washingtonpost.com/business/economy/comcast-time-warner-agree-to-merge-in-45-billion-deal/2014/02/13/7b778d60-9469-11e3-84e1-27626c5ef5fb_story.html; http://www.hollywoodreporter.com/news/why-cable-mergers-could-dominate-666144; http://www.reuters.com/article/2014/02/13/us-comcast-timewarnercable-idUSBREA1C05A20140213; http://venturebeat.com/2014/02/25/the-comcast-time-warner-cable-merger-goes-in-front-of-the-senate-march-26/; http://www.naturalnews.com/044025_Obama_administration_FCC_Ministry_of_Truth.html

Time Warner

CNN
Home Box Office (HBO)
Time Inc.
Turner Broadcasting System, Inc.
Warner Bros. Entertainment Inc.
CW Network (partial ownership)
TMZ
New Line Cinema
Time Warner Cable
Cinemax
Cartoon Network
TBS
TNT
America Online
MapQuest
Moviefone
Castle Rock
Sports Illustrated
Fortune
Marie Claire
DC Comics
People

Walt Disney

ABC Television Network
Disney Publishing
ESPN Inc.
Disney Channel
History Channel
SOAPnet
A&E

Lifetime
Buena Vista Home Entertainment
Buena Vista Theatrical Productions
Buena Vista Records
Disney Records
Hollywood Records
Miramax Films
Touchstone Pictures
Walt Disney Pictures
Pixar Animation Studios
277 Radio Stations
Buena Vista Games
Hyperion Books

Viacom

Paramount Pictures
Paramount Home Entertainment
Black Entertainment Television (BET)
Comedy Central
Country Music Television (CMT)
Logo
MTV
MTV Canada
MTV2
Nickelodeon Magazine
Nick at Nite
Nick Jr.
Nickelodeon
Noggin
Spike TV
The Movie Channel
TV Land
VH1

News Corporation

Dow Jones & Company, Inc.
Fox Television Stations
New York Post
TV Guide
Fox Searchlight Pictures
Beliefnet
Fox Business Network
Fox Kids Europe
Fox News Channel
Fox Sports Net
Fox Television Network
FX
My Network TV
MySpace
News Limited News
Phoenix InfoNews Channel
Phoenix Movies Channel
Sky PerfecTV
Speed Channel
STAR TV India
STAR TV Taiwan
STAR World
Times Higher Education
Times Literary Supplement
Times of London
20th Century Fox Home Entertainment
20th Century Fox International
20th Century Fox Studios
20th Century Fox Television
BSkyB
DIRECTV
Wall Street Journal
Fox Broadcasting Company

Fox Interactive Media
FOXTEL
HarperCollins Publishers
National Geographic Channel
National Rugby League
News Interactive
News Outdoor
Radio Veronica
ReganBooks
Sky Italia
Sky Radio Denmark
Sky Radio Germany
Sky Radio Netherlands
STAR
Zondervan

CBS Corporation

CBS News
CBS Sports
CBS Television Network
CNET
Showtime
TV.com
CBS Radio Inc. (130 stations)
CBS Consumer Products
CBS Outdoor
CW Network (50 percent ownership)
Infinity Broadcasting
Simon & Schuster (Pocket Books, Scribner)
Westwood One Radio Network

Comcast

NBC
Bravo
CNBC
NBC News
MSNBC
NBC Sports
NBC Television Network
Oxygen
Sci Fi Magazine
Syfy (Sci Fi Channel)
Telemundo
USA Network
The Weather Channel
Focus Features
NBC Universal Television Distribution
NBC Universal Television Studio
Paxson Communications (partial ownership)
Hulu
Universal Parks & Resorts
Universal Pictures
Universal Studios Home Video

The average American watches over 150 hours of television per month, and most begin to feel physically uncomfortable after a long period without some form of media consumption.19 Our addiction to media grows more insatiable by the moment, while the media itself was long ago bought and sold to cold and inhuman greed.

The prostitution of our information and media, as well as our right to free speech, is appalling. However, even with all the money

---

[19] See, for example, David Hinckly, "Americans spend 34 hours a week watching TV, according to Nielsen numbers, "New York Daily News (September 19, 2012), http://www.nydailynews.com/entertainment/tv-movies/americans-spend-34-hours-week-watching-tv-nielsen-numbers-article-1.1162285.

and power in the world, institutions and authorities require all common people, including you and I, to submit.

All of us are responsible. Shamefaced and subservient, we stand on the front lines. Brothers and sisters, we have made this so.

Happily, by coming together, we can fix it.

Let us consider John Perkins again. He was a chief economist at a major international consulting firm, where he advised the World Bank, United Nations, IMF, U.S. Department of the Treasury, and Fortune 500 corporations, as well as countries in Africa, Asia, Latin America, and the Middle East. He has worked directly with heads of state and CEOs of major companies. His books on economics and geopolitics have sold more than one million copies, spent many months on best-seller lists, and are published in over thirty languages.

Confessions of an Economic Hit Man details his work for the NSA. While working as a hit man for the government, he was ordered to defraud countries around the world and shackle them with enormous debt, forcing them to acquiesce to rule by the United States.20

John shares how the economic-hit-man techniques first came to pass during the illuminating movie series The Power Principle.21 We learn that Colonel Kermit Roosevelt was the forerunner of the economic hit men and jackals who, today, further government interests via official positions within private organizations.

Roosevelt worked with the British M16 on behalf of the American CIA and successfully instigated the overthrow of the democratically elected prime minister of Iran Mohammad Mosaddegh in 1953.22 The techniques used in Iran set the stage for the ensuing violent overthrowing of leaders and subversion of nations around the world.23

---

[20] Confessions of an Economic Hit Man…[add page]
[21] "Part I: Empire," "Part II: Propaganda," "Part III: Apocalypse," The Power Principle, Top Documentaries Web site, http://topdocumentaryfilms.com/power-principle/.
[22] Confessions of an Economic Hit Man, 18
[23] Confessions of an Economic Hit Man, 114.

Examine United States foreign involvement and you will discover new, stronger forms of financial control. Countries and leaders who refuse to play by the bankers' new rules are murdered or experience a coup d'état or definitive career change.

Now consider that the following quote from over a hundred years ago, which despite being very likely forged in the name of The Rothschild brothers of London writing to associates in New York, still points to a strategic reality that seems to be undeniably evident in a much more evolved sense today.

> *"The few who understand the system will either be so interested in its profits or be so dependent upon its favours that there will be no opposition from that class, while on the other hand, the great body of people, mentally incapable of comprehending the tremendous advantage that capital derives from the system, will bear its burdens without complaint, and perhaps without even suspecting that the system is inimical to their interests."*
> *- The Rothschild Brothers -*

Lies and injustice are everywhere. Our slavery is brassy and unquestionable. If this material was news to you, we commend you for having the courage to listen. If you find this stuff frightening, we understand, but we ask you not to walk away. In your sidelong glances and shrugged shoulders, together we meet our doom.

> *"You can present the material, but you can't make me care."*[24]
> *- Bill Watterson -*

---

[24] Calvin and Hobbes.

> *"The tragedy of modern man is not that he knows less and less about the meaning of his own life but that it bothers him less and less."* 25
> *- Vaclav Havel -*

> *"Apathy is one of the characteristic responses of any living organism when it is subjected to stimuli too intense or too complicated to cope with. The cure for apathy is comprehension."* 26
> *- John Dos Passos -*

Many leaders – courageous luminaries all – have done all they can to warn and educate us, to protect our world's common resources and common people's rights, and to fight for us.

You have seen the trend at every turn, in every field. You have seen people who expose crime in politics or promote and provide effective methods to liberate the common man and free us from enslavement being killed. One way or another, their messages are debunked and destroyed by PR campaigns with no budgetary or technical limits.

> *"The drive of the Rockefellers and their allies is to create a one-world government combining super capitalism and Communism under the same tent, all under their control…Do I mean conspiracy? Yes I do. I am convinced there is such a plot,*

---

[25] Letters to Olga (New York: Henry Holt & Co., 1989), 237.

[26] Apathy_is_one_of_the_characteristic_responses_of. Dictionary.com. Columbia World of Quotations. Columbia University Press, 1996. http://quotes.dictionary.com/Apathy_is_one_of_the_characteristic_responses_of (accessed: February 03, 2014).

international in scope, generations old in planning, and incredibly evil in intent."27
- Larry P. McDonald -

These facts are not presented to scare or shock you.

Acknowledging them prepares us to make informed and healthy decisions about our future. Do not take at face value the next slanderous story you read about a fellow human being. In reality, he or she may be working hard to make the world a better place. We need to interpret the information institution hands us as primarily a means to control.

Humanity is busy self-educating on critical thinking practices, investigation techniques, and sustainable solutions. No matter where you are in the education process, each one of us has so much more to learn and there are ways we can help each other gain new knowledge.

Here is a tiny list of people who many consider to have been assassinated for standing up to the banker elites: Abraham Lincoln, Andrew Jackson, James Garfield, and John F. Kennedy.

That is four United States Presidents.28

---

[27] Quoted by Gary Allen in The Rockefeller File (Buccaneer Books, 1998).
[28] "U.S. Presidents Murdered by the Rothschild Banking Cartel: Lincoln's Private War, the Trail of Blood," (2009), http://rense.com/general86/pres.htm "All Wars Are Bankster Wars," Extreme Prejudice Web site (September 1, 2013), http://extremeprejudiceusa.wordpress.com/2013/09/01/all-wars-are-bankster-wars/; "The Bankster Gangster Crowd Has Killed Our Presidents, So What Do They Have Planned for OWS People?" Goon Squad Web site (October 14, 2011), http://careandwashingofthebrain.blogspot.ca/2011/10/bankster-gangster-crowd-has-killed-our.html; "Bilderbergs Issue Assassination Orders, Bilderberg Swiss Bankers Pay the Contract Kill Fees," Fourwinds10.com (June 8, 2011), http://www.fourwinds10.net/siterun_data/government/new_world_order/news.php?q=1307545048; "Federal Reserve Bank (Inc.), A Murderous History, Banksters the World's Worst Gangsters," Liberty for Life Association Web site (n.d.), http://www.libertyforlife.com/banking/federal_reserve_bank.html. http://rense.com/general86/pres.htm; http://www.youtube.com/watch?v=THlaMUq6MKU

Today's leaders face the very same threat. If countries stand up to the bankers, the leaders are eliminated and the nations are forced back into banking dependence.

The answer is solidarity.

> *"The death of Lincoln was a disaster for Christendom. There was no man in the United States great enough to wear his boots and the bankers went anew to grab the riches. I fear that foreign bankers with their craftiness and tortuous tricks will entirely control the exuberant riches of America and use it to systematically corrupt civilization."* 29
> - Conrad Siem -

In 1835, President Andrew Jackson stated his abhorrence for banking elite as such. "You are a den of vipers. I intend to rout you out, and by the Eternal God I will rout you out. If the people only understood the rank injustice of our money and banking system, there would be a revolution before morning." 30

Torture, death, depravity, and the drowning of human potential are guaranteed returns on the world's investment in privately owned monetary systems. The evidence is far too overwhelming; we cannot hold on to these dead and deadly ideas and systems. Take a bigger step backward friend, and see that the world's banking elite do not work for the common good.

If you still believe, understandably so, that your fellow human beings could never be so callous, careless, and cold, the following quotation brings to light the potential darkness in us all. "A very senior executive of one of the 5 big Canadian Banks made the

---

[29] The C.S.L.T., containing views of Abraham Lincoln as expressed by Bismarck in 1878, from the recollections of Conrad von Bauditz Siem (1915).

[30] Quoted by Stan V. Henkels, Andrew Jackson and the Bank of the United States (Privately Printed, 1928), 4.

following (ill-advised) comment the other day in a private gathering: 'Our credit card business is still the rock-star; we don't love it when people max out their cards and then make the minimum payment. We love it when they are late once, we increase their rate to 24%, and then they make their new minimum payment forever and a day. I will retire very well because of their stupidity.'"31

Once you accept these truths, you might desperately want to know who all these awful people are. The "who" does not matter, and neither does the why. We only need to understand how to weed the planetary garden properly.

For now, our focus needs to remain on things we can easily agree on and things we can improve when implementing the next stage of humanity's best ideas and solutions.

The money machine is built of old tricks, which have always put the majority of wealth in the hands of smaller numbers. In modern times, however, the divide between rich and poor has cancered into a chasm. Ever more human wealth is in the hands of an ever-smaller number of people.

Because of this, the massive potential of humanity is locked away from the entirety of humankind. We, the common people, are given a tiny percentage of 5–15% to live on, all at an increasing interest.

Bear in mind this monstrous divide is still growing at a ferocious rate.

Despite our best efforts, most of us cannot really comprehend this divide very well. Here is a jaw dropping six-minute video called "Nine Out of Ten Americans are Completely Wrong about this Mind-Blowing Fact" that visualizes the concept brilliantly and whose title speaks to our inability to even comprehend this gap.32

---

[31] Unidentified speaker quoted by "Ian in Perplexing," "Illegal Interest Rate Price Fixing by The Big 5 Canadian Banks," Chronically Perplexed (Blog, February 18, 2013), https://chronicallyperplexed.wordpress.com/tag/credit-card-rates/.

[32] http://www.utrend.tv/v/9-out-of-10-americans-are-completely-wrong-about-this-mind-blowing-fact/.

The world's money problems can seem incredibly difficult to both understand and solve. They are not. Easy solutions are available and support for them grows every day.

Scarcity is a very real aspect of the free market and determines supply and demand. However, if we face the raw truth, we learn that scarcity is another large, divisive lie. Consider that six billion people could fit side-by-side, arms stretched out, on Vancouver Island—one square meter for each person. The same six billion people could then each be given two acres of land from Australia's landmass alone, and roughly, 10 to 15 percent of the land would still be left.

The planet has space for many trillions or more. Resources are much more abundant than we are led to believe.

Abundance is the rule of life. Free enterprise will discover its healthy potential when a transparent community ethic governs the world. Sharing is an innate impulse. As we assume rightful ownership of our global inheritance, we will come to understand the meaning of nature, life, and abundance. These three terms are interchangeable.

It can be tough to understand this possibility, but it is one of the most delightful problems we will ever face.

Global fiscal soundness is assured with even 50 percent of the planet's resources and abundance in our common hands.

Now think about how these funds will help us reshape the world.

How do we reclaim the planet's wealth and fix this fiscal nightmare?

We start by politely saying, "Fuck off" to the International Monetary Fund, the international banking elite, and all connected debt.

Then we sit back and watch life shift for the better instantly.

People are already doing it.

Iceland recently did just that: told the International Monetary Fund to fuck off.

The Freedom Handbook

The country now retains better control over printing its own currency. The common people of Iceland even forced members of their government to resign. Remarkably, they then installed two protestors as new members of parliament.

Iceland nationalized the banks and refused to pay the debt supposedly owed to the international banking elite. The real kicker was that all of this was done in a completely peaceful manner.33

There is nothing stopping the rest of us.

Iceland's recent banking rebirth has been coined the "pots and pans revolution," so named because Icelanders taking to the streets to protest made themselves heard by banging pots and pans. Their protest is captured in a short video from the Dumb Planet called "How to Start a Revolution: Learn from Iceland!"34

Now, we humbly present another list, this time of the top four things we as individuals and groups can do right now to plug in and create healthy change in our money systems:

Kick out the banking elite and print our own currencies. Let us make our global voice the dominant force it is meant to be through pots, pans, and demonstrations in the streets. We need only our computers, mobile phones, tablets, and occasionally a small contribution from our wallets. Join the rest of us and be the change. Your voice is needed.

Undermine the current system and increase personal wealth by avoiding interest, debt, and service charges through alternative currencies. This is a short- and long-term solution.

BitCoin is currently the global leader in alternative currency. For a terrific lesson on the nature of BitCoin and why alternative currencies are the way to go, check out Stefan Molyneux's two talks

---

[33] "2008-11 Icelandic financial crisis," Wikipedia Web site (February 15, 2014), http://en.wikipedia.org/wiki/2008%E2%80%9311_Icelandic_financial_crisis.

[34] "How to start a revolution: Learn from Iceland!" The Dumb Planet (n.d.), http://www.youtube.com/watch?v=8-SiYQ8s_6I.

on the subject: "The True Value of Bitcoin: What You Really Need To Know," published on November 30, 2013,35 and the earlier "The Truth About Bitcoin," published on 27 Sep 2013.36

Alternative currency is one of the most potent tools at our disposal. Through it, we can liberate our fiscal activities immediately and non-violently before taking on the larger, more time-consuming task of removing international banking influence altogether. The best part of this plan is that all the tools needed to implement it already exist. It only needs more support before the scales tip in our favor, forever.

Decentralized peer-to-peer crypto-currencies like Bitcoin provide a huge numbers of game-changing benefits. For example, Stephan explains that they can eliminate as much as 10 percent of global economic spending, represented by the financial services industry.37

All this money goes back into the hands of the common people.

This is only a single benefit. There are many more, such as limited legal fees for all kinds of transactions. For a detailed explanation, watch the first of Stefan Molyneux's two talks, where he compares this digital currency innovation to the theory of relativity and the heliocentric model of the universe, in regards to both size and scope.

A few more specifics about alternative currency are covered later on, but it would take another chapter at minimum to scratch the surface of the benefits this emerging economy will grant to all of us.

Stop paying taxes, which in large part pay for criminal interest charges on immoral national debt to bankers.

Get involved in online exchange and commerce communities that trade, barter, and collaborate outside the sphere of current institution.

Think about the collective power that we will have when our mobile phones can locate organizations that share our views and economic

---

[35] http://www.youtube.com/watch?v=Cs6F91dFYCs
[36] http://www.youtube.com/watch?v=w4HGVJjqDVk.
[37] http://www.youtube.com/watch?v=Cs6F91dFYCs

practice, like not contributing tax to the system. Collaborating in this way is an invaluable tactic to help us gain momentum.

Adam Kokesh can teach us more about this type of collaboration.

Adam is a decorated Iraq war veteran who now advocates nonviolent resistance to authority. He is a recognized American activist fighting for freedom and liberty and hosts a popular radio show, identifying with voluntarism, agorism, anarchism, and libertarianism. Adam's story is yet another example of how positive forces in our world are perpetually persecuted. In this video with Stefan Molyneux, he defines the term agorism as a libertarian social philosophy that advocates creating a society in which all relations between people are voluntary exchanges by means of counter-economics, thus engaging in a manner with aspects of peaceful revolution.38 This term can be used to describe many of the voluntary exchange practices discussed in this book.

Agorism, as a complementary force, is a highly effective technique when used to remove unruly authorities. It immediately allows humanity to enjoy the fruits of her labor without interference from the state or any other unwanted party.

In essence, agorism cuts out the middleman. By getting government out of our pockets and stripping it of the resources to control us, we free ourselves to re-purpose our infrastructure as we see fit. In Iceland, agorism was employed as added pressure to effectively strip the corrupt government of power over the masses.

So, to recap: use alternative forms of currency as often as you can and help build and support new tools and/or even fix the old ones if we want.

Pretty simple, right?

---

[38] "Agorism," Wikipedia Web site, http://en.wikipedia.org/wiki/Agorism; "Samuel Edward Konkin III," Wikipedia Web site, http://en.wikipedia.org/wiki/Samuel_Edward_Konkin_III; The Tireless Agorist blog, http://tirelessagorist.blogspot.ca/.

Thank you for taking this journey so far.

Now it is time to take off our gloves and get serious about solution. In the last five chapters, we answer the two toughest questions. Is humanity ready for freedom, and, if so, how do we make it happen quickly and peacefully?

The simple fact is that some of us are ready and some are not. No matter what, though, change is coming. Whether you accept it now, or are run over and lambasted by it tomorrow, is a choice you need to make.

With that in mind, let us test our mettle and see what we are truly made of.

CHAPTER TWELVE

- The Problems: A Summary -

"Nothing appears more surprising to those who consider human affairs with a philosophical eye, than the ease with which the many are governed by the few."1
- David Hume -

"I never could believe that Providence had sent a few men into the world, ready booted and spurred to ride, and millions ready saddled and bridled to be ridden."2
- Richard Rumbold -

If you feel surprised, bamboozled, or enraged by the information that we have discussed so far, do not worry – you are not alone. We are being ridden by a royal, blackened, and charred handful of our fellow women and men who have done things that are unimaginable to the rest of us.

The beginning of this book promised that the reading it would be one of the wildest rides of your life. The story began with a snapshot of the problems we all face, the evils standing between freedom and

---

[1] "Essay 4: Of the First Principles of Government," Essays, Moral, Political, and Literary (1758), full text at Library of Economics and Liberty Web site, http://www.econlib.org/library/LFBooks/Hume/hmMPL.html.
[2] Speech on the Scaffold (Edinburg, 1685), I_never_could_believe_that_Providence_had_sent. Dictionary.com. Columbia World of Quotations. Columbia University Press, 1996. http://quotes.dictionary.com/I_never_could_believe_that_Providence_had_sent (accessed: February 05, 2014).

us. You have been with us as we have traveled down this strange road with an open mind, listening to truths that are anything but comfortable.

Now, take a moment. Look down upon our earth, our home, and examine what we have learned. Think about the road behind without losing sight of the path to the future, because four tasks still demand our attention.

1. We must lock down a consensus regarding the global problems we have been discussing and spread an understanding of the truths contained herein. More of us need to better understand what is happening, and be able to express that understanding on at least a basic level.
2. We must prepare individually for the future and help our friends with accepting the world as it is, and deciding how we can make it better. Understanding is all well and good, but it still leaves massive ground that must be covered on the road to recognition. Guidance, community, and acceptance are critical during the whole world's dark night of the soul, and people need to come together. We must all come to terms with individual and collective problems if we are going to solve anything.
3. We must focus on potential game-changing hazards and dangerous distractions. First, all distracting and irrelevant issues need to be recognized as such. Taking out the trash from our conversations allows us to focus on the core issues. Focus also means developing the discernment to identify the core truths that lie hidden in a sea of half-truths and outright lies. This level of self-education, critical thinking, and collaboration ensures that no matter how severe the propaganda, public relations efforts, or false flag events, divide-and-conquer and distraction techniques will not work anymore.

4. We must finalize plans and solutions to change the world. We must identify issues in current activities and plans, adjust together accordingly, and then act on the decisions that we have made. In addition, above all else, we must continually experiment and adjust for maximum effectiveness. In a changing world, this process is and always will be ongoing.

The final confrontation with all of the barricades to our freedom is at hand.

In this chapter, we tackle the first task on the list, but before we go further, it might be helpful to briefly examine the idea of and need for revolution.

> *"Remember, remember always, that all of us, and you and I especially, are descended from immigrants and revolutionists."*[3]
> *- Franklin D. Roosevelt -*

> *They Live*[4]
>
> *Imagine you find a really cool pair of sunglasses at a gas station. When trying them on, you notice everything looks a bit strange, but the cashier's impatience and a long line forming both distract you, so you quickly pay for them and leave. Just before driving away, you inspect the glasses and remove a small tag, which you had not noticed*

---

[3] Remarks before the Daughters of the American Revolution, Washington, D.C., April 21, 1938, *The Public Papers and Addresses of Franklin D. Roosevelt, 1938*, (1941) 259.

[4] Directed by John Carpenter, written by Ray Nelson and John Carpenter (Universal Studios, 1988).; http://www.imdb.com/title/tt0096256/

earlier. It says, "Revo-shades reveal truth and help stir the molten fires of courage, if you dare..."

The following quotations are similar insurgent lenses that will help us examine the rest of the book and the need for revolution with discerning clarity.

"Revolution is not something fixed in ideology, nor is it something fashioned to a particular decade. It is a perpetual process embedded in the human spirit."[5]
- Abbie Hoffman -

"A revolution is not a trail of roses.... A revolution is a fight to the death between the future and the past."[6]
- Fidel Castro -

"We used to think that revolutions are the cause of change. Actually it is the other way around: change prepares the ground for revolution."[7]
- Eric Hoffer -

"I learned that courage was not the absence of fear, but the triumph over it. The brave man is not he who does not feel afraid, but he who conquers that fear."[8]
- Nelson Mandela -

---

[5] Soon to be a Major Motion Picture (New York: Putnam, 1980), 297.
[6] "Speech on the second anniversary of the triumph of the revolution" (January 2, 2961).
[7] "A Time of Juveniles," The Temper of Our Times (1967).
[8] Long Walk to Freedom: The Autobiography of Nelson Mandela (Hachette Book Group, 1995), 148.

> *"Courage is being scared to death but saddling up anyway."*
> *- John Wayne -*

To prepare for global rebirth, we need to reach global consensus, a great many of us standing united and together. How many people does it take, exactly, to win our freedom? The answer comes toward the end of the next chapter, and it is guaranteed to leave you slightly more optimistic about our chances.

First, to help us reach consensus, here is a final look at the problems covered so far. This summary was designed to marshal the rest, to motivate everyone to take back their lives, lands, homes, humanity, rights, responsibilities, planetary resources, personal paychecks, potential joy, and pure freedom.

If it is not already, your fight will soon be ready.

> *"If you want to know the taste of a pear, you must change the pear by eating it yourself. If you want to know the theory and methods of revolution, you must take part in revolution. All genuine knowledge originates in direct experience."9*
> *- Mao Zedong -*

> *"A revolution is an idea which has found its bayonets."10*
> *- Napoleon Bonaparte -*

---

9 If_you_want_to_know_the_taste_of. Dictionary.com. Columbia World of Quotations. Columbia University Press, 1996. http://quotes.dictionary.com/If_you_want_to_know_the_taste_of (accessed: February 05, 2014)

10 Journal of International Affairs, by Columbia University, School of International Affairs (1976), 94.

> "You can jail a Revolutionary, but you can't jail the Revolution."11
> - Huey Newton -

> "I began revolution with 82 men. If I had to do it again, I would do it with 10 or 15 and absolute faith. It does not matter how small you are if you have faith and a plan of action."12
> - Fidel Castro -

This journey began by looking at government. We know we can do better. Debate is over. We need to end the expired, oppressive insanity of all current forms of government and institution.

> "What good fortune for governments that the people do not think."
> - Adolf Hitler -

> "Government is not reason; it is not eloquent; it is force. Like fire, it is a dangerous servant and a fearful master."13
> - W.M.

---

[11] Quoted on "Free Huey," The Black Panther Black Community News Service, http://xroads.virginia.edu/~UG01/barillari/pantherchap2.html (accessed February 6, 2014).

[12] Yale Book of Quotations, ed. Fred R. Shapiro (Yale University Press, 2006), 139, quoting article in New York Times (April 22, 1959).

[13] "Liberty and Government," The Christian Science Journal, vol. XX, No. 8, ed. Mary Baker Eddy (November 1902), 465.

A Profound Testimonial

"To be <u>governed</u> is to be watched over, inspected, spied on, directed, legislated at, regulated, docketed, indoctrinated, preached at, controlled, assessed, weighed, censored, ordered about, by men who have neither the <u>right</u>, nor the <u>knowledge</u>, nor the <u>virtue</u>. ...

To be governed is to be at every operation, at every transaction, noted, registered, enrolled, taxed, stamped, measured, numbered, assessed, licensed, authorized, admonished, forbidden, reformed, corrected, punished. It is, under the pretext of public utility, and in the name of the general interest, to be placed under contribution, trained, ransomed, exploited, monopolized, extorted, squeezed, mystified, robbed; then, at the slightest resistance, the first word of complaint, to be repressed, fined, despised, harassed, tracked, abused, clubbed, disarmed, choked, imprisoned, judged, condemned, shot, deported, sacrificed, sold, betrayed; and, to crown all, mocked, ridiculed, outraged, dishonoured. That is government; that is its justice; that is its morality."14
- Pierre-Joseph Proudhon -

Have you ever felt wronged by the state? Have you been treated unfairly by the tax collector, the police, or any government institution?

---

[14] Pierre-Joseph Proudhon, from Idée Générale de la Révolution au XIXe Siècle (1851), in James Joll, The Anarchists, trans. James Joll (Grosset and Dunlap, 1964).

Have you ever needed help with something and been run through a state wringer that only made your problems worse?

If not, think about how many people you know who might have. Most people on the planet have stories like this to tell. This is our family. Let us do this better. Let us self-govern.

Symbiotic transparency has three basic pillars of freedom that are instrumental and already evident in our world. The plan is solid. It is not complete, nor is it quite right – it needs you and many more of us to lovingly test and tweak it to perfection in the company of our global community.

Symbiotic transparency drove Luke and I to create a single, overarching term to describe the "the unbridled, transparent, symbiotic, and organic nature of humanity's organizing self." By replacing the entire spectrum of "isms" with two common-sense truths – symbiosis and transparency – humanity can surrender old political ideas. By removing authority's arbitrary restrictions, humanity can discover its true symbiotic nature.

> *"And a new philosophy emerged called quantum physics, which suggest that the individual's function is to inform and be informed. You really exist only when you're in a field sharing and exchanging information. You create the realities you inhabit."*[15]
> *- Timothy Leary -*

Now we can move on to the next topic.

Social programs and taxes are an undertaking to discuss. The bulk of our work ahead lies here. Together, we have come to understand unequivocally, the corruption of current institutions. The abuse, lies, and theft must come to an end, here and now. Our social programs are undergoing a management change.

Systems remain – only the nature of authority shifts.

---

[15] Chaos and Culture (Berkeley, CA: Ronin Publishing, 1994)

Brothers and sisters, unite and let us paint a new world. We will be rewarded with the reclaimed and realized true abundance that our planet can provide everyone. You will be compensated, as great artisans truly should; the riches will be yours and yours alone to lovingly share with family and neighbor.

> *"Yes. We both have a bad feeling. Tonight we shall take our bad feelings and share them, and face them. We shall mourn. We shall drain the bitter dregs of mortality. Pain shared, my brother, is pain not doubled, but halved. No man is an island."*[16]
> *- Neil Gaiman -*

We need to come together in thought and action.

We need to establish a few new patterns and habits.

No big deal. As Nietzsche reminds us, victory is assured the moment we realize we have been fighting the wrong battle.

Hearts heal with fast grace in the hands of a friend.

Have you ever needed better social programming? How many people have you met who do? We can certainly do better. We need only common sense upgrades and to remove arbitrary authority from the equation.

Come on Filipino kaibigans and Afrikaans vriends – all the earth's common crew, gather around; let us talk education.

> *"Knowledge will forever govern ignorance; and a people who mean to be their own governors must arm themselves with the power which knowledge gives."*[17]
> *-James Madison -*

---

[16] Anansi Boys (New York: HarperCollins, 2005), 63.
[17] Letter to W.T. Barry (August 4, 1822), http://press-pubs.uchicago.edu/founders/documents/v1ch18s35.html.

> *"Next in importance to freedom and justice is popular education, without which neither freedom nor justice can be permanently maintained."*[18]
> *- James A. Garfield -*

Education is a no-brainer. We can do this better. We must. Thankfully, there is already a wealth of healthier options available.

> *"You must unlearn what you have been programmed to believe since birth. That software no longer serves you if you want to live in a world where all things are possible."*[19]
> *- Jacqueline E. Purcell -*

How many kids do you know who have been shorted by the education system? Were you one of them? Inciting curiosity and the human imagination is not hard, and neither is presenting the right tools and getting out of the way. This is how we set the stage for education and human potential to grow organically. It is easy. It happens every day through homeschooling, unschooling, open source schooling, and many other environments.

Let us join in.

Consensus calls to you, our Indian dost, our Chinese péngyou, friends from around the world. Listen...collective human potential is singing a healing song.

With respect to health, we cannot even imagine what we are actually capable of accomplishing. We know that cures for many current ailments have been discovered and consequently suppressed at one point or another. Therefore, it will not take long to rediscover,

---

[18] Letter accepting the Republican nomination for president (July 12, 1880), http://www.presidency.ucsb.edu/ws/index.php?pid=76221.

[19] Quoted by Michael Leroux in Revolution of the Heart (Xlibris, 2013), 242.

redistribute, or breed new solutions as inconceivable levels of control, manipulation, and hindrance are removed.

> *"The most common commodity in this country is unrealized potential."*
> *- Calvin Coolidge -*

> *"The only way to discover the limits of the possible is to go beyond them into the impossible."*[20]
> *- Arthur C. Clarke –*

> *"Our aspirations are our possibilities."*
> *- Robert Browning –*

How many of your family members have to get sick with modern illnesses or be killed by our health systems, or lack of access to them, before you stop taking government's prescription of allopathic (often toxic) medicine, believing it's the only possible answer to health? How do you feel about your health and your health system's relationship to it? If you and your family have no serious complaints so far, can you say the same for everyone you love, or even for your neighbors?

Let us let every man decide for himself the healer of his choosing. Let us focus on curing our diseases instead of on treatment.

We can do health better than this.

Subjugation calls to you, Russian prijátel. It commands every one of us to kneel, obey, and get in line, or be destroyed. Let us take a final look at man's law.

> *Then a lawyer said, But what of our Laws, master?*
> *And he answered:*

---

[20] "Hazards of Prophecy: Failure of Imagination," *Profiles of the Future* (1962).

You delight in laying down laws,
Yet you delight more in breaking them.
Like children playing by the ocean
who build sand-towers with constancy
and then destroy them with laughter.
But while you build your sand-towers
the ocean brings more sand to the shore,
And when you destroy them the ocean laughs with you.
Verily the ocean laughs always with the innocent.
But what of those to whom life is not an ocean,
and man-made laws are not sand-towers,
But to whom life is a rock, and the law a chisel
with which they would carve it in their own likeness?
What of the cripple who hates dancers?
What of the ox who loves his yoke and deems the elk
and deer of the forest stray and vagrant things?
What of the old serpent who cannot shed his skin,
and calls all others naked and shameless?
And of him who comes early to the wedding-feast,
and when overfed and tired goes his way saying
that all feasts are violation and all feasters lawbreakers?
What shall I say of these
save that they too stand in the sunlight,
but with their backs to the sun?
They see only their shadows,
and their shadows are their laws.[21]
- Kahlil Gibran -

---

[21] The Prophet.

The idea of having no written laws can be tough to come to terms with.

You have known nothing your whole life aside from a world filled with law, limitation, legislation, legalese, restriction, rule, and rhetoric, and these are only a few arrows in legalized oppression's quiver.

We have learned that human-made laws and the act of writing them down only serve as a means to enslave. When we drop this old habit of telling each other what to do, we'll not only have the freedom to discover humanity's innovative potential, but we'll also build necessary togetherness, trust, and collaborative skills.

> *"A law is not a law without coercion behind it."*[22]
> *- James A. Garfield -*

If you still have an issue with the idea of no written laws, the very fact that you are worried is indicative of humanity's undeniable basic goodness.

The people you are afraid of do not exist. We have been tricked into fearing one another. The truth is, you and your neighbor will meet at the coffee shop and the grocery store, and not much will change. When written law is a memory, the coffee shop and grocery story will not be more dangerous.

It is, in fact, quite the opposite.

Remember, criminal choices will always be made, but for those who believe that this lawlessness is a golden opportunity to throw portions of their pock-ridden moral garb in the trash, trouble will paint the horizon a brazen red.

The new world of justice is a whole lot more efficient and deters harmful behavior much more effectively. In short, justice hath arrived.

Be safe, delighted, and warned.

---

[22] Quoted by Joslyn Pine in Wit and Wisdom of American Presidents (Courier Dove Publications, 2000), 32.

When Luke first sat down to pen solutions for a new world, he ran up against a huge wall of rules. He wondered if it was even possible to improve on previous sets of instructions for life. He told me that it felt preposterous to try to improve on brilliant documents like the Bill of Rights or the United States Constitution.

He found himself equally disturbed by a certain perennial fact: the ruling class breaks golden, noble rules with the same ease as minor ones.

He realized that the very act of writing down a rule was a problem in and of itself. Before he shared with me this linchpin of our freedom, I walked the earth in a broken daze, unsure like many of us how to manifest the big changes, the all-over solutions we all so desperately seek.

Therefore, Luke came to embrace Anarchy.

> *"If this is the price to be paid for an idea, then let us pay. There is no need of being troubled about it, afraid, or ashamed. This is the time to boldly say, "Yes, I believe in the displacement of this system of injustice by a just one; I believe in the end of starvation, exposure, and the crimes caused by them; I believe in the human soul regnant over all laws which man has made or will make; I believe there is no peace now, and there will never be peace, so long as one rules over another; I believe in the total disintegration and dissolution of the principle and practice of authority; I am an Anarchist, and if for this you condemn me, I stand ready to receive your condemnation."*[23]
> *- Voltairine de Cleyre -*

---

[23] "Our Present Attitude," Mother Earth 3.2 (1908), opa. 7, 78-80, http://praxeology.net/VC-OPA.htm.

Do not let the word anarchy scare you. It is one of the most manipulated terms in the English language. Research it and discover its true history and potential. Furthermore, realize that like the rest of the world, this idea is rapidly shifting to fit our contemporary shape. Modern tweaks that breathe fresh life into this older concept are discussed further on.

> *"Even if the absence of Government really meant anarchy in the negative, disorderly sense of that word – which is far from being the case – even then no anarchical disorder could be worse than the position to which Governments have already led their peoples, and to which they are leading them."*[24]
> *- Leo Tolstoy -*

We do not need to dissolve all large, centralized forms of structure and live in chaos. You do not need to move to the hills or abandon all material wealth. Just look in the mirror and be honest with yourself. Trust yourself and your fellow human beings.

Let us work together with more compassion and effectiveness than the rulers we have endured for millennia.

We can definitely do better.

I trust in you, friend, and if we falter, I trust in the power of our community to catch us both. Community will stitch humanity's future efforts with artistry, love, and new efficiency, born of our age-old struggle and eventual lessons learned.

Has the law ever hurt you? Has it ever hurt someone you loved or knew? Have you ever felt restricted by senseless legislation? If not,

---

[24] Quoted by Thomas E. Hachey and Ralph Edward Weber in European Ideologies Since 1789: Rebels, Radicals, and Political Ferment (Krieger Publishing Co., 1981), 104.

talk to a business owner you know and ask her how she feels about her experiences with the institution of regulation and law. Business owners are also good people with whom to discuss the tax collector, other forms of government, banks, and institution in general. Private business owners are leading the charge for collaborative institution's growth. Would you like to help remove law's restrictions and inject integrity back into our justice systems? With transparency as our main guide, let us do this better.

Come friend, cara, chingu—time to talk about drugs.

The war on drugs is done. This is a health concern, not a criminal one. War is strictly a means to divide and conquer.

> *"Anyway, no drug, not even alcohol, causes the fundamental ills of society. If we're looking for the source of our troubles, we shouldn't test people for drugs, we should test them for stupidity, ignorance, greed and love of power."*[25]
> *- P.J. O'Rourke -*

> *"In a free society, how can you commit a crime against yourself?"*[26]
> *- Jesse Ventura -*

Most already agree that the war on drugs is a plague on humankind that needs to be abolished immediately. Think about how

---

[25] No_drug_not_even_alcohol_causes_the_fundamental. Dictionary.com. Columbia World of Quotations. Columbia University Press, 1996. (accessed: February 07, 2014).

[26] Kevin Kelly, "Jesse Ventura: the First, Second, and Fourth Amendment are gone," The Washington Times (June 24, 2013), http://communities.washingtontimes.com/neighborhood/remnant/2013/jun/24/jesse-ventura-first-second-and-fourth-amendment-ar/

inspiring it must have felt to be part of the Underground Railroad or the Abolition Movement.

Let us liberate our bodies and minds from slavery.

Because the war on drugs is already teetering on very shaky ground, with monstrous opposition firmly in place, we can use it as a means to motivate. Ending this war will significantly bolster global solidarity, and increase our resolve in the continuing fight for freedom.

What is most exciting is that because global opinion is already rather unanimous, and organized regarding the issue, we should be able to end the entire war on drugs around the world with the right types of added pressure.

How do you feel about drugs and the right for human beings to choose for themselves? How do you feel about treating this issue like a health concern instead of a criminal one? Has the drug war hurt you, your family, or anyone you know? There is no doubt we can do this better. How would you like to help?

Hey, tomodachi, Japanese buddy, grab an Albanian mik or make one; we have arrived at our discussion of war. In fact, Hungarian barát, you are in charge of taking roll call before we begin. German freund, can you please stop talking to your Australian mate for one bloody second!

> *"First they came for the Socialists, and I did not speak out—because I was not a Socialist. Then they came for the Trade Unionists, and I did not speak out—because I was not a Trade Unionist. Then they came for the Jews, and I did not speak out—because I was not a Jew. Then they came for me—and there was no one left to speak for me."*[27]
> *- Martin Niemöller -*

---

[27] Harold Marcuse, "Martin Niemöller's famous quotation: 'First they came for the Communists . . .,'" Niemöller Quotation Page (February 28, 2013), http://www.history.ucsb.edu/faculty/marcuse/niem.htm#discsources.

> *"The fact that war is the word we use for almost everything—on terrorism, drugs, even poverty—has certainly helped to desensitize us to its invocation; if we wage wars on everything, how bad can they be?"28*
> *- Glenn Greenwald -*

This thing called war, its divisiveness, torture, scorching pain and hatred, has been our own doing through servitude to feral animals. The ruling elite's reign has come to an end.

> *"The West's post-Holocaust pledge that genocide would never again be tolerated proved to be hollow, and for all the fine sentiments inspired by the memory of Auschwitz, the problem remains that denouncing evil is a far cry from doing good."29*
> *- Philip Gourevitch -*

The Gulf of Tonkin incident, Urgent Fury, PBSUCCESS (the covert CIA operation that overthrew Jacobo Arbenz Guzman, the second legally elected president in Guatemalan history), the assassination of Patrice Lumumba30 (the first democratically elected leader of Congo), the United States' 2002 attempt to remove the president of Venezuela, Hugo Chávez, from office,31 and even 9/11 are all the same type of event – a lie.32

---

28 A Tragic Legacy: How a Good vs. Evil Mentality Destroyed the Bush Presidency (Broadway Books, 2008).
29 We Wish to Inform You That Tomorrow We Will Be Killed with Our Families: Stories from Rwanda (Picador, 1999).
30 John Perkins, The Secret History of the American Empire (Dutton, 2007), 14, 249.
31 John Perkins, The Secret History of the American Empire, 110-113
32 http://www.truth-out.org/news/item/19551-us-invasion-of-grenada-a-30-year-retrospective; http://www.globalresearch.ca/operation-agent-fury-the-1983-us-invasion-of-grenada/5360313; http://www.globalresearch.ca/thirty-years-after-the-u-s-invasion-of-grenada-the-first-neoliberal-war/5355916; http://www.

They are lies designed to control and suppress the independence and strength of the common classes. Horrified, we shrink away and chastise the whistle-blowing messenger, willing anything else to be true.

*"War is peace. Freedom is slavery. Ignorance is strength."*33
- George Orwell -

"Though the contradictions of war seem sudden and simultaneous, history stalks before it strikes. Something tolerated soon becomes something good." 34
- Anne Michaels -

"All war is a symptom of man's failure as a thinking animal." 35
- John Steinbeck -

"If everyone fought for their own convictions there would be no war." 36
- Leo Tolstoy -

---

miamiherald.com/2013/10/24/3709792/us-invasion-of-grenada-30-years.html; Power Principle (Grenada); http://www.consortiumnews.com/archive/story38.html; http://www2.gwu.edu/~nsarchiv/NSAEBB/NSAEBB4/; http://www.nytimes.com/2011/10/21/world/americas/an-apology-for-a-guatemalan-coup-57-years-later.html?_r=0; http://historicalmemoryproject.com/Historical_Memory_Project/index.html; Power Principle; http://news.bbc.co.uk/hi/english/static/audio_video/programmes/correspondent/transcripts/974745.txt; https://www.wsws.org/en/articles/2013/04/18/lumu-a18.html; http://www.thehindu.com/news/international/world/british-peer-reveals-mi6-role-in-lumumba-killing/article4567513.ece

33 Nineteen Eighty-four, Chapter I.
34 Fugitive Pieces (Toronto: McClelland & Stewart, 1996).
35 Once There Was a War.
36 *War and Peace* (1869).

> *"War is over. If you want it."* [37]
> *- John Lennon -*

Do we need to ask you if war has hurt you directly?

The pain of war is something all of us can feel with a little empathetic effort. Few wounds are more universally felt than those caused by war. Refugees from war-torn areas of the world seek safety in our "peaceful nations."

If you have not seen, been a victim of, or intimately come to understand the pain of war, then you have people living close to you who have. Ask them about it.

Let us start talking to each other, teaching each other, consoling each other. Together we can heal this pain and build a world with no war.

If this issue moves you, then roll up your sleeves and get serious.

Before summarizing everything we have learned together about religious institution, we need to open a vile and hidden-away box of religious secrets. The Catholic Church has, perhaps, more blood on its hands than any other religious institution, but we are demanding your attention not to talk about war, but about our children being sexually assaulted.

According to some counts, as many as eighty percent of Catholic priests are pedophiles. In other words, at one point or another, our kids have accused eight out of ten priests of sexual abuse.

Who cares what the numbers are.

They are huge, and so gross that there are no words.

The Catholic Church leaders' policy for dealing with the most heinous of human acts is to shovel them under the rug, silence the victims and families, and move the accused to another territory to prey.

In his powerful book Mortal Sins, Michael D'Antonio observed, "In the course of the continuous scandal, more than 6,100 priests

---

[37] Bed-in for Peace, Montreal, Quebec (June 1, 1969).

were deemed by the Church itself to be 'not implausibly' or 'credibly' accused of sexual crimes against more than 16,000 underage victims in the United States alone."

Given that Church leaders were denying and covering up the crimes committed by the priests, its recognition that thousands of priests at a minimum were implicated is damning indeed.38

You and I need to stop praying with these people.
We cannot ask or allow them to lead us. We cannot stay silent anymore with our eyes on the ground, while their hands are in our pockets and raping our children.

Celibacy is a human-made rule. Common sense tells us to do away with this arcane rule/foolishness. No one should be told how to live. That being said, people are always free to choose their own roads, so there is always space to make that personal celibacy decision.
Even for the majority of our spiritual leaders, the path of asceticism and restriction long ago evolved into the Buddha's Middle Path, or the French's philosophy of sugar and spice in equal measure.

When we use common sense to examine celibacy in religious institutions, another striking contradiction becomes evident.
Think about all the parents you know. Would any of them even consider taking parenting advice from their friends who do not have kids? It is likely not. My own conversations with my sisters who have children have made this abundantly clear.
The fact still remains that many parents feel that (apparently) celibate, self-exalted religious leaders can somehow offer sage, well-rounded parenting and family advice.

The current institution of church is unhealthy and unnecessary.

---

[38] Michael D'Antonio, Mortal Sins: Sex, Crime, and the Era of Catholic Scandal (New York: Thomas Dunne Books, 2013).

Free, we will educate our children and our neighbors on the good in our hearts and our traditions. We need no ruler or compass in the hands of the individual or tired organizations. Alternatively, we need a new paradigm for celebrating our spiritual ideas and the golden rule.

> *"Some go to church to see and be seen, Some go there to say they have been, Some go there to sleep and nod, But few go there to worship God."*
> *- Proverb -*

> *"Clearly the person who accepts the Church as an infallible guide will believe whatever the Church teaches."*[39]
> *- St. Thomas Aquinas -*

> *"The church says the earth is flat, but I know that it is round, for I have seen the shadow on the moon, and I have more faith in a shadow than in the church."*[40]
> *- Robert Green Ingersoll -*

> *"Church isn't where you meet. Church isn't a building. Church is what you do. Church is who you are. Church is the human outworking of the person of Jesus Christ. Let's not go to Church, let's be the Church."*
> *- Bridget Willard -*

---

[39] Sumna Theologica, second part of the second part, question five, article three, under the heading "Whether a man who disbelieves one article of faith, can have lifeless faith in the other articles?"(1265-1274).

[40] Individuality (1873), http://infidels.org/library/historical/robert_ingersoll/individuality.html.

How has religious institution impacted your life?

If you have religious beliefs, are there certain things you take with a grain of salt? Have you modernized the message to address the issues you have with old-fashioned moral material?

Humanity can learn to celebrate in peace. The great majority of us are already happy to. Institutions are the ones who like to fight and instigate fundamentalist attitudes. It takes organization and institutions to grow sick ideas beyond individual outbursts.

With collaborative institution, harmony rules the day. Look in your community and in your heart and you will know that we can do this better.

The truth behind humanity's monetary systems offers us a clear view of some of the most potent ways rulers have machined our slavery. This knowledge about money and its powerful motivating capacity makes it easier to stir significant sedition.

Imagine what we will do with 99 percent or even 50 percent of the whole world's wealth back in our neighborhoods, personal piggy banks, and children's trusts.

> *"All the perplexities, confusion and distress in America arise not from defects in their Constitution or Confederation, nor from want of honor or virtue, so much as downright ignorance of the nature of coin, credit, and circulation."* 41
> - John Adams -

> *"When you or I write a check there must be sufficient funds in our account to cover that check, but when the Federal Reserve writes a check, it is creating money."* 42

---

[41] Letter to Thomas Jefferson, August 23, 1787, Works of John Adams.
[42] Putting It Simply—The Federal Reserve, Federal Reserve Bank of Boston, Public Service Department (1984).

- Federal Reserve Bank -

"In a small Swiss city sits an international organization so obscure and secretive...Control of the institution, the Bank for International Settlements, lies with some of the world's most powerful and least visible men: the heads of 32 central banks, officials able to shift billions of dollars and alter the course of economies at the stroke of a pen." 43
- Keith Bradsher -

"A great industrial nation is controlled by its system of credit. Our system of credit is concentrated. The growth of the nation, therefore, and all our activities are in the hands of a few men." 44

We have come to be one of the worst ruled, one of the most completely controlled and dominated Governments in the civilised world—no longer a Government by free opinion, no longer a Government by conviction and the vote of the majority, but a Government by the opinion and duress of a small group of men." 45
- President Woodrow Wilson -

---

43 "Obscure Global Bank Moves Into the Light," New York Times (August 5, 1995), http://www.nytimes.com/1995/08/05/business/international-business-obscure-global-bank-moves-into-the-light.html.
44 Woodrow Wilson, "Monopoly or Opportunity?" The New Freedom: A Call for the Emancipation of the Generous Energies of a People (1913), Section VII, 185.
45 "Benevolence, or Justice?" The New Freedom: A Call for the Emancipation of the Generous Energies of a People (1913), Section IX, 201.

> *"The issue which has swept down the centuries and which will have to be fought sooner or later is the people versus the banks."*[46]
> - Lord Acton -

No matter where you stand on the economic scale, you can likely admit we have big problems. Do not worry - there are things you personally can do to make this better. Money is one of those subjects that most of us want to work hard to understand. We can participate in its evolution.

Let us discover what abundance really feels like and perform better with our money.

We have arrived at the end, sadeaky. This marks the conclusion of humanity's excruciating tale of corruption, tyranny, and slavery. This is a story as old as our oldest books, a tale that has finally and in perfect, natural order, ended.

Now it is time to examine and experiment with the tools needed for the human being to change. Oh, how she fights change with her last, dying breath. The next chapter addresses humanity's coming of age and coming to terms – death and rebirth.

To end the darkest part of our journey, it is appropriate to shift the focus to humanity's embryonic, infinite talent.

> *"The greatest waste in the world is the difference between what we are and what we could become."*[47]
> - Ben Herbster -

---

[46] As quoted in Maxed Out: Hard Times, Easy Credit, and the Era of Predatory Lenders (2007) by James D. Scurlock.

[47] Quoted by Robin Ryan in Soaring on Your Strengths (Penguin Books, 2005), Part 3.

> "We all have possibilities we don't know about. We can do things we don't even dream we can do."[48]
> - Dale Carnegie -

> "Never underestimate the power of dreams and the influence of the human spirit. We are all the same in this notion: The potential for greatness lives within each of us."[49]
> - Wilma Rudolph -

> "Research shows that you begin learning in the womb and go right on learning until the moment you pass on. Your brain has a capacity for learning that is virtually limitless, which makes every human a potential genius."[50]
> - Michael J. Gelb -

> "In the depth of winter I finally learned that within me there lay an invincible summer."[51]
> - Albert Camus -

What dreams have you abandoned? Where is your imagination hiding?

---

[48] Dale Carnegie Training Leadership Posts, Facebook (June 19, 2013), https://www.facebook.com/Dale.Carnegie.Training.Leadership/posts/10151522031432842.

[49] Quoted in "The Fastest Woman in the World: Wilma Rudolph," by Graciela Sholander, http://www.rodneyohebsion.com/wilma-rudolph.htm (n.d.).

[50] Quoted in The Unprocessed Child: Living Without School, by Valerie Fitzenreiter (Lake Charles, LA: Unbounded Books, 2003), 141.

[51] As translated in The Unquiet Vision: Mirrors of Man in Existentialism by Nathan A. Scott (New York: World Pub. Co., 1969), 116

The Freedom Handbook

Who are you meant to be?
What is locked up inside you, waiting for its marching orders?

Come on; let us go catch a few fireflies, a little hell from the ignorant, a hard-earned lesson or two along the way, and surely some of our wildest dreams.

CHAPTER THIRTEEN

- A Whole World's Dark Night of the Soul -

When your eyes are tired
the world is tired also.

When your vision has gone
no part of the world can find you.

Time to go into the dark
where the night has eyes
to recognize its own.

There you can be sure
you are not beyond love.

The dark will be your womb
tonight.

The night will give you a horizon
further than you can see.

You must learn one thing:
the world was made to be free in.

Give up all the other worlds
except the one to which you belong.

Sometimes it takes darkness and the sweet
confinement of your aloneness
to learn

anything or anyone
that does not bring you alive
is too small for you.
- David Whyte, "Sweet Darkness" 1 -

---

[1] House of Belonging (Many Rivers Press, 1997).

My brother came by to see me the other day with a friend I had never met.

Naturally, I asked the man to read Chapter One of this book and answer five quick questions. He had a great many things to say, but these statements said it all: "I've got friends that are into all this stuff...I had to stop watching Zeitgeist, and I cannot really handle looking at these things. I just get too upset and do not know what to do about it. Nothing makes sense and I feel like running around in a crazy rage, screaming truth at people and anger at the world."

He perfectly described the battle we all face with ourselves.

This book strains to stretch us, to push us far outside the realm of comfort and familiarity and lead us to our deaths so that we can be reborn. The conversation about a dark night of the human soul, although not as shocking on the surface as other topics, is certain to ruffle almost everyone's feathers.

> *"One must still have chaos in oneself to be able to give birth to a dancing star."*[2]
> *- Friedrich Nietzsche -*

You need to take courageous steps, far into your pitch-black fear, to find truth in the dark. You need to read between the lines. You need to go deep inside yourself to pose questions and wait for answers.

> *"It's beautiful to be alone. To be alone does not mean to be lonely. It means the mind is not influenced and contaminated by society."*
> *- Jiddu Krishnamurti -*

---

[2] Thus Spake Zarathustra (1885), prologue 5.

Whether the human difficulty shared in these pages was old news to you or new, the world has a special job for you. You are to be the investigator, the torchbearer, and the revolutionary.

You are to be the savior of humankind.

> *"Friendship is always a sweet responsibility, never an opportunity."* 3
> - Kahlil Gibran -

We have been talking together about friendship, sharing, and collaboration. Now, let us explore what it takes to shed pain, fear, and loss.

Community is a big part of the answer. Part of building stronger communities means being there for one another, emotionally, as the best of friends in the worst of times.

Nothing less will do.

> *"But let there be spaces in your togetherness and let the winds of the heavens dance between you. Love one another but make not a bond of love: let it rather be a moving sea between the shores of your souls."* 4
> - Kahlil Gibran -

If you are not ready to be free of old habits of judgment and willing enough to be there for your neighbor by really being there, meaning it, and helping them, then you are not ready to lead the charge yet. Instead, look inward first, and then to others in order to help you get there.

Once we are strong enough, we can offer healthy support to our neighbors.

---

[3] Sand and Foam (1926).
[4] The Prophet, 103.

This might sound silly, but we are driving at what lies at the very center of all solutions, as well as within this dark night of our collective souls. You and I can make this journey as individuals, and indeed, we must. A good portion of the journey is deeply personal, and no one can be carried across a bridge he or she does not want to cross.

Still, there is enormous potential amidst such big change to help each other cope. Together, we can achieve our highest potential quite a bit sooner. Together, we will reach home and be free with far less pain and fallout.

Moreover, this is why those of you that already know the truth are here.

> *"The person you consider ignorant and insignificant is the one who came from God, that he might learn bliss from grief and knowledge from gloom."*[5]
> *- Kahlil Gibran -*

> *"A few great minds are enough to endow humanity with monstrous power, but a few great hearts are not enough to make us worthy of using it."*[6]
> *- Jean Rostand -*

We all face the same tasks, to love our neighbors as ourselves. It does not sound so difficult or complicated, but it will take some getting used to, without a doubt.

> *"This is the mystical experience of the 'dark night of the soul,' when old convictions and conformities dissolve into nothingness and we are called to stand naked to the terror of the unknown. We must let*

---

[5] The Treasured Writings of Kahlil Gibran
[6] The Substance of Man (Doubleday, 1962), 85.

> *the process move through us—one which is much greater than we can comprehend. We can never force our way back to the light. It is only in this place of absolute surrender that the new possibility can emerge. We don't just have one dark night in our lives, but again and again, as we are called to continue releasing the images we cling to so tightly."7*
> *- Christine Valters Paintner -*

Writing this book has been as wild of a ride as the one you are on. Luke and I have both read numerous accounts of all the gross and unimaginable problems our world faces, and we have studied many intriguing solutions. Like many of you, we were always left wondering, "Now what?"

This experience was intensely frustrating.

This book is not just an examination of human strife or the combination of both with a few suggestions for change. It is a cohesive, total solution.

As a trail is slashed to the heart of humanity's concerns and distractions are removed, viable solutions are revealed.

This is, in essence, the whole dilemma and a surefire response.

Luke and I constantly wonder, what will everyone think when face-to-face with truth? How will people of all places, mind-sets, ideologies, and ages feel?

We have endeavored to create a work of liquid fire, difficult but impossible not to hold on to. We want you to feel compelled to share this with everyone you meet.

---

[7] "Giving Up A Too-Small God," Pantheos Progressive Christian Web site (May 1, 2012), http://www.patheos.com/Progressive-Christian/Giving-Up-a-Too-Small-God-Christine-Paintner-05-02-2012.html; Christine Valters Paintner, www.AbbeyoftheArts.com.

Even if it is horribly presented, can this collection of ideas still help humanity turn the tides forever? If it is legible enough, will the world just take the core and run, never looking back? Will they leave the useless bits and forgotten authors behind and strive for the new future?

Will people read it? Will they pass it along? Will their hearts-force them to? Will the coup be fully realized quickly? How fast – and where – will revolution's biggest changes happen first?

The pain of holding terrible knowledge in your heart can be overwhelming.

Both Luke and I know well the splintering sensation that comes with a fuller awareness of the state of our world. This is cognitive dissonance at its climax.

Awareness of humanity's comatose state can smash some people's sanity. Others hold on to the truth for a time, running far, and telling as many as they dare. Then, they fade in a lonely battle with themselves, slavery, the entire world of structure, and more often than not, you.

> *"Just look at us. Everything is backwards, everything is upside down. Doctors destroy health, lawyers destroy justice, psychiatrists destroy minds, scientists destroy truth, major media destroys information, religion destroys spirituality and government destroys freedom."*
> - Michael Ellner -

There are a few heroes, however, who refuse to surrender to pain, to the vast unknown, to slavery. They quietly rally our hearts and minds.

Enlightened leaders, healers, speakers, and humanity's greatest teachers, all the kings and queens of our modern hearts, it is time to give it everything you have.

> *"Cowardice asks the question, "is it safe?" Expediency asks the question, "Is it politic?" And Vanity comes along and asks the question, "Is it popular?" But conscience asks the question, "Is it right? And there comes a time when one must take a position that is neither safe, nor politic, nor popular; but one must take it because Conscience tells him it is right."* 8
> - Martin Luther King, Jr. -

Let us look again at the individual's role, the common person's call to action.

All of us will fight this war internally, in our minds, hearts, and spirits. Coming of age is tough. Coming to terms with the awful truths in the world can be terrifying and confusing. Holding fast to our convictions under untold pressures can be even more challenging.

> *"In oneself lies the whole world, and if you know how to look and learn, the door is there and the key is in your hand. Nobody on earth can give you either the key or the door to open, except yourself."* 9
> - Jiddu Krishnamurti -

Jiddu Krishnamurti was a terrific spiritual human being and an impressive teacher in our recent past. His entire life, he spoke about how humankind's revolution is an internal one. The Krishnamurti

---

8 "Remaining Awake Through a Great Revolution," sermon at the National Cathedral, Washington, DC, March 31, 1968, published in Martin Luther King, Jr., A Testament of Hope: The Essential Writings of Martin Luther King Jr., ed. J.M. Washington (New York: Harper & Row, 1986).

9 As quoted in Perfecting Ourselves: Coordinating Body, Mind, and Spirit (2002) by Aaron Hoopes, (Wethersfield CT: Turtle Press), 64.

University Online,10 among many other sources, states this about his philosophy: "He constantly stressed the need for a revolution in the psyche of every human being and emphasized that such revolution cannot be brought about by any external entity, be it religious, political, or social."11

He is wholeheartedly right.

> "When you have an efficient government, you have a dictatorship."12
> - Harry S. Truman -

> "When dictatorship is a fact, revolution becomes a right."
> - Victor Hugo -

> "No real social change has ever been brought about without a revolution...revolution is but thought carried into action."13
> - Emma Goldman -

In his or her own way, every single person on the planet thinks about how screwed up things are. Since we all have these thoughts, and repeatedly, the dragon of revolution stirs from its slumber. When we all come to share thoughts about similar kinds of solutions, victory will be realized.

People say over and over again, "This can't be. You have it wrong. There must be more to the story. No one could possibly exhibit such

---

[10] As quoted in Perfecting Ourselves: Coordinating Body, Mind, and Spirit (2002) by Aaron Hoopes, (Wethersfield CT: Turtle Press), 64.
[11] Home page, Jiddu Krishnamurti University, http://jkvarsity.org/.
[12] Lecture, Columbia University (April 28, 1959).
[13] Emma Goldman. BrainyQuote.com, Xplore Inc, 2014. http://www.brainyquote.com/quotes/quotes/e/emmagoldma125064.html, accessed March 17, 2014.

barefaced evil. I refuse to believe all this lying could go on under our very noses. It's impossible."

If you find the facts of our slavery and the unspeakable atrocities everywhere hard to swallow, the reason is that you are moral and made of love. Good people cannot comprehend how anyone could knowingly behave with such disregard for all that it means to be human.

> *"A great deal of intelligence can be invested in ignorance."* 14
> *- Saul Bellow -*

> *"Propaganda is to a democracy what the bludgeon is to a totalitarian state."* 15
> *- Noam Chomsky -*

Think about how humans shed beliefs.

Some will fight to the death defending old, dead ideas. Change has always been hard, but we are breaking new ground and shattering old paradigms of change, acceptance, and growth with new forms of sharing and collaboration.

In this grand unfolding, we can foresee so little, as the language of our future knows no bounds, and we come from a world of restricted dreams. Old beliefs die in the face of courage alone. We must find the courage to face our shame, humiliation, vulnerability, and responsibility.

Here is another way to look at this big idea of a dark night for humanity's collective soul: imagine you are young, around the age of twelve, in the midst of a long journey. Your parents are among the

---

[14] To Jerusalem and Back: A Personal Account (1976), 127.
[15] Interview on WBAI (January 1992), http://www.chomsky.info/interviews/199201--.htm.

first in hundreds of years to decide to make the dangerous journey to a strange, faraway place called Modeerf.

You are moving from your cherished home, the only home you have ever known. Along the seemingly impossible journey through desert, jungle, forest, and plains, on a dark night when the moon is hidden from sight, you lose your way.

Frantic when you realize you are alone, you scream for help but no one hears. You search for hours, only making things worse, and eventually fall asleep exhausted in a teary heap.

When you awake, your feet ache, your eyes sting, and you are still alone.

Suddenly you remember that your papa sewed a small note into the hem of your left pant leg, just in case you ever lost your way on the journey to Modeerf. Eagerly tearing open the seam, you pull out a white cloth. Stitched into it is the following message:

"Son, I'm so sorry you've lost your way. Life is so big; we never really know what is around the corner. All you can do is listen to the love, and not the fear, in your heart, and then decide who you want to be. You are never limited by the past. You should always strive to redefine yourself in healthier ways. Do this with a brand new, reborn openness in each fresh moment. Life is built of change.

"Now, son, I need to tell you something that will be hard to hear at first. Be patient - men are not grown overnight.

"You aren't my son. Your mother and I have loved and cared for you as our own, but now, we may never see you again. You need to know that your real parents are out there somewhere. You were stolen from Modeerf as a baby, when travelers were teaching in our lands. I can tell you nothing more of your people or real home, only this – a powerful freedom lives in your people, my beautiful boy, a power that can move any mountain if love wills it be done.

"Go; find your love, family, and home."

As a blurry haze of wandering hours and days go by, you realize more fully what it is to be alone. Understanding wells inside. Your family cannot come back for you.

They must go on.

You must go on, but you have absolutely no idea where to begin. You remember your father repeating mysterious words about the lands you seek:

"Modeerf is a wild and natural place, son; there are no rules other than those that live in your heart. Fear it not, for humanity's collective heart knows only insane beauty, cascading abundance, everlasting love, and all things heavenly; but only the bravest, most courageous, and purest of heart will ever find their way.

"Take my hand, my son. I will always be right here beside you.

"I love you."

Many of us have ridden on oceans of loneliness all our lives.

It can often be easier to connect with all that is, than with the person in front of us. We all come to times and places where we cry those same lost tears as the young boy in our story.

He knows nothing. Can you imagine his colossal fear? With no possible clue where to begin, he must. First though, he needs to understand what has befallen him. He must find the courage to face the truth about his beginnings. He needs to face all his fears and move forward.

Without a perfect plan, he has to make some hard choices about direction.

Modeerf, or freedom, is a feeling, waiting to be discovered and shared.

> *"Refuse to fall down. If you cannot refuse to fall down, refuse to stay down. If you cannot refuse to stay down, lift your heart toward heaven, and like a hungry beggar, ask that it be filled, and it will be*

> *filled. You may be pushed down. You may be kept from rising. But no one can keep you from lifting your heart toward heaven."*16
> *- Dr. Clarissa Pinkola Estés -*

As the boy came into being, I realized we have all known him forever, this tiny dark knight; and our hearts swell and shiver with him in the cold black. Our boy moves through apathy like lightning, beyond insurmountable fear and doubt.

He is alone and must survive or die.

For modern humans in first world countries, apathy is generally a rule due to constant architectural fear and distraction. We can easily lose perspective about ourselves and the world we live in.

> *"For the great majority of mankind are satisfied with appearances, as though they were realities, and are often more influenced by the things that seem than by those that are."*17
> *- Niccolò Machiavelli -*

Superficial stimuli from current power systems keep us at bay. Drunk with sensory pleasure and high on judgment's horse, we live by apathy's rule and with cynicism's perverse delight.

> *"But if you say, you can still pass the violations over, then I ask, hath your house been burnt? Hath your property been destroyed before your face? Are your wife and children destitute of a bed to lie on, or bread to live on? Have you lost a parent or a child by their hands, and yourself the ruined and wretched*

---

[16] The Faithful Gardener: A Wise Tale about That Which Can Never Die.
[17] Quoted by George Seddes in Great Thoughts, rev. ed. (Random House: 2011).

> survivor? If you have not, then you are not a judge of those who have. But if you have, and can still shake hands with the murderers, then you are unworthy of the name of husband, father, friend, or lover, and whatever may be your rank or title in life, you have the heart of a coward and the spirit of a sycophant." 18
> - Thomas Paine -

> "The apathy of the people is enough to make every statue leap from its pedestal and hasten the resurrection of the dead." 19
> - William Lloyd Garrison -

> "People have moved beyond apathy, beyond skepticism into deep cynicism."20
> - Elliot Richardson -

You might be tired of this discussion on apathy, but there is no greater task for us than reclaiming our individual voices and roles in our lives and our world. Everybody needs to explore the rusty intersection of ignorance and understanding and find the road to action. Cynicism is a rabid dog we need to corner and put down. Born of apathy, ignorance, and unhealthy skepticism, this communicative scourge must be strung up.

---

[18] Common Sense (3rd ed., 1776), http://www.ushistory.org/PAINE/commonsense/singlehtml.htm.

[19] "To the Public," No. 1 (January 1, 1831), quoted in William Lloyd Garrison and the Fight Against --- by – Cain (Bedford Books, St. Martin's Press: 1984), http://www.pbs.org/wgbh/aia/part4/4h2928t.html.

[20] Elliot Richardson. BrainyQuote.com, Xplore Inc, 2014. http://www.brainyquote.com/quotes/quotes/e/elliotrich298999.html, accessed March 17, 2014.

"All over the place, from the popular culture to the propaganda system, there is constant pressure to make people feel that they are helpless, that the only role they can have is to ratify decisions and to consume."[21]
- Noam Chomsky -

"Peel off these dusty wool blankets of apathy and antipathy and cynical desiccation. I want life in all its stupid sticky rawness."[22]
- Isaac Marion -

Briefly consider indifference and ignorance, two playmates of apathy.

"The opposite of love is not hate, it's indifference. The opposite of art is not ugliness, it's indifference. The opposite of faith is not heresy, it's indifference. And the opposite of life is not death, it's indifference."[23]
- Elie Wiesel -

"Genuine ignorance is...profitable because it is likely to be accompanied by humility, curiosity, and open mindedness; whereas ability to repeat catch-phrases, can't terms, familiar propositions, gives the conceit of learning and coats the mind with varnish waterproof to new ideas."[24]
- John Dewey -

---

[21] Quoted by Jean Bricmont, Noam Chomsky, and Julie Franck in Chomsky (Éd. de l'Heme, 2007), 218
[22] Warm Bodies
[23] Quoted in U.S. News Report (October 27, 1986).
[24] How We Think (London: DC Heath, 1909), 177.

Our young boy needs to come to terms with his past and present situation, and so do we. He needs to begin his journey regardless, his pain alive and screaming. He needs to figure out where to go. In wild new lands with unseen possibilities, an open mind is key.

With what we know, we need to take those first steps down the road. We need to begin walking, despite our salty wounds.

We can talk and heal along the way.

With freedom comes responsibility. Responsibility means personal and collective accountability. This is the crux of our new world.

We need to become communally omnipotent and individually engaged.

Everyone needs to ask questions and challenge authority. There is no shelter in individual ignorance or diseased prayers to the powers that be. They will not build our world/cages with love or the common good at heart.

> *"Most people live, whether physically, intellectually or morally, in a very restricted circle of their potential being. They make very small use of their possible consciousness, and of their soul's resources in general, much like a man who, out of his whole bodily organism, should get into a habit of using and moving only his little finger."*[25]
> *- William James -*

Find acceptance through action.

Examine the things that need to be done to ensure you are on the right path, for your family and children's sake, if not for your own. Look at the ways you contribute to systems and ideas that

---

[25] Letter to W. Lutoslawski (May 6, 1906).

perpetuate our problems, and then get engaged in the areas you feel most passionate about.

That's good enough, unless your community asks you for something else, in which case you get to decide if and how you'd like to contribute.

Here is an inspiring reality to think about as we move on to discuss violence: freedom transmutes violence with the sheer presence of its blinding light.

Violence is the language of slavery.

> *"Violence is not merely killing another. It is violence when we use a sharp word, when we make a gesture to brush away a person, when we obey because there is fear. So violence isn't merely organized butchery in the name of God, in the name of society or country. Violence is much more subtle, much deeper."* 26
> *- Jiddu Krishnamurti -*

Violent struggle has always been at the core of common people's fight for freedom, across time and the world. At this point in our evolution, with such astounding levels of communication and collaboration developing, the dynamics of this age-old fight can change.

During transition, perhaps nonviolence can rule the day, with tiny elements of physical resistance. However, we need to stand tall, united, and ready, physically prepared to fight for freedom in the name of our children, countless generations to come, and ourselves.

Humans can now access and share collective knowledge in ways we never could have imagined. Our spectacular new tools possess previously unheard of possibility.

---

[26] Freedom from the Known (1975), Ch. 6, http://www.jkrishnamurti.org/krishnamurti-teachings/view-text.php?tid=48&chid=56789&w=&.

We also have all the tried and tested weapons of our past. This is freedom's unstoppable one-two punch, which is already transforming the world's darkness to compassionate, vivid beauty. With the best old and new tools ever created, we are already beginning to heal the world.

We introduce the topic of violence to prepare for a discussion with our military leaders and all those wearing violence's uniform. Larger-scale specifics are addressed further on but our focus here is the individual's role.

Freedom's responsibility demands we single out those of you in uniform.

If we want freedom, then you, our military and uniformed family, eventually need to quit your job. If you can afford to quit now, do it. If you still need the job, we need you to fight with us from within the expiring systems, until restructuring provides new types of jobs.

Do not follow orders that are not right. Refuse to be violent. Refuse to harass the innocent. Refuse to cause harm. Band together and form organizations like LEAP for all issues, on an international scale.

These organizations can dismantle the established patterns of persecution for not following orders.

When the time comes, abandon your posts around the world and disband on the home front. Take your guns; we paid for them. We will need your help upholding peace and protecting our world from those rare few who will see opportunity for harm in this shifting.

We will also need you to help arrest the world's most heinous criminals, responsible for the greatest crimes against humanity that ever were. There is no more impressive way for you to sign off on that career.

Again, humanity cannot have a bunch of trained killers sitting around with nothing to do. Otherwise, something will be dreamt up to justify violent action.

> "Our country is now geared to an arms economy bred in an artificially induced psychosis of war hysteria and an incessant propaganda of fear."[27]
> - Douglas MacArthur -

Smedley Butler was a major general in the US Marine Corps, the highest rank in his time, and died the most decorated marine in US history.

After a thirty-four-year career, he wrote a book called War Is a Racket. If you work in the military, consider Butler's words: "I helped make Mexico, especially Tampico, safe for American oil interests in 1914. I helped make Haiti and Cuba a decent place for the National City Bank boys to collect revenues in...I helped purify Nicaragua for the international banking house of Brown Brothers in 1909-1912. I brought light to the Dominican Republic for American sugar interests in 1916. In China I helped to see to it that Standard Oil went its way unmolested."

Let us end this deranged "support the troops" mentality right now.

We need to ask ourselves what exactly we are supporting. Common people's real concerns are liberty, freedom, health, happiness, and family.

We care about our sons and daughters in uniform. We are creatures of love.

> "Love is friendship that has caught fire. It is quiet understanding, mutual confidence, sharing and forgiving. It is loyalty through good and bad times. It settles for less than perfection and makes allowances for human weaknesses."[28]
> - Ann Landers -

---

[27] Speech to the Michigan legislature, in Lansing, Michigan (May 15, 1952), published in General MacArthur Speeches and Reports 1908-1964 (2000) by Edward T. Imparato, 206

[28] Margo Howard, Ann Landers in Her Own Words: Personal Letters to Her Daughter (Hachette Digital Inc., 2007). Letter of February 28 or 29, 1959.

Do not follow orders that do not feel right. Refuse to go anywhere to fight and refuse to kill when the orders come. Nobody wants to leave their loved ones, lives, communities, and homes and go off to fight a war. Be joyful knowing we are making it possible for our children to live in a world with no war. Without law, rules, government, or a standing military, there will be no mechanism left to convince a nation of men and woman to fight a war.

> *"War is organized murder, and nothing else."* [29]
> *- Harry Patch, last surviving soldier of WWI -*

> *"Why do we electrocute men for murdering an individual and then pin a purple heart on them for mass slaughter of someone arbitrarily labeled 'enemy'?"* [30]
> *- Sylvia Plath -*

It has been said there are three types of people who join the military.

The first type of person does it out of misguided patriotism, at times generations in the making. The second is just looking for a decent job. The third is looking for legal means to support murderous or evil intent.

To this third type: humanity's dark alleys and hidden corners are filling with the light of liberated human potential, unchained. If you cling to the ideas of old and try to chain us down, then in your attack, you will meet your undoing.

Instead, accept the outstretched hand of humanity and join us. We will happily accept those who reach for a better life, who help us instead of hurt us, and who reach for their family's forgiveness.

---

[29] "The last of the noblest generation," The Independent (July 26, 2009), http://www.independent.co.uk/news/uk/home-news/the-last-of-the-noblest-generation-1761467.html.

[30] The Unabridged Journals of Sylvia Plath, ed. Karen V. Kukil (Anchor Press: 2000).

> *"Look now—in all of history men have been taught that killing of men is an evil thing not to be countenanced. Any man who kills must be destroyed because this is a great sin, maybe the worst we know. And then we take a soldier and put murder in his hands and we say to him, 'Use it well, use it wisely.' We put no checks on him. Go out and kill as many of a certain kind of classification of your brothers as you can. And we will reward you for it because it is a violation of your early training."* [31]
> - John Steinbeck -

On that note, humanity owes its deepest apologies to these same brothers and sisters whose minds and souls are left like battlefields because of our apathetic agreement to train killers.

We unearth our salvation, community, and freedom inside our empathy for one another.

To the second type: everyone knows that government institutions all around the world are full of good people who mean well. If you need the job, look for ways to help support the coming change in management.

Eventually, you will need a new job too. Your communities need you. No problem; roll up your sleeves, because there is always work to be found for strong hands.

> *"The revolution is not an apple that falls when it is ripe. You have to make it fall."* [32]
> - Che Guevara -

---

[31] East of Eden, Centennial Edition (London: Penguin Books, 2002), 24.
[32] Che Guevara speaks: Selected Speeches and Writings (1967).

To the first type: for your loyalty and those lofty contributions of generations past, our ancestors and our own hearts thank you.

True honor is now found fighting the only battle humankind has left to fight – the final struggle where we defeat our masters, our ruling-class family.

Friends, fight with us and together we will free the world. We can free our children and neighborhoods from pain, hunger, disease, restriction, and torture. Stand with us and fight for your honor, fight for your lives, fight for our family.

Where will togetherness lead us?

Even at a glance, there is immeasurable space for us to improve the world, but first we need to transform personally. Then, as individuals coming together, we will discover the full potential of our power, revolution, and freedom.

> *"Personal transformation can and does have global effects. As we go, so goes the world, for the world is us. The revolution that will save the world is ultimately a personal one."*
> *- Marianne Williamson -*

> *"The only freedom which deserves the name is that of pursuing our own good, in our own way, so long as we do not attempt to deprive others of theirs, or impede their efforts to obtain it."*[33]
> *- John Stuart Mill –*

All types of people, right down to you, can make all the difference in the world.

---

[33] Three Essays: On Liberty, Representative Government, The Subjection of Women (Oxford University Press, 1975), 18.

As we unite, self-governance is unstoppable. It is time to strengthen the bonds of friendship between all of us.

> "Part of the healing process is sharing with other people who care."34
> - Jerry Cantrell -

> "In the sweetness of friendship let there be laughter, and sharing of pleasures. For in the dew of little things the heart finds its morning and is refreshed." 35
> - Kahlil Gibran -

> "Friendship marks a life even more deeply than love. Love risks degenerating into obsession, friendship is never anything but sharing." 36
> - Elie Wiesel -

Institutional friends, if you work with or for any of the world's governments, be it in health care, educational, legal, judicial, law enforcement, financial, or corporate systems, all those warm fuzzy answers you are searching for are coming. Your global family has your back.

If you cannot commit any hours above your present position within the system to build its replacements, then support those of us who are in every way you can. Imagine if throngs of government employees the world over began wearing shirts and hats to work that said, "I work for all human beings and am ruled by none," or "Undergoing a change in management."

---

[34] Jerry Cantrell. BrainyQuote.com, Xplore Inc, 2014. http://www.brainyquote.com/quotes/quotes/j/jerrycantr434394.html, accessed March 17, 2014.
[35] The Prophet
[36] The Gates of the Forest.

For now, know that everyone understands that most of you are great people. We need your help; contribute in your own ways. In fact, humanity can soon afford to employ the world's unemployed in all kinds of fun and fabulous jobs.

Again, details are coming. Just know that you are desperately needed. We are all equally to blame, unless you are found to be at the heart of the problem, though 99 percent of us will not be.

Dealing with the 1 percent will be ethically challenging.

The differences between old and new systems are vast. However, the alterations are simple, elegant, and righteous. No one can argue with transparency, social justice, and accountability. Everyone wants abundance for all and an end to poverty, hunger, and oppression.

We need to remove arbitrary authority altogether, but we are scared.

Fear and doubt steal enormous energy and momentum from our positive aims. If left unchecked, they can paralyze and potentially destroy our dreams.

Establishing the inner strength to conquer fear only manifests through keen, developed observation. We need to watch our own emotional and thinking patterns. As luminaries point out all through history, doing so is the only path to self-knowledge, virtue, true awareness and critical-thinking skills, as well as peace, and freedom.

> *"You tell me it's the institution/well, you know you better free your mind instead."*
> *- The Beatles, "Revolution"*[37]

There are lots of big ideas and questions in the world. Remember that the answers must come from inside.

---

[37] Performed by the Beatles, written by John Lennon and Paul McCartney (Apple, 1968); http://www.metrolyrics.com/revolution-lyrics-john-lennon.html.

Hence, nothing is really that complicated. Sit and wait for the answers if you become confused or doubtful. No matter how committed you might be to social justice, change, and freedom, we all find ourselves slammed up against confusion and doubt from time to time.

Confusion and doubt signal fear's presence. When you encounter inevitable thoughts such as "This world certainly has gone astray, but we must be able to fix or improve the existing structures," or "Institutions and things in general are bad, but certainly slavery is a bit extreme," or, "Can people really learn to get along and/or critically think?" know that this is what fear sounds like.

> *"No sooner does man discover intelligence than he tries to involve it in his own stupidity."*[38]
> *- Jacques Yves Cousteau -*

Whenever you find yourself doubting the same things you felt with all your heart a moment ago, usually fear is to blame. Talk to someone you love or respect, reread this book, or do some of your own research.

Ideally, get involved in the new solutions popping up in your community or online. There are countless ways to deal with our inner negative tapes and fear's natural push back.

The bottom line is that you must be strong and ask yourself again to dig deeper. Cultivate the most important conversation you will ever have: the internal one.

Humanity is counting on you.

Most of us could use some help conquering the dragon of resistance, doubt, and fear in all its forms, so read Do the Work by Steven Pressfield.[39] Steven's amazing book lit the path when I was lost and helped ensure this book realized its potential.

---

[38] Quoted by David Day, The Environmental Wars (Ballantine Books, 1991), 135.
[39] (The Domino Project, 2011).

Do the Work was designed to help individuals or groups through any project, be it a book, a ballet, a new business venture, a philanthropic enterprise, or anything else. It is a perfect road map for changing the world by overcoming fear's various forms.

A great friend sent the book to me as a Christmas gift in my darkest hour. This is an example of how community, collaboration, and sharing can often help us with the most private tasks.

We hope you are ready to accept responsibility for creating a better world. No leader or Heaven-sent wonder is going to hand us our freedom.

It is up to us.

The math behind revolution is simple and so encouraging you may feel like screaming and shouting for joy. Though it has been criticized, the mathematical law called the Law of Diffusion of Innovation can be used as a common sense indicator of how, why, and at roughly what rate innovation spreads through human culture.40

Those unfamiliar with the mathematical theory can view the concept below.

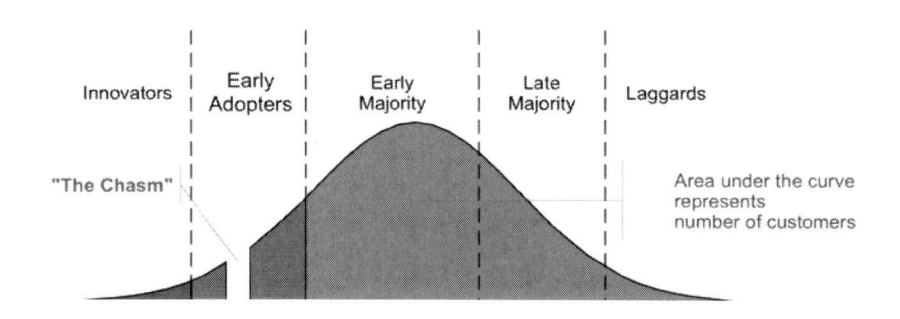

---

[40] Everett M. Rogers, Diffusion of Innovation, 5th ed. (Free Press: 2003); Simon Sinek, "Law of Diffusion of Innovation," TED Talk (October 12, 2012), http://www.youtube.com/watch?v=zU3fIEPfctQ.

The law breaks society into five categories.

The first group, the innovators, represents only 2.5% of the world's population. These visionaries, inventors, and experimenters change and define our world.

The second category, the early adopters, represents 13.5% of the population. These folks love to connect with innovators and try new ideas out.

The third, early majority group makes up 34%. Those in this category are quick to adopt the tried and tested ideas after the early adopters.

Curiously, the fourth group, called late majority also represents exactly 34% percent of us. This group is reluctant to try that innovative new idea or product until the early majority has reached a positive conclusion about it.

The last category, which totals 16% percent of the population, contains the conscientious rejecters, or the laggards. These people might still have rotary phones and talk about how much they hate their computers, cell phones, etc.

There is debate over where the tipping point is and how to navigate the chasm as well as how valid this principle is in regards to broad social issues. However, no matter how you slice it, the fact remains that it doesn't take many leaders to create a movement and it doesn't take long before people who don't see the benefit of innovations like the Internet or smart phones join the crowd and try it out for themselves.

> *"...it does not require a majority to prevail, but rather an irate tireless minority keen to set brush fires in people's minds..."*
> *- Unknown Author -*

> *"Apathy can be overcome by enthusiasm, and enthusiasm can only be aroused by two things: first, an ideal, which takes the imagination by storm, and second, a definite intelligible plan for carrying that ideal into practice."*[41]
> - Arnold J. Toynbee -

The innovators and their ideas are already out there, and the early adopters' acceptance is gaining momentum fast. The early adopters are those of us working on the front lines, carrying the torch, spreading the message.

Be glad and know that this bunch of folks can listen to reason and possess the vision, foresight, and courage to jump aboard a rolling train headed for an unknown but improved future.

Perhaps not enough of this segment is fully aboard yet.

You, however, could very well represent the end of our required list.

On the other hand, there may be enough of us already, and as Arnold J. Toynbee said, we just need a solid, innovative plan that early adopters and the rest of us can agree on.

We do not even need to discuss the rest of the population because people will jump aboard in due course. Humanity only needs a tiny fraction of the total population, the innovators and their closest allies, to agree on the shape of our new solutions, and then big change will spread around the world like the hottest new toy.

<u>This slideshow</u> introduces a few helpful books that examine human innovations from varying perspectives. It also outlines a major key to successfully navigating the tipping point or chasm. After a certain level of success and social proof from early adopters, it becomes easy for the rest of the population to see tangible benefits.

---

[41] Quoted by Eric Robert Morse in Juggernaut (New Classic Books, 2010), 454.

Earlier, we discussed this concept of creating small successes, which can then be replicated around the world, and this is how it is done. This trend in innovation might even be considered an expression of the infamous hundredth monkey theorem,42 another inspiring element of natural evolution.

If you have not heard of the concept, ask someone you trust or respect about it. Start engaging with others and forward our collective discussion.

> *"How few there are who have courage enough to own their faults, or resolution enough to mend them."* 43
> *- Benjamin Franklin -*

> *"You will never do anything in this world without courage. It is the greatest quality of the mind next to honor."* 44
> *- James Lane Allen -*

> *"Courage is not simply one of the virtues, but the form of every virtue at the testing point."* 45
> *- C. S. Lewis -*

> *"Don't make assumptions. Find the courage to ask questions and to express what you really want.*

---

[42] Lyall Watson, Foreword to Lawrence Blair, Rhythms of Vision: The Changing Patterns of Belief (London: Croom Held Ltd., 1975); Ken Keyes, The Hundredth Monkey (Camarillo: DeVorss & Co., 1984).

[43] Proverb #253, Poor Richard's Almanac, 1914 edition (Waterloo, Iowa: The U.S.C. Publishing Co, 1914), http://www.archive.org/stream/poorrichardsalma00franrich/poorrichardsalma00franrich_djvu.txt.

[44] Quoted by Bob Kelly in Worth Repeating (Kregel Academic, 2003), 67.

[45] Screwtape Letters and Screwtape Proposes a Toast, Harper Collins Adobe digital edition (HarperCollins eBooks: 2009), 114.

> *Communicate with others as clearly as you can to avoid misunderstandings, sadness and drama. With just this one agreement, you can completely transform your life."46*
> *- Miguel Angel Ruiz -*

> *"Men make history and not the other way around. In periods where there is no leadership, society stands still. Progress occurs when courageous, skillful leaders seize the opportunity to change things for the better."47*
> *- Harry S. Truman -*

Global courage is at an all-time high. Our creative capacity continues to grow at an incredible pace. Our common leaders are stronger, better informed, and more numerous than ever before in recorded history.

Most exciting, our collective voice is immeasurably stronger than ever before. You can join common folk rallying everywhere. We are all helping each other come to terms with coming together and creating a better world.

> *"Yesterday we obeyed kings and bent our necks before emperors. But today we kneel only to truth, follow only beauty, and obey only love."48*
> *- Kahlil Gibran -*

---

46 The Four Agreements (San Rafael, CA: Amber-Allen Publishing Inc., 1997).

47 Quoted by John Hamm in Unusually Excellent: The Necessary Nine Skills for the Practice of Great Leadership (John Wiley & Sons, 2011), 123.

48 Quoted in The Complete Idiot's Guide to Quotations for All Occasions (Penguin, 2008), 174; Kahlil Gibran, The Vision—Reflections on the Way of the Soul (1994).

The Freedom Handbook

In the first chapter, you were asked about the pain in your heart. You were asked to look carefully and without turning away, at the pain in our world, and in our communities and families. You were asked to follow along with a genuine openness and with love as your only real guide.

Now, your courage is needed most.

Let the whole world see your lion's heart. Let courage guide you. Let it help you decide how to participate, as you discover a growing number of ways to take part in the amazing changes going on. Let your courage roar like thunder.

We are all kings and queens of these jungles.

> *Rise like Lions after slumber / in unvanquishable number / shake your chains to earth like dew / which in sleep had fallen on you / ye are many - they are few*
> *- Percy Bysshe Shelley49 -*

---

[49] The Mask of Anarchy (1819), St. 91

CHAPTER FOURTEEN

- Moot Points and Potential Game Changers -

"We can easily forgive a child who is afraid of the dark; the real tragedy of life is when men are afraid of the light."
- Unknown -

"There is a crack in everything. That's how the light gets in." [1]
- Leonard Cohen -

With a better understanding of society's ruling mechanisms, it is easy to get caught in a viscous obsession with questions such as, "Who are these people?" "Why do they do these things?" "How could they?" "What exactly is going on behind closed doors?"

It will certainly be liberating to finally expose the truth and satisfy humanity's deep, long-held curiosity. Together, we will discover truths about our history, culture, and pieces of ourselves, an inheritance that the ruling class has kept hidden from the masses.

All that has been hidden, in thousands of places all over the world, will be revealed in the light of our transparent, collective sun. Humankind will open the Vatican vaults and all other storehouses of our collective accomplishments, exposing our secret legacy from which everyone can learn.

The archaeological secrets alone are exciting to contemplate.

All things hidden are hidden for one purpose – control.

The means of this control are confusion, propaganda, technology turned against the public, theft, abuse, slavery, and death. Its ends

---

[1] Leonard Cohen (Writer, Performer), "Anthem," *The Future* (1992). http://www.youtube.com/watch?v=mDTph7mer3I

include the dumbing down and degradation of a species to a perfectly manageable state of servitude, productivity, and complacent apathy.

> *"The very word 'secrecy' is repugnant in a free and open society; and we are as a people inherently and historically opposed to secret societies, to secret oaths, and to secret proceedings."*[2]
> *- John F. Kennedy -*

> *"The further a society drifts from Truth, the more it will hate those that speak it."*[3]
> *- Jsnip5 -*

Big questions haunt us.

People wonder about fluoride in the water and chemtrails. They worry about HAARP and technology's role in global mind control. The questions regarding secret societies and reported black magic are undoubtedly important, as are those about the technology the rulers secretly possess.

Technology is decades, if not centuries, ahead of popular purview. We need to be asking what kind of weaponry authorities can unleash on humanity if we push back.

In addition, of course, there is all this talk of aliens and the reptilians...

Hang on...

We have worked hard to differentiate between opinion and fact. By and large, all the facts in this book are just that. For example, there is little room for debate about fluoride in the water anymore. Look

---

[2] Address before the American Newspaper Publishers Associations (April 27, 1961). Audio: http://www.jfklibrary.org/Asset-Viewer/Archives/JFKWHA-025-001.aspx.

[3] Post to RealistNews.net forum (February 14, 2011), quoting opinion piece by Selwyn Duke (May 6, 2009).

for yourself if you have any doubts and make your own decision.[4] Only 5 percent of the world's population's water supply is currently being fluoridated.[5]

In the United States, more people drink fluoridated water than the rest of the world combined, at 55% of global consumption.

Indisputably, fluoride is highly toxic to the human body. The regions of the world where higher levels of fluoride naturally occur in the water also have systems in place to remove it. Countries that do not fluoridate their water supplies do not have higher rates of tooth decay.

You can see a complete list of the twenty-seven countries that have a water fluoridation program, along with the status of OECD nations and a few other healthy resources, in the bibliography.[6]

Fluoridation is unethical and a major health risk for human beings.

Dr. Paul Connett, the director of the global organization Fluoride Action Network (FAN), wrote a terrific article entitled "50 Reasons to Oppose Fluoridation," as well as a book called The Case Against Fluoride.[7]

---

[4] Paul Connett, James Beck, and H.S. Micklem, *The Case Against Fluoride: How Hazardous Waste Ended Up in Our Drinking Water and the Bad Scientists and Powerful Politics That Keep It There* (White River Junction, VT: Chelsea Green Publishing, 2010).

[5] "Water Fluoridation Status in OECD Nations," *Fluoride Action Network* (August 2012), http://fluoridealert.org/content/oecd_nations/.

[6] "Water Fluoridation Status in OECD Nations," *Fluoride Action Network* (August 2012), http://fluoridealert.org/content/oecd_nations/; http://skeptics.stackexchange.com/questions/10717/has-99-of-the-western-continental-europe-banned-water-fluoridationhttp://fluoridealert.org/content/oecd_nations/http://fluoridealert.org/content/bfs-2012/http://fluoridealert.org/studies/dental_fluorosis02/)

[7] Dr. Paul Connett, Ph.D.; Dr. James Beck, M.D., Ph.D., and Dr. H.S. Micklem, D.Phil., *The Case Against Fluoride: How Hazardous Waste Ended Up in Our Drinking Water and the Bad Science and Powerful Politics that Keep It There* (White River Junction, VT: Chelsea Green Publishing, 2010).

While at home for the holidays one year as a young man, a conversation around the dinner table took a turn I will never forget. A respected and intelligent scientist sat across the table, so I could not resist asking her about fluoride in the water.

"Isn't it dangerous?" I asked, intensely curious about what an intellectual might think of all the data floating around.

"Fluoride has accepted health benefits, and anything else is a ridiculous assertion," she responded.

We cannot really blame her.

Any other conclusion would mean that popular opinion and even science and education were being manipulated for nefarious ends, a heartbreaking idea for any scientist and human being.

Fluoride was easy to discuss briefly, but some subjects are not. Everything that was not discussed in the book was for good reason. Everyone is dying to know the details of the power structure's secret inner workings.

However, we need to answer these questions together, in due course. When the time comes, humanity will deal with them effectively and in transparent fashion.

Then, we will all share in the good feelings that come with uncovering the truth.

For now, realize that the distraction of these questions can become an impossible problem and the consequences of too much focus on the problem can often destroy individual and collective hope for freedom by distracting us from the solutions we are moving towards.

Yet, the high levels of legitimate, as well as incited, controversy surrounding these intriguing topics make them almost too confusing to discuss. The world needs more of us to help solve her core concerns, and avoiding these troublesome questions makes it easier for people to join in.

We all need to agree that the conversations about the roots of humanity's problems are messy and that we do not need to agree on the mess before agreeing to start making things better.

We can begin to self-govern and vastly improve our situation by first focusing on small models that we can replicate on a large scale. One step, one region, and one industry at a time, this process will free and open up the world.

Along the way, we will equip and train ourselves to deliver justice in the most difficult cases, not to mention answer all the toughest questions.

The perilous debates will end themselves when the time is right.

Most of these issues do not matter anymore than rotary phones or pagers.

They are all old realities—museum worthy.

The last and largest reason for not discussing such irrelevant and hypnotic topics: Luke and I just are not those guys. For us, exploring problems just is not as much fun as exploring our imaginations, our potential. There is more than enough conjecture about the darkly fascinating irrelevancies already.

We need a plan of action for the problems we can agree on, rather than debates as moot as whether the unseen atom exists in the wake of the microscope.

Over the coming months and years, as we common folk remove the ruling class through our collective voice and transparency, we will continually and naturally refine our techniques for handling local, regional, and global issues.

Humanity was destined to form tribes and then build civilizations, to build on knowledge until various forms of oligarchy and authority developed into self-governance. It is our logical destiny to self-govern.

Only unchecked power and greed can destroy these dreams.

Symbiotic transparency offers all the tools we need to dismantle the old systems and build new ones. Symbiotic transparency offers humanity real social justice. Symbiotic transparency is an evolving idea that the world is welcome to continually re-invent.

A living document is one that is always evolving.[8] If you dislike the definition of symbiotic transparency, then try to improve on it and ask the world to decide what is best. The same goes for all its components; the term does not have to live on, but the collaborative opportunity to make things better is what people need to embrace.

> *"For me, forgiveness and compassion are always linked: how do we hold people accountable for wrongdoing and yet at the same time remain in touch with their humanity enough to believe in their capacity to be transformed?"*[9]
> *- Bell Hooks -*

> *"It is not only the slave or serf who is ameliorated in becoming free...the master himself did not gain less in every point of view...for absolute power corrupts the best natures."*[10]
> *- Alphonse Marie L. de Prat de Lamartine -*

Before moving on to discuss the game changers, we need to look at something terrible.

This horrifying reality should motivate every one of us. Akin to the section on the horrors of child abuse we discussed in religion, this is the darkest discussion in the book. We will cover it as quickly as we can, but we need to do so. In the bibliography, you will find several links and references to support the discussion and help guide you to the best places to plug in and ways to help put an end to these crimes.

---

[8] http://en.wikipedia.org/wiki/Living_document; I http://onlineslangdictionary.com/meaning-definition-of/living-document

[9] *Feminism Is for Everybody* (Pluto Press, 2000).

[10] Alphonse Marie L. de Prat de Lamartine, trans. from the French (London: H.G. Clarke, Fifth edition, 1848), 24.

Pedophilia is an ugly reality. Logic dictates that it exists in all parts of society, including elite circles. Numerous sophisticated and highly commercialized global child-abuse rings, which involve pedophiles from all occupations, including those involved in organized crime, have been acknowledged and successfully prosecuted.

The following German documentary, <u>Ritual Child Abuse in France</u>, covers three powerfully disturbing accounts:[11] It looks at the evidence and testimonies provided by three alleged victims of satanic ritual abuse: Deborah, Robert, and Noemi.

Recounting identical details, the children describe candles, robes, masks, underground cages, and tunnel systems. They even discuss how they recognized one another's names and faces in video evidence, despite living hundreds of miles apart and never meeting one another elsewhere.

Beyond the sexual, physical, and emotional abuse these kids endured, they talk about participating in much more extreme torture than is considered "normal" such as child murders and sacrifice, and even instances of cannibalism.

During the '80s and '90s, the world was rocked by numerous allegations of ritual child abuse. Claims of satanic cults, organized pedophilia rings, and high-level criminal and government official participation began surfacing in America and parts of Europe.

Frances and Dan Keller are among as many as six people who have recently been released from prison for being wrongfully accused of similar crimes. Tom Dart tells us in his December 5, 2013, article for the Guardian, "Texas Pair Released After Serving 21 Years for 'Satanic Abuse.'" "The only physical evidence against the Kellers was the testimony of Dr. Michael Mouw, who examined the girl in the emergency room of a local hospital after the therapy session and said he found tears in her hymen that potentially indicated that she was molested. Mouw signed an affidavit last January in which he affirms

---

[11] "Ritual Child Abuse in France," Pt I (n.d.), http://www.youtube.com/watch?v=MUzQ7aqFyiU

that he now realizes his inexperience led him to a conclusion that 'is not scientifically or medically valid, and that I was mistaken.'"

In the Slate.com's January 7, 2014, article "The Real Victims of Satanic Ritual Abuse," Linda Rodriguez McRobbie adds, "Their release may also finally mark the end to one of the strangest, widest-reaching, and most damaging moral panics in America's history: the satanic ritual abuse panic of the 1980s and 1990s."

The Kellers' case, freedom for the "San Antonio Four" a few weeks earlier, and the release of the trio dubbed the "West Memphis Three" indicate that we need to be very careful when investigating and prosecuting people for these claims.

Wrongful conviction is horrible, and it happens across the spectrum of alleged criminal activity. The potential for extraordinarily harmful repercussions when it comes to these specific types of accusations and wrongful prosecutions means that humanity needs to be extra patient and methodical when investigating these cases.

Suggestive interview techniques, shoddy scientific evidence, and questionable testimony are all huge problems the entire justice system faces.

Currently, many people share a growing opinion that this entire idea of ritualized abuse, be it satanic or elitist or whatever, is a not only a misconception but a complete falsehood. The wild and fanciful stories told by children in the Keller case as well as the interview techniques used were certainly highly questionable.

However, the testimonies of the victims in the German documentary have been consistent over years of questioning, and seem to be more than credible.

The appalling stories our children tell are very similar the world over.

Many recorded cases of child abuse involve not only the abuse and murder of children, but also the constant presence of video and camera equipment used to produce child abuse and snuff films for extremely demanding and wealthy clientele, in addition to material for the run-of-mill pedophile.

At the time the German documentary was released, it was estimated that the global child-abuse industry earned over 300 billion euros a year. In Germany alone at the time, the figure was thought to be over 1 billion euros a year.

Deborah Muir and Mark Hecht explore the virtual world of criminal child abuse in their report Violence Against Children in Cyberspace and confirm that even the global industry in trade of child sexual abuse images is a multibillion-dollar business. [12]

To watch a child die, the film claims people pay from twenty-five thousand up to a million euros. One of the filmmakers tells us that the most extreme child abuse and snuff films only exist because of a rich audience.

Rumors suggest that the most extreme kinds of pedophile networks, like the ones described in the German documentary, are more common than most people realize. The Casa Pia case in Portugal, the Dutroux case in Belgium, the Franklin affair in the United States of America, and the Zandvoort affair in the Netherlands are just a few.

In each of these cases, like so many others around the world, there have been allegations of cover-ups and the involvement of people in leading societal roles. Investigations in such cases rarely lead to an acceptable or moral outcome, despite things like video proof and due to things such as lost police reports and other forms of evidence.

Surprisingly, in the Portuguese Casa Pia scandal, politicians and a national TV-show host were actually convicted, which happens intolerably rarely.

---

[12] Deborah Muir and Mark E. Hecht, *Violence Against Children in Cyberspace*, ECPAT (September 2005), *www.**ecpat**.net/sites/default/files/Cyberspace_ENG_0.pdf*.

Despite the growing opinion to the contrary, it is estimated that over 60 percent of the United States population believes that organized and ritualized abuse is a distinct reality.

In the following quote, Michael Salter, author of Organised Sexual Abuse, shares some insight into the group dynamic of abuse as well as the obvious need to return to our common senses and listen to these victims:

"Allegations of multi-perpetrator and multi-victim sexual abuse emerged to public awareness in the early 1980s contemporaneously with the denials of the accused and their supporters. Multi-perpetrator sexual offences are typically more sadistic than solo offences and organized sexual abuse is no exception. Adults and children with histories of organized abuse have described lives marked by torturous and sometimes ritualistic sexual abuse arranged by family members and other caregivers and authority figures. It is widely acknowledged, at least in theory, that sexual abuse can take severe forms, but when disclosures of such abuse occur, they are routinely subject to contestation and challenge. People accused of organized, sadistic or ritualistic abuse have protested that their accusers are liars and fantasists, or else innocents led astray by overly zealous investigators. This was an argument that many journalists and academics have found more convincing than the testimony of alleged victims."[13]

Do your own research and make up your own mind.

There are thousands of people from all around the world with similar stories of ritual abuse at the hands of normal folks and, more importantly, our world leaders. It is absolutely ridiculous and sickeningly irresponsible to assume that all of these children and adults are lying.

---

[13] Michael Salter, *Organised Sexual Abuse* (Routledge: 2013), 1; http://www.goodreads.com/quotes/tag/pedophile-rings

What is much more likely, however, is that the safest place for criminal rings to survive[14] is among the near-impossible-to-prosecute ruling class, the unchallengeable global elite.

---

[14] "Four men jailed over global paedophile ring," *BBC News Lincolnshire* Web site (June 13, 2011), http://www.bbc.co.uk/news/uk-england-lincolnshire-13711329; John Henley, "French paedophile ring case turns into judicial fiasco," *The Guardian* Web site (December 2, 2005), http://www.theguardian.com/world/2005/dec/02/france.jonhenley; Robert Rich, "Enormous 400 child pedophile ring busted," *MR Conservative* Web site (November 15, 2013), http://www.mrconservative.com/2013/11/27359-enormous-400-child-pedophile-ring-busted/; "Marc Dutroux," *Wikipedia* Wikipedia Web Site (March 6, 2014), http://en.wikipedia.org/wiki/Marc_Dutroux; Lewis Smith, "Sixty children saved from abuse in UK as paedophile ring is broken," *The Independent* Web site (March 17, 2011), http://www.independent.co.uk/news/uk/crime/sixty-children-saved-from-abuse-in-uk-as-paedophile-ring-is-broken-2244014.html; Belinda Merhab, "Catholic order had a 'pedophile ring' in Vic," *The Sydney Morning Herald* Web site (November 9, 2012), http://news.smh.com.au/breaking-news-national/catholic-order-had-pedophile-ring-in-vic-20121109-292d9.html; Danica Kirka and Jim Gomez, "Authorities break up international pedophile ring that streamed live child abuse in Philippines," *Global News* Web site (January 16, 2014), http://globalnews.ca/news/1086250/authorities-break-up-pedophile-ring-involving-streaming-of-live-child-abuse-in-philippines/; EddyTheCat7, "Satanic ritual abuse and Project Monarch in the UK - an alleged case" (January 16, 2013), http://www.youtube.com/watch?v=dokzA0IQLZU; EddyTheCat7, "Satanic ritual abuse in the UK - Scotland Part 2" (January 16, 2013), http://www.youtube.com/watch?v=Uq-Tm3cyUoA; "Victims of Cardiff Social Services and South Wales Police: Missing Dossier on Top Child Abuse Rings" (February 28, 2013), https://www.facebook.com/VictimsofCardiffSocialServices/posts/607407062618596; Roxine, Tree Climbers: Sandusky Child Porn Ring - Pedophile Ring?, *Daily Kos* Web site (August 10, 2012), http://www.dailykos.com/story/2012/08/10/1118768/-Tree-Climbers-Sandusky-Child-Porn-Ring-Pedophile-Ring; Great article:, Nicholas West, "Child Sex Rings Reveal Unspeakable Acts of Power Elite," *Activist Post* Web site (November 14, 2012), http://www.activistpost.com/2012/11/child-sex-rings-reveal-worst-of-power.html; "Savile victims allege pedophile ring existed at the BBC," *The Daily Star* Web site (October 25, 2013), http://www.dailystar.com.lb/News/International/2012/Oct-25/192651-savile-victims-allege-pedophile-ring-existed-at-the-bbc.ashx; "Boy raised by global pedophile ring," *Before It's News* Web site (June 23, 2013), http://beforeitsnews.com/alternative/2013/06/boy-raised-by-global-pedophile-ring-2697596.html

The documentary Scientology, the CIA and MIVILUDES: Cults of Abuse corroborates many specific details about the most extreme forms of child abuse mentioned in the German documentary that child victims testify to.[15]

The Christian church, Scientology, and even many high level Jewish rabbis have been accused of rampant and systemic child sexual abuse.

Long-time Hasidic activist Rabbi Nuchem Rosenberg has been a victim of some of the classic examples of suppression we have described. He has endured several extremely violent attempts to silence him and end his work exposing child abuse, assisting the victims, and helping his community with prevention. Rabbi Rosenberh has had bleach thrown in his face by relatives of the convicted sex offender Baruch Lebovits, whose conviction was overturned in April 2013.

In Julian Kossoff's article "Sex Abuse Scandals Rock Orthodox Jewry in New York and London" for International Business Times UK Edition from January 9, 2013, he tells us, "This was not the first time that Rabbi Rosenberg was assaulted. Back in 2008, he was stopped on the street several times at knifepoint while being warned to shut down a hotline in which he provides information in Yiddish regarding how to protect children from sexual predators. It was around this same time he was shot in the head after not obeying the warnings."

Julian starts off by telling us that "Jewish leader Nechemya Weberman is due to be sent to prison after being found guilty on 60 charges of child sex abuse, for molesting a girl he was counselling over a three-year span beginning when the girl was 12. Weberman is a member of the fiercely private Satmar Hasidic sect, one of the largest and most powerful within the Charedi (ultra-Orthodox) world. In the run up to his trial in December 2012, four Satmar members were arrested for allegedly trying to bribe the victim."

---

[15] *The Big Story* series, Carlton Television, UK, http://www.youtube.com/watch?v=KOQzmtU1SjM.

A large number of the stories of child abuse, whether ritualized or not, seem to be undeniably supported and often organized by some of the world's top political and religious leaders. This trend leads to some serious and difficult-to-answer questions about the purpose and extent of these atrocities throughout history and today.

There is no uncertainty about the horrifying guilt within the Christian church or the substantial number of victims in the Jewish community. Very little doubt seems to remain about the systemic involvement of religious institution in the widespread propagation of child abuse and the protection of pedophiles and child abusers.

Religious, political and top leaders from all aspects of society are the toughest people on the planet to prosecute for any type of criminal behavior. This imbalance is the root of much of humanity's suffering.

Another deeply connected topic surfaces here and demands investigation. As discussed, the ruling class has been pooling research data on human mind control for centuries, if not millennia. Modern examples are the declassified secret government mind-control programs[16] and their logical contemporary counterparts.

---

[16] *Educate-Yourself* Web site, http://educate-yourself.org/mc/; "CIA Mind Control Child Victims Abused After Program Closed?" (December 17, 2013), http://article.wn.com/view/2013/12/17/CIA_Mind_Control_Child_Victims_Abused_After_Program_Closed/; Kathleen Sullivan, "Ritual Abuse and Mind Control," http://www.whale.to/b/sullivan.html; Ron Patton, "Project Monarch: Nazi Mind Control," *The Evolution of Project MKULTRA*," (n.d.), http://www.bibliotecapleyades.net/sociopolitica/esp_sociopol_mindcon02.htm; Joe, U.S. Mind Control Child Ritual Abuse Victims Public Testimony Full A-C, Human Experiments," *Resisting the New World* Order Web Site (October 21, 2012), http://12160.info/video/u-s-mind-control-child-ritual-abuse-victims-public-testimony-full; http://www.earthops.org/cult/; "Origins and Techniques of Monarch Mind Control," *The Vigilant Citizen* Web site (December 12, 2012), http://vigilantcitizen.com/hidden-knowledge/origins-and-techniques-of-monarch-mind-control/; "Survivorship Ritual Abuse and Child Abuse 2014 Conference," *Survivorship* Web site, https://survivorship.org/survivorship-ritual-abuse-and-child-abuse-2014-conference/;"Federal

The CIA claims its criminal experiments on humans ended in 1964, however government abuse survivors born after 1964 were tortured throughout childhood in state mind control programs. In fact, 317 ritual abuse survivors responded to the 2007 Extreme Abuse Surveys, claiming they were child victims of United States and Canadian government mind control experiments, with over 2000 cases reported worldwide.[17]

"Government-funded tortuous brainwashing experiments on children could be happening today. Some survivors of government mind-control experiments believe there are still children out there being subjected to the same torture as they endured throughout childhood" stated Judy Byington, CEO of Child Abuse Recovery in this article,[18] which also covers a brief introduction into the declassified beginnings of the CIA's MK-Ultra mind control program.

Mind Control Experiments on Unwilling Subjects, Cult Cut-Outs, the "False Memory" Cover Story & Mass Media Concealment of the Nazi-Style Atrocities," *Prison Planet* Web site forum, http://forum.prisonplanet.com/index.php?topic=231197.0;wap2; Eleanor White, "The State of Unclassified and Commercial Technology Capable of Some Electronic Mind Control Effects," Constitution.org Web site, http://www.constitution.org/abus/mkt/uncom.htm; http://www.mindcontrol.se/?page_id=7394; "Satanic Ritual Abuse And Secret Societies - Part 1," Followers of Jesus Christ (Inc.), 1995, uploaded by TyrannosaurusRadio (November 2, 2011), http://www.youtube.com/watch?v=GI4Gz7kKx6g; "Elite child sex slaves "1981" forgotten documentary," uploaded to Youtube by elevenplaneteleven (July 17, 2011), http://www.youtube.com/watch?v=_6FKEwjPmHQ

[17] Judy Byington, "CIA Mind Control Child Victims Abused After the Program Closed?" *Examiner.com* Web site (August 16, 2013), http://www.examiner.com/article/cia-mind-control-victims-abused-after-program-closed; "Child Extreme Abuse Survey," (2007) http://extreme-abuse-survey.net/; "Judy Byington, Saratoga Springs Child Abuse Examiner," *Examiner.com*Web site, http://www.examiner.com/child-abuse-in-provo/judy-byington; Trauma and Dissociation Conferences, *Child Abuse Recovery* Web site, http://childabuserecovery.com/

[18] Judy Byington, "CIA Mind Control Child Victims Abused After the Program Closed?" *Examiner.com* Web site (August 16, 2013), http://www.examiner.com/article/cia-mind-control-victims-abused-after-program-closed

All these victims and their therapists explain that the acute forms of sexual abuse effectively splinter the human personality. This is a naturally occurring, now clinically recognized, coping mechanism to the most extreme forms of trauma.[19] Imagine what repeatedly watching other children being raped and murdered would do to you.

This splintered human being offers uniquely malleable characteristics, which can turn him or her into a valuable asset for government agencies.

A video called "U.S. Mind Control Child Ritual Abuse Victims Public Testimony" covers a few American victims and their stories.[20] Cathy O'Brien is another American victim who tells her own, much more controversial, story[21] in this talk at the Granada Forum, October 31, 1996. She goes into further detail in her book Trance: Formation of America.[22]

She makes some pretty outrageous claims, but the estimated fiscal gain from her book sales, etc., compared to the ridicule she received

---

[19] Alejandra Swartz, "Dissociative Identity Disorder," *AllPsych Online* Web site (December 10, 2001), http://allpsych.com/journal/did.html; Ralph B. Allison, "Understanding the Splintered Mind," *Dissociation.com* Web site (April 13, 2005), http://www.dissociation.com/2007/docReader.asp?url=/docs/Understanding%20the%20Splintered%20Mind.txt; "All of Me," *Sixty Minutes Australia* Web site (September 30, 2011), http://sixtyminutes.ninemsn.com.au/stories/8354008/all-of-me.

[20] "U.S. Human Experiments—Mind Control, Ritual Child Abuse? Victims Public Testimony" by Valerie B. Wolf (clinical social worker), Claudia S. Mullen and Chris deNicola Ebner before President Clinton's Advisory Committee on Human Radiation Experiments (Washington D.C., March 15, 1995), Part II, uploaded October 20, 2012, Pt. 1 http://www.youtube.com/watch?v=IfmTAScPofs; Pt.II, http://www.youtube.com/watch?v=fBNKBCU5YQ4.

[21] Rapist in the White House watch, "MKULTRA sex slave testimony verified via 'Cheney's member' in recent news pic?" *Portland Independent Media Center* Web site (October 18, 2005), http://portland.indymedia.org/en/2005/10/326950.shtml; "I finally saw that picture of Dick Cheney's huge cock," *Poor Mojo Newswire* Web site (n.d.), http://www.poormojo.org/pmjadaily/archives/001883.html; Ray Bilger, "The True Story about Mark Phillips," *Rense.com* Web site (July 12, 2000),

[22] (Reality Marketing Inc., 1995).

sure seems like little reason to go public. Whether Cathy's story is true or not, Mark Dice had this to say about her claims of ritual sexual abuse at the Bohemian Grove, in an article where he examines her claims:[23]

"Numerous children have come forward saying that they were sexually abused in the Bohemian Grove and were forced to participate in child pornography and snuff films, allegations that Ted Gunderson, former Senior Special Agent In Charge of the Los Angeles [sic] FBI confirms. So such abuse has been alleged to occur in the past, and by young children with no books to sell, and who are not even aware of what the Bohemian Grove is, or who its membership consists of."

Perhaps the most convincing and emotionally challenging case you will ever come across is the recently publicized story of Toos Nijenhuis, a fifty-four-year-old Dutch woman. Her case is being documented in the European office of the International Tribunal into Crimes of Church and State (ITCCS), to be used as evidence in future hearings.[24] Listen to this courageous woman tell her story here.[25]

ITCCS is a powerful organization working for human rights that needs everyone's support. First, learn about Kevin Annett,[26] as his example is the most compelling we can offer. This amazing man, with the help of ITCCS, is pursuing legal methods to prosecute some of

---

[23] Mark Dice, "Cathy O'Brien's Claims of Being an MK-Ultra Victim," http://www.markdice.com/index.php?option=com_content&view=article&id=126:cathy-obriens-claims-of-being-an-mk-ultra-victim

[24] If anybody has been ritually abused, or has any information that can help with our investigations, please get in touch with us: info@freedomcentral.info; www.freedomcentral.info; www.itccs.org; www.itccs.tv

[25] "International Ritual Child Sacrifice, Torture and Trafficking: A Survivor Speaks Out," ITCCS, uploaded May 14, 2013, http://www.youtube.com/watch?v=XhnG76vwNms

[26] *Kevin Annett* Web site, www.kevinannett.com; "Welcome to ITCCS.ORG and the International Tribunal into Crimes of Church and State," *ITCSS* Web site, http://itccs.org/.

the world's most powerful and heinous criminals. A copy of his book Hidden No Longer: Genocide in Canada, Past and Present is available free online <u>here</u>.

In learning about him, you will find evidence of genocide in Canada and of church- and state-organized child abuse and murder.

> *"I gave Kevin Annett his Indian name, Eagle Strong Voice, in 2004 when I adopted him into our Anishinabe Nation. He carries that name proudly because he is doing the job he was sent to do, to tell his people of their wrongs. He speaks strongly and with truth. He speaks for our stolen and murdered children. I ask everyone to listen to him and welcome him."*[27]
> *- Chief Louis Daniels -*

These atrocities exist.

Governments have admitted to these practices in the past, and we are lying to ourselves if we think they do not happen today. The topics of ritual abuse and mind control are important. The practices are not the same, but they do support each other.

We can put an end to this kind of abuse. Use the enormous and indescribable feelings that these crimes can evoke to fuel your motivation.

As a final call to recognize the inevitable abuse of technology and information to control the general population, just imagine the potentially negative uses that might exist for biotechnology, being explored in Rhiannon Williams's Telegraph article "<u>Prisoners could serve 1,000 year sentence in eight hours</u>."

Williams tells us that "Speaking to Aeon magazine, Dr. Roache said drugs could be developed to distort prisoners' minds into thinking time was passing more slowly. 'There are a number of psychoactive drugs that distort people's sense of time, so you could

---

[27] "Tag Archives: Rev. Kevin Annett," *2012 The Big Picture* Web site (March 4, 2013), **http://2012thebigpicture.wordpress.com/tag/rev-kevin-annett/**.

imagine developing a pill or a liquid that made someone feel like they were serving a 1,000-year sentence,' she said."

The only way to prevent technology and information from being used against us for ill and to help us appreciate the positive benefits without risk is to abolish arbitrary authority.

First, let us start listening more closely to these victims.

It is time for the world to investigate these crimes together, with a real display of human capacity for a change. With that being said, the darkest and most elite forms of these potential crimes might unfortunately be too difficult to fully investigate – like all crimes committed by government and the ruling elite – until we have secured larger levels of global solidarity and success in other areas.

Still, spend some real time investigating these issues yourself. Your desire to learn more, to make a change, to find justice, along with your powerful emotions, can all be used to motivate many more of us to join the initiatives that exist to expose these crimes and prosecute the criminals.

There are two large, and uniquely problematic, game changers left to discuss.

These issues are revolutionary in themselves. In fact, the controlling powers of today could use this subject matter in a last-ditch effort to maintain control under serious threat of global coup.

The potential for massive stores of hidden technology, human history, and archaeology. Secret technology is a given: the question is how advanced we really are. Human history could also be very different from what we believe it to be. There seems to be large amounts of archeological evidence to support radical shifts in our thinking.

The potential for extraterrestrial existence.

We are not here to debate these topics. However, Luke, I, and untold millions of you question and in some cases firmly believe that science supports strong evidence for both.

If you are truly curious about either subject, Dr. Steven Grier is among those leading the global charge for what he calls the "disclosure of the ET presence." For an expanded archaeological perspective on human history, check out both Graham Hancock and Michael Cremo.

The critical issue at hand, however, is the ruling elite's capacity to use such groundbreaking subject matter to galvanize common opinion on new perceived threats or massive shifts in our belief systems. A paradigm-shifting event that humanity has never seen the likes of or a threat so large we cannot understand it: two perfect scenarios in which the powers that be can step in and save the world from a manufactured threat while scared people sit at home and watch a theatre of pandemonium unfold.

If the world we knew came crashing down, we would habitually – not naturally – seek shelter and confidence from up on high, as we have been trained to do over millennia.

The actual phrase "the powers that be" needs to be expunged from our vocabulary. It is insane. We need to be vigilant. There is no possible excuse for surrendering our right to self-govern our global community.

> *"The world belongs to humanity, not this leader, that leader, kings or religious leaders. The world belongs to humanity. Each country belongs essentially to their own people."*[28]
> *- The Dalai Lama -*

There are no problems the human race cannot face and overcome. We are quite capable of managing our collective and individual selves, but society needs protection from greed and individual

---

[28] Catherine Shoichet, "Dalai Lama: World belongs to 'humanity,' not leaders," WTVR-CBS (April 26, 2012), quoting interview on "Piers Morgan Tonight," CNN (April 25, 2012), http://wtvr.com/2012/04/26/dalai-lama-world-belongs-to-humanity-not-leaders/

power. Transparency is the answer, the linchpin, and inherent in this information revolution.

The only question is how long it will take us to route around the censorship of our information.

It has been proven that a few Rockefellers and rogue elitists caused the stock market crash of 1929. They upended the national financial system in the United States and swooped in with the Federal Reserve private banking solution, the very same Federal Reserve System in place today.

At the time, the public was educated and very wary about oppressive banking solutions, right up until the seemingly insurmountable financial crisis presented itself. After the crisis, the same elitist puppeteers bought up property and corporations for pennies on the dollar in what some consider to be the largest single act of robbery in history.

Individual or institutional authority cannot be used to solve any of humanity's problems. Transparent, collective authority is the only kind left. At the end of humankind's current evolution, you sure would not want to be a former elitist.

> *"No man can put a chain about the ankle of his fellow man without at last finding the other end fastened about his own neck."* [29]
> *- Frederick Douglass -*

Remember this conversation if some earth shattering false flag scenario should take place. The world's authorities are practiced masters at manipulating popular opinion through crises' such as economic collapses, terrorist attacks, false reports of enemy military action and human rights violations, and so on.

The Boston Marathon bombing shows many telltale signs of a false flag event, as do many of the "mass shootings" of late. Financial crashes, 9/11, and almost every single moment of crisis or savagery

---

[29] Speech at Civil Rights Mass Meeting, Washington DC (October 22, 1883).

you can think of, nearly all are contrived crisis, lies, often interwoven with partial truths.

> *"No matter how big the lie; repeat it often enough and the masses will regard it as the truth."- John F. Kennedy -*

> *"How easy it is to make people believe a lie, and how hard it is to undo that work again!"*
> *- Mark Twain -*

Hollywood-style false footage and propagandized news have reached impressive technical heights. We common folk need to work together to strengthen our voice, transparency's power, and our collective critical-thinking skills.

There is even speculation that advanced holographic communication techniques might be used as part of a future global false flag event. If it exists – and it is not that big a stretch – this type of technology could produce images and audio in the skies around the world in different languages, to impersonate the commands of a higher spiritual power or alien race.

> *"...as all history informs us, there has been in every State & Kingdom a constant kind of warfare between the governing & governed...And this has alone occasioned great convulsions, actual civil wars, ending either in dethroning of the Princes, or enslaving of the people...There is scarce a king in a hundred who would not, if he could, follow the example of Pharaoh, get first all the people's money, then all their lands, and then make them and their children servants forever."* [30]
> *- Benjamin Franklin -*

---

[30] Speech in Constitutional Convention, 1787, as quoted in Bryan, William Jennings, ed. *The World's Famous Orations*. New York: Funk and Wagnalls, 1906; New York: Bartleby.com, 2003. www.bartleby.com/268 (accessed February 12, 2014).

A large number of global conflicts are in fact, aggressions against leaders who support the interests of the common people, such as the CIA-orchestrated coups against Mossadegh of Iran, Qasim of Iraq, Arbenz of Guatemala, and Lumumba of the Congo.[31]

Our history and media tell a completely different story.

We must think for ourselves and absorb insanity's lesson on learning from our mistakes, which applies here more than anywhere. Manufacturing crises is a strategy that has been around for millennia and is by far one of the most effective.

The only way to find truth is to think critically and participate. Asking honest questions individually and then acting together with transparency is how we unearth freedom. There is no security, only guaranteed tragedy, in not thinking for yourself and jumping aboard the closest train of accepted thought.

> *"Questions provide the key to unlocking our unlimited potential."*[32]
> *- Anthony Robbins -*

> *"One man alone can be pretty dumb sometimes, but for real bona fide stupidity, there ain't nothin' can beat teamwork."*[33]
> *- Edward Abbey -*

Think about how tragedies the world over have been used to create desperate fear and violent, tyrannical cycles. Generations before have fought to warn and protect us. We need tremendous courage to hold on to truth in our hearts, spread the word, and act out revolution for our children.

---

[31] John Perkins, *The Secret History of the American Empire*, 14.
[32] *Awaken the Giant Within* (New York: Simon and Schuster, 2012).
[33] *The Monkey Wrench Gang* (Philadelphia: Lippincott Williams & Wilkins, 1975), 313.

> *"War is just a racket. A racket is best described, I believe, as something that is not what it seems to the majority of people. Only a small inside group knows what it is about. It is conducted for the benefit of the very few at the expense of the masses."* [34]
> *- General Smedley Butler -*

You do not even need to believe the extremes of our problems – easy, common-sense improvements are available on surface level.

No matter the atrocity, whether real or contrived, humanity is never safer or better off with corporate or individual protection. The human spirit is transcendent over law, but achieving freedom is an ongoing effort that can lose ground quickly if autocratic authority still breathes. We need to look together and inward for freedom's seed.

Our next challenge is accepting the truth and acting on it.

We must find the raw courage to do something about it, the courage to fight back. More people continue to join the positive movements already in place and build on them every day. We are forming new habits for setting the stage around our problems and ideas. Global and local collaboration is growing into new forms of community and institution, the best aspects of the ancient village combined with all the possibility of modern humanity.

Our revolution begins and ends with collaborative action and open discussion.

Think about how inspiring this is.

Even if Castro and revolution's math was right, and we do only need a tiny fraction of the population's support, let us give acceptance a little push and get as many more on board as possible, quickly. The transition will be proportionately more fun, and easier.

So, grab a friend or neighbor if you get it, or parts of it, and patiently help him understand and then come to terms. Spread the message.

---

[34] "War is a racket" pamphlet, based on *History Is a Weapon: War Is a Racket*, www.historyisaweapon.org/defcon1/warracket.html.

> *"One man with courage is a majority."*[35]
> *- President Andrew Jackson -*

> *"Courage is contagious. When a brave man takes a stand, the spines of others are often stiffened."*[36]
> *- Billy Graham -*

Love, driven by our fiery courage, conquers all evil and like light, overpowers any darkness. Let us grow our collective human love big enough, strong enough, and nothing will stand in our caring way.

> *"Who could refrain that had a heart to love and in that heart courage to make love known?"*[37]
> *- William Shakespeare -*

Most people are feeling ready for a change, but you have noticed a few holes in the plan as outlined so far.

Let us talk about that.

---

[35] As quoted by Pres. Ronald Reagan.
[36] "A Time for Moral Courage," *Reader's Digest* (July 1964).
[37] *The Tragedy of MacBeth,* Vol. XLVI, Part 4, The Harvard Classics. (New York: P.F. Collier & Son, 1909-14), Bartleby.com, 2001, www.bartleby.com/46/4 (accessed February 12, 2014).

CHAPTER FIFTEEN

- Holes In the Plan -

"You can never plan the future by the past." [1]
- Edmund Burke -

In the beginning of this book, we wrote "What humanity needs more than anything is a viable solution: a plan of action with absolute merit. We need a common understanding, a common goal, and an agreed-upon stratagem. Leaders need solid direction, as information rules the day and consensus is nowhere to be found."

This book holds within it the pivotal beating heart of our freedom. Humanity's problems are constantly discussed but rarely compiled and analyzed as a whole. The world's most inspiring solutions and ideas already existed, but now they are all together and clearly offering opportunities for healthy improvements and self-governance.

Jettisoning irrelevancy and magnetizing focus on essential and simple strategies, we have honed in on the core issues. Quantitative reasoning, discernment, and critical thinking are synonymous which allow us to pick our fights, pick our agreements, pick our starting points, act quickly with far less planning and use vastly different strategies.

Humans are nimble, changing, and creative creatures.

We will all fight this war internally, in our minds, hearts, and spirits. It is insane to attempt to silence the voices in your heart and mind with popular behavior and thought.

---

[1] Letter to a Member of the National Assembly (1791)

> *"Enlightenment, peace and joy will not be granted by someone else. The well is within us, and if we dig deeply in the present moment, the water will spring forth."* 2
> - Thich Nhat Hahn -

With new forms of sharing and collaboration, we can shatter old paradigms of change, acceptance, and growth. Remember that in the grand unfolding we foresee little, as the language of our future knows no bounds despite being born in a world of restricted dreams.

> *"Man cannot discover new oceans unless he has the courage to lose sight of the shore."* 3
> - Andre Gide -

Beliefs die in the face of courage alone, courage to face your vulnerability and responsibility.

We have said that this is not a complete plan, that you could not possibly squeeze all of humanity's questions as well as the answers to them into a single book. However, we have also stated that this is the complete problem and the complete solution. We have acknowledged humanity's tendency to make plans, and we have said that these tendencies are largely unnecessary in our new world. Then we talked of consensus, saying we need it.

Now, we will say we don't and we do; it's all about timing and application.

Where are the lines, amidst all this contradiction?

Questions about how to implement the changes we have spoken about naturally surface and some of these will be addressed

---

[2] Peace Is in Every Step: The Path of Mindfulness in Everyday Life (New York: Bantam Books, 1991), 41.
[3] Les faux-monnayeurs [The Counterfeiters] (1925)

specifically. However, some bridges cannot be crossed until we arrive and see the lay of the land. What we common folk know for sure is that we need some big improvements to the ways we have been dealing with our problems.

Here and in the final chapter, we will discuss the looks of some of these bridges. Remember though, that the only thing we really need to agree on to begin the revolution is humanity's right and responsibility to create healthy change. We are rediscovering and learning to fully embody the idea of the sovereign human being.

> *"Liberty does not consist in mere declarations of the rights of man. It consists in the translation of those declarations into definite action."*
> *- Woodrow Wilson -*

People do not have to agree on what to do individually during battle. Everyone has different thresholds. So long as humanity possesses the courage to fight for freedom combined with a lucid and living plan, we will win.

Let us look at a few specifics regarding the uncertainties of this plan.

Consider self-harm through the lens of the war on drugs.

The idea of the sovereign human being and our unquestionable right to govern our own bodies makes complete sense to most of us. Nevertheless, we can still be left wondering: "How will we deal with people who harm themselves with drugs?"

Great question.

Justice, as we have relearned, is unique in each case, and categorized rules do not effectively address retribution or rehabilitation. Adult human beings cannot be forced to make inner changes. Humanity cannot legislate good behavior. People need to choose for themselves.

Luke has a brother who is addicted to some pretty harmful drugs, and Luke's wife's mother is drinking herself to death despite the family's best efforts to help her stop. Luke and Maria's families have attempted all manners of counselling, support, and love with these self-destructing individuals to no avail. Luke is adamant about the fact that it is impossible to make real change through force, and this issue sparked our most heated discussions.

For people with doubts left, here is a final story Luke told me on the topic that can help. It is a story about two brothers. The elder we will call James. James was heavily addicted to crack cocaine. James's brother, Michael, loved James deeply and wanted to help end his brother's suffering.

Michael's love was so powerful it drove him to plan a yearlong trip for the two of them, deep in the jungles of a faraway country. James knew that Michael had chosen this specific country because its drug laws were so extreme that being caught in possession of or using drugs would mean certain imprisonment.

Michael employed every method he could think of throughout their time together to rekindle his brother's will to heal, live, and thrive. He watched his brother closely and was both proud and happy that James did not consume any drugs at all. At the end of their year in the jungle together, while flying home atop an ocean of sunlit clouds, Michael felt a comforting warmth settle in, a happy confidence that a major shift had occurred for his brother.

Two days after returning to Canada, James was back on the streets using drugs. It makes no difference how much you love someone or what you do; the decision to change must come from inside the person in question.

Change cannot be forced, but you can support it.

In some situations, people like James choose to heal. Compassionate support and counselling make a major difference for lots of people. Through caring, transparent, and collected efforts, huge improvements can be made across all social platforms. Drugs are a health problem, not a criminal one.

In short, let us focus on learning to help people heal instead of fruitless attempts to restrict adult human behavior.

Protecting the environment and ensuring corporate accountability seem to be two of the largest holes. There are no exceptions to humanity's golden principles of self-governance. No written rules, no arbitrary or individual authority, and complete transparency in all activities must be the order of the day.

> *"Government is an unnecessary evil. Human beings, when accustomed to taking responsibility for their own behavior, can cooperate on a basis of mutual trust and helpfulness."*[4]
> *- Fred Woodworth -*

The world can easily handle both environmental and corporate accountability concerns using a simple new technique. We need shareholder and employee accountability in all corporate activities.

Guidelines for dealing with criminal issues in general were handled earlier, but more specific corporate accountability questions remain "How do we hold people and corporations accountable," "Who's really responsible and to what extent," and "What does true justice even look like?"

The answers to all these questions are hardly complicated. Every person who owns shares or works for a company would liable for everything that company does during the time frame he or she works there. Every employee, shareholder, investor, and even subcontractor should be held liable.

On the surface it sounds unreasonable to make the secretary and everybody else working within a large corporation liable for the decisions of every manager, who could have perhaps been coerced by an executive superior, but life is simple: either everybody's responsible for the world we live in or nobody is.

---

[4] The Match.

Socialists, libertarians, anarchists, and fans of democracy alike can all find common ground and answers to valid concerns in this strikingly straightforward strategy. Debate between right and left factions that are concerned about social justice and how to balance ethics and commerce will end.

When profit is involved, the only way to make people do the right thing is shared accountability. Currently around the world, shareholders cannot be held responsible for anything their company does. Companies may face lawsuits and go out of business, but in most cases, they receive nominal fines and then continue doing whatever they want.

> "Companies, to date, have often used the excuse that they are only beholden to their shareholders, but we need shareholders to think of themselves as stakeholders in the well being of society as well." 5
> - Simon Mainwaring -

Now consider the rules and regulations that politicians continually compile and then exempt themselves from as well as their favorite groups.

For example, in the United States, insider trading is against the law, and even a very famous and wealthy Martha Stewart went to jail for it. Yet United States senators and members of congress consistently stole millions, if not billions, in exactly the same criminal fashion, year after year.

Despite this article from the April 2012 Wall Street Journal detailing new legislation, which finally made sections of this activity illegal, hypocrisy exists and infects all levels of American government.6

---

5   "Blake Mycoskie on TOMS new One for One Eyewear: Part," The We First Blog (June 24, 2011), http://simonmainwaring.com/future/blake-mycoskie-on-toms-new-one-for-one-eyewear-part-2/.

6   http://www.techdirt.com/articles/20130416/08344222725/congress-quickly-quietly-rolls-back-insider-trading-rules-itself.shtml; http://blogs.wsj.com/

> *"It is interesting to observe that in the year 1935 the average individual's incurious attitude towards the phenomenon of the State is precisely what his attitude was towards the phenomenon of the Church in the year, say, 1500. The State was then a very weak institution; the Church was very strong. The individual was born into the Church, as his ancestors had been for generations, in precisely the formal, documented fashion in which he is now born into the State. He was taxed for the Church's support, as he now is for the State's support. He was supposed to accept the official theory and doctrine of the Church, to conform to its discipline, and in a general way to do as it told him; again, precisely the sanctions that the State now lays upon him. If he were reluctant or recalcitrant, the Church made a satisfactory amount of trouble for him, as the State now does. Notwithstanding all this, it does not appear to have occurred to the Church-citizen of that day, any more than it occurs to the State-citizen of the present, to ask what sort of institution it was that claimed his allegiance."7*
> *- Albert Jay Nock -*

Trashing and re-creating our old systems to improve how we address humanity's concerns is hardly the problem people perceive it to be.

---

corruption-currents/2012/04/04/obama-signs-ban-on-congressional-insider-trading/

[7] Our Enemy, the State (1935), Chapter I, Part V, http://flag.blackened.net/daver/anarchism/nock/oets1.htm.

The truth is that the human race cannot possibly arrive anywhere remotely close to the terrible place that we are in right now. The fears people have of chaos, confusion, and failure are almost totally imaginary. Problems, adjustments, learning, and improvements are all natural parts of any process, including the processes we currently use.

The only thing we are changing is who is in charge.

Transparency and community are all we need to rebuild the world. It is impossible not to improve on systems that are so archaic, riddled with corruption and disease.

It would go against every law in our nature for us not to improve ourselves using transparency.

Let us return to the issues of the environment and corporate accountability. If there were no special protection for you, as an employee or investor, you would not want to work for or invest in an organization that polluted or operated unethically.

Therefore, the common-sense solution for any decent employee who becomes aware of criminal activities is to take measures to expose the truth, and then leave the company. If you were working for a company and discovered nefarious activities, you would be responsible for exposing the harmful behavior to the company and media.

Then, you could easily prove to any victims or a jury that you did your part.

By employing these techniques, humanity assures that all private enterprise is continually held accountable to the most contemporary standards of ethics and environmental stewardship.

Think about what will happen when people in the first country to adopt this principle unite. The lone example would help the rest of the world in many ways. At this, some people naturally inquire, "What if this country couldn't compete economically anymore," or "Why would companies continue to do business there, if they could avoid the limitations elsewhere?"

We simply publicize, ostracize, and pressure with new transparent zeal any organizations that avoid humankind's only global principle for environmental stewardship and general ethics. Continued exposure and pressure is more than any structure or organization can take, especially as we gain momentum.

Even a small coalition of participating countries can begin a landslide of global pressure that quickly converts the remaining regions of the planet.

Common people are the world; we make things run, and now it is time to decide for ourselves, into which machines we will put our quarters. We are building new machines and re-tooling our old systems where possible. All new systems will function with ultimate transparency.

Big, polluting corporations or pharmaceutical companies that murder for profit will not be able to conduct business in any region. We would begin testing and refining this principle in small areas and then we would be able to scale our healthy ideas and models all around the world in no time.

We know we can do it.

Imagine what it will be like when all businesses are ethical and environmentally sustainable.

Soulless corporations will not survive for long as they run and hide within the last dark vestiges of humanity. Change is funny that way; when the time comes, there is no turning back. Organizations that try to fight it will find themselves quickly forced to acclimate or die.

Environmentally responsible countries will certainly entice corporations and individuals to come do business, especially when no one pays any tax at all.

Luke runs his own company, and he would be first in line to start operating by the new principles. Think about how those countries will help his organization by being a more productive and capable contributor to the community and world we all share.

Untold tax dollars funnel into corrupt pockets, war, propaganda, and unhealthy systems that cannot operate efficiently or profitably.

Let us stop this.

Imagine the potential if the resources of every business and individual in the world were in the hands of the individuals who had earned them. Look around. There are more than enough people concerned about every issue we have to deal with.

"I live in and operate my business in a free country."

This powerful statement attracts. In many regimes, common people flock to escape over real and political walls, built to keep them in. Real liberty and freedom is magnetic and attracts participation. Imagine saying, "We don't pollute, our companies operate in harmony with the planet, and our corporations pay zero taxes, allowing us to build and fund our own social programs."

Next, we come to the need for consensus, which many people look at as a hole in the plan. Consensus can seem impossible because of our mental conditioning and training. Deep inside, we know how to engage with one another naturally; you have been pushed, prodded, and persecuted into believing your brothers and sisters are enemies.

Everyone understands the need for community, collaboration, creativity, compassion, sharing, and agility. However, the truth is that we are just fearful of our neighbors and doubt our abilities to get along.

This fear blocks the path to corrected, collected living. There are many ways to rediscover trust in each other through healthy communication.

To achieve solidarity we need to understand that the objecting party is always right. The objection itself requires that we sit down beside members of our community and help them understand that we do care about their points of view. When you really try to understand another person or group's point of view, it often become clear there is room for compromise and a strong win-win scenario.

It is also tremendously empowering to realize that most often, disagreements become outright conflict because of underdeveloped communicative habits, not in differences of opinion.

Conflict stems from the approaches we take.

> *"10% of Conflicts is due to difference in opinion. 90% is due to wrong tone of voice."*
> *- Unknown -*

Remember, you cannot pick people up, carry them across the bridge, and plop them down in healthier territory. We have to listen to each other, talk to each other, and help everyone come around. We have to talk until we reach consensus or until every known effort has been made to achieve it, and the majority can then move forward with sound, transparent activities.

You do this all the time already. We all know exactly how it works.

Look around. We all reach agreements with our coworkers, neighbors, and friends all day long without the help of authority. Moreover, in our new world, when we cannot agree our transparent community will help us discover fair and customized solutions that make sense.

New habits for sharing all our information and every ounce of responsibility will take time to form, but this is the best and healthiest kind of challenge to have.

Most of the time people get along. We just need a little practice to relearn to live and work openly together in all aspects of life.

We do not need parents. We only need enough trust in each other to take the first scary steps, and even our first steps will be humungous improvements. This is our rite of passage, our coming of age into full adulthood and freedom.

> *"It is easier to love humanity as a whole than to love one's neighbor."* 8
> - Eric Hoffer -

> *"Wherever there is degeneration and apathy, there also is sexual perversion, cold depravity, miscarriage, premature old age, grumbling youth, there is a decline in the arts, indifference to science, and injustice in all its forms."* 9
> - Anton Chekhov -

Now that we have come to understand that common folks are currently treated as tender and property to be traded, discarded, and destroyed at will by an age-old ruling class, hopefully you have realized that you have been being treated like assets.

If we hesitate with half measures and fear, we will quickly discover a real New World Order of brutal physical slavery.

> *"It is easy to sit up and take notice. What is difficult is getting up and taking action."* 10
> - Al Batt -

---

[8] The Ordeal of Change (1963), Chapter 11
[9] Letter to A.S. Suvorin (November 1889).
[10] Quoted in Quotable Quotes: Wit and Wisdom from the Greatest Minds of Our Times, Editors of Reader's Digest (n.d.).

> "Inaction breeds doubt and fear. Action breeds confidence and courage. If you want to conquer fear, do not sit at home and think about it. Go out and get busy."[11]
> - Dale Carnegie -

If you act on the horror and nausea you feel in your heart, this already ongoing shift will fully fruit much faster. It relies solely on our levels of cooperation and collective action.

> "Of life's two chief prizes, beauty and truth, I found the first in a loving heart and the second in a laborer's hand."[12]
> - Kahlil Gibran -

The need to free ourselves from top-down decisions coming from corrupted and diseased heights is like a scream slicing us to bits, bunching our shoulders and necks, and awakening all the pores on our skin; a scream that cuts a pitch-black night into jagged pieces.

We cannot be deaf anymore to the cries of our future's children. The only way we will successfully face our problems is with critical minds and acceptance of our responsibility to meet them ourselves instead of outsourcing them to authority in exchange for false security. We also need transparency, the life force of our world, running through our blood.

The principles of life and in this book are oh so simple.

Their simplicity elicits feelings that many of us cannot wait to act on, but first, some want to know every step they will need to take along the way. People frequently see any uncertainty as another hole.

---

[11] Dale Carnegie. BrainyQuote.com, Xplore Inc, 2014. http://www.brainyquote.com/quotes/quotes/d/dalecarneg132157.html, accessed March 24, 2014.

[12] The Treasured Writings of Kahlil Gibran (Open Road Media, 2011).

You need to embrace the unknown and your innovative and loving nature. This is planning versus agility.

Pema Chödrön is a famous American Buddhist nun in the lineage of Chögyam Trungpa, the renowned Tibetan meditation master. She is also a prolific author and a favorite Buddhist scholar and teacher of mine. Her book Comfortable with Uncertainty changed my life forever. I have purchased it for half a dozen or more loved ones over the years.

In the book, she asks a great question: [13] "Do I prefer to grow up and relate to life directly, or do I choose to live and die in fear?"

She also points out "a warrior accepts that we can never know what will happen to us next. We can try to control the uncontrollable by looking for security and predictability, always hoping to be comfortable and safe. But the truth is that we can never avoid uncertainty. This not-knowing is a part of the adventure. It's also what makes us afraid."

Her words can inspire us to understand that looking for security and predictability in the ruling elite, instead of accepting our lives, responsibilities, and the great unknown, is madness.

Humankind must embrace its fool.

The Fool in the tarot's major arcana represents the moment in life's journey when steps forward into the unknown must be taken. There is no doubt that trials and tribulations are in store. However, new discoveries and all of the future's glory also await your first courageous, unknowing steps.

Learn to trust that if our world needs something done, people will naturally respond.

That is what happens now. People speak out, and we rely on the ruling class and the government to respond. If you trust people to

---

[13] Comfortable with Uncertainty: 108 Teachings on Cultivating Fearlessness and Compassion (Boston: Shambhala, 2008), 5-6.

care and react by engaging with government now, then trust people to continue to care.

Let us hire each other instead, without any authority to get in the way and pillage the process.

People will naturally create common-sense solutions in the wake of crumbling, broken government and corporate dictatorship. The law of supply and demand is equally applicable to social behavior. Look a little deeper into Spain's revolution of 1931, on top of the many other conflicts we have mentioned, if you still have any doubts as to how humans respond to self-governance.14

The fast version goes like this: Spanish peasants and workers took control over production, consumption and social life across large parts of the country, at which point in a rare display, fascist and democratic countries joined forces to oppose them and put an end to their system of self-government. Common folk had proven that they had the capacity to self-govern very effectively. This display of the true power us common folk have, posed a major threat to all forms of government.15

Incidentally, the common rebels called themselves anarchists. In the first of the Power Principle Documentaries, while discussing this Spanish revolution, Noam Chomsky and some of the rebels shed a touch more light on the situation for us:16

"In the media and general commentary the term anarchy is used to indicate chaos, bomb throwing, disruption, criminality. The actual meaning of the term is quite different:it involves mutual aid, cooperation; it's as close as you can get to pure democracy, real popular control over all institutions. Sometimes resistance is leaderless resistance. That's partly ignorance and partly a way to

---

[14] "Empire," The Power Principle (Metanoia Films, 2012), at 1:18.
[15] The Power Principle (Metanoia Films, 2012).
[16] http://dotsub.com/view/e74f7d45-ee6c-4dd9-b039-e597ecd556b5/viewTranscript/eng

undermine efforts to try to achieve a cooperative society with popular control which of course is obviously very much opposed by elite interests.17

"When the collective was formed, when it was created, the vast majority of the people accepted it easily and there were no union people or anarchists at all. There was a big blackboard in the union office. Any worker who had a complaint would write it on the blackboard and it would be discussed in the assembly. If a person suggested something, it was to find out what others thought and if they would accept that proposal. If people agreed, fine; if not, they'd do something else, but always by consensus." 18

"How did the liberal democracies respond? Exactly as you'd expect them to. They despise democracy, for very good reasons: the masters do not want the ignorant meddlesome outsiders to run their own affairs, because they'll do it in their own interest. You lose hierarchy, dominion, and centralized control: all the values that the masters naturally want. So the liberal democracies essentially joined forces with the fascists and the communists to destroy the revolution, then they started fighting amongst themselves. But the first task, for the year, was to make sure that the popular revolution was crushed."19

Collaborating left- and right-wing political leaders have crushed self-government movements in Haiti, Spain, and all around the world.20 Together, you and I can prevent small uprisings and positive changes from being stifled. All we have to do is gather the global voice and defend each other. Our voice is already strong enough – we just need to focus it through a single, agreed-upon microphone, and then take part in the actions that are decided.

---

[17] "Empire," The Power Principle, at 1:19.
[18] "Empire," The Power Principle, at 1:19:20 (Metanoia Films, 2012).
[19] "Empire," The Power Principle, at 1:22.
[20] The Power Principle.

One of the largest battles that remain is wrapping our collective heads around the idea of the sovereign human being. When you truly understand "freedom," you will be able to answer many of the big questions yourself.

That being said, some matters will require professional guidance so we can make informed collective decisions. Therefore, we have to start with what we know and gather the human resources required to address issues that are more complex.

Our global community needs to begin with all "perfect-enough" plans. The best equipped of us will no doubt step forward and tweak the sense into them where required.

It is exciting to consider that most of you would be floored if you truly understood your own problem-solving abilities, or those of the average person. If you have a suggestion to make things better, the world is listening, waiting for you to get out of that chair, or sit and use an electronic device and engage.

All the tools we have at our disposal can eliminate the last bits of your fear and any remaining perceived holes in the plan.

Another large tool we have is our collected wealth and working capital, so to speak. Imagine 99% or even 10% of the planet's sweat equity, rightfully owned resources, and our cold hard cash back in our collective hands to spend as we choose. Just a portion of a single year's near two-trillion-dollar global military budget will address enormous concerns.

Most of you would openly share material wealth with a child, woman, man, or family dealing with trauma and crisis. When problems arise, so does the natural, unchained human spirit built of compassion and infinite imagination.

We need to support each other in coming to terms with reality. The pain and lies are hard to swallow and difficult to process alone. Once privy, we can never again hide in our apathetic shells of indifference.

The truth will tear us to pieces.

> "Once you awake, it's hard to go back to sheep."
> - Unknown -

> "All knowledge hurts." 21
> - Cassandra Clare, City of Bones -

The anticlimactic irritation people can feel at this stage of the book is often indicative of an internal fight with acceptance and/or responsibility.

> "An individual has not started living until he can rise above the narrow confines of his individualistic concerns to the broader concerns of all humanity." 22
> - Martin Luther King, Jr. -

People wonder how the strongest among us will help and lead the charge. So, I say to you: leaders and visionaries, those who rally our hearts and minds, the heroes who have refused to surrender all along to pain, to the vast unknown, to slavery - the time has come for you, our strongest global voices, to glow a deep crimson, the color of our righteous justice.

Ripe change calls you to action and your family calls you to lead. You know what to do.

Let us turn the page in our evolution, and at last find out what real revolution is all about.

---

[21] City of Bones (New York: Simon and Schuster, 2009), 232.
[22] "Conquering Self-Centeredness" Speech in Montgomery, Alabama (August 11, 1957)

CHAPTER SIXTEEN

- Freedom -

How do we change the world?

People tend to shut off when they hear the question. The problem seems too immense. Even when we hunger desperately for change, the first steps toward it can be terrifying.

> *"Liberty means responsibility. That is why most men dread it."*[1]
> *- George Bernard Shaw -*

> *"Our lives improve only when we take chances—and the first and most difficult risk we can take is to be honest with ourselves."*[2]
> *- Walter Anderson -*

The reality is, we possess all the resources, as well as the physical and psychological labor required for revolution. Implementing global changes will be much easier than you might imagine.

This final chapter addresses the following:

1. Ways to cultivate inner strength, so we can create the outer solutions everyone so desperately wants.
2. Potential pitfalls and areas of deep concern.

---

[1] "Maxims for Revolutionists," Man and Superman (1903), http://en.wikisource.org/wiki/Man_and_Superman

[2] As quoted in Everyone Communicates, Few Connect: What the Most Effective People Do Differently (Thomas Nelson, Inc., 2010), by John C. Maxwell, 241.

3. The full plan in all its glorious detail. Hold on to your hats—some of the specifics just might put your hair on end in raw excitement.

Some ideas might seem familiar, even tiresome, but if you skip ahead or your mind wanders, you squander solidarity and hemorrhage potential.

> *"To read without reflecting is like eating without digesting." 3*
> *- Edmund Burke -*

Take a few seconds to breathe, to draw in the strength required to be a warrior. We all need to learn to fight for what is right. To fight with honor, you need to know what you are fighting for and possess a willingness to make some serious sacrifices for victory.

Although some will be willing to sacrifice more than others will, all of us must personally prepare for the battle ahead. Don't worry, be happy. Not everyone needs to be on the front lines. There are more than enough of us willing and ready to lead the charge.

Still, we all must be prepared.

Common women, children, and men of the world, we will be attacked with machinations and weaponry we have never even seen before, along with all the ancient and modern controlling mechanisms we are all too familiar with.

> *"Be not intimidated...nor suffer yourselves to be wheedled out of your liberties by any pretense of politeness, delicacy, or decency. These, as they*

---

[3] Quoted by Lilless McPherson Shilling and Linda K. Fuller in Dictionary of Quotations in Communications (Greenwood Publishing Group, 1997), 189.

> *are often used, are but three different names for hypocrisy, chicanery and cowardice."4*
> *- John Adams -*

To prepare our inner warriors, let us slow right down before taking off at a run through the external specifics of freedom's final revolution.

> *"Without inner peace, outer peace is impossible. We all wish for world peace, but world peace will never be achieved unless we first establish peace within our own minds. We can send so-called 'peacekeeping forces' into areas of conflict, but peace cannot be opposed from the outside with guns. Only by creating peace within our own mind and helping others to do the same can we hope to achieve peace in this world."5*
> *- Geshe Kelsang Gyatso -*

This battle is yours to general. Protect yourself first.

This is the most important job you have. If you are weak enough energetically, spiritually, or personally in any way, the authorities will do everything in their power to limit, subvert, and enslave you. Remember, we all need to face the dark night of the soul, the feeling of fear rising to nauseating levels.

On the other hand, do not be too scared or prideful to ask for help. We can often make this solitary journey more quickly with assistance.

---

[4] A Dissertation on the Canon and Feudal Law (1765), http://teachingamericanhistory.org/library/document/a-dissertation-on-the-canon-and-feudal-law/.

[5] Transform Your Life: A Blissful Journey (Glen Spey, NY: Tharpa Publications, 2001), 11.

You will come out on the other side, stronger than ever, and then you must prepare for a mental, emotional, physical, and spiritual battle on every front. It will be conflict the likes of which humankind has never seen before. The only way to prepare is to strengthen the inner tools, ideas, and feelings you hold dear.

> *"What we achieve inwardly will change outer reality."*[6]
> *- Plutarch -*

Be centered in your heart at all times. Our hearts are the only possible guides when facing a world of dark choices in a battle for freedom. Remember, the best answers surface only when we make a little space for higher guidance to come through. Sometimes you have to be quiet inside while being screamed at to hear solution's call.

Those of you strong in your centers, lend an energetic hand to your neighbors, friends, and loved ones. Be a guide modeling right action and loving compassion, transforming destructive and divisive behavior. We have all been in situations where we could have stood up taller against injustice and for the people around us. It is time to make friends and make examples that the world can follow, that can really inspire.

> *"Safeguarding the rights of others is the most noble and beautiful end of a human being."*[7]
> *- Kahlil Gibran -*

All human tribes have been pitted against one another. We are trained to stick together and support our own to survive. We are

---

[6] As quoted by J.K. Rowling, Commencement Speech, Harvard University (September 15, 2011), http://www.youtube.com/watch?v=wHGqp8lz36c.

[7] Selected Quotes in Treasured Writings of Kahlil Gibran, tr. Martin L. Wolf, Anthony Ferris, and Andrew Dib Sherfan, Kindle ed. (Open Road Media, 2011).

conditioned to avoid contact with other tribes and to be suspicious of one another.

It is time to break out of that old mold. We do not need it anymore. Now, we teach our kids, our neighbors, and ourselves that everyone's basic interests and rights are the same. The only way to meet everyone's needs fairly is to remove arbitrary authority and cooperate in transparent fashion.

People often need to see things to believe in them, so to achieve this goal of cooperation we will need to display all kinds of gestures along the way.

Each person, all over the world, needs to set a new tone and send a strong new message to one another. Ask yourself in each fresh moment what you can do, to show your neighbors that you trust them and that you believe in them. Show them you know they are part of one big common family that needs to learn to get along through the good times and the bad. Finally, show them that you, with all your heart, have their best interests at heart.

> *"Be the change that you wish to see in the world."*8
> *- Mahatma Gandhi -*

> *"A mediocre person tells. A good person explains. A superior person demonstrates. A great person inspires others to see for themselves."*9
> *- Harvey Mackay -*

> *"In everyone's life, at some time, our inner fire goes out. It is then burst into flame by an encounter with*

---

[8] From Arun Gandhi in "Arun Gandhi Shares the Mahatma's Message," by Michel W. Potts, India—West (San Leandro, CA), Vol. 27, No. 13 (February 1, 2002, A 34.

[9] Swim with the Sharks without Being Eaten Alive (HarperCollins, 2009).

> *another human being. We should all be thankful for those people who rekindle the inner spirit."* 10
> *- Albert Schweitzer -*

Grab ahold of all that you know in your heart to be good and true while envisioning our potential. A vision of our potential is the only focus we need.

> *"If I were to wish for anything, I should not wish for wealth and power but for the passionate sense of the potential, for the eye which, ever young and ardent, sees the possible. Pleasure disappoints, possibility never."* 11
> *- Søren Kierkegaard -*

Hold on to this focus when in doubt about the right to fight; when in doubt about our victory; when staring fear in the face. Believe in your enormous human potential. Engage your most powerful weapon: your imagination.

Life is a canvas and everyone has a paintbrush, so stop painting what you have been told and paint something from your own heart! Have faith in the collective artistry of the unrestricted global community.

We will agree on a world that is fair.

If we hand over the reins to any individual, he or she will be naturally corrupted by absolute power and we will be left with a

---

[10] As quoted in Don't Let the Fire Go Out! (University of Missouri Press, 2004), by Jean Carnahan, p. 3.

[11] If_I_were_to_wish_for_anything_I. Dictionary.com. Columbia World of Quotations. Columbia University Press, 1996. http://quotes.dictionary.com/If_I_were_to_wish_for_anything_I (accessed: February 14, 2014).

tyrannical, narcissistic monarch or authoritative structure to paint our future for us.

Consider Buddha's famous confrontation with Mara, a demon considered to be the personification of temptation in Buddhism. During this famous duel, the Buddha sat peacefully beneath the tree of knowledge while Mara hurled blazing rocks and his huge, terrifying army-shot arrows, all of which Buddha turned into flowers.

In the same way, we can and will, transmute problems into paradise.

The power of light is a thousand times more powerful than that of darkness.

Creating lasting positive change can require significant time and energy, but if positive choices were not more powerful than negative ones, no one would ever change for the better. Other times we can purge even the longest-held negative habits immediately. Sometimes we wake up and say to ourselves, "Enough of that. I do not want X in my life anymore. I choose a different path from now on."

The power of positive action and thought is immeasurable.

Understanding how humans navigate change can help marshal some extra faith, inspiration, and courage for the good fight.

> *"Again I say to you that if two of you agree on earth concerning anything that they ask, it will be done for them by My Father in heaven. For where two or three are gathered together in My name, I am there in the midst of them."*
> *- Matthew 18:19–20, NKJV -*

Many positive changes have been accomplished with small numbers, and many people refer to the above quotation from the Bible to show that prayers and/or focused efforts made in concert are more often rewarded.

However, why are our intentions and prayers answered at certain times and not others? Consider how many people are focusing energy on a conflicting outcome. This could be a possible major reason.

> *"Two heads are better than one."* [12]
> *- John Heywood -*

Imagine what would happen if common folk everywhere banded together to create global solidarity on a level never seen before. A few of humanity's biggest and purest dreams might become a reality this time.

Life's seasonal changes prepare the ground for revolution, not the other way around. Nature has already started this revolution. A big, fast, unstoppable shift in human culture is already happening all around us.

Our ability to communicate and interact with life is developing at a tremendous rate. As we change, so does the entire symbiotic world.

Over the last fifty years or so there has been much discussion about the need to manage our technological growth ethically, emotionally, and even mentally. All imbalance and corruption are eradicated through absolute transparency.

All knowledge can be used for good or ill. It is your call this time. It is finally becoming our collective reality and responsibility to fully manage our ethics. The common human voice is now powerful and connected.

There is no going back once you have seen the truth, and the common world is coming to understand the responsibility at hand.

Revolution's first requirement, acceptance, demands awareness. Through awareness, we can work through the necessary stages of comprehension to reach acceptance.

---

[12] Proverbs, Part I, Chap. 9 (1546).

> *"When you make the finding yourself—even if you're the last person on Earth to see the light—you'll never forget it."* 13
> *- Carl Sagan -*

Consider the difference between knowing we have a planet full of slavery and depravity and actually coming to terms with this mind-blowing reality and sharing the truth, no matter the pain.

> *"Owning our story can be hard but not nearly as difficult as spending our lives running from it. Embracing our vulnerabilities is risky but not nearly as dangerous as giving up on love and belonging and joy—the experiences that make us the most vulnerable. Only when we are brave enough to explore the darkness will we discover the infinite power of our light."* 14
> *- Brené Brown -*

Revolution comes alive through courageous action, which is the second requirement. Inevitably, a conscious and aware human being, knowing natural law and his or her responsibility to uphold it, acts with courage.

Let us consider the world's whistle-blowers, the people who tell the truth with tremendous courage under extreme pressure. Mainstream media and the propaganda machine call their actions treasonous and

---

[13] Quoted by Jack Canfield, Mark Victor Hansen and Tom Lagana in Chicken Soup for the Prisoner's Soul (Open Road Media, 2012).

[14] The Gifts of Imperfection (Center City, MN: Hazelden, 2010), 12-13. (Brown 2010).

seek your approval to persecute your brethren as if they were traitors and serial killers.

This sticking sack of criminal lies has always been used to kill or imprison people who threaten the establishment's secrecy and ironclad control of the masses.

To be a traitor, a person must significantly oppose his or her state or government authority, all according to that authority's own subjective opinion, but if this authority happens to be the common people themselves, rising against arbitrary authority itself, then treason and sedition become right and lawful.

Thus, exposing the truth is a moral certainty, and the obligatory act of a good person.

> *"To learn who rules over you, simply find out who you are not allowed to criticise."*
> *- Unknown Author -*

Heroes like Eric Snowden (NSA), who came out publicly just before we began writing this book, Jesselyn Radack (Justice Dept.), Thomas Drake (NSA), William Binney (NSA), Mark Klein (AT&T), Sibel Edmonds (FBI), Susan Lindauer (CIA), Colonel Anthony Shaffer (Military), Joe Banister (IRS), Chelsea Manning (US Army), and Julian Assange (WikiLeaks) need our protection, gratitude, and support.

We need more whistle-blowers to blow this world's corruption wide open.

All of you people who are aware, it is time to come out and expose the truth.

To pave the way and encourage our fellow women and men, we need to make a global announcement and say to our brave brothers and sisters that it is time to do the right thing, and it is safer to do it now! Let go of fears of abuse and ignore government threats of all kinds. We will do our best to protect you, we promise.

To honor our commitment, we will gather our voice on the street and on the web, pool resources and donate to our cause, and demand/enforce sanctuary and protection for these heroes. These things are being done already; we only need the people who already care about these issues to unify their efforts and a few more of you to join with us, and then we can protect our brothers and sisters. Our numbers and strength will soon be unstoppable.

We can't stress enough how important it is to spend some time looking into and thinking about the aforementioned heroes, along with John Perkins's Confessions of an Economic Hit Man, which we discussed during the chapter on war. John's phenomenal exposé offers deep insight into the inner workings of the elite's control mechanisms, war, and national leadership, among other things.

Thinking about humanity's untapped potential can be distressing. The gap is so big between what we see and what we feel is possible, and this distinction can cause massive cognitive dissonance and learned helplessness.

Consider this: we have huge portions of the planet's population to put to work. Unemployment and poverty rates can be eradicated. Large groups of people need, and many more will desire, a major career change.

Details and plans come in a few pages, a place in which you will find the encouragement to imagine our collaborative potential.

Now, we rally our hearts and minds.

John F. Kennedy called the United States to reach for the heights of human potential. He said we could, and many of us from around the world did, help NASA reach the moon. If JFK were here today and gave the entire world a speech to live by, to dream by, to fight by, to reach our rightful freedom and peace by, imagine what he would say.

The Freedom Handbook

Have you seen the movie Braveheart?15 Have you heard William Wallace's battle cry? Did you hear his final, tortured call, a single word that has the power to echo forever in our hearts and minds?

All of humanity's greatest leaders light the fires of our inspiration and imagination. They awaken our hearts and stir our emotions. They ask us to feel, to become painfully alive. They remind us of, and excite, our immense ability. They arouse our deepest feelings, if only for a few brief moments.

Revolution makes us feel truly alive. Freedom is our right, our nature, and it is exhilarating. At the rally cry, humanity emerges and when the trumpets sound, our hearts hear them. In listening, our powers awake.

Global revolution comes down to only one word, William Wallace's word.

This word cuts darkness in half and allows light to race forward with liberation in hand. This single word we will use to stay true, together, and triumphant: freedom.

We shall be free.16

Sisters and brothers, citizens of the world: no matter how these words found their way to you, listen. Listen, as you never have before. Listen with all your heart and being.

At the beginning, you were asked for the same, in order to understand the devastating suffering of all life on the planet. Now go deeper. Go right to your center and be still...

... Listen...

... think about all the hurt in the world.

---

[15] Randall Wallace (writer); Mel Gibson (director); Bruce Davey, Mel Gibson, and Alan Ladd Jr. (producers); Icon Entertainment and The Ladd Co. (production companies), Paramount (distributor) (1995).

[16] Garth Brooks, We Shall Be Free, Concent of the Century (Washington, 1999), http://www.youtube.com/watch?v=AQjyE_ldm1M, We Shall Be Free, http://www.youtube.com/watch?v=UtxqJGmq-Pk.

Can you feel it? Imagine looking into the eyes of the countless children, men, and women, broken from violent rape. Imagine holding them and trying to help them deal with those feelings. Picture living in one of the many villages, cities, or countries massacred by war. Picture losing every person you love. Imagine all the fates worse than death, which your brothers and sisters are living with.

How well do you know the depravity, torture, starvation, and loss that your family is suffering? Can you feel their pain?

Touching these scorching ideas, you feel.

We all hurt. We are the same. We all can imagine how it would feel if the person killed or raped was our sister, our mother, our child, our brother, our father, or our neighbor.

You and I are the same.

If common people unite, nothing can hold us back.

Gather together. Just ask yourself, ask your neighbor and your sister to look at the undeniable truth. Completely transparent, common-sense driven, self-governance is our destiny. Individual power, corruption, and greed know no end when given free reign. Humanity's need for, and age of, rulers is over.

> *"But the most brilliant propagandist technique will yield no success unless one fundamental principle is borne in mind constantly and with unflagging attention. It must confine itself to a few points and repeat them over and over. Here, as so often in this world, persistence is the first and most important requirement for success."*[17]
> *- Adolf Hitler -*

---

[17] vol. 1, chap. 6 (1925)

> *"If you repeat a lie often enough, people will believe it."*[18]
> *- Joseph Goebbels -*

To all the evil in our world, be warned.

The vengeance of all the brothers, sisters, husbands, wives, parents, and family of the women, children, and men you have raped and killed will be nothing compared to the wrath of the whole human world.

Born with the light of potential, common women, men, children, this is your call. Fear nothing, for nothing can harm you unless you allow it. Be distracted by nothing, especially the fate of the few devils among us.

We will follow freedom's light and call to action. This call will build togetherness, confidence, and the capacity to self-govern, all around the world.

With a deafening roar, jungle cats, lion hearts among you, rise, rally the rest, and fight. Fight now. It is time for humanity's final uprising, our truest destiny. Finally, we will come to know and live true, infinite freedom.

As discussed, fear and distraction can be tough. Courage and an unfailing focus on our potential, currently in chains, are all we need to defeat those chains and gain our freedom.

Individual sovereign strength is establishing itself, and common people's solidarity is growing at a phenomenal pace.

Still, a mesmerizing distraction and potential pitfall waits in the dark to pounce on and crush any efforts made and any hope for self-governance. This beast was named "potential game-changers," and it can wear many disguises - libraries of secrets, aliens, mythical creatures, advanced technology, gods, lies, and actual realities.

---

[18] Publications Relating to Various Aspects of Communism (1946), by United States Congress, House Committee on Un-American Activities, Issues 1-15, p.19

The beast in any of these forms could be used to subjugate humankind all over again under a new pretext.

No matter how fantastic or unbelievable the world may become, freedom always means two things. First, no one has the right to any level of authority over another person, and, second, no human being can be forced to do anything, even if society deems it to be in his or her best interests, unless the person was involved in criminal activity that caused actual harm.

As you collect inner strength, you become ready for the definitive shift to the outer-action plan. Whilst doing battle, always remember the three basic steps of revolution:

Acceptance
Courageous action
Setting the stage for new solution

As humanity's revolution picks up its pace, people will be all over the map. You have to be ready to understand and help, not make things worse with divisive behavior and thinking.

> *"If you can't control your anger, you are as helpless as a city without walls waiting to be attacked."*[19]
> *- Proverbs 25:28 -*

My anger has gotten the best of me at times.

Passion is a good thing, but we need to be able to temper it with self-observation. Making space for new solutions by quickly observing your mental, emotional, and even physical intensity can be a tough task, even when we are practiced and highly motivated to do so.

This is a core element of our work, both individually and collectively. If we cannot find patience and objective perspective while engaged in highly emotional and stimulating conversations

---

[19] Good News Translation.

with our friends and neighbors, consensus will become much more challenging. It will become time consuming, painful, and at times even impossible.

The only choice we have is between violence and words.

I know I let my anger go too far sometimes. All human beings are riddled with faults. Each one of us can make mistakes through attachment to anger, but, again, teamwork is typically more effective than smaller groups or solo efforts.

Larger miscommunications can be avoided when we support each other in groups and assist the individuals who have become too attached to emotion to think clearly. The cool thing is that humans naturally reach out when we have knowledge or experience that can help someone else.

When communicating with family and friends about the world we live in, things can get really tough. In fact, most freedom fighters can readily identify with feeling like some sort of communicative scourge, even with friends and family, when discussing the big issues in life. Sometimes our negative tendencies will get the best of us and lead us to various forms of communication breakdown.

It's important to recognize all communication breakdown as having both the potential for violence that needs to be avoided with all your might as well as the potential to be a powerful learning experience.

Through our mistakes, we discover success, humbly. We learn to apologize, to forgive, and to communicate with directness and a lack of drama.

On the other hand, powerful emotions like anger and pain can also be very useful tools for focusing individual and collective energy, so long as we do not become too attached to these emotions and allow them to cloud our judgment and actions.

Rage, fear, and loss can be frightening, but they can provide extra encouragement to take the fool's intimidating first steps.

Humanity needs the rightful, natural anger in sovereign human beings to rise from our current slavery. Your fury is calling, but it needs understanding, acceptance, and somewhere to focus its transformative power.

> *"Step follows step / hope follows courage / set your face towards danger / set your heart on victory."*[20]
> *- Gail Carson Levine -*

Not only your anger, but also your love, friendship, and forgiveness are needed too.

You need to accept the truth and spread the word. We need to make friends, forgive ourselves, each other, and then take hands in our expanding knowledge and responsibility.

You need to believe in the sovereign human being. You need to believe in your sovereign self.

Only then, will you be fully compelled and empowered to take small, everyday actions to help spread the message and be the positive change we need.

> *"Action is the real measure of intelligence."*[21]
> *- Napoleon Hill -*

> *"Actions express priorities."*[22]
> *- Charles Garfield -*

There are four main ways to take action. Through:

---

[20] The Two Princesses of Bamarre (New York: HarperCollins, 2001), 2.
[21] Napoleon Hill. BrainyQuote.com, Xplore Inc, 2014. http://www.brainyquote.com/quotes/quotes/n/napoleonhi152837.html, accessed March 23, 2014.
[22] Peak Performers (New York: Harper Collins, 1987).

1. Communication, friendship, and solidarity
2. Defiance and simple forms of resistance
3. Skillful defiance (the world's professional and creative minds)
4. The battle on the front lines (warriors of all kinds)

Communication, friendship, and solidarity have been discussed at length.

Now, we will explore together specific details and activities that take these concepts to a whole new level, and that people everywhere can participate in.

Just remember that you know the truth. Once you know how to take action, there is no escaping the responsibility. Before you know it, your neighbors might in fact be the ones informing you of these kinds of responsibilities.

> *"Success comes from taking the initiative and following up...persisting...eloquently expressing the depth of your love. What simple action could you take today to produce a new momentum toward success in your life?"*[23]
> *- Anthony Robbins -*

Spread the message.

Our first task is to spread truth like wildfire. In the beginning, use this book as a helpful font of truth, as a battle horn the entire world can hear.

---

[23] Giant Steps: Small Changes to Make a Big Difference (New York: Simon and Schuster, 2011), 9.

> "Man reading should be man intensely alive. The book should be a ball of light in one's hand."24
> - Ezra Pound -

> "Every time there's a revolution, it comes from somebody reading a book about revolution. David Walker wrote a book and Nat Turner did his thing."25
> - Mike Tyson -

As we have learned, the power of information is the greatest tool of all, aside from our togetherness. We cannot gather together, however, without ideas to gather around.

The media, face-to-face conversations, social media and the Internet, and of course books are a few of the most potent tools the world has for sharing and growing our collective knowledge. Use all the tools at your disposal with greater tenacity and stubbornness than ever before.

Ideas change the world.

Spread the message.

To help facilitate mass dissemination, FREE, easily sharable digital copies of this entire book loaded with 600+references, 300+quotes and a plethora of live links to powerful content. In our assessment this just might be the most valuable gated content anywhere on the Internet that anyone can have in exchange for your email. Cheap paperback and hardcover copies of this book are also waiting for you to enjoy and share as a means to support these ideas and Incite Insight, a global think tank and trailblazing new media channel dedicated to the total dissolution of the practice of arbitrary authority and honoring humanity's absolute freedom.

---

[24] Quoted by Stephen Richards Graubard and Paul Omer Leclerc in Books, Bricks and Bytes: Libraries in the 21st Century (Transaction Publishers, 1997), 75.

[25] Robert E. Johnson, "Mike Tyson," Ebony (September 1995), 82.

Visit incite-insight.com to learn more and download free copies to share.

We want to make sure this message is free and easy to share in larger numbers than normal. Send a few emails, a hundred or a thousand.

Pass all kinds of catalytic books on to the people you love first, of course, but do not forget random acts of kindness.

We all need to become family, neighbors, and friends.

Tied intimately to the call to spread freedom's message is the need to arouse our deadened media outlets and personalities into honesty. These people are paid handsomely to lead us. Using stubborn harassment techniques in larger numbers, we will easily force many of our so-called leaders and freedom fighters into reclaiming their responsibility to seek and report on truth.

In so doing, we enable these soldiers of our information's freedom to blaze a righteous and empowering path for us using the mighty weapons of our media and dignity.

Your dignity is in the hands of our supposed journalists, politicians, judges, and leaders of all kinds. This is what we pay them for, so exceedingly well. The behavior of our media and institutional leaders makes many of us sovereign human beings livid.

> *"No honest journalist should be willing to describe himself or herself as 'embedded.' To say, 'I'm an embedded journalist' is to say, 'I'm a government Propagandist."* [26]
> *- Noam Chomsky -*

---

[26] Interview with David Barsamiam, "Collateral Language," Z Magazine (July-August, 2003), http://www.chomsky.info/interviews/200307--.htm.

Barrett Brown is an investigative journalist who was imprisoned for looking into the wrong kinds of state activity. What kinds of state activity was he investigating? The private firms he focused on are all allegedly involved in collecting intelligence on you and me and surveilling public citizens.

Private contractors are an established legal shield for the state's criminal and immoral activities, and not just with respect to surveillance. The legal case against the United States' illegal and immoral spying on nearly the whole world is gaining ground all the time. This spying is considered by some to be one of the largest attacks on modern civil liberties to date.

For a full list of the companies Barrett Brown was investigating before the government threw him in jail, read Kevin Gallagher's article from the Daily Dot "The legacy of imprisoned investigative journalist Barrett Brown."27 To understand the case even better, do a little research on your own. Kevin offers another worthy starting point in his post "Why Barrett Brown should not be in jail."28

The truth is hard to swallow.

We need to separate the wheat from the chaff.

In plainer terms, we need to identify people working for our dignity, like Barrett Brown, and protect them more efficiently. We need to reclaim our dignity and integrity from our alleged servants of common good, the leaders and protectors who claim to be the few who understand the system and, as such, are interested in its profits or dependent upon its favors.

If you feel like picking up the phone and calling a journalist, banker, politician, or a judge, then do it. Your country folk are

---

[27] http://www.dailydot.com/opinion/barrett-brown-private-intelligence-industry/

[28] "Barrett Brown Court Dates," Free Barrett Brown Web site (n.d.), http://freebarrettbrown.org/; http://www.dailydot.com/opinion/free-barrett-brown-anonymous-house-cards/.

begging you. Humanity will continue to be the servants of insatiably greedy individual power if you do not.

Understand that spreading the message and unravelling truth leads to solidarity, new solutions, and success. Only together can we face the roughest terrain and the potential heights of this amazing transformation. Spreading the message is more than accepting a measure of our vast problems and communicating the truth. We must insist that our leaders and public figures take up the call.

We must join hands. We must re-learn to sit down and talk, this time on a global scale. These discussions will get easier as we practice and much more so, as we reclaim the media as a viable platform for discussion.

Truth and information alone will transform our world.

This happens, in part, by prodding the right people.

Next, visit the world's new online home for collected activity.

Think of it as a place where we common people can house our discussions and initiate operations. With open source technology, the globe is already reorganizing itself as a whole and on regional levels. The possibilities are infinite. Undoubtedly, reality will be more awesome than anything anyone could imagine.

Humanity's transparent hub will continually evolve.

Within the online hub, let us build a continually updated list of people from around the world in media, journalism, education, health, and politics. You name the field and we will list the criminal people, as well as folks who, with luck, just need more pressure on them to leverage their names and resources for the common good instead.

Confrontation is required, but remember that the tone we bring to our discussions can make all the difference in the world. Let us invite our sisters and brothers to join us in building a free world. Chastisement alone only divides, and our goal is togetherness.

A focus on forgiveness, empathy, our potential unchained, and collaboration builds strength and unity.

When addressing any particular group, remember that we all find ourselves in different camps regarding different issues at different times.

The apathetic slave and the hero live in each and every one of us.

> *"To understand the heart and mind of a person, look not at what he has already achieved, but at what he aspires to."* [29]
> - Kahlil Gibran -

Friendship, collaboration, and community come from openness, acceptance, and compassion. Let us make amends. Let us become the best of friends. Our shame and empty fears about ourselves and each other are the only things standing in the way.

> *"If the other person injures you, you may forget the injury; but if you injure him you will always remember."* [30]
> - Kahlil Gibran -

Technology is a vital part of modern communication. The technological aspect of revolution is equally central. Here are eight quick ways any of us who enjoy or can use technology are able to pitch in and help:

Help protect the freedom to use technology for good and transparency.

---

[29] As quoted in Become a Conscious Creator: A Return to Self-Empowerment (2007) by Lisa Ford, p. 44
[30] Sand and Foam, in Kahlil Gibran: The Collected Works (New York: Alfred A. Knopf, Borzoi Books, 2007), 200.

Our voice is much stronger with all technology's modern tools. We need to protect their integrity, because they actually protect our integrity. This is freedom.

The freedoms naturally afforded by all the new technological platforms are under continual attack. Around the world, there are massive attempts to restrict, subvert, and control all technologies. These are our technologies. They embody the very idea of freedom, which knows no bounds and no rules other than natural law, common sense, and ethical consensus.

We need to protect our technologies with the same unshakable resolve used to protect our rights and our families. Stand up, use your voice, and perhaps even donate. This means gathering together and making things happen online and on the ground. The tools are there; we only need to work together, unified with a laser-like focus. Our global voice is already unstoppable.

With your help, humanity can enforce total transparency on the Internet and in all technologies. Transparency is a key standard in operations and requires all the existing movements around the world to start working together. It is vital that we stitch these movements together and unite our global voice for all causes, especially transparency.

Use technology to gather around social issues. Seek out new systems and ideas online and on the ground and lend a hand.

Common folk built Wikipedia and taught corporatocracy a tough lesson. Moreover, the effects of platforms such as Wikipedia are only just beginning to reverberate throughout our global culture.

It is finally time to use the very best of human knowledge and upgrade education, social programs of all kinds, business, social justice, spirituality, food systems, and life in general. This means getting involved in discussions and activities that pertain to the things in life you are most passionate about.

Your phone, computer, tablet, inner voice, and your wallet are all ways to plug in. On the other hand, you can walk out of your front door and plug in with friends, neighbors, and strangers.

Gather together, tech-gods, and produce the heart of revolution's technical business.

Serious tech-warriors for freedom who are already engaged around the world, healthy hackers, common technical folk, Anonymous world – thank you for all your hard work and service to freedom. Thank you for helping to ensure our technology is still as transparent and helpful as it is. Now humanity requires your help more than ever. There are many new, exciting things to do. The world needs you to build us a secure online home.

Help create for your brothers and sisters a safe and inviting place to organize global revolution and global operations in all their forms. This web-home will house the early and perhaps even the long-term needs of our planetary administration. We only request that the world's future needs to be open sourced, so please, build it for everyone by everyone, and make it completely transparent.

The best types of new systems possess a dexterity that more closely matches humanity's own potential for agility. Even our first major open-sourced efforts for self-governance can grow with us.

InsightIncite is currently working on a global invitation and outlining a rudimentary foundation, but humanity needs the world's technical saviors to take over. Lead the way. Help us recruit and stitch together humanity's positive efforts and build a fair and righteous home for humanity's self-governance.

Help with the primary need to build a secure collective voting process on global and regional levels.

> *"The people who cast the votes decide nothing. The people who count the votes decide everything."* [31]
> *- Joseph Stalin –*

---

[31] Said in 1923, as quoted in <u>The Memoirs of Stalin's Former Secretary</u> (1992) by Boris Bazhanov [Saint Petersburg], http://lib.ru/MEMUARY/BAZHANOW/stalin.txt (in Russian).

Fight corrupt global monetary systems by increasing support for secure, alternate forms of digital currency like BitCoin.

Technical and knowledgeable friends, alternate currency can play a tremendously powerful role in humanity's rebirth. You likely understand this better than most, but you need to help spread the message about its potency and transformative opportunity with newfound stubbornness. Help and invite your fellow women and men to understand, and use, new forms of currency and exchange.

Help reclaim and protect the rightful inheritance and stolen global resources of the planet's common people. With respect to money, all along this revolutionary road and into the future, you tech-warriors will be called to help protect and secure our systems and wealth.

Think how exciting it will be to empty all those bank accounts! It is finally time to liberate abundance from millennia-old chains. Time to be a real, sustainable Robin Hood for our starving and dying family and supply the entire planet's unemployed with jobs.

Build freedom apps. Security and solidarity can be found more easily and bolstered to unstoppable heights through mobile apps that help freed services and individuals connect, collaborate, and support one another when under duress and in general. This technology will help all aspects of healthy change grow.

Think of how effectively Twitter, Facebook, and many other social networking sites have exposed corruption and added strength and a global voice to localized movements and injustice.

Just as people check Google to find information on businesses, common folk can use powerful mobile apps to instantly connect with a world of concerned and motivated citizen activists and find resources and support.

Yes, Google Facebook, Twitter, YouTube, Avaaz and most of our favourite online resources and utilities have been subverted long ago and perhaps at inception, however, the power is in our voice, #WorldVoice, not the microphone we use.

We now know how to be build better, networked microphones. Let's get to work building better more secure and open-sourced upgrades.

Most important, this strategic application of everyday technology offers huge leaps in safety and security. Common people could unite and finally feel safe as individuals when taking a stand or facing potential harassment. Imagine knowing this technology is there to help ensure appropriate support is always just a click or two away.

First and foremost, hackers, computer specialists, and leaders everywhere, blanket the Internet and every corner of the world with truth, coup, and freedom's call. Spread the message.

This means building on our collective voice in numbers that have never been seen before. It means focusing on central goals and central platforms. Once we agree, and take our first few major steps, we will be undefeatable. Use your phones, computers, face-to-face conversations, alternate forms of media, and our mainstream channels if they have started covering real issues.

Share the truth and the call.

Imagine the colossal power of our collected voice when we all join together. Imagine what the world will look like when 20 to 50 percent of the information being shared over social media is tied to the self-governance movement. By then, we will be working out the kinks and the ruling elite will become bedtime stories for our kids.

Now that we have looked at technology specifically, let us dig a little deeper into the second major form of positive action: defiance and simple forms of resistance.

Everyone can participate in this, regardless of skills, resources, and level of dedication to the movement. All the average person has been asked to do so far, is be prepared to vote on community issues, spread the message, and start thinking about and practicing healthier forms of community, i.e., becoming better friends with neighbors.

You have been asked to educate yourself and make up your own mind about everything instead of buying propagandized popular opinion.

Last, you have been asked to believe in and encourage positive change wherever you can.

Nothing too tough yet.

For those willing and able to take extra steps, here is a list of four things you can do to help stoke the flames of resistance and transformation to revolutionary heights:

1. Stop paying all taxes, right now. Do not pay income tax, corporate tax, property tax, or any other tax you can easily separate from the price of the goods in question. An exception to this rule, to start, would be fuel tax, as the tax is usually built into the price of gasoline at the pumps.

Stop paying sales taxes at the businesses you frequent. The owners should not be paying them anymore, so do not pay the extra. This is an age-old favorite form of common rebellion, simple "no tax" agreements between common folk. For as long as time has been counted and rulers and tyrants have taxed their serfs and slaves, common folk have eagerly eliminated the greedy, useless middleman whenever possible when conducting private business with one another.

This is freedom, and classic agorism at its finest.

2. Stop paying all government, student, and bank loans immediately. The bottom line for now: the only people hurt by our not paying these fraudulent loans are those same few who have stolen our money.

Stop obeying like lemmings your villages', towns', cities', and countries' arbitrary dictations. For example, if you do not feel like waiting at the red light if it is obviously safe to proceed, then do not. Go for it and feel truly free. Just remember to be safe and respectful. If you hurt someone, there will still be justice.

Alternatively, perhaps you could help stop bylaw officers from illegally robbing the common people. I once saw a T-shirt that read "I am completely FREE...I have all the licenses and permits to prove it."

Just the other day a bylaw officer tried to stop me and give me a ticket while I was walking my dog. I simply told the individual that I paid no respect to his authority or chosen profession and was going to continue on my way no matter what he said. However, I have been forced to hand over ID and wait for a ticket under threat of arrest when attempting a similar approach with actual police wearing guns and handcuffs.

To stand up to police effectively, common people need to band together through mobile apps and every other means necessary. Hopefully, some of our sisters and brothers in blue will help support us, as well, simply by letting us walk away, protest, gather, and live in any way we choose, as long as it is peaceful.

4. Stop involving thieves in commercial transactions with one another. When shopping for products and services, insist on freed services. If you own a business, make new signage and include the freed message in your advertising. Business owners and consumers alike can connect with the new freedom apps and technology.

Common folk all over the world need to begin insisting on freed medical services, freed financial services, freed automobile and insurance services. Insist that your accountant take steps to acclimate with revolutionary, transparent, and healthy trends. Speaking of health, make sure your doctor is willing to provide or help source the type of treatment you are looking for.

Online tools and mobile apps will make all these connections easier and will soon keep you in constant connection with the growing global community of freed businesses and individuals.

Simple defiance is just that: little things that can be done each day, to proudly let the world know that you are a free, sovereign human being.

We will learn together how to speak for ourselves with infallible personal power.

Be vigilant. Your freed hearts and minds will tell you when, where, and how to take a stand. Remember that it is critical to remain diplomatic, peaceful, and spiritually centered in your defiance. You will not often get a chance to stick it to "the powers that be" directly, so realize that primarily your fellow women and men will challenge your defiance.

These people are your future friends who do not yet understand freedom and its inevitable coming as well as you do.

Remember: communication, friendship, solidarity.

> *"Treat people as if they were what they ought to be and you help them to become what they are capable of being."*
> *- Unknown -*

> *"There are many ways to calm a negative energy without suppressing or fighting it. You recognize it, you smile to it, and you invite something nicer to come up and replace it; you read some inspiring words, you listen to a piece of beautiful music, you go somewhere in nature, or you do some walking meditation."* [32]
> *- Thich Nhat Hanh -*

With respect to refusing to pay taxes and loans, many might wonder "Won't we be thrown in jail? How will the roads be fixed? How will our services be paid for?"

First, remember that our actual collective wealth is hidden on a much larger scale than just the CAFR in Canada points to.[33] Most

---

[32] The Art of Power (New York: HarperOne, 2007), 19.
[33] Introduction to the CAFR - Why You Can't Get Ahead, http://www.youtube.com/watch?v=T2aif0Wk9E0; The CAFR Swindle - The Biggest Game In Town,

of the world's wealth has always been in the hands of the ruling class. This fact alone makes it impossible to say how much wealth there actually is in the world, especially when you factor in all the confusion and corruption within our monetary systems. What we know for sure is that common humans live on next to nothing, and with a fraction of what we know exists, we could totally rebuild the world.

Roads are paid for by fuel tax, which for a time will continue as is. The money that was lent to you never existed; the loans are fraudulent. Lastly, we are only discussing who manages our money. Humanity will still decide that the roads need fixing and that grandmothers who live on pension checks need support, etc.

Global economics have also proven time and again over the centuries that in the absence of heavy taxation and regulation, countries and economies boom and social structures are surprisingly sustainable, self-sufficient, and compassionately effective.

> *"The instant formal government is abolished, society begins to act. A general association takes place, and common interest produces common security."*34
> *- Thomas Paine -*

> *"Government is an unnecessary evil. Human beings, when accustomed to taking responsibility for their own behavior, can cooperate on a basis of mutual trust and helpfulness."*35
> *- Fred Woodworth -*

---

http://www.youtube.com/watch?v=1pRPBKJQnyU.

[34] Rights of Man, Common Sense, and Other Political Writings (Oxford: Oxford University Press, 1998), 215.

[35] The Match.

If you feel that equally taxing the rich and increasing corporate taxes – ideas recently popularized by the media – are answers, do a little more research into our monetary systems. You will quickly find it explained that all the wealth in the world is locked away. Instead, we are loaned imaginary notes that represent a false economy, inflated and depressed at will.

Most of the billions and trillions that your government is stealing from you go toward paying back massive loans from the IMF and Federal Reserve, which are private, elitist organizations.

We can take better care of social programs and the roads than they can. Private industry and people like John Stossel provide evidence of this daily. Put your money into your community, not the government.

The only question to ask yourself is if you want to manage your money or give it to the ruling elite.

A final tax reality - when our communities' monies are in transparent accounts, we will find out exactly how abundant the world truly is. As well as the full extent of how much more effective private efforts are, than governments or institutions of old.

If you cannot see how our tax dollars are not going where you think they are, leave it, do some more research. Perhaps instead you can simply fight the fight where and when you are comfortable. Then, get involved in the global discussions and investigations later. You will likely come around on these fiscal issues with the help of some people more qualified than Luke and I.

Perhaps even your neighbor, brother, mother, or aunt will help.

Let us leave you with a few final words on revolution's secondary actions, such as defiance and simple other forms of resistance.

Picture this: you are driving down the road on a Saturday afternoon feeling inspired by the book you just read and the liberated movement increasing around the world. In your heart, it feels as though the common good is rapidly approaching critical mass and ultimate victory.

You are feeling so free in the moment that you decide to ignore a stop sign, a calculated, safe action that caused no harm. However, a police officer decides to pull you over to give you a ticket. In possession of so much truth and your sovereign strength, you decide to use your new mobile freedom app that helps freedom's individuals and groups find each other.

Through the app, you quickly send out an alert and a request for a roadside motor-vehicle traffic-ticket support team. Now imagine that as all this is going on, you never stop driving. You refuse to pull over while driving safely and respectfully enough not to cause harm.

You also remember to film the police and the entire event.

After you calmly drive for approximately five minutes, cars begin showing up from all directions. Honking, they fall into the fold. You quickly gain enough support to feel comfortable pulling over. You are now free to tell the police officer to go fight real crime and steal money from someone else.

That is solidarity in action.

This type of resistance is not for everyone. It will not even be possible until we have thousands of people connecting and sharing in small, targeted local areas – not to mention our tech-buddies need to build the app first.

Imagine how exciting things will get after we have worked out the bugs and evidenced a landslide of proof-positive examples to encourage the rest of the common world to join in. That kind of solidarity and strength in voice and action can accomplish anything.

If you are excited by this conversation, and realize that as you read these words, the discussion and actual work has already begun and is gaining ground fast, both online and offline. Join in!

As changes develop and take shape, many other specific concerns and suggestions will arise out of all our experiences. Look online for growing, contemporary, and more robust solutions than Luke and I can put forth.

This next story shows how similar types of resistance are easily accomplished. Recently in British Columbia, more than 150 bikers refused to pull off the road for a police check when stopped during their annual ride between Nanaimo and Victoria. The large group of bikers told a decent-sized multi-departmental gathering of police officers to fuck off and go home while they sat there peacefully, blocking the Trans-Canada Highway. 36

The event makes one simple and powerful point. United we can stand against authority and divided we will fall.

The police, after making countless phone calls and wasting a huge amount of time and money, eventually packed up and went on their way, as did the bikers, after proving their point. Eloquently and peacefully, one might add, despite the media's fear-mongering reports of the incident.

Despite how controversial biker clubs are, these BC riders still show the rest of us how any group of people can stand against the police peacefully.

Brothers and sisters in uniform, men and women driving those police cars or even sitting behind our government counters, friends: please stop performing unlawful and ineffective tasks, such as writing traffic tickets and enforcing municipal fines, fees, and useless regulations/pseudo-obligations that are designed to engender dependence, division, and servitude.

Protect against harm and do not allow yourself to become the perpetrator of it. Protect common sense, not arbitrary laws written

---

[36] Louise Dickson, "Trans-Canada Highway blocked as Island convoy of Hells Angels refuses to pull off for police check," Times Colonist (May 4, 2013), http://www.timescolonist.com/news/local/trans-canada-highway-blocked-as-island-convoy-of-hells-angels-refuses-to-pull-off-for-police-check-1.14618; Stephanie Ip, "More than 150 Hells Angels and other bikers block road during police showdown on Vancouver Island," The Province (May 5, 2013), http://globalnews.ca/news/537207/more-than-150-hells-angels-and-other-bikers-block-road-during-police-showdown-on-vancouver-island/.

by the ruling class that rarely serve common interests. We can take this old, ugly red-tape world and create new transparent ties that do not bind our potential but free it.

Support LEAP and our police so they can stand up and protect all our human rights for a change. With our help, police can take a stand by refusing to arrest nonviolent drug users. This is just one easy-to-identify example to start with.

> *"As I watch government at all levels daily eat away at our freedom, I keep thinking how prosperity and government largesse have combined to make most of us fat and lazy and indifferent to, or actually in favor of, the limits being placed on that freedom."*[37]
> *- Lyn Nofziger -*

If you decide to continue to show up to work and fight the good fight from within old institutions, tweak your efforts with common sense. The world trusts you as a fellow human being to make human decisions that ease the blatantly insane burdens, red tape, and headaches that violate our rights.

Let us turn a few of our old institutional buildings into new community centers like indoor agricultural centers, shared spaces, farmers markets, art galleries, or even new types of social structures that operate with common sense.

We can manage our resources in a transparent and sensible fashion. We can solve our own problems. The human race no longer has a need for kings, rulers, and individual authority to parent society in any way.

Everyone has varying thresholds when it comes to rebellion, so people will naturally engage in all manner of reform activities using subtle, as well as in-your-face tactics.

---

[37] As quoted by Michael Spalding in We Still Hold These Truths (ISI Books, 2009).

Let us turn our attention to the third action in our four-pronged attack on oppression and all the limitations imposed on humanity over the past few thousand years: skillful defiance.

You and I are beginning to demand to be treated fairly, freely. Now, we need to recruit the help of skilled professionals and leaders of all kinds.

As a kid, when you wanted to do something cool, sometimes you needed a friend's help to make it happen. Think about how many times that buddy with great ideas, a new toy, a car, or vacationing parents came in handy.

The excitement you felt creating games, finding new ways to experience life, chasing fun, this is the kind of enthusiasm and joy you can find while working on your dreams. As humanity really begins to engage and collaborate, what fun we will learn to have again.

Imagine working on projects that liberate humanity. Imagine working on our biggest dreams. Imagine working for freedom.

> *"Work is love made visible. And if you cannot work with love but only with distaste, it is better that you should leave your work and sit at the gate of the temple and take alms of those who work with joy."* [38]
> *- Kahlil Gibran -*

People from all lifestyles are needed, from skilled laborers and trades-people to government workers, police officers, military personnel, educators, researchers, scientists, medical staff, financial analysts, recent legal graduates, and academics of all kinds.

---

[38] The Prophet: The Collected Works (New York: Alfred A. Knopf, Borzoi Books, 2007), 115.

> *"No matter what the level of your ability, you have more potential than you can ever develop in a lifetime."* [39]
> *- James T. McCay -*

Search for the highest potential, within yourself, within your work.

This means educating and strengthening yourself first. Then, choose the things you care about most and get involved in solution. Through your work, all kinds of potential ways to get involved in the fight for freedom can arise. Some of you can simply shift your focus and change how you do your job.

Listen to your common sense and, instead of purely profits, support morality and the common good more courageously and more often from now on.

All you professional minds out there, doing things better instead of bigger will make all the difference in the world. The Story of Solutions video mentioned in Chapter Five presents an insightful and inspiring look at this specific adjustment in our perspective, and how this singular change in our attitude can help the world heal and thrive.

Given all our various roles in life, the specifics of skillful defiance will look very different for everyone and will naturally develop out of broad ideas. One of the most powerful changes we can apply right now, though, is a much stronger can-do attitude.

We have been conditioned to live in a state of learned helplessness that prevents us from addressing life directly. The ruling elite are not blessed with special brains or magical powers that enable them to make astute parenting decisions that a supposed childlike human race cannot make on its own.

---

[39] Quoted in Eat that Frog: 21 Great Ways to Stop Procrastinating and Get More Done in Less Time, Google eBook by Brian Tracy (Berrett-Koehler Publishers, 2007), 56.

Men and women, people like you and me, are, in truth, running the world now. We are responsible for every ounce of dirty and sophisticated work there is. The only problem is that the whole world takes orders from a tiny few people.

Rulers hire us with our money – which is plundered from us at every turn – to solve our own problems while we live and work by sets of rules and restrictions that serve them. We do all there is to do, yet choose to take orders instead of making our own decisions?

This is crazy and it must stop, right now.

We can do this.

> *"Few men desire liberty; most men wish only for a just master."* 40
> *- Sallust -*

Luke described to me a scenario that exemplifies the strength of this simple but radical shift to a can-do perspective.

Imagine a gathering of people with various strengths in a room with a large whiteboard. When confronted with a truly innovative idea, most respond with a statement along the lines of "it can't be done." This type of response means the group is on the right track. On the contrary, if everyone says, "that's doable," the group is not being innovative.

After the skeptical attitude is established in the room, a truly innovative and lofty goal is written at the top of the board. Then, the group is then tasked with coming up with ideas to reach the goal. The only twist is that no one is allowed to voice any can't-be-done statements. If one is made, the group simply shouts out "Next!" and moves on to other ideas.

Picture the excitement and the positivity in a room like that.

---

[40] Sallust (Gaius Sallustius Crispus), *Histories*.

Professionals and skilled workers can also apply themselves immediately by supporting the ideas and people, which in the past have been pushed aside or persecuted. Ridicule is nothing more than a stage along the road to acceptance and has been a part of every major change in human thinking. Think about the things we are all ridiculing now that could help lead us into the future, into the truth. Stop divisive behavior and let us better support anyone who is working on human potential and healthy change.

It's time to say no to corruption and unjust persecution, and put an end to unchecked corporate and political abuse of humanity's freedom fighters of all kinds. They are our educators (the John Gatto's), lawyers (the Jesselyn Radack's), scientists (the Nikola Tesla's), doctors (the Harvey Bigelsen's), journalists (the Barrett Brown's), and our geniuses and brightest minds (the Aaron Swartz's).

They need more support.

These few familiar names speak to a reality that is all around us. Our brothers and sisters are being trampled on for trying to do the right thing. First, we better support people who show the enormous courage it takes to do the right thing in yesterday's world.

Then, we firmly establish a new era - a powerful, protected today that encourages a global tidal wave of whistle-blowers and human beings doing the right thing.

Look at what we have learned from just a handful of whistle-blowers.

Imagine what we will learn from just the first few thousand more.

This simple act of better supporting the right people and projects might be one of many potential deal breakers that brings fast success and freedom for all. Go find someone who is doing work that you are really impressed with and lend some sort of support.

We all get to do some fun research, which, if you choose, could also lead to activities and collaborative opportunities. Protecting and participating in the future's still-ridiculed ideas is some very cool work.

Imagine how capable humanity will be when we all become friends. Now, picture removing divisive and can't-do attitudes. Imagine if all new ideas were held up, admired, and inspected with open minds instead of being ridiculed and ostracized.

As we learn to engage our imaginations and reduce our self-restriction and self-persecution, we will discover almost anything is possible for the human race.

Protect each other and band together.

Grouping together is the key to everything. We may need to leverage our skills outside of our regular jobs and help construct various replacement systems.

No matter your field or specific skill set, your primary job is uniting with everyone to form a common voice. Create new groups at work and outside of work. Grow the healthy freedom fighting groups that exist, then stitch them all together and humanity will have both a microphone and a sword that will not meet any opposition.

Government workers, for the most part, will eventually need to find new jobs. Governments are the largest employers of common people the world over, so this is a delicate and important issue for many.

Lots of you may decide to work in a similar capacity. There is still a need for huge numbers of you to continue to serve your neighbors, through community and privately funded services. Help in your chosen field, in a connected one, or try something completely new.

As technology evolves and manual labor jobs become automated, some people worry about job security in the common workforce in the future. This is the all-too-familiar fear of the unknown. It is natural but is easily diffused when recognized for what it is: irrational fear.

This fear also evaporates in the face of new kinds of jobs, which always arise. As technology changes more rapidly than ever before, the nature of humanity's working world is also changing fast.

First on the chopping block is arbitrary authority.

There are two kinds of government workers. There are good people who need decent jobs and want to help others, and those who have become misguided and even authority hungry.

Government workers should not feel picked on though, because many things are changing. Friendship, respect for one another, and new forms of collaboration will revolutionize how we treat each other. Service will shine. Today things are especially hard for all you government workers, but you will experience some of the greatest joys and largest changes, so be happy – the public is looking forward to working, once again, with good friends who trust and enjoy working together and helping each other.

We will look each other in the eye, attend to business, and know that there are not any backroom agendas, third-party thieves, or arbitrary measures of right and wrong.

We are essentially going to be using all the best parts of humanity's global institutions and tossing out the garbage. There is nothing to fear. Things that work well today will only get better.

Things that need improvement will get better too. All kinds of people might really enjoy working within the new administrative community. The nature of many jobs is changing for the better.

If you can be bossy and authority-hungry, you need an attitude adjustment, just like the rest of us. Power corrupts human beings as reliably as warming ice and snow make water. The only cure is the transparent and watchful collective eye and sometimes guidance and support from our fellow women and men.

We all need big adjustments in the way we interact with each other. With the end of arbitrary authority and the realization of global self-governance, all authority-driven positions will undergo the biggest types of changes.

In our new world, our public figures no longer have authority, from the police officer, doctor, educator, and religious leader right down to the meter attendant, tax collector, and average bureaucratic staff member.

No longer will they tell other people what to do.

The good news is that there are new ways to do things, and they can eliminate the resentment people often feel toward government employees. The public's hostility can unfortunately often make for the toughest days and moments in a public servant's career.

On the other side, talk to your average human being and he will have horror stories about dealing with government, tax collectors, the health industry, and all forms of institution and authority.

The majority of this resentment is actually misdirected frustration with the massive injustice in our current systems.

Imagine how our communities will feel and how you will feel when we, common people are attending to the needs of the day and to one another. Imagine airing our grievances and sorting out our issues amongst ourselves in transparent and communal fashion. You become part of the team and part of the solution, instead of part of the problem.

Work should be fun. Work is supposed to feel liberating. It is supposed to allow us to explore our skills and curiosity. Our technology, information, food, medicine, relationships, and work throughout history have all been restricted and bent into tools for control instead of freedom.

Humanity is not going to listen to rhetoric, dogma, or unhealthy ideas any longer.

Each individual must find a way to free their services, so that we all ensure that we are helping people honestly. For some of us, this will require very little change. Join your voice with the global common voice for freedom. Utilize agorism's many forms, and participate in some of the discussions online, and that is all it takes to remove your support for the old and invest in a healthier world.

Those who will need new jobs will be glad because they will enjoy their new job and day-to-day working life way more!

Simply imagine the possibilities. The real question is, what do you want to do?
Asking your inner child can be a great place to start.

If you find yourself out of work because of new methods of running the world, there will be many new kinds of work in every single field on the planet, so pick your fancy. There will also be resources aplenty to pay you more than fairly. Most of you are sure to find work that makes you giggle with the glee of a school kid.
Hopefully, by now you can really picture what it will be like when we, in small pieces and then sweeping chunks, successfully replace old systems with new ones, or effectively convert them.

A very powerful tactic has been used all throughout history to upend unruly authorities. It also affords the opportunity to very quickly repurpose public assets. This technique falls under revolution's final action: the battle on the front lines.
It is also one of the most volatile and risky techniques and needs to be used with extreme caution. These types of tactics become safer and more fun as solidarity among common people increases.

This decision to battle is a distinct choice that some people, countries, regions, and industries may make, and the possibility needs to be addressed. There is still some ground to cover regarding the specific details of skillful defiance. While doing so, we will examine a few potential applications of this tactic that people may naturally decide on.
The strategy is simple: we are the world—and we reclaim it.

When people get angry enough with their government or rulers, they decide to dispose of them. This has happened throughout history. Most often, this strategy takes the form of common people repossessing main government buildings and evicting the current tenants.

We are the proprietors of this earth, you, I, and the rest together.

Our global assets are in need of transparent redistribution and assessment.

Here is an exciting scenario. Picture the day when all the government workers in a given building or area peacefully and in unison empty the state location of resources. They will not trash things in violence that threatens their fellow humans, but a bit of long overdue destruction in the name of freedom and self-governance, well, that will feel amazing to be a part of, and definitely trump the best videos on YouTube to date.

At this stage of the revolution, your community just might decide that all city vehicles are now the property of city workers. Imagine if your community said, "Take them home; you now own them. Thank you for your service."

Perhaps you would help someone out by offering him or her a lift.

By now, you might be feeling a bit better about life's rewards and coming justice.

Hang on to that huge can of worms for a minute and let us talk about cops. We know there are good people out there, but an awful lot of our police officers are just overgrown bullies. With all the recent attention on bullying amongst our youth, this behavior is now even easier to identify.

Just as humans need to learn social skills on the playground as children, now we need to learn how to relate better to one another as adults. We need to support one another, and this includes rehabilitating bullies.

This is the only way to overcome all our various social struggles and heal.

If you can be a bully sometimes, think about why. The cause of your violence is likely insecurity, fear, and pain. No one will judge you for this, because we have all felt these things. Human beings are compassionate.

Forgive yourself, because we are ready when you are, to make a different choice.

Back to our good guys who joined the force to protect and serve their communities. Even if you have lost your way over the years under pressures that no human should face, your community understands and is willing to forgive. Humanity needs your heartfelt apology in the form of moral behavior and help rebuilding, securing, and serving freedom.

The days of serving institution and the old-school chain of command are over.

We are not angry about yesterday but we need you to stand with us today.

Further, the prison systems may be full of nonviolent drug offenders now, but those of you who take sides with the ruling elite over your common brethren will be occupying those lonely, half-empty halls next week.

> *"I hear much of people's calling out to punish the guilty, but very few are concerned to clear the innocent."* [41]
> *- Daniel Defoe-*

---

[41] The Works of Daniel De Foe, ed. W. Hazlitt (London: J. Baker, 1715), clxxix.

The moment you have the courage and enough of us are banded together, we need freed justice officials and legal personnel to empty the jailhouses of nonviolent drug offenders and unjustly incarcerated political prisoners, one cell, one prison at a time.

This activity alone will provide lots of work and healthy changes for health workers, social program staff, and legal professionals as well as all forms of police and justice staff. Moreover, even regular folks like you and me have the chance to be these desperately needed changes by helping to apply all sorts of pressure to the current system.

In addition, starting immediately, we will need your help filling a small measure of that newly created space in the prison system. We need to fill those cells with the few tyrants and leaders of the past, who refuse to acclimate to more evolved behavior and those whom humanity deems guilty of crimes of oppression. They will not be allowed to live free among us.

Police and military personnel, your whole human family is gathering together and desperately needs you to fulfill the essence of your sworn oaths. Protect us common folk, the innocent everywhere, from tyrannical dictatorship and real, harmful crime.

Any debate about how to affect total global coup without violent resistance can only be settled through our actions. Debate will never end if we allow it.

It is time to begin the journey.

The nature of our future and our survival depends on it.

With respect to the use of force, if there is anyone who is qualified to fight and resist oppression with force, it is you, our soldiers and protectors.

Police and military brethren, the ruling elite need your physical obedience, your hand, to enslave the common people. Bankers and individual human rulers need your servitude the most. You, our police and military protectors are their monopoly on force.

Protect humanity, not institution, individuals, or government. You are the only ones who can allow them to impose martial law and/or actual war.

It is time to refuse.

No one wants to be remembered as part of the security force of tyranny.

Remember, that decision can even be life threatening, as the many soldiers tried for human rights violations prove.

Friends, neighbors, brothers, sisters, and family members, refuse to take arms against us; instead, obey your hearts, listen to the orders of your community at large. We beg you to stand with us and for us, as you have always dreamed you would.

Build with us a new peace, a new, human order: a transparent and common world safe from individual power, greed, and oppression of the masses, once and for all.

Police officers and those who provide similar services can do the same as the government workers and drive your cars home, too. Most importantly, empty the weapons caches and take all the contents home. Better yet, take over the buildings and use them to facilitate our rebirth.

You are, we are, the majority.

If you are human, you probably feel the tremendous tug of truth in the world. If you wear a gun to work, the job you signed up for has finally arrived. It is time to serve humankind.

Generals and top military leaders of the world, stop taking orders from the ruling elite of the world and start taking order from us. Imagine the potential of an open sourced Avaaz-like microphone gathering our global voice daily and commanding the common global freedom force, which will slowly eradicate unruly authority and old, unethical systems.

Military folks from every nation on earth, let us talk. Alphabet soup agencies of the world, perk up your highly trained ears too. If you consider yourself a true warrior, this next message is for you.

You are the true action heroes in the greatest movie of all time.

You will be the ones on the front lines, as always, but this time fighting for good, for justice, and for freedom instead of for private agendas so compartmentalized and corrupt, that they forced you to look away or put the issue out of your mind.

Imagine how it will feel to know in your whole heart that you are working for good for a change, for what is right.

When humans do things that require us to shut off parts of our hearts and minds, we fall perilously out of touch with our humanity itself. Very few of us would ever want to become like that. You have been tricked.

Be excited. You will be the heroes responsible for turning the majority of the world's wealth and abundance back over to your neighbors, some of whom just lost the jobs they hated. You can be among the real Robin Hoods who fill the global accounts with our stolen wealth, which will clothe, feed, shelter, and employ an entire planet of your brothers and sisters.

Make the arrests.

Open the secret vaults of knowledge and wealth.

Help us discover the real truth behind all the conspiracy theories.

You are the ones who understand best how compartmentalized the truth really is. Please confirm. The truth is wilder than the craziest Hollywood movies, at minimum. Help us focus our efforts on the right targets and motivate the world.

As we open the world's vaults, be warned, you must recognize when you come across the Ark of the Covenant or some other potential world-controlling power or information store. The world is watching, likely over your shoulder, waiting to see your integrity rise to its rightful place. We know you have it in you.

Once the world's evils have been rooted out, most of you will likely retire and find new ways to enjoy the rest of your lives.

Picture living them out as the real heroes you were always meant to be.

Over time, we humans have heard from many shattered warriors, especially lately, who have told us that they are sickened and heartbroken by the lack of integrity in wars, causes, and governments.

Billions of history's soldiers learned the truth too late and died worthlessly. Millions have taught and spoken about this. Listen to soldiers like Paul Chappell,[42] General Smedley Butler,[43] and Harry Patch,[44] the last survivor of the Western Front carnage in WWI, before it is too late and you are staring a worthless death in the face.

We see this last-minute realization again and again, even in Hollywood movies. Warriors, now you have a real fight on your hands.

What are you going to do? Which side will you choose? We have a real battle on our hands, one for the freedom of the human race; we need you.

Specifically, we would love it if you took control of all the most sophisticated systems, infrastructure, and assets of all kinds. Turn them into resources that serve freedom. You could even use this equipment for your own personal enjoyment at times, provided no one comes to harm as a result.

Most of the world's resources and infrastructure can probably remain as is.

Initially, the only change will be where the orders are coming from. However, you likely know better than Luke or I, which weapons

---

[42] Peace Leadership Director, Nuclear Age Foundation (September 21, 2011), http://www.youtube.com/watch?v=VuKUJCPMly8.
[43] War Is A Racket (New York: Round Table Press, 1935).
[44] "The last of the noblest generation," The Independent (July 26, 2009), http://www.independent.co.uk/news/uk/home-news/the-last-of-the-noblest-generation-1761467.html.

and systems will need to be confiscated, so to speak, so they cannot be used against us.

Most importantly though would be to transfer all weaponry as well as your assistance, to the service of freedom.

Your human family trusts that you can imagine how we would like you to integrate all of these assets, especially the hard-core technical infrastructure, into our global self-governance and freedom movement.

It cannot be stressed enough how key the technological aspect is.

Eventually all the hard drives, laptops, files and documents of all kinds, and even your telephones will be taken home, taken elsewhere, or taken over. All these assets belong to the common citizens of the world and are ours to be employed transparently in the defense of common sense, all things good, and solidarity.

Imagine not only the world's mightiest warriors, but all the mental giants in white coats as well, finally leveraging all the greatest skills and talents of the human race for good—instead of selling themselves, our potential, and the whole world out behind closed doors. Our best and brightest are being forced to become tools used to control, divide, and enslave the rest of us. We will come back to scientists, researchers, and other forms of skilled resistance after finishing off our discussion on the element of force and its counterpart: fear.

Imagine the untapped potential of humanity's crème de la crème locked into servitude to systems of war and control. Look beyond the trillions wasted every year and imagine what we could really do if we used our minds and technology for good.

Imagine eventually reaching the point where bases around the world are emptying. Imagine tanks, planes, and all the weapons of war, being driven home and sporadically placed throughout our communities. It is likely safer to spread these assets out to all corners of our countries instead of centralizing our resistance, which might make us easier targets.

With that being said, if you do not feel comfortable taking our property or weapons home, that is okay. It is enough for most of you folks to do one of two things.

One, simply go home. Abandon your government posts in droves and find a new way to engage with the community and support yourself. If you are concerned about money or employment, connect with the new administration, as there will undoubtedly be new positions and wages. Job boards will take on a whole new role as humanity re-purposes a large part of the world's workforce. Take a look online before making the big move, and collaborate with your coworkers. Leave in large or small numbers, but remember that greater solidarity instills even greater confidence in others, so you may want to grab a few friends.

Two, if you need to stay, join those who decide to take orders from freedom's central command instead, or even just think about where exactly you are going to draw the line. It is vital to ask yourself what orders you will not follow. Those orders are going to come eventually, if they have not already. Successful refusal, remember, becomes easier as we band together in groups, so if you've got to stay, connect in and build on support systems for moral conduct.

If enough of you listen to reason, listen to your hearts, your neighbors, your family and friends, who are begging you to come home and serve us for a change, then there won't be enough assets or personnel left to wage oppressive war against the masses with any real success.

The idea at its most basic is that the greater our numbers, the smaller the chance of actual fighting breaking out. All humans can join together and help out online and on the ground.

First and foremost, everyone needs to spread the message, especially at work.

Already there are secret and open groups of military, police, and even professionals of all kinds, preparing for a change in management.

Collections of the world's leading minds are also eagerly waiting to clear the global halls of corruption and lies. Lies that allow your comrades to be killed, your honor, and the greatest gifts that live inside you to be stolen. Lies used to kill, to control, and to enslave your parents, siblings, and children.

Soldiers and trained warriors, you should see more clearly than most exactly how much a person has to be manipulated and controlled in order to murder another human being in cold blood.
We have been convinced to fear each other, and make war.
Since it is humanity's largest adversary, let us explore this concept of fear more fully. Trained to view the light as dark and the darkness as light, common people are bound to feel utter confusion when faced with the decision of whether to trust another person. However, the human mind is changed most easily through experience.
Much of the darkness in the world is baseless fear, which we have been made to worship. Step-by-step, we will all witness firsthand how amazing the human spirit and our neighbors really are. We will easily come together and make collective decisions locally and globally that the majority of us agree on. We will discover the true nature of fear, a decision and a perspective with rarely an ounce of reality to substantiate its arousal.

> *"My wife was afraid of the dark. Then she saw me naked and now she's afraid of the light."* [45]
> *- Rodney Dangerfield -*

Fear is an illusion and a decision, pure and simple.
We cannot stop fear's arousal, but we can change our reaction to it. You do not need protection from yourself. The rest of us likely do not need protection from you. When exceptions occur, transparent

---

[45] Quoted in How to Laugh Your Way Through life: A Psychoanalyst's Advice by Paul Marcus (Kamac Books, 2013), 34.

justice is in the hands of the common world, and this fact should make everyone sleep much easier.

For anyone in doubt, watch, wait, and see how your future friends display their common good and sense. Take a look around now at the best examples of human goodness in action. You will be a true believer in the human spirit very soon.

If you want some added inspiration to gather your present courage, look to where there is trouble now. You will always find numerous examples of kindness, sharing, and the human being in all its peaceful glory. Despite living in a world filled with tragedy and pain, if you look closely and with the right eye, you will see much more hope, compassion, and happiness than is ever reported on.

We can change that too and make it easier for everyone to see our collective greatness, our goodness, by reporting on these stories in the freed media and global open sourced hubs.

Perspective is a tool at everyone's disposal.

We can focus it just as we always have, or we can choose how to focus it. Through our choices, our world emerges.

If you have mountainous fear about the choices and changes happening around you, have faith and search for positive signs. Hopefully, a more positive-minded friend or neighbor can take you on a virtual tour through the true nature of our manufactured world and our budding potential. You will soon see that almost all of us, the planet over, hold the same peaceful, loving goals in our hearts.

At one point, I had a long conversation with one of my two fathers about the book. Running through the center of the discussion was this subject of fear.

We explored questions such as, "How much is there to really fear in one another?" "How many fanatical people are there?" and "How can we convince people that there's nothing to be scared of?"

We asked the tough questions like, "Why do people have such a tough time seeing that we can manage our own systems more effectively?" and "Why do people put up with ruling elite and leaders who promise only to protect us from one another and ourselves?"

Overcoming these types of fears will be the largest struggle for common people at the very beginning of the transition. Once we have covered a little more ground though, we will come to our senses, with so much exposure to the true harmony in collective activity.

Fight the good fight inside first. When you have conquered your fears or reached an impasse, a point where you need input and communication, then follow your instincts and connect with the world around you to work through the difficulty.

As time goes on and you establish or re-establish a sense of understanding, engage in the changes as you see fit. However, remember that spending a little time helping others arrive at the same answers to your own toughest questions is one of the most important parts of the entire process.

Spread the message and join the discussions.

At times, our brilliant potential all by itself can lead us naturally and joyfully to consensus. It is time to reach out and claim our freedom.

We will find ourselves drawn to all aspects of our potential, if we let our imaginations and hearts lead the way. Dreams of humanity's potential are dreams that need to be worked on and shared with newfound vigor, so that we can discover security and success in our fight for freedom.

Dream big, dream together, dream much more often, then get to work building these dreams and we will reach the summit of our shared vision for self-governance.

> *"Humanity has the stars in its future, and that future is too important to be lost under the burden of juvenile folly and ignorant superstition."* [46]
> - Isaac Asimov -

Let us move on and discuss the financial systems and job markets.

On a quick side note, if you have lots of money in the banks and financial markets, you might want to withdraw that cash before you-know-who steals it.

Take a look at Cyprus. The Cypriot government recently froze its citizens' bank accounts and stole what it needed to fill empty government bank accounts.

That being said, accrued wealth will hopefully largely be protected and retained during the transition. That is, aside from any property deemed to be illegally obtained.

If you work at a bank, if you are a stockbroker or a financial analyst or planner, you will probably need a new job, too. New standards dictate far fewer old-world brick-and-mortar infrastructure and fewer staff, although some people will be needed to help us design, build, and manage the new fiscal systems.

On that note, even if it is just for your own sake, learn more about the emerging trends and potential solutions that are available. If you want to help rebuild the world's fiscal soundness and transparency, then get involved and support those initiatives.

When the time comes, unite with your coworkers peacefully and empty the place of everything you can. "Disrupt and disempower" could be a powerful nonviolent tactic. Since safety and security are primary concerns, dismantling will require enough military and police support to help prevent violence.

---

[46] Isaac Asimov. BrainyQuote.com, Xplore Inc, 2014. http://www.brainyquote.com/quotes/quotes/i/isaacasimo148289.html, accessed February 17, 2014.

Just be glad knowing the eventual dismantling and repurposing of the broken system is ongoing, regardless of specific tactics, or speed. To write a book or accomplish any large task, you just need to put one foot in front of the other in stubborn fashion.

In addition, there are millions upon millions of us already on the march.

Join us and lend your voice.

Fiscal friends, do not forget to encourage your coworkers and community to join in and learn the good word. We need to move on and address some concerns that may be rising.

How will services be replaced fast enough to make sure our kids have schools to attend during coup? How will we ensure there are no mishaps with people's bank accounts? How will we prevent overall chaos during such big changes? After tearing down existing walls, won't we be standing amidst rubble, wondering what have we done?

Yes and no.

Surrender to your human fool. Embrace the unknown. What does this really mean, and how does all this theory translate into our kids having schools to attend, for example?

First, teachers have choices to make as individuals. Do you want to teach? If so, what do you want your future career to look like? Some communities and teachers may decide to keep things moving in a shuffle similar to yesterdays until new options surface.

In some cases though, old systems may crumble before the new ones are ready to take their place, and this is okay. It is natural and necessary.

It is called death and rebirth, or, quite simply, change.

We will not endure any more suffering than we have in the past. For that matter, nothing will be worse than the depravity and suffering occurring today. In truth, the human spirit is so capable, compassionate, and creative that we will all be living in a reborn, free world before you know it.

Our children, in rare cases, may have to spend a few weeks to six months or even a year or so at home with us, but this is not necessarily a bad thing. The family unit is damaged, and our children need better support. Six months to a year is a rough estimate, based on common sense.

The old systems will not be broken long at all before brilliant, sustainable ones are built to replace them and in most cases, our new systems can be built, while the current ones continue along. Operations can be transferred in stages as new systems come online.

Current systems are beyond toxic and disempowering.

The time it takes humanity to deal with all this natural shifting we could think of as spring, a quick thing that assuredly leads to a long, warm summer lush with the fruits of our labor.

Imagine what people will say and what you will say, in five, ten, or fifty years about learning to band together and the time it took, about the enormous struggle, and the reward of freedom from millennia-old rulers.

If we look a little deeper, we can see a large, budding truth emerging. All the vulnerability and communal compassion required to weather precisely this kind of storm is exactly what we humans, as a race, need to become friends again. Learning to co-create and co-govern our own lives in peace and abundance is just what the doctor ordered.

This spring will bring us all healing.

Social engineering requires generations of educational training. To reverse unhealthy trends generations in the making, immediate education reform is the foundation. Removing our children from old systems instantly prevents further social degeneration and harm.

If you're still concerned about schools possibly being shut down during our global spring cleaning, remember that we've already discussed how your kids are better off being homeschooled or unschooled. They can find success participating in open source schooling, or even utilizing the many new, continually emerging platforms for self-education.

An entire generation of the world's kids could learn the basic primary and secondary school skills from parents and communities with far greater efficacy. Home schooling and all kinds of new community education programs will easily fill the gap.

All our biggest dreams are beginning to come true.

It is time to set new goals, beyond just attaining our freedom from slavery. What are we capable of? It is hard to say when all our focus is consumed by the need to identify and remove the many layers of our shackles, but it is a beautiful thing to perceive freedom and let our imaginations and creativity see the big, wide-open sky, and the endless possibilities that for so long have been restricted.

Take a moment, close your eyes, and imagine what it will be like to see what the human race can really do, without all the corruption and restrictive, unethical, and arbitrary control.

Take heart because this transition will also unveil, with unadulterated new focus, our true and freed good sense. Have faith. There is no room for pessimism anymore. Healthy debate, yes, but we must abandon our fearful, negative thinking.

Engaging with a can-do attitude, we set the stage for our inevitable failures and eventual success.

> *"The number of times I succeed is in direct proportion to the number of times I can fail and keep on trying."*
> *- Tom Hopkins -*

Let us quickly recap two important ideas:

Fear

It is natural to fear the unknown, but we need to trust that our nervous first steps will lead us somewhere that makes sense. We will discover that courage grows with each new experience.

> *"When you get to the end of all the light you know and it's time to step into the darkness of the unknown, faith is knowing that one of two things shall happen: either you will be given something solid to stand on, or you will be taught how to fly."* [47]
> *- Edward Teller -*

Fear has infinite forms. Fear is illusory, but a paralyzing and polarizing protagonist. Humans find freedom from our various fears by learning to sit with them and examine them and/or taking those courageous first few steps into the unknown despite them. Through self-observation and those first courageous steps toward one another, our fears will evaporate in the light of our shared human goodness.

> *"If man is to survive, he will have learned to take a delight in the essential differences between men and between cultures. He will learn that differences in ideas and attitudes are a delight, part of life's exciting variety, not something to fear."*
> *- Gene Roddenberry -*

---

[47] As quoted by Jane M. Frutchey in Starting and Running an Editorial Consulting Business (2002), 121.

Setting the stage

> *"It's quite fashionable to say that the education system's broken—it's not broken, it's wonderfully constructed. It's just that we don't need it anymore. It's outdated."*48
> *- Sugata Mitra -*

Setting the stage for humanity's unchained potential to rise is a glorious challenge. Even though the ideas are simple and easy to apply, it can take a little time to train our human emotions and form new patterns out of old habits.

Imagine the wonder and new solutions bound to arise as we learn to set the stage and get out of the way. As concerned parties gather, lay the problems and tools on the table, and then get out of the way, watch fresh solutions unfold. Especially as we learn to fully awaken our imaginations, or at least eliminate the pessimistic "can't" attitude from our discussions and shift the focus to the question of how.

> *"In nine months, a group of children left alone with a computer in any language will reach the same standard as an office secretary in the West."*49
> *- Sugata Mitra -*

Remember that these concepts of learning, discovery, and collaboration apply to adults, too.

> *"Education is a self-organizing system, where learning is an emergent phenomenon."*

---

48 "Speakers—Sugata Mitra: Education Researcher," TED, https://www.ted.com/speakers/sugata_mitra.html.
49 "Speakers—Sugata Mitra: Education Researcher," TED, https://www.ted.com/speakers/sugata_mitra.html.

- Sugata Mitra -

When in doubt as to how to set the stage, or when searching for a new solution that works for everyone, look to nature.

Nature has always been, and will always be, our best guide.

"Come forth into the light of things, let nature be your teacher." 50
- William Wordsworth -

Truth also comes from within, so if you do not know what to do, go deep inside. Ask the questions. Wait for answers. You should know when, where, how to act, and very soon indeed.

Truth can also found in collaboration so if you are still at a loss, talk to a friend, neighbor, coworker or family member. If you are alone, go make a friend in our community.

Collective action and consensus ask that you join in a few discussions, so get online, go to various planetary hubs for information and collaborative action, and plug in to the discussion you care most about...or start one.

Let us move forward to the final set of actions: the battle on the front lines.

Get involved. Let us all get off our asses and make the world around us a better one. We are all equally and collectively responsible for shaping humanity's ongoing season of big changes.

If we are not driving this bus, rulers will. It is time we grab the wheel and create our own lives. We will learn together to uphold the responsibilities of transparent self-governance.

Some people's wish for just leaders may come true after all. You and I are these leaders, united in transparent fashion to ensure unique and ethical justice for all.

---

50 The Tables Turned, st. 4 (1798).

It is time to gather generals, serious warriors, and the captains of our freedom. This could be you. Any of us can help lead the way. To you mental titans across all walks of life, become the truest cerebral cats you were born to be, come and help us redefine how you apply your acuity and join the fight for freedom.

The following is a run-through of most major ways people can get involved and help to cultivate global self-governance.

Industry Leaders

Ask yourself the tough moral questions so you know when and where to draw the line. Everyone in the world needs to do this. We all need to know where we stand and why, and what we are going to do about it.

Ask yourself if you support the ruling class or your fellow humans as a whole. No one can make this decision for you. Indecision and apathy got us here, and if you do not decide for yourself, uncertainty will allow those lines to be pushed further than you ever would have agreed to otherwise. Unchecked greed and power will eventually lead to our self-destruction, by any reasonable estimation. All empires crumble. We can dismantle the idea of empires and power struggles by joining hands and taking responsibility for our own lives.

Group together. Grouping together in new, transparent form, across all industry and social categories, makes the tough personal decisions mentioned above much easier. The group is the central model for all new and old human systems. Instead of organizing our goals and ourselves around an expired institution, let us gather our shared knowledge and form new habits for decision-making and operational methods as a new collective.

Lend your special skills to the emerging groups and healthier efforts in your industry. We need new organizations and we need to repurpose and restructure the ones that remain. We need your expertise and collaboration. Part of being human is adapting to change, be it changing careers, paths, or interests. The global changes afoot also bring with them renewed opportunity for personal rebirth. Your acquired skills may come in handy if you want to help some fresh faces take over your old responsibilities. If you are interested in something new, join these groups too. Everyone will be glad to have you, and new opportunities are popping up all the time.

Gather together in numbers that do not take no for an answer. Grouping together provides humanity all the security and safety it needs. Everyone understands the basics of safety in numbers. This process of grouping together across industry and in general is the only way to accomplish our goals and minimize, even eliminate, violent suffering along the way.

Professionals, Scientists, and Academics of all kinds

Group together. Be safer. Be stronger. Be better.

Help the term whistle-blower became fully embodied. Industry is rampant with corruption. The world needs to be aflame with non-stop-shouters sharing stacks of documentation that exposes all the theft, human rights violations, and real criminals of the world. Tell the truth. Go find it. Expose corruption everywhere. When we have new whistle-blowers every day, we will learn to protect them better and turn these tides forever. Look at how powerfully disruptive a tiny few key whistle-blowers like Daniel Ellsberg, Edward Snowden, and Julian Assange have been for the ruling class. Look at Ellsberg's case alone and how frighteningly worse off we are now. Today's government is at war with whistle-blowers. That says it all. Let us multiply their efforts by a thousand, then ten thousand and a hundred thousand. This is one powerful weapon, and if every industry faced massive whistle-blowing trends, unhealthy and criminal practices would quickly come to an end. Let us build a huge, global, whistle-blowing team.

Police Officers

Decide which orders you will not follow and where you personally will draw the lines that define your life.

Group together. Be safer. Be stronger. Be better. Perhaps this means fracturing current forces, militia style. Help your coworkers make the right call and help protect us from those who do not.

Protect your whole human family from violence and oppression. This means helping arm common people. Refuse to disarm your family. Furthermore, if you are willing, quit the old systems. If it is safe, along the way, transform the weapon systems so they can be used to protect the public within the new systems.

Work for true justice and help us all discover it together, in transparency.

Join the whistle-blowing team.

Military Operatives

Decide which orders you will not follow, where you draw the line, and how the world will remember you.

Group together. Be safer. Be stronger. Be better.

Stop killing. You have been lied to, and if you look deep enough inside, you will see that war is killing you and the rest of us too.

Help us minimize violence in humanity's current revolution by standing with us. If enough of you do, the ruling class will not have anyone left to fight for them.

Join and help lead the whistle-blowing team. Your old, corrupt bosses possess, and many of you work with. the biggest, deadliest, and most criminal secrets in the world.

Intelligence Gatherers

Group together. Be safer. Be stronger. Be better.

Play for something that really matters. Play for the right team. Your bullet points are similar to the military, but your skills are some of the most dangerous in our battle for humankind's future. Your family is watching you with careful attention. We need you to touch that human place in you. We need your specialties, too. Let us redefine them together.

Help secure the safety of freedom's fighters with your expertise. We trust you will figure it out.

Lead the charge to uncover and corner our truth, our justice.

Join and add serious substance to the whistle-blowing team.

Here is an idea: head over to Area 51 and similar installations and empty the locations of all their secrets. Bring humanity our heritage and our discoveries. Bring us some game changers. Bring everything to the center of town, for everyone to see. Secrecy has no place in a transparent new world. Let us open the floodgates of secret projects, financed with our stolen money. We have the need and right to seize these assets, to open all closed doors and shine a light in all the dark corners.

Media Producers

Redeem yourselves and help us reclaim our dignity.

Group together. Be safer. Be stronger. Be better.

Report on truth for a change, inspire us instead of using your services to play on instinctual fear, and help broaden control.

Report on the corruption and hidden structures of the ruling elite. Seriously, it is time. You could play a major role in motivating and helping to free the world.

Share and advertise better information in a healthy fashion. The promotion of truth in all forms, even this book, and most certainly revolution itself rely heavily on the enlightened behavior of you, our media, and your skills.

Stop selling fear. Show us our solidarity, our power, our passion, our potential, and our plans at work.

Join and take up your integrity's vital part in the whistle-blowing team.

Politicians

Decide which orders you will not follow, where you draw the line, and how the world will remember you.

Group together. Be safer. Be stronger. Be better.

Help us tear down broken systems and build better ones. On the other hand, perhaps you would like a new home in an echo-filled prison…what is it going to be?

Join and honor your integrity's vital part in the whistle-blowing team.

Rise above the rules of old. Humanity is forgiving. We would love to have you with us. Politics may be over in traditional form, but your skills as communicators alone can be super tools for good.

Join us, and in turn redefine and redeem yourselves.

Bankers and Financial Experts

Decide which orders you will not follow, where you draw the line, and how the world will remember you.

Group together. Be safer. Be stronger. Be better.

Be the change, co-create solutions, be vulnerable, ask for forgiveness or face criminal consequences. Elite professionals of the world, the message is becoming clear.

Lend your expertise, financial professionals, to emerging forms of alternate currency, agorism in general, education, and the replacement of old systems as well as the operations of new ones. Some of you might be tired of working in money and will prefer a career change. No problem, just pick your fancy and get engaged.

Help the world understand truth and join the whistle-blowing team. People deserve to know the truth.

Legal Professionals

Decide which orders you will not follow, where you draw the line, and how the world will remember you.

Group together. Be safer. Be stronger. Be better.

Help us facilitate the legal battles. As stated, humanity still has a need for a smaller justice system and various forms of civil mediation. We need the best of you.

Lend humanity your professional opinions and expertise. Many of you are no strangers to the limitations imposed on human capacity. It is time for us common folk to assemble our defiance, to get methodically and menacingly prepared, to tear down and reconstruct all our establishments.

Join the whistle-blowing team. Judges and lawyers both, the secrets that some of you keep are colossal. With respect to the bar, oaths, fealty, admiralty law, common law, and secret societies, the time for truth has come. Too few of you have come forward with evidence of the true depth of the lies. People deserve to know. Help us understand these horrors and find all the forgiveness and understanding you need.

Our greatest minds and strategists, along with every other willing and interested contributor

Lead the charge, all you creative and brilliant among us. Everyone is welcome to participate, but we had better get serious about getting together in one place. We need to gather solidarity and consensus like there is no tomorrow.

Re-define our think tanks' purposes and practices.

Help us, you intellectuals of the world, to understand some of the most amazing truths. Join the whistle-blowing team. Many of you white coats and great minds of our time work in secret, for the system. Not everyone harbors secrets, obviously. However, at the very top of the chain, compartmentalized as reality may be, awareness and opportunity to shed light on parts of the problem are present. Humanity deserves the truth.

Decide which orders you will not follow, where you draw the line, and how the world will remember you.

Group together. Be safer. Be stronger. Be better.

You, if you're willing

Steer away from the treacherous waters of neutrality and the sidelines. Humanity needs as many of us as possible to accept responsibility for a portion of the front lines. This responsibility is internal, dark, terrifying, and transformative.

> *"Men, it has been well said, think in herds; it will be seen that they go mad in herds, while they only recover their senses slowly, and one by one."*[51]
> *- Charles Mackay -*

Talk to those around you and seek out sensible support if you feel frozen by fear or inexperience. You will find all the help you need and build more than enough courage.

Speak if you possess any information that can help the human race. Many people take secrets to their grave. Others tell the world their stories late in life. End secrecy and end this silence in service to the elite. Make your legacy really count.

Decide which orders you will not follow, where you draw the line, and how the world will remember you.

Group together. Be safer. Be stronger. Be better.

---

[51] Extraordinary Popular Delusions and the Madness of Crowds (R. Bentley, 1841).

> *"If you are neutral in situations, you have chosen the side of the oppressor."* [52]
> *- Desmond Tutu -*

> *"Forget about having an identity crisis and get some identity capital…Do something that adds value to who you are. Do something that's an investment in who you might want to be next."* [53]
> *- Meg Jay -*

Here are a few more exciting ways that everyone can join the front lines:

a. Pressure and help make it easier for family, friends, coworkers, and leaders to join the team. You can do this by spreading the message and helping people come to terms and accept the truth. Then you can help them research, reach out, and get involved. Some people will need help navigating the changes afoot and finding new forms of employment. Industry and education will naturally work together to retrain the workforce where needed. Pressure can be applied in many ways, depending on the objective. Use your common sense and ask for help if you want to find out how your voice can help topple oppressive systems.

This applies to everyone, and especially those in the list above. It is up to us to demand that our fellow women and men in positions of power make positive changes.

---

[52] As quoted in Ending Poverty As We Know It: Guaranteeing a Right to a Job at a Living Wage (2003) by William P. Quigley, p. 8.
[53] The Defining Decade: Why Your Twenties Matter—And How to Make the Most of Them Now (Hachette Digital, 2012).

b. Really take a stand and become a community spokesperson or freedom-movement leader in some capacity. This means spreading the message with meticulous fervor. Leverage your existing audience, your voice. Expand and transform your present efforts to become a messenger for freedom. Spread the message and incite the discussions.

c. Get involved with a social cause you care about. Charities around the world are a perfect example of how committed humanity is to social justice. Let us refocus our efforts by removing the corrupt middleman from all our institutions. Building on our knowledge while creating and sharing more success stories is all it takes to initiate a widespread global systems upgrade.

d. You can pressure authority figures through peaceful protest and disengagement from the system. Refuse to participate in and contribute to flawed and corrupted systems. Develop the front lines of the sovereign human movement in every way, shape, and form you can imagine.

Since her first video in November 2013, Josie the Outlaw has been educating us and applying increasing pressure on men and women in uniform using simple YouTube videos. She is one person.

Imagine if the world joined together and had multiple groups of our police working for freedom. Imagine if all of them joined forces with LEAP, Josie, Veterans Against Police Abuse, countless other new and old organizations, and you and me. Imagine if they sent laser-focused directives, messages, and initiatives down the pipe, one after another.

e. You can pressure local communities and businesses, even your bosses. Imagine twenty-five, fifty, or a hundred people walking into your local big-chain grocery store and demanding to be served without the application of sales taxes.

Imagine how that would affect other people who happened to be shopping at the same, carefully chosen, busy moment.

There is nothing stopping all the staff members of small and large companies alike from demanding a similar equivalent to Canada's independent contractor status. The United States also uses the same term. Independent contractors do not have taxes removed from their paychecks and are responsible for dealing with the government directly, which restores your right to refuse or modify the way you chose to do so. In the United States, FICA taxes are payroll deductions that are paid by both the employee and the employer 50/50.[54] There is no doubt companies would be delighted to avoid paying for all the paperwork, headaches, and tax contributions associated with employees.

f. Common professionals, gather. Form new collectives and spread freed services and information. Unplug from the restricted settings you are currently chained to. Create new platforms for all our needs and services. Alternatively, you can tweak the systems you are working within so they acclimate to transparent, ethical practices. We are all learning new ways to collaborate, research, work, and solve our problems with freedom and joy.

g. To our youth, free thinkers, students, the occupy movement, and others: it is time to get serious and pull no punches when it comes to defending our divine right to self-govern. It is insanely obvious we can do better. The '60s were the precursor; let us show the ruling class this next generation of rebellious youth doesn't take no for an answer and sees right through the sugar-laced poison ideas.

h. Everyone, get online and help. The Web version of freedom has enormous communicative, technical, and logistical

---

[54] Federal Insurance Contribution Act, 26 U.S. Code Chapter 21.

demands. Humanity's healthiest potential is waiting for every one of us to walk out our front doors or get online and start talking and working together. We humans are going to recapture our resources from banks, institutions, corrupt leaders, and politicians, and the list goes on. The faster disease and discontent turns to dissent and revolution, the faster we can fund the global population's full-time employment in jobs that people choose and love to do.

The possibilities for when, where, and how to plug in with the changes going on, and the dreams inside of you, are infinite. As common folk, go get the job, start the business, chase the dream you have always wanted to. You can even try a few things out and see which experiences you like the best.

Common people around the world can also help support and facilitate the justice movement's efforts. We need to hold those who have caused harm accountable for their actions and reclaim our global resources. This requires enormous collaboration and cohesive solidarity; namely, pressure.

Therefore, we must break out the pots and pans and hit the streets in numbers that our rulers have never seen. We must build new global microphones and keep improving on the Avaaz model. We will make our voice heard, and that global, transparent, and compassionate voice shall rule forever.

Empires and rulers inevitably perish; the transparent global collective will live on until our planet cannot house us anymore. By then, we will no doubt have somewhere else to be, anyway.

For the work being done within the confines of our broken system, Join Kevin Annett[55] was nominated for the 2013 Nobel Peace

---

[55] Kevin Annett, Hidden No Longer: Genocide in Canada, Past and Present, http://hiddennolonger.com/; www.kevinannett.com; Kevin Annett, www.kevin annett.com.

Prize by academics from Canada and around the world. He is a true hero. He is working furiously to bring rulers like the Queen, the Prime Minister of Canada, and others to justice. He is leading the charge, beginning to establish methods and enough solidarity among international human rights organizations to hold top global leaders accountable for their monstrous crimes.

Every single one of us needs to concentrate on the undeniable, documented evidence and witness testimonies provided by victims of political and corporate persecution, sex crimes, ritual and organized abuse, human experimentation, human-trafficking, forced prostitution, mind control, and unthinkable forms of abuse and torture. These practices have always been most rampant among the ruling elite. These horrifying facts need your attention.

Countless illegal and terrifying acts of violence and enslavement run through the highest levels of the Vatican and throughout political arenas, elitist institutions, and secret societies.

No one wants to believe these things could be true. It can be very difficult to process such incomprehensible evil. Part of you likely wants desperately to disbelieve and forget the things you have just heard, but despite the fear and skepticism, go and see for yourself. The evidence is undeniable and it will change you.

Dig and then dig deeper. Expose and eradicate evils that we CANNOT stand for. Let these be some of the first entry points into the darkest chasms of humanity's secret lairs. Let the uncovering of these repulsions be the beginning of secrecy's end.

Our common hearts cannot tolerate a single day more. Fathers, mothers, every last human being reading this - it is time you do something about it.

Kevin Annett and the ITCCS have been so successful that they have forced resignations and brought tough legal action against the popes and top church officials, as well as the Queen herself and the current prime minister of Canada, Stephen Harper, as mentioned. With a little more help from the rest of the world, people like Kevin

Annett and others can lead us to justice and fairness and can liberate our children from torture, rape, and death.

Millions of individuals and groups of warriors everywhere are screaming for our support and attention as they struggle with every ounce of their humanity to free us from tyranny, oppression, slavery, and pain. Imagine what will happen when all our righteous causes and all the true global compatriots of freedom get the help and support of the common people.

On the other hand, there may be enough of us for victory already. Even if no new freedom fighters joined the fold and only those of us already on the field joined forces and began working together, we could eliminate the problems and then invite the rest of humanity to enjoy the fruits of freedom and help re-imagine the world.

The world's problems are too much to bear individually. Thankfully, we have each other. An entire planet of 6 or 7 billion non-elites, we will figure it out together.

It is sometimes hard to imagine what something different might look like, but despite enormous fear, tremendous change is not overly arduous. It is only the idea of change and the first few steps that are the most difficult.

Once we get moving in earnest, re-creating ourselves will be joyous and laborious, but not excessively backbreaking. Every step we make as a civilization lessons our physical demands and requires more of humans only mentally and emotionally. For too long humanity has been staring fearfully at the need to balance technology and capacity with compassion and sense. It is time.

When push comes to shove, we only need to acknowledge the global population, versus how many people are really in charge. This is all we need to know to free ourselves.

The numbers that stand against us are pitiful. Imagine how you would protect yourself in a street fight with, say, three hundred people. Picture trying to fight three thousand, thirty thousand, or three hundred thousand people by yourself and no one even needs to do the math. We only need to realize that the ruling elite lose all power when common people simply stop following their orders. They have no power other than that which we offer them.

I am well beyond finished supporting authority of all kinds, and Luke is a ferocious tiger, ready to tear into anyone who tries to impose his or her will on another human being. We are just two average people, in a great sea of you amazing folks who have come before us and who stand beside us.

Thanks to the many of you who inspire us. Thanks for helping us figure things out when we were struggling. Moreover, thanks for welcoming us into the community that is so rapidly stitching all of humanity's different groups together.

For those not quite ready to join the ranks and build a self-governed future, think about the things you are worried about specifically and then connect with the freedom community after you are done reading. Go online or go meet with some people and ask the world around you the toughest questions that you are still grappling with.

As we reclaim our resources, or even a tiny fraction of them, we can immediately fund even the biggest kinds of changes, provided we have had time to decide together on the initial details. Imagine the feeling of knowing the accounts are full and we can make healthy, transparent decisions together, as both large and small communities.

In the meantime, let us gather together and discuss all aspects of our lives.

When we are ready with replacements, we get to demolish the walls of existing structures which will be guaranteed fun. All the while, we will look for ways to support the natural decay and rebirth that accompanies change.

It is important to note that if a region or group of people is comfortable with patchworked interim solutions, the option exists to force the rebuilding phase immediately via stronger methods of disregarding, disempowering, and demolishing old systems. To be as safe as can be, this type of fast-tracking will require effective support from the new justice movements.

Again, true success requires greater numbers of us working together. That is it. Imagine protecting the land, becoming the stewards of the planet we are meant to be, and being free to enjoy and travel the entire abundant globe as you see fit.

Nothing will make or break our success other than a stubborn commitment to it or against it.

All of the ideas in this book are just opportunities and examples of the best we have. It includes many things that we have learned and a few good places to start. We can all start by doing the simple things with which we feel completely comfortable. Comfort levels will vary greatly and shift too, as we get stronger.

It's everyone's first job to spread the message. Speak with your community and, of course, share all the information you can with each other.

Many agree that the biggest fear most of us face is each other. We lack trust in each other's basic goodness, as well in as our ability to get along and agree. The only way we will overcome these fears and our misguided dependence on authority to protect us from ourselves is to try. We will learn to trust each other again while sharing the experience of rebuilding the world in transparent, healthier fashion.

Forming new habits for everything and setting the stage for new solutions to take shape will be a challenging but equally joyful process. Remember, we are only changing who is in charge, and it would be impossible not to improve on current systems.

> *"There are two ways of spreading light: to be the candle or the mirror that reflects it."* [56]
> *- Edith Wharton -*

Go. Get warm by the glow of someone strong.

---

[56] "Vesalius in Zante (1564)" North American Review (November 1902), 631.

Be inspired by the highest ideals that live deep in your heart.

Light the path for others along the way.

In the greatest season of change the world has ever seen, what is your role? As humanity's imagination and curiosity comes fully alive, what would you really like to do?

Manufactured by Amazon.ca
Acheson, AB